D1452075

*The German Military in the
Age of Total War*

The German Military in the Age of Total War

EDITED BY
Wilhelm Deist

WITH A FOREWORD BY
Paul Kennedy

BERG

Berg Publishers Ltd
24 Binswood Avenue, Leamington Spa,
Warwickshire CV32 5SQ, UK
51 Washington Street, Dover,
New Hampshire 03820, USA

First published 1985
© Berg Publishers 1985

British Library Cataloguing in Publication Data
The German military in the age of total war.
1. Germany — Armed Forces — History
I. Deist, Wilhelm   II. McMurry, Dean S.
355'.00943   UA710

ISBN 0–907582–14–1

Library of Congress Cataloging in Publication Data
Main entry under title:

The German military in the age of total war.

1. Germany—Armed Forces—History—20th century—
Addresses, essays, lectures. 2. Germany—History,
Military—20th century—Addresses, essays, lectures.
I. Deist, Wilhelm.
UA710.G432 1985   355'.00943   84–73479
ISBN 0–907582–14–1

Printed in Great Britain by Billings & Sons, Worcester

Contents

PAUL KENNEDY

Foreword

Over the past two decades, military history has expanded in so many directions that the subject has quite transformed itself. Formerly concentrated rather specifically around the history of great generals, famous regiments and classic campaigns, it has increasingly been studied of late within a far wider context — that of the entire society in which the armed forces existed. In consequence, armies and soldiers throughout history are now being analysed in relation to economic changes and technological advances, to the social structure and class relations of their country, and to the 'political structure' and national traditions. Armed forces, whether operating in peacetime or in war, seem to offer raw material not only for different *types* of historians, but also for sociologists, political scientists and, even, psychologists and anthropologists.

This trend has perhaps been particularly to the fore in Anglo-American countries in recent years (although there also exist very important French-language studies, especially by distinguished scholars like Philippe Contamine and André Corvisier,[1] on 'War and Society' themes). In Britain, one of the most popular courses offered by the Open University in the 1970s was that on 'War and Society', which familiarised thousands of readers and viewers with these new approaches. In the USA, the famous Shelby Cullom Davis Center at Princeton recently focused upon 'War and Society' as its two-year seminar theme. Moreover, journals on *War and Society* and *Armed Forces and Society* have sprung up, a *War and Society Newsletter* flourishes, and a popular multi-volume series[2] of textbooks on *War and European Society* provides a final confirma-

1

tion that the subject has arrived. So overwhelming have these trends appeared in Britain and the USA, for example, that certain historians have begun to make 'a modest plea for drums and trumpets'[3] — that is, to call for the actual conduct of battles not to be totally ignored!

In Germany, by contrast, the large-scale development of studies upon 'War and Society' is of much more recent origin. There are, it is true, some now-classic works in this genre such as Karl Demeter's *Das deutsche Offizierkorps in Gesellschaft und Staat*, Volker Berghahn's *Der Tirpitz-Plan*, and Jürgen Kocka's *Klassengesellschaft im Kriege;*[4] but it would be fair to say that only over the past few years have a significantly larger number of German historians directed their attention to the relationship between military forces on the one hand, and economic, technological, social and political events on the other.[5] Thanks to a recent surge of scholarly German-language publications, it is now possible to see the new directions which are being taken in the study of German 'War and Society', to observe the chief questions which are being asked, and to compare the results which are emerging. The essays which follow are intended to offer a signpost to these newer explorations.

Although the interaction between 'armed forces' and 'society' can just as well be studied for the pre-industrial and (especially) for the feudal period, it is not surprising that the heaviest concentration of recent German-language works has been in the period between the late-nineteenth century and the end of the Second World War. The most obvious reason for such a concentration is that so much of German history itself in those decades relates to the origins, course, and consequences of two appallingly deadly wars. In the second place, this entire period was strongly influenced by the dynamics of technological and social change, which in turn forced the German military and naval commands to grapple with the twin problems of waging *industrialised* mass warfare and simultaneously retaining the support of an increasingly urbanised and democratised population. Preserving a certain 'gap' between the armed forces and the greater part of German society, as many senior officers of the older type favoured, was no longer possible in the century of 'total war'. Exactly how the army and the navy related to the newer social forces — whether of the Left or of the Right — and how the military's claims for autonomy could be reconciled with its own growing demands upon the national economy and the mass of the population, were problems which would not go away. As a large number of the essays in this excellent collection show, the German armed forces' leadership was forced to grapple (usually unsuccessfully) with the long-term consequences of the 'unbound Prometheus' of technological and social change. Since this was, of course, a problem for leaders in other advanced societies (Britain, the USA, France, Italy — not to mention the Soviet Union and Japan), these essays offer us a starting-point for some useful comparisons across national boundaries.

One further reason for the concentration of scholarly attention upon German 'war and society' in the twentieth century is the sheer richness of available sources now that the mountains of documents captured by the Allies in 1945 have been returned to the Federal Military Archives (*Bundesarchiv-Militärarchiv*) in Freiburg. It is by no great coincidence that Freiburg is also the home of that unique institution, the Military History Research Office (*Militärgeschichtliches Forschungsamt*), where both historically-minded serving officers and, most notably, professionally-trained historians have combined to produce a remarkable outpouring of works: monographs, bibliographies, handbooks, multi-volume studies (e.g. on Germany and the Second World War), the excellent journal *Militärgeschichtliche Mitteilungen*, and conference proceedings, all attest to the wide-ranging and fertile state of German military studies at this present time, thanks chiefly to the Freiburg centre. That the editor of this collection, and many of the contributors to it, are members of the Military History Research Office is a further testimony to the unequalled reputation which it has acquired in the German-speaking world for its investigations into all aspects of military history, from battlefield encounters to larger 'war and society' issues.

If, with the present publication of these essays, readers in the English language are enabled to get some sense of the exciting new research occurring in the Federal Republic, then all those who have encouraged and contributed to this book will be well satisfied.

Notes

1. Both recently translated into English as: P. Contamine, *War in the Middle Ages* (Basil Blackwell, Oxford/New York, 1984), and A. Corvisier, *Armies and Societies in Europe 1494–1789* (Indiana University Press, Bloomington/London, 1979). The bibliographies, especially Contamine's, give a good sense of how much research has been done in this earlier period.
2. By Fontana Books, under the general editorship of Geoffrey Best.
3. This is the title of Denis Showalter's excellent article in *Military Affairs*, 39(1975), pp. 71–4.
4. K. Demeter, *Das deutsche Offizierkorps in Gesellschaft und Staat*, Frankfurt, 1964; V. R. Berghahn, *Der Tirpitz-Plan*, Düsseldorff, 1971; J. Kocka, *Klassengesellschaft im Kriege*, Göttingen, 1978 (transl. as *Facing Total War: German Society 1914–1918*, Leamington Spa, 1984).
5. Note that path-breaking English-language studies such as Gerald Feldman's *Army, Industry and Labour in Germany 1914–1918*, and Alan Milward's *The German Economy at War*, were published as early as 1966 and 1965 respectively.

WILHELM DEIST

Introduction

The phenomenon of war, unleashed military force, has
always held a strange fascination for many people and has consequently been a favourite subject of all types of literature. War
studies fill entire libraries. A glance through any bookshop will
show an abundance of publications of the most varied kind and
quality in the field of military history, particularly that of the first
half of the twentieth century. Scholars have studied the origins,
underlying causes and consequences of the two World Wars intensively and have included military developments in their analyses.[1]
In Anglo-Saxon countries particularly, German military problems,
successes and failures in the two wars have received great attention.[2]
Although the present volume provides much information about
previously unknown developments, its publication has another
objective.

In recent decades the study of history has expanded to include
many new areas, thereby giving rise to new questions and enriching
historical scholarship with new knowledge about conditions of
development in state and society.[3] It is thus all the more astonishing
that up to now this expansion has little affected the approach of
historical scholarship to the study of military establishments and of
war, although their significance to industrial societies in the twentieth century is not disputed. It is generally recognised that the
rapidly accelerating advance of industrialisation, technology and
automation has, in comparison with earlier times, completely changed
the nature of military conflict. This recognition has not as yet had

Transl. from the German by Dean S. McMurry.

great influence on the approaches and perspectives of most historians concerned with military history. In choosing the contributions for this volume the editor has, therefore, sought to further the required broadening of the military historical perspective. Research in this area in the Federal Republic of Germany has made considerable progress during the past two decades, developing ideas and concepts related to the military history of Germany in the nineteenth and twentieth centuries which can offer fruitful starting-points for the study of the military history of other industrialised nations. The present volume does not claim to present a balanced picture of this field in Germany; rather the individual contributions demonstrate, in exemplary fashion, the possibilities of gaining new knowledge by using the methods of modern military historical research.

In spite of a number of important works by individual historians — for example Max Jähns,[4] Hans Delbrück,[5] Eberhard Kessel,[6] Gerhard Ritter[7] and Hans Herzfeld[8] — military historiography in Germany has been influenced persistently by the work of military institutions: the Historical Department of the General Staff and, after the First World War, the Naval Archive.[9] The type of military historiography developed in the voluminous series published by these institutions generally served a dual purpose. It represented reports designed to legitimise recent German military achievements, while at the same time constituting one of the basic elements of tactical training for officers. Neither of these functions was conducive to a critical analysis of historical events, leading rather to a restriction of the subject to purely military developments. Even during the Weimar Republic, when the writing of the 'official' history of the First World War was entrusted to the newly established 'Reichs-Archiv', the attempt to give adequate space to the analysis of political and economic factors before and during the war was unsuccessful. Finally, in the Second World War the activity of the corresponding military institutions degenerated into thinly disguised propaganda with the aim of indoctrinating and training the nation in the National Socialist military spirit.[10]

For these reasons it was obvious that a continuation of the earlier tradition of German military history could not be considered when the armed forces of the Federal Republic were organised in the 1950s. Fortunately however, Hans Meier-Welcker was appointed as director of historical research in the *Dienststelle Blank* (Blank Office, the precursor of what is now the ministry of defence). He was an uncompromising advocate of the view that military history was part of the study of history in general and, influenced by the discipline's methodology and procedures, was able from the beginning to exert a strong influence on the development of military historical research in the Federal Republic.[11]

At that time the Americans were employing a considerable number of former high-ranking Wehrmacht officers in the Operational History (German) Section, under the direction of Franz Halder, an army chief of staff in the Second World War; another group, the Naval Historical Team, worked under ex-Admiral Schniewind for the US navy. During the next few years these officers produced a large number of studies of German operations in the Second World War, written from a traditional military history perspective. These studies were frequently influenced by the political climate of the Cold War and were often written from a utilitarian perspective.[12] At no time, however, did these writings, or the series on the history of the Second World War published by the victors, have any influence on the goals and work of the institution which Meier-Welcker had founded, the Office of Military Historical Research in Freiburg. Rather the idea of a modern approach to military history assumed an increasingly clear form in the publications of the office and finally became itself the subject of numerous articles concerned with principles and definitions as a specific genre of historiography.[13]

Modern military history has as its primary subject the 'role of the military as an instrument of policy in the hands of the state and the role of the armed forces as a factor and centre of power in the state'.[14] This broad description also means that, in addition to the still central task of analysing the military conduct of war and its increasing involvement in, and effects on, almost all aspects of state and society, military history must examine the relationships between the military, both as institution and as political factor, and the rest of society — in its social, intellectual, cultural and economic interest groups. Manfred Messerschmidt has described the aim of such a military history of the Second World War as the writing of 'a history of society at war'.[15] This ambitious aim illuminates the great difference between traditional and modern military history. It is not surprising, therefore, that the modern approach is often rejected; demands are often heard that military history should have some immediate, practical application, in order to compensate for a lack of actual war experience by the use of historical examples. It is surprising, however, that military history is scarcely studied at universities in the Federal Republic of Germany. Even the military history of the unified German state has attracted the interest of only a few university lecturers. One can only speculate about the causes of this situation; it seems probable, however, that the disasters of the First and Second World Wars have led to this distinct lack of interest in the military aspects of German history from 1871 to 1945.

The selection of contributions for the present volume has been determined by the comprehensive concept of military history outlined above. The separate essays are intended to make readers aware of how well both military and related institutions are suited to provide perspectives from which general as well as particular phenomena in state and society can be examined and understood. The selection has been deliberately restricted to topics of German military history. Its primary purpose is to inform the English-speaking reader about new research in this area — specifically, research based on the 'modern' concept of military history — and thus to promote the international exchange of ideas by helping to overcome the language barrier and the difficulties presented by the growing mass of publications in this field. For this reason, all the contributions are by historians in or from the Federal Republic of Germany, even though, following the example of such pioneering scholars as John Wheeler-Bennett, Gordon Craig and Francis L. Carsten,[16] large numbers of historians in English-speaking countries still write about German military history.

The restriction of the scope of the present volume to the particular period implied in the title requires an explanation. In the history of Central Europe it becomes possible to speak of the phenomenon of 'total' war only since the beginning of this century, although those who fought in the First and Second World Wars probably did not experience these conflicts with the same clarity and precision that this concept now conveys.[17] Since military planning and preparation for total war can never be restricted to wartime and necessarily extends to the years before and after, an expansion of the scope of this book to include the years after the Second World War seemed logical at first, particularly as a number of publications on the security policy of the Federal Republic are available.[18] But the assumptions and conditions under which the German military functioned before and after 1945 differed so completely that it was decided, in order to preserve the unity of the frame of reference, not to extend the period under consideration to the first years of the Federal Republic. Moreover, the fact that few recent works on military subjects deal with the earlier periods of modern German history made it necessary to confine the scope of this volume to the period from 1871 to 1945.[19] It would have been impossible to offer an even partially satisfactory survey of important earlier periods.

The concentration of this volume on that period was not, however, only a result of the external factors mentioned above. For well-known reasons those seventy-four years, more than any other in German history, have been intensively researched and analysed in recent decades and are considered an historical unit.[20] Of its various military historical aspects, it is primarily those dealing with the direct exertion of political influence by the armed forces which have been studied. To give the reader some idea of the decisive influence of the military as 'a political force within the state', it is sufficient to name the two Moltkes, Schlieffen, Tirpitz, Ludendorff, Seeckt and Beck. Gerhard Ritter, Francis L. Carsten, Thilo Vogelsang, Wolfgang Sauer, Klaus-Jürgen Müller and Manfred Messerschmidt have documented and comprehensively described the political role of the hierarchically structured military élite and its representatives, as well as their assumptions and aims.[21] The 'historical-sociological' foundations of this élite have also been analysed in detail.[22]

In the past two decades it has been primarily scholars working in the long-neglected fields of economic and social history who have given us a clearer and more varied picture of developments in German society during the period from 1871 to 1945. In this picture the extremely complex ideological, political, economic and social effects of the industrial revolution and the continuing industrialisation under the specific conditions of the German state have acquired a central significance. This is, of course, especially true of the history of Imperial Germany and, with somewhat different points of emphasis, of the Weimar Republic and the Third Reich.

Military historical research has only begun to answer the questions of how the German armed forces reacted to industrialisation, how their structure was changed by it, and what effects these changes had on state and society.[23] The present volume tries to make a modest contribution to this very complicated subject. The idea of total war refers to a phenomenon which first became really important as a result of industrial economic developments.[24] To be sure, its ideological roots date back to the French Revolution and, in Germany, to the struggle against Napoleon, but it first received its modern meaning as a result of the effects of continuing industrialisation on the armed forces. The First World War is rightly considered to have been the first 'total' war on the European continent. Its distinguishing characteristic was the 'industrialisation of war' — as it was described at the time in France[25] — with far-reaching political, military, economic and social consequences. Thus the title of this book implies the question of the nature of the tensions between the German military and a German society shaped increasingly by ongoing industrialisation, a question which had its roots far back in the nineteenth century.

In his history of Imperial Germany, Hans-Ulrich Wehler stresses the decisive role of the absolutist forces — the army, the bureaucracy and the diplomatic service — within the formal framework of the country's constitutional monarchy; Wolfgang Sauer has described the army as the 'hard core' of the whole state.[26] It seems appropriate, therefore, to proceed from these insights to an analysis of the tensions between the military and society. In this volume, *Wolfgang Petter* sees the main feature of this situation embodied in the compromise between the army and the German bourgeoisie as a result of the Prussian constitutional conflict of the 1860s. This compromise guaranteed the extra-constitutional position of the army as well as the social and economic power of the middle class. It confirmed and strengthened the politically stabilising role of the military as the protector of the existing domestic power structure, a role considered just as important as the task of maintaining the external security of the country. Yet industrialisation among other factors made the fulfilment of both these tasks impossible; the circle could not be squared. Thus Tirpitz's naval construction programme not only resulted in increased hostility of other powers towards Germany but also endangered the foundations of the 'fundamental compromise'. For the army this danger, as a consequence of industrialisation, was most evident in the constantly growing number of supporters of the Social Democrats; no defence or immunisation strategy was effective against these 'Reichsfeinde' (enemies of the state). Yet Schlieffen's operational plans could not be implemented without the huge numbers of conscripts from the industrial working class, which was 'infected' with Social Democratic ideas.[27] The generally accepted fact that the political constitution, which was based on the above-mentioned compromise, no longer corresponded to the rapidly changing social and economic structure was clearly demonstrated by this dilemma of the military.[28] In the First World War the compromise in its original form collapsed completely under the pressure of having to mobilise for the war effort the resources of the entire nation, including the manpower of the former Reichsfeinde. Moreover, the uncompromising war aims of the military leaders finally destroyed German society's broad-based support for the army and navy as national institutions.

This real and deep crisis of the German armed forces in the years immediately after Versailles was made bearable for the military leaders by the decision of the victors to permit Germany to maintain only a small professional army, the 'Reichswehr'.[29] This arrangement, which all politically and socially influential groups considered only temporary, spared the army leadership the necessity of establishing a new relationship with the rest of German society on the basis of the experiences of the first 'industrialised war'. This inconclusive situation and the political conditions in the Weimar Republic permitted the military to continue practising methods of exercising power which had not corresponded to German social reality even before the First World War and which, in the 1920s, tended to turn the army into the police and border guard desired by the victors.[30]

The moment, however, that the primary military tasks again became important, the armed forces' awareness of their dependence on state and society grew. Recent studies have shown that, in order to maintain their ability to function militarily, the armed forces were forced, after 1926, to revise the cool, reserved attitude towards the state and society of the republic advocated by von Seeckt.[31] Compared with the ideal, the preventive organisation of state and society for war, these first changes were extremely limited, but they still permitted the planning and realisation of systematic, co-ordinated armaments programmes. This difficult way to co-operation, which implied a dependence on the political decisions of changing majorities in both government and parliament, remained controversial within the Reichswehr itself; it was incompatible with the traditional conviction of many leading officers that the armed forces as a state institution should enjoy a special, elevated position.

What other possible ways were there to reach the common goal sought by both groups in the Reichswehr, that is, the broadest possible support for the armed forces? As *Wolfram Wette* has demonstrated, the crisis of the party state, of the democratic system in the final years of the Weimar Republic,[32] was marked by a 'remilitarisation of public opinion'. One result of this was that the previously successful policy of peaceful revision in small steps, pursued by the parties of the Weimar coalition, received less and less support. To the military the various forms of martial nationalism, together with the election victories of the National Socialists, gave rise to the belief that this political movement represented a real alternative to the co-operation policy of the Reichswehr leadership. This hope was not disappointed. Hitler's statement that the 'strengthening by all means of the German will to fight' formed the decisive precondition for his policy meant,[33] for the generals and admirals, the elimination of politically motivated resistance to the purely military organisation of the country's defence. A few months after Hitler's coming to power, it became clear that the programme of 'rebuilding the German capacity to fight' had as its first goal the establishment of a militarised national-racial community ('Volksgemeinschaft'). This seemed to accord perfectly with the interests of the military. The programme was carried out with great energy and expense and formed the basis of a solid co-operation which was never, could never, be questioned by the Reichswehr and later the Wehrmacht leaders, as they considered the appropriate military organisation of all social groups the prerequisite for effective action. They believed that only in this way could a recurrence of the negative developments of the First World War — the outbreaks of unrest among the workers and the soldiers' strikes — be prevented.

This 'rebuilding', which was carried out without significant difficulties, formed the basis for military policy decisions and planning after 1933. The political actions of the military and the political-ideological relationship of the leaders of the Reichswehr, and later the Wehrmacht, to National Socialism have been frequently examined in recent years, though by no means exhaustively. The phrase coined by Manfred Messerschmidt, a 'partial identity of goals', accurately describes this relationship.[34] Only recently have the military activities of the leading institutions of the armed forces received more attention, with the purpose of producing a clearer picture of the consequences of the aims of military policy, that is, of the organisational decisions of the armed forces and the methods used to realise or in the attempt to realise them.[35] Both areas of research are represented in this volume.

The decision to rearm unilaterally, made at the time of Hitler's coming to power, was connected in the minds of German military leaders with the goal of regaining the Great Power status Germany had enjoyed before 1914, without reflecting the consequences of such an ambitious aim. *Michael Geyer* stresses the fundamental importance of this decision for the course of German history, national and international, and examines, above all, the repercussions of a permanently accelerating process of armament on the army command's way of acting. The futile striving for military security became the decisive factor of this acceleration, in the process of which the military leader's controlling rationality fell a prey to the dynamics of armament. In this respect General Beck's resignation as chief of the army general staff in the summer of 1938 appears to be both the consequent result of his armament policy and the abrupt end of the traditional, so to speak self-evident claim of the military in case of war to take the strategic decisions and to control their implementation. The development of the navy in the interwar period presents a similar picture, whose determining factors are outlined by *Jost Dülffer*. In contrast to the rearmament in the army and air force it is clear that, in the interest of his ideologically determined policy towards Britain, Hitler exerted a decisive influence on the individual phases of naval rearmament. But it is also obvious that for a long time there was no clear idea in the navy itself as to the military policy aims of naval rearmament. The organisational and technical prerequisites were at the same time more complex and less developed than in the army.

In addition to the submarine, the First World War demonstrated the importance of three new weapons which inspired the imagination of military theorists: the aeroplane, the tank and poison gas.[36] It seemed to many strategists that a future war fought with these weapons would lead either to a total victory or to a total defeat; the distinction between Front and home front disappeared completely. Germany circumvented the prohibitions of the Treaty of Versailles against the new weapons with the help of the Soviet Union and was able to put the abundant experience acquired there to good use after 1933.[37] The detailed survey by *Rolf-Dieter Müller* not only gives a picture of the various phases of the planning for the use of poison gas but also shows the influence and methods of the interested industrialists. In selling their products, the directors of IG-Farben by no means restricted themselves to technical matters and aspects of quality control. They also recommended the use of poison gas for strategic and ideological reasons. The military planners and lobbyists failed, however, because of Hitler's veto.

The use of large formations of bombers against military and civilian targets played a role similar to that of poison gas in the plans of military thinkers. Consequently, in the planning phase of the German air force build-up, ideas which generally speaking implied the terrorising of the civilian population of the enemy in a future air war were discussed by the responsible officers. In his essay *Klaus A. Maier* largely rejects prevailing opinion and points out that, in spite of the lack of four-engined strategic bombers in the German air force, its leaders did indeed intend to conduct a strategic air war against civilian populations. In particular, they planned to employ this form of war against Britain, with London as the main target. Strongly influenced by ideological factors, the German generals believed that the superiority of their system guaranteed victory over the politically divided democratic societies of the West.

Not surprisingly, the essays in this volume give the general impression that German military planning and actions after 1933 were first made possible and then sustained by the awareness of a secure relationship between the armed forces and the nation; this was quite aside from the striving of the various military branches and departments for efficiency. This relationship was best expressed in the National Socialist ideology of the national-racial community. Conflicts might develop about aims, methods of rule, and questions of practice,[38] but the basic ideological foundation remained unaffected. *Bernd Wegner* touches upon one of these conflicts, the dispute between the armed forces and the armed SS, the military instrument of the National Socialist movement. With the consistent and rapid build-up of the armed SS, Himmler and other SS leaders pursued a goal which threatened the position of the armed forces as the legitimate executive instrument of the state. The vision of a pan-Germanic army united with the armed, ideologically indoctrinated *Staatsschutzkorps* (state defence corps) of the 'order' in Germany in a Europe dominated by National Socialism foreshadowed a new relationship between the armed forces and the organised national-racial community based on the idea of a master race.

In spite of the constant growth of the SS empire, and the power of the SS as the ubiquitous police instrument of the regime, its leaders were not able to influence German strategic considerations and decisions during the war. Such decisions remained the domain of the armed forces, their high command and, above all, Hitler, who was accepted more than ever as the undisputed political and strategic leader after the triumph over France. *Gerhard Schreiber*'s study of the relationship between Hitler's ideological programme and German military planning is concerned with the question of whether in the summer and autumn of 1940 alternative strategies to Hitler's programme actually existed in the German leadership. The suggestions of the foreign minister, von Ribbentrop, and the commander-in-chief of the navy, Admiral Raeder, (each representing different perceptions and goals) to continue the war against the Anglo-Saxon sea powers instead of attacking the Soviet Union were indeed such strategies; but an examination of German political initiatives and military planning with regard to the Mediterranean makes clear that Hitler's irrevocable strategic decision to attack the Soviet Union was made at a conference with his military advisers on 31 July 1940. In other words, the suggested alternatives in western and southern Europe had no chance of replacing Hitler's ideological-programmatic goal — the conquest of living space in the east, which he had developed as early as the 1920s.

This aim determined not only the strategic decision but also the manner in which it was carried out. In the spring of 1941 Hitler left no doubt that his goal was not only to expand the area under German domination but also to 'annihilate Jewish Bolshevism' at the same time. The resulting measures, which corresponded to Hitler's social Darwinist programme and made the war against the Soviet Union the 'most shocking war of conquest, enslavement, and annihilation' in modern times, have already been thoroughly examined.[39] But the usual answers to the question of how this complete rejection of accepted humane values was possible in a nation that proudly considered itself a civilised country are still unsatisfactory. *Manfred Messerschmidt*'s contribution on the subject of the jurisdiction of the German military in the Second World War details the intellectual-historical background which must be examined to understand the causes of the perversion of legal thinking and practice in the Third Reich. Here too it is clear that defeat in the First World War and all the accompanying developments left deep marks and changed the thoughts and actions of the leading German classes.[40] To prevent a disintegration of the nation, as had happened in 1918, the German military justice system accepted the task of maintaining the national-racial community by all means and regarded the sacrosanct *Führerwille* (will of the leader) as the absolute law. As *Jürgen Förster* shows, this strongly ideological attitude, which was also the cause of violence directed against other Germans, explains to some degree why Hitler's annihilation strategy against Jews, Bolsheviks and the hostile Slavic population found such a surprisingly strong echo in the leadership of the armed forces. In no other area was the influence of the total war ideology on military decisions and actions so strong. The fact that the organised mass murder cannot be blamed on Himmler's SS alone is regarded as provocative by influential circles in the Federal Republic, concerned with establishing a legitimising military tradition. At the same time, the historian could well find it difficult to explain if the German armed forces, as a traditional élite, had proved able to resist the pervasive attraction of a perverted nationalistic thinking.

The two contributions by *Lothar Burchardt* and *Bernhard R. Kroener* are concerned with entirely different aspects of the Second World War, but they also show the decisive influence of the experiences of the First World War. Unlike the situation in 1914–18, the militarised national-racial community seemed to offer the possibility of organising the nation for an industrialised war through centrally controlled, effective measures in all areas of society. This theoretical plan was, however, frustrated by the structure of the *Führerstaat* (leader state).[41] By analysing the methods of allocating personnel between the armed forces and the economy, Kroener shows that there was simply no effective planning or organisation in this extremely critical area in the first years of the war. He rejects the still widespread opinion that the victories over Poland and France were the results of a comprehensive plan for a 'Blitzkrieg' (lightning war) and comes to the conclusion that, if any of Hitler's wars fitted that description, it was the one against the Soviet Union, not only in a military but also in an economic sense. Kroener's study is concerned with a previously neglected subject offering important insights into the structure of the Third Reich under war conditions.

Also fruitful are comparative studies of the preconditions, conditions and effects of the conduct of the First World War from 1914 to 1918 and the Second World War from 1939 to 1945, an approach neglected in the past. Burchardt's many-sided comparison of the food supply system for the civilian population conveys, among other things, an impression of the efforts the National Socialist regime made to avoid any alarm in this area. The traumatic experience of the First World War caused the German leaders to regard the maintaining of the home front as an important, separate goal, which was achieved by the 'carrot and stick' method. The total industrialised war was conceivable and realisable only with the co-operation of the workers and soldiers. In making his plans Hitler had to take into consideration what General Wilhelm Groener had realised in 1916, that the war could not be won against the workers,[42] and what Ludendorff had understood in the summer of 1918, that a war could not even be conducted against the will of the mass of ordinary soldiers.[43]

The editor hopes that the selected essays not only throw new light on central themes of research but also offer guidelines for studying the history of the German national state which has been determined to a large extent by the sword. The areas of possible research are by no means all covered by the contributions published here. Studies of certain aspects of the educational system,[44] the control of public opinion,[45] or of economic[46] and social[47] conditions and the effects of the activities of the military give one an idea of the possibilities for further research in military history. An example of the synthesis possible in this field is offered in the conclusion of the first volume of the history of the Second World War, published by the Office of Military Historical Research in Freiburg, and printed here as the last contribution. The reader may have the impression that the study of the military as an institution, or of the organisational and social problems of its internal structure or, primarily, the description of military events themselves might be neglected in favour of the deliberate expansion of the framework of military history. That this impression is wrong may be seen, for example, in the organisation of the series about the Second World War mentioned above. The major shortcoming of military history in Germany from 1871 to 1945 was rather its failure to examine the effects of the continuing industrialisation on the internal structure and the political and military freedom of action of the armed forces. The growing dependence on economic factors and armaments technology and the increasing bureaucracy in all areas of life, including the military, are only the key words for developments whose significance for the armed forces cannot yet be measured. There is, after all, no international basis of comparison, although the need for it in all areas of historical studies has already been pointed out so often and with such emphasis — though without success — that nothing more can be added in this regard here.

In conclusion the editor, on behalf of all the authors, would like to thank the publisher, Dr Marion Berghahn, for the care and prudence with which she has prepared and assisted in the publication of this book. Most importantly, she made the suggestion to publish this volume, a truly rare example of a publisher's interest and initiative in spreading knowledge of a specialised discipline, which is all too often an unprofitable undertaking.

Notes

1. A selection of the extensive periodical literature on military historical subjects can be found in the *War and Society Newsletter*, published as a supplement to the *Militärgeschichtliche Mitteilungen* since 1975. As an exceptional guide, see D. E. Showalter, *German Military History, 1648–1982. A Critical Bibliography*, New York/London, 1984.

2. For example, in the works of Sir Basil Liddell Hart (on Liddell Hart see B. Bond, *Liddell Hart: A Study of his Military Thought*, London, 1977) and the extensive Rommel literature (e.g. David Irving, *The Trail of the Fox: The Life of Field Marshal Erwin Rommel*, London, 1977). The number of translations of the memoirs of German generals is also remarkable: for example, Erich von Manstein, *Lost Victories*, London, 1958. In this respect see Andreas Hillgruber, 'Generalfeldmarschall Erich von Manstein in der Sicht des kritischen Historikers', in U. von Gersdorff (ed.), *Geschichte und Militärgeschichte*, Frankfurt/M., 1974, pp. 349ff.

3. For the Federal Republic of Germany cf. for example the numerous volumes of the historical series of the Neue Wissenschaftliche Bibliothek which have been published since the 1960s, originally by Kiepenheuer & Witsch; cf. also the periodical *Geschichte und Gesellschaft: Zeitschrift für historische Sozialwissenschaft* (since 1975).

4. M. Jähns, *Geschichte der Kriegswissenschaften vornehmlich in Deutschland*, three vols., Berlin, 1920–36.

5. H. Delbrück, *Geschichte der Kriegskunst im Rahmen der politischen Geschichte*, seven vols., Berlin, 1920–36.

6. E. Kessel, *Moltke*, Stuttgart, 1957.

7. G. Ritter, *Staatskunst und Kriegshandwerk: Das Problem des 'Militarismus' in Deutschland*, four vols., Munich, 1958–64 (transl. as *The Sword and the Sceptre: the Problem of Militarism in Germany*, London, 1972).

8. H. Herzfeld, *Das Problem des deutschen Heeres 1919–1945*, Laumpheim, 1952.

9. Cf. the contributions by G. Sandhofer, H. Umbreit and K. Köhler in R. Higham (ed.), *Official Histories*, Manhattan/Kansas, 1970, pp. 147ff.

10. M. Messerschmidt, *Die Wehrmacht im NS-Staat: Zeit der Indoktrinierung*, Hamburg, 1969, pp. 339ff. On the aims and methods of military historiography see *Militärgeschichtliche Mitteilungen*, 20 (1976), pp. 15.

11. N. Wiggershaus, 'Die amtliche Militärgeschichtsforschung in der Dienststelle Blank und im Bundesministerium für Verteidigung 1952 bis 1956', *Militärgeschichtliche Mitteilungen*, 20(1976), pp. 115ff.

12. G. Greiner, ' "Operational History (German) Section" und "Naval Historical Team": Deutsches militärstrategisches Denken im Dienst der amerikanischen Streitkräfte von 1946 bis 1950', in M. Messerschmidt, K. A. Maier, W. Rahn and B. Thoss (eds.), *Militärgeschichte*, Stuttgart, 1982, pp. 409ff.; C. B. Burdick, 'Vom Schwert zur Feder. Deutsche Kriegsgefangene im Dienst der Vorbereitung der amerika-

nischen Kriegsgeschichtsschreibung über den Zweiten Weltkrieg: Die organisatorische Entwicklung der Operational History (German) Section', *Militärgeschichtliche Mitteilungen*, 10(1971), pp. 69ff.

13. Cf. the contributions in Messerschmidt et al. (eds.), *Militärgeschichte*, pp. 18–59.

14. R. Wohlfeil, 'Wehr-, Kriegs- oder Militärgeschichte?' *Militärgeschichtliche Mitteilungen*, 1 (1967), p. 25.

15. *Das Deutsche Reich und der Zweite Weltkrieg*, I, *Ursachen und Voraussetzungen der deutschen Kriegspolitik*, Stuttgart, 1979, p. 17.

16. J. Wheeler-Bennett, *The Nemesis of Power*, London, 1964; G. Craig, *The Politics of the Prussian Army 1650–1945*, London, 1968; F. L. Carsten, *The Reichswehr and Politics 1918 to 1933*, (Berkeley, Calif., 1973).

17. H.-U. Wehler, ' "Absoluter" und "totaler" Krieg: Von Clausewitz bis Ludendorff', in von Gersdorff (ed.), *Geschichte und Militärgeschichte*, pp. 273ff.

18. Cf. *Anfänge westdeutscher Sicherheitspolitik 1945–1956*, I, *Von der Kapitulation bis zum Pleven-Plan*, Munich/Vienna, 1982.

19. Cf. B. Kroener, 'Literaturbericht zum Kriegswesen 1648–1888', in *Handbuch zur deutschen Militärgeschichte 1648–1939*, V, Munich, 1979, pp. 587–633; cf. also *War and Society Newsletter*.

20. Cf. K. D. Erdmann, *Die Zeit der Weltkriege*, ninth edn, *Gebhardt Handbuch der deutschen Geschichte*, IV, Stuttgart, 1973, 1976.

21. Ritter, *Staatskunst*; Carsten, *Reichswehr*; T. Vogelsang, *Reichswehr, Staat und NSDAP: Beiträge zur deutschen Geschichte 1930–1932*, Stuttgart, 1962; W. Sauer, 'Die Mobilmachung der Gewalt', in K. D. Bracher, W. Sauer and G. Schulz, *Die nationalsozialistische Machtergreifung*, Cologne/Opladen, 1960, pp. 685–972; K.-J. Müller, *Das Heer und Hitler: Armee und nationalsozialistisches Regime 1933–1940*, Stuttgart, 1969; Messerschmidt, *Wehrmacht*.

22. K. Demeter, *Das deutsche Offizierkorps in Gesellschaft und Staat: 1650–1945*, fourth revised and enlarged edn., Frankfurt/M, 1965; H. H. Hofmann (ed.), *Das deutsche Offizierkorps 1860–1960*, Boppard, 1980; R. Stumpf, *Die Wehrmacht-Elite, Rang- und Herkunftsstruktur der deutschen Generale und Admirale 1933–1945*, Boppard, 1982.

23. The best example of this is V. R. Berghahn, *Der Tirpitz-Plan: Genesis und Verfall einer innenpolitischen Krisenstrategie unter Wilhelm II.*, Düsseldorf, 1971; see also M. Geyer, *Aufrüstung oder Sicherheit: Die Reichswehr in der Krise der Machtpolitik 1924–1936*, Wiesbaden, 1980; V. R. Berghahn, *Militarism: The History of an International Debate*, 1861–1979, Leamington Spa, 1982.

24. Cf. Wehler, *Krieg*.

25. I. Saatmann, *Parlament, Rüstung und Armee in Frankreich 1914/1918*, Düsseldorf, 1978, p. 455.

26. H.-U. Wehler, *Das Deutsche Kaiserreich 1871–1918*, Göttingen, 1973, pp. 62, 149 (transl. as *The German Empire 1871–1918*, Leamington Spa, 1985); W. Sauer, 'Das Problem des deutschen Nationalstates', in Wehler (ed.), *Moderne deutsche Sozialgeschichte*, second edn., Cologne, 1968, p. 432.

27. W. Deist, 'Armee und Arbeiterschaft', in Messerschmidt et al. (eds.), *Militärgeschichte*, pp. 171ff.
28. W. Mommsen, 'Die latente Krise des Deutschen Reiches 1909–1914', in Brandt, Meyer and Just, *Handbuch der deutschen Geschichte*, Frankfurt/M., 1973, IV/1, p. 5.
29. Cf. M. Geyer's literature report, 'Die Wehrmacht der deutschen Republik ist die Reichswehr', *Militärgeschichtliche Mitteilungen*, 14(1973), pp. 152ff.
30. H. Hürten, *Reichswehr und Ausnahmezustand: Ein Beitrag zur Verfassungsproblematik der Weimarer Republik in ihrem ersten Jahrfünft*, Opladen, 1977.
31. Geyer, *Aufrüstung*; cf. also the contributions in K.-J. Müller and E. Opitz (eds.), *Militär und Militarismus in der Weimarer Republik*, Düsseldorf, 1978; W. Rahn, *Reichsmarine und Landesverteidigung, 1919–1928: Konzeption und Führung der Marine in der Weimarer Republik*, Munich, 1976; E. W. Bennett, *German Rearmament and the West, 1932–1933*, Princeton, NJ, 1979.
32. E. Matthias and R. Morsey (eds.), *Das Ende der Parteien*, Düsseldorf, 1960; K. D. Bracher, *Die Auflösung der Weimarer Republik: Eine Studie zum Problem des Machtverfalls in der Demokratie*, fifth edn, Villingen, 1971.
33. At a meeting on 3 February 1933. Cf. T. Vogelsang, 'Neue Dokumente zur Geschichte der Reichswehr 1930–1933', *Vierteljahreshefte für Zeitgeschichte*, 2(1954), pp. 434f.
34. Messerschmidt, *Wehrmacht*, p. 1.
35. Cf. the contribution by W. Deist in *Ursachen und Voraussetzungen*, pp. 371ff.
36. Cf. for example M. Schwarte, *Der Krieg der Zukunft*, Leipzig, 1931.
37. Geyer, *Aufrüstung*, pp. 149ff.
38. Cf. the studies by Müller, *Heer*, and Messerschmidt, *Wehrmacht*, as well as K.-J. Müller, *Ludwig Beck: Studien und Dokumente zur politisch-militärischen Vorstellungswelt und Tätigkeit des Generalstabschefs des deutschen Heeres 1933–1938*, Boppard, 1980; W. Deist, *The Wehrmacht and German Rearmament*, London, 1981.
39. J. Förster in *Das Deutsche Reich*, IV, *Der Angriff auf die Sowjetunion*, Stuttgart, 1983, pp. 413ff.; C. R. Browning, 'Wehrmacht reprisal policy and the mass murder of Jews in Serbia', *Militärgeschichtliche Mitteilungen*, 33(1983), pp. 311f.
40. As an introduction see A. Flitner (ed.), *Deutsches Geistesleben und Nationalsozialismus*, Tübingen, 1965.
41. G. Hirschfeld and L. Kettenacker (eds.), *The 'Führer State': Myth and Reality, Studies on the Structure and Politics of the Third Reich*, Stuttgart, 1981; see particularly the introduction by W. Mommsen, pp. 9ff.
42. Deist, 'Armee', p. 179.
43. Cf. *Militär und Innenpolitik im Weltkrieg 1914–1918*, W. Deist (ed.), Düsseldorf, 1970, p. 1250, n. 13.
44. Cf. for example M. Messerschmidt, 'Bildung und Erziehung im "zivilen" und militärischen System des NS-Staates', in Messer-

schmidt et al. (eds.), *Militärgeschichte*, pp. 190ff.

45. W. Wette, 'Deutsche Kriegspropaganda während des Zweiten Weltkriegs', in Messerschmidt et al. (eds.), *Militärgeschichte*, pp. 311ff.
46. F. Forstmeier and H.-E. Volkmann (eds.), *Wirtschaft und Rüstung am Vorabend des Zweiten Weltkriegs*, 2nd ed., Düsseldorf, 1977; F. Forstmeier and H.-E. Volkmann (eds.), *Kriegswirtschaft und Rüstung 1939–1945*, Düsseldorf, 1977.
47. M. Geyer, 'Ein Vorbote des Wohlfahrtsstaates. Die Kriegsopferversorgung in Frankreich, Deutschland und Grossbritannien nach dem Ersten Weltkrieg', *Geschichte und Gesellschaft*, 9(1983), pp. 230ff.

WOLFGANG PETTER

'Enemies' and 'Reich Enemies'. An Analysis of Threat Perceptions and Political Strategy in Imperial Germany, 1871–1914

1

It was, of course, an exaggeration when a contemporary observer described the Prussia of Frederick the Great as being not a state with an army but an army with a state.* *Bons môts* are seldom completely true, but they do usually contain a grain of truth; the Prussian state with its claim to self-preservation and the maintaining of its own power provided the *raison d'être* for the army, and wars were waged not in the interest of the army but in that of the state. But it is also a commonplace of history that the army was among the most important components of the Prussian state and that the country appeared to be a single enormous army depot organisation. This was the deeper meaning of the proverbial expression 'travailler pour le roi de la Prusse'. It was decisive that war was intended to

---

*The following essay spans such a wide range of sources that notes would not provide adequate references. A Select Bibliography (p. 39) provides a basic reading list for those who wish to pursue the matter further. A thematically similar work by the author has been published under the title 'Der Kompromiss zwischen Militär und Gesellschaft im kaiserlichen Deutschland 1871 bis 1918', in *Revue d'Allemagne*, 11(1979), pp. 346–62.

Transl. from the German by Dean S. McMurry.

benefit not Frederick's subjects but the bureaucratic organisation 'state', for whose sake enormous sums were spent. Among the categorical imperatives of service to this bloodless apparatus, however, the tendency to degenerate into an end in itself was inherent in the subapparatus army and its service. The essence of the old Prussia became clear after her devastating defeat in 1806, when she demanded not patriotism but 'calm and order' as the appropriate duty of her subjects.

After the reforms of the following years, the crown could no longer make independent decisions about war and peace or conduct a war for reasons that it alone understood. It was dependent on the harmony of its interests with those of the groups which provided the conscripts, the non-professional officers and the necessary funds. The rebellion of the East Prussian gentry, which began the war of liberation against Napoleon in 1813, or conversely the mutinies of 'Landwehr' troops in May 1849, which accompanied the struggle of Friedrich Wilhelm IV against the national movement and, finally, the refusal of the Prussian parliament to approve the budget during Bismarck's war against Denmark in 1864, showed that an army drawn from the mass of the population inevitably reflected the opinions of that population, who had to be persuaded of the necessity of winning a war. This was accomplished superbly in June 1870 and August 1914, by describing the hoped-for conflicts as defensive wars with aims that enjoyed widespread support. Military traditions die hard; many dyed-in-the-wool soldiers could not accept the change in the nature of the Prussian military state and the shift of its main point of reference. It was considered noble to shed or to sacrifice blood for the state and its personification, the monarch. But the demands of the ordinary people, that their lives and well-being, as they understood and articulated these concepts politically, be defended were met with contempt. This anachronistic attitude was expressed most strikingly in connection with the Schlieffen Plan; many officers no longer considered 'civilian' policy to be the basis for waging a war and determining its goals. Rather they regarded the main task of such policy to be the creating of a favourable starting-point for military operations. After the end of the monarchy, this attitude lived on in Seeckt's almost 'old-Prussian' observation: 'The army serves the state and only the state, for it is the state'.

In Imperial Germany this view was widespread but by no means obligatory. Even then German leaders were thinking in terms of a total socio-political strategy in which the meaning and purpose of war was not simply victory but the preservation of larger interests. In March 1912, in an argument with Kaiser Wilhelm II, the chancellor of the 'Reich', Theobald von Bethmann Hollweg, did refer to 'honour' as the first morally justifiable reason for war, but he also added some very concrete ideas about the 'vital interests' of Germany. The basis of his ideas in this respect was the compromise which had developed in the Prussian constitutional controversy of 1862–6 between two social groups, the military and the bourgeoisie. This was not an agreement between leading representatives of the government and the parties but rather a relationship of trust and confidence between these two groups. By their strict adherence to the constitution during the conflict both groups had contributed to overcoming the traumas of the revolution and counter-revolution of 1848 and 1849. In the constitutional conflict the bourgeoisie had sought to prevent the army from turning to a doctrinaire conservative policy, which it seemed to be doing by the elimination of the militia-like Landwehr as field troops and the extension of military service for the purpose of the better training of conscripts in a blind obedience. For its part, the army had mistakenly believed that its extra-constitutional position was in danger, but the opposition wanted only to keep the military out of politics. Any reservations the bourgeoisie had about the army were eliminated by its function as a convincing instrument of liberal 'Realpolitik' practised, surprisingly, by Bismarck. Even in the Empire the bourgeoisie guaranteed the sovereign position to which the army was accustomed. In addition, they proved to be such a good source of human material for the army that the proportion of men of bourgeois origin in the officer corps had risen from one- to two-thirds by 1914 without affecting the outlook of that social group. The number of reserve officers, mostly middle-class, grew to several times the size of the professional officer corps between 1914 and 1918. Even the non-Prussian bourgeoisie proudly renounced the traditional use of paid substitutes to avoid military service, for which purpose insurance policies had occasionally been taken out for children. The military rewarded this support by accepting the gradual loss of power of the nobility, although its mentality continued to be shaped by the values of that class, and it even guaranteed the power of the bourgeoisie. This compromise was so strong and so generally accepted that it survived until almost the end of the First World War, collapsing only after the crown and those groups directly connected with it had irrevocably lost their authority.

In the classical view, military policy is closely associated with foreign policy. Of course even Clausewitz, who was the first and perhaps the only contemporary to communicate fully the importance of the Prussian civil and military reforms after the collapse of Frederick the Great's system, did not mean this one component but policy as a whole when he spoke of war being its continuation 'by other means'. In fact after the Paris Commune of 1871, at the latest, those in responsible positions in Germany no longer viewed the armed forces as merely an important figure in the chess game of foreign relations and clearly separated from domestic politics and social conditions. Henceforth the military and war were viewed in broader contexts, in connection with the social order. As the perceptive Jakob Burckhardt expressed it, even Bismarck profited from the 'great advantage that the entire world believed that only Louis Napoleon was waging war for domestic reasons'. Of course the purpose of Imperial German foreign policy was ostensibly limited to maintaining the Great Power position of the Reich, but this itself was already a one-sided view. Power, which in itself is neutral, has been defined by Max Weber as 'the possession of the means to realise one's intentions'. In the final analysis, the intentions of Imperial Germany were determined to a considerable degree by what were considered the common interests of society as well as by group interests.

Prussian Germany's measure of her status as a Great Power — the ability, without losing that status, to keep herself free of alliances in which she could not control her partners in decisive areas — was objectively dangerous and, in its irrationality, a cause of justified concern for neighbouring states. Such a standard was perhaps still suitable for the half-industrialised Prussia of 1866, who was unable to prevent the desertion of her partners in the 'Zollverein' during the brief inter-German war and did not long feel that loss. For the industrialised German Empire, however, which was increasingly dependent on foreign markets for selling and purchasing goods as well as for labour and investment, this standard inevitably impaired the powers of judgement of its leaders to the point of producing misperceptions of reality. Only in this way can the unanimous view of those involved in the German management of the July Crisis be explained — that they had stumbled into the crisis and had been overwhelmed by the automatic functioning of the military-diplomatic mechanism which led to the outbreak of war. Without wishing to take sides, belatedly, in the Fritz Fischer controversy of the 1960s and 1970s, we must point out that all German leaders were agreed that sooner or later a great war would be necessary to stabilise the system by establishing an economic imperium in Central Europe. For the German leaders, who could imagine international co-operation only as a *societas leonina*, the alternatives were 'world-power status or decline', a choice which the retired cavalry general Friedrich von Bernhardi made popular in 1912, giving as his reasons 'the struggle for jobs' and — a sign that he was far behind in his understanding of domestic political developments — 'socialism and the means to overcome it'.

2

In the final analysis it may be seen that the total German socio-political strategy had as its purpose the defence of the compromise between conservative and progressive elements in German society against a world of real and imagined enemies, foreign and domestic. For this reason any opposition or protest group was labelled a 'Reichsfeind' (Reich enemy) and subjected to the most severe attacks as soon as it was perceived by those in power to represent even a remote threat to the established order. Conversely, even the most disliked domestic political opponent provoked only disputes within the system so long as he was not suspected of constituting a danger for it as a whole. An example here is the proto-fascism organised by Adolf Stoecker in 1878, which had disastrous consequences later. Bismarck wanted to use the Socialist Law to suppress the abusive agitation of this movement in 1880, but the Kaiser, in agreement with the general staff, rejected his recommendation.

If we consider another aspect, Britain became an object of public hate in Germany after the turn of the century, in this respect completely overshadowing feelings against France, the more traditional enemy. This was after interested groups led by Admiral Alfred von Tirpitz had infected everyone with their own deep fear that 'perfidious Albion' was in a position to disrupt Germany's economic and social order at will through her control of world trade. A certain animosity between Germany and the United States, which was to grow into open hostility in the spring of 1917, developed as a result of a concern dating from the Bismarck era. The high emigration figures of the 1880s* gave rise to apprehension owing to the loss of especially desirable conscripts from farming areas. The German government sought to counteract the 'pull effect' of America by repression, without really understanding that the main cause was the negative effect of the agricultural crisis, which reached its full intensity after 1879. Intending emigrants were ostracised.

The oldest opponents of the compromise between the bourgeoisie and the military were the left-wing Liberals, or *Fortschrittspartei*, a party founded in 1861. As they defended the military organisation of the Prussian reform period with its middle-class component, the Landwehr, they were sharply attacked politically and, until 1866, in some cases physically. After the founding of the Empire and their reluctant acceptance of the compromise, they were again attacked because of their demand that the Imperial constitution be converted into a parliamentary system. Bismarck implied that they had not only ideological but also concrete political connections with Britain, as he considered them soldiers of the 'Crown Prince *fronde*' around the Kaiser-to-be, Friedrich III, and his English consort Victoria. Only after the Crown Prince had explicitly rejected a 'German Gladstone cabinet' were the left-wing Liberals no longer accused of treasonable tendencies and thus enabled to embark on a development which eventually made them once again the main representatives of the bourgeoisie.

After the Prussian annexation of Hanover in 1866, the Guelphs, a socially conservative and politically pro-Austrian regional movement for the re-establishment of the province of Hanover as a kingdom, appeared as a second internal/external enemy. In the beginning they had both the means and the fanaticism to organise an exile army, the so-called *Welfenlegion*, but they ran out of money and rapidly lost followers after the outbreak of the Franco-Prussian War in the spring of 1870. After the founding of the Empire the militant Guelphs slowly degenerated into a lukewarm protest party which was never able to win national support, even though it survived into the Federal Republic.

In December 1870 political Catholicism also began to articulate its goals as a protector of the Catholic minority against the 'Prottestant monarchy'. With its policy of preventive negation, it succeeded

---

*Between 1880 and 1893 1.8 million Germans emigrated to the United States.

from the start in mobilising for its party, the Centre, one-third of German Catholics.* As early as 1871 the state, which was dominated by right-wing liberalism, began its counter-attack, the 'Kulturkampf', which it continued with varying severity until 1886–7. Political Catholicism acquired the label of a Reichfeind in the categories of contemporary threat analysis, which included above all religious and tactical ties to other countries and to the national minorities with their separatist tendencies. At the height of the Kulturkampf half of the Catholic bishops and one-quarter of the priests in Prussia were either arrested or expelled, but the Centre was still able to double its share of the vote in the national and state parliamentary elections of the early 1870s. Nevertheless, the loyalty of Catholics to the state remained unbroken; the number of Catholics supporting the Centre rose from one-third to only about one-half (16.88 per cent of all persons entitled to vote) in 1874 and stabilised at something definitely less than a half in 1877. Tyrannicide was confined to an isolated attempt on Bismarck's life in 1874. In 1876 Bismarck began to reduce the discrimination and to integrate Catholicism into his political calculations. The Catholics responded with especially warm support for the compromise. Within the framework of the constitutional system the Centre can even be considered as a party which supported the government in the years 1878–86, 1893–1906 and 1908–18. Catholics were underrepresented in the élites of the Empire and the German states, for example in the officer corps and among professors, compared with their numbers in the population as a whole, but this was only to a small degree a result of discrimination. The causes of the Catholic educational deficit, evident for example in the fact that only 0.033 per cent of Catholic men attended a university, compared to 0.054 per cent among Protestant men, are too complex to be discussed here. The relative under-representation existed even in such predominantly Catholic areas as Bavaria. If at times the only Catholic in the Prussian ministry of the interior was the chancellery errand boy, this was intentional, but no conclusions regarding a strategy of domestic diversion from real problems can be drawn from the general under-representation, although such a strategy is frequently assumed. We can say that German Catholics as such were never

---

*Catholics made up one-third of the total population (36 per cent minus the national minorities). Thus the Centre Party attracted 9.38 per cent of those entitled to vote.

regarded as a danger to the Reich and political Catholicism was considered a threat only temporarily. With its idea of class reconciliation, it was even an important stabilising factor in maintaining the socio-political structure and thus incorporated in the total socio-political strategy.

In no other areas were the dubiousness and the strength of the compromise between the military leaders and the bourgeoisie so clear as in their converging and diverging attitudes towards the workers. For a long time the threat analysis and the total strategy took these attitudes as their point of orientation; as we now know, this was a misinterpretation of reality. The reasons for this orientation can be explained primarily as the enormous dynamism of the radical economic changes which transformed Germany from an agrarian to an industrial state during the course of the nineteenth century. In the period 1860 to 1869 the relative agricultural and industrial shares of the net domestic product were 44:25; by 1890 they were equal; in 1910 to 1913 they were 23:45. Wolfram Fischer summarises this development:

> In 1850 only 44 per cent of a population of 35 million were employed. In 1913, on the other hand, the figure was 46 per cent of a population of 67 million. The number of jobs in mining, industry and handicrafts tripled in this way from 3.8 million in 1852 to almost 11.5 million in 1913, whereas the number of persons employed in agriculture, the fishing industry and forestry only rose from 8.3 million to 10.7 million. The rise in services (business, transportation, public service and the military), which employed around 3 million people in 1850 but about 8.5 million in 1913, was only slightly behind employment in the production sector. Only the simultaneous rise of both sectors marks the change from an agricultural to an industrial society; in the first phase the production and in the second phase the service areas tend to grow more rapidly — a development clearly recognisable in Germany.

The change in the nature of the lower classes of the social order, which took place during this transformation, was the most decisive factor in German military history during the Empire (the change in that of the middle class was the second most important). The industrial working class, with the exception of a not insignificant number of socially declassed artisans, had developed from the lower class of craftsmen of pre-industrial times. As a group the industrial workers included one-twentieth of the population in 1846, one-fifth in 1871, a quarter in 1884 and one-third in 1907. In terms of size they completely replaced the economically irrelevant pauperism of pre-industrial times. As an indispensable factor in the modern production process they were of much greater importance, since it was possible for them to raise the price of their labour by strikes. However, the mentality of most Germans lagged far behind the actual material changes; the self-image of the industrial working class and its recognition by other social groups adjusted only slowly to the new situation. The two partners in the compromise abandoned only hesitantly their pre-industrial attitude which, under the changed conditions of production, may be described, negatively, as a class struggle from above or, positively, as patriarchal. Some individuals in both groups never changed their views in this respect. The workers' movement had been suppressed since its beginnings in 1835, as had all political organisations of the period before the 1848 revolution. The revolt of the French workers in June 1848 had the effect of an alarm signal on most European governments and, in Germany, led to harsh persecution of the workers' movement. Only in 1863, in its struggle against the bourgeoisie, did the Prussian government permit the development of an organisation which referred to itself in its statutes as, among other things, the 'Social Democratic Party of Germany'. The first trade unions were formed in 1865–6.

The hope of the government to use this tactic to divide the opposition was realised. The social-liberal Hirsch-Duncker Works Union, founded as a bourgeois counter-move in 1868–9, never attracted many members, but the authorities, who were in principle favourably disposed towards the workers' movement, had granted it the right to strike in 1866 and guaranteed that right in 1869, soon renewed their suspicions of the movement. In 1870 the left wing of the workers' movement, which belonged to the First International, refused to vote for war credits, and after Sedan all politically organised workers spoke of a 'just defensive war' of the French, which ought to be ended without annexations or reparations. When August Bebel, in the 'Reichstag' on 25 May 1871, praised the Paris Commune as the 'herald of a new society' and prophesied that revenge would be taken for the *semaine sanglante*, he gave the authorities reason to view the workers' movement itself as an enemy. The thesis of the East German historian Horst Bartel, that 'the historical importance of the unification of Germany is determined by the effects of the Paris Commune', is one-sided and exaggerated if one considers the total development. It is, however, an accurate description of the military-historical aspect of the situation; the German military were occupied for a very long time and very intensively with the struggle against socialism. After 1872 the state again resorted to suppression of the politically organised workers. Their parties were dissolved by police order in Saxony (1872), Bavaria (1874) and Prussia (1875) because of alleged revolutionary agitation. In the Ruhr and the Saar industrialists organised large-scale counter-measures against the workers' movement in their own factories. Perhaps for this reason many workers began to support the party which proclaimed itself their representative; in 1871 the Social Democrats won 1.33 per cent, in 1874 4.13 per cent and in 1877 5.52 per cent of the votes of all the enfranchised, one-quarter of the working class.

In its threat analysis after the election of 1877 the crown had to consider no fewer than 31.5 per cent of all its subjects as active Reichsfeinde of varying degrees of hostility. This was the sum of all opposition votes, but it certainly did not represent the limits of opposition. At the same time the decline in election abstentions (between 1871 and 1877 the number fell from 49.0 per cent to 39.4 per cent) indicated that the subjects were becoming increasingly politicised. Only 29.1 per cent of those entitled to vote supported the government. This development coincided with the first general European Balkan crisis, which resulted from the Russo-Turkish War (April 1877 to February 1878). Moreover, the Crown Prince, who was considered in some circles to be a left-wing liberal, temporarily assumed the leadership of the government around the middle of 1878. In the categories of threat analysis these developments indicated a major crisis for the Reich. In the summer of 1878 Bismarck parried the external and the liberal components of the internal threat with the Congress of Berlin, at which he succeeded in shifting an international conflict from the centre to the periphery of Europe and in making himself indispensable to the Prince Regent as a puller of strings in European diplomacy. He was thus able greatly to reduce the prospects of the development of parliamentary government in Germany. The active terrorism of anarchist sympathisers of Social Democracy gave him the desired weapon for the main internal struggle. After a Reichstag election held in a climate of crisis and hysteria the government pushed through a law against the 'socially dangerous activities of Social Democracy' (*Sozialistengesetz*) on 21 October 1878. With this law the government hoped to drive a wedge between the workers and the workers' movement.

The number of workers supporting the Social Democrats did indeed decline, to 4.79 per cent in 1878 and to 3.43 per cent in 1881. When the illegal party expelled its anarchist wing under J. J. Most, it was able to avoid being associated with the great wave of terrorist attacks on the élites of the Empire and the German states in 1883. When it became known how seriously the remaining groups of the party were debating whether to adopt a revolutionary strategy or one within the system, the Prussian minister of the interior, Robert von Puttkamer, ordered the *Sozialistengesetz* to be implemented in a 'mild' form between 1881 and 1886. The result was the victory of that wing of the Social Democrats which favoured working within the existing system; unexpectedly the revolutionary group accepted this decision. Election support for the Social Democrats grew to 7.8 per cent in 1887. Measures then adopted by the government to combat this tendency, such as the model forms of social welfare introduced in 1883 and constantly improved thereafter, did not achieve their purpose, as the workers fully understood the government's intentions. The intervention of the new Kaiser, Wilhelm II, in the first great miners' strike in the Ruhr in May 1889 — against the advice of his own government and the military — and the repeal of the *Sozialistengesetz* at the beginning of 1890 were regarded by the workers as a legalisation of the moderate Socialist Party. Their support for the party doubled in 1890 to 14.07 per cent, which amounted to at least half of all German workers. Until 1912 this figure rose constantly and finally reached 29.43 per cent, which included most of the workers and a considerable number of persons from other social groups.

It scarcely needs to be mentioned that questions of autonomy and the protest movements of the national minorities were a cause of great concern to the ruling circles of the Reich. The question of Alsace–Lorraine and related issues contributed significantly to the fall of the monarchy. It was hoped that in the course of time the inhabitants of Alsace–Lorraine (3.5 per cent of the total German population) could eventually be re-Germanised and considerable progress was made in this direction. But the permanent confrontation with France resulting from the annexation prevented the German government from regarding and treating the inhabitants of the area other than as unreliable civilians living on a military glacis. For a generation all recruits from Alsace–Lorraine were assigned to units outside the 'Reichsland'. Only after 1903 were 25 per cent of them permitted to serve there. Alsace–Lorraine provided few professional and reserve officers for the German army (the last Prussian minister of war, Heinrich Scheüch, was an exception), whereas it had provided 170 French generals! The Zabern Incident of 1913, an unprovoked military action against demonstrators, had little to do with the question of Alsace–Lorraine itself, but it would hardly have been conceivable if the German military had not felt that it was in hostile country.

A settlement defused the North Schleswig conflict to the point where complete ships' crews from the Danish minority (0.3 per cent) could be used as blockade runners during the First World War. However, after the war the majority decided in a plebiscite to rejoin Denmark.

The disloyalty of the Poles in the Prussian eastern provinces (6.5 per cent), in the event of the re-establishment of their country as a national state, was simply assumed. For this reason systematic and, after 1908, illegal pressure was exerted to Germanise them. Poles were accepted as troops in the eastern provinces, but the professional and reserve officers of their regiments were almost all Germans.

The German–Jewish population (1 per cent) was not included in the threat analysis. In the Franco-Prussian War of 1870–1 there were, in addition to the 9,000 Jewish conscripts, 150 Jewish officers in the German army, including a large proportion of medical officers. After 1880, however, antisemitism spread in Prussia as a result of the struggle against left-wing liberalism, which gave rise to 'anti-plutocratic' emotions directed especially against the Jews. The position of Jews in the army became much worse after the Conservative parties began to include antisemitism in their programmes. Although not forbidden by regulations, no unbaptised Jew was made an officer in a German regiment before the First World War, even though 30,000 were qualified. Of 1,500 baptised Jews 300 achieved reserve officer rank and a few even became professional officers. Only a few Jews became non-commissioned officers. It was argued that, given the widespread antisemitism in Germany, no Jew would have the necessary authority over his men, which the military considered the main prerequisite for such positions.

3

The political change of course in 1890, when Kaiser Wilhelm II dismissed Bismarck and began his 'personal government', marked a break in many other respects. For German military history it was especially important that the emphasis was shifted from threat analysis to total strategy. The will to realise certain goals replaced the previous defensive attitude. 'Nothing works any more.' With these words the press had described the end of the Bismarck era, an era dominated by the defence of the status quo and the fear of losing what had been won in 1871 and 1878. In the end this policy seemed to be nothing more than stagnation. Under these circumstances, Bismarck's dismissal was felt by many Germans to be a liberation. Kaiser Wilhelm II considered himself the spokesman of those who branded the caution of the Reich outside Europe as the cardinal error of previous German foreign policy. The motto of that policy had been 'Germany, Germany above everything else', with the implicit meaning that every German should regard the fatherland as his most valuable possession. But after 1890 the term 'Germany' was critically analysed and presented as something whose unification had been only a 'silly youthful prank' which 'the nation played on its old age and which, because of its costs, should have been avoided if it was to be only the conclusion of previous developments and not the starting-point for German policy as a world power' (Max Weber).

After the decision as to the future course of German policy had been made, the question of the instrument for the realisation of German world power claims and how it should be used presented itself. It was obvious that this instrument had to be a fleet and, in counting up the possible enemies, the responsible German naval strategists discovered that all expected conflicts abroad, as far as their location was concerned, were of secondary importance compared to Britain's control of the sea approaches to Germany. Logically, then, the German leaders came to believe themselves threatened by Britain and began to view the British insistence on 'splendid isolation' as hostility.

The development of this threat analysis on the basis of the total strategy is especially clear in the thinking of Rear-Admiral Alfred Tirpitz, who was appointed naval minister in the summer of 1897 to supervise the expansion of the navy. Tirpitz supported the 'New Course' of 1890, which Bismarck's successor, General Count Leo von Caprivi, paraphrased with the words: 'We must export; either we export goods or we export people; with a growing population we are not able to live without industry'. Tirpitz's own contribution consisted of combining Caprivi's trade policy, which aimed at establishing an economic bloc in Central Europe, with German policy towards the rest of the world, which had until then consisted largely of ceaseless and aimless activity not based on any overriding material interests. In a great propaganda campaign full of whole, half and apparent truths Tirpitz persuaded the public that firstly, in future, well-being and social peace could be maintained only by keeping overseas markets open, secondly, John Bull was guarding the gate to these markets and thirdly, a large battle fleet was the only way to remove him. In itself this argument was consistent, although in 1891 Tirpitz had argued only for expanding the coastal defences against France and Russia to the high seas and had begun to prepare arguments to persuade the Reichstag to approve the necessary number of ships. Then in 1897, when he was able to determine the shape of the future fleet himself, Tirpitz observed succinctly: 'As a basis for our naval policy we must assume the most difficult military situation in which our fleet could possibly find itself. For Germany, Britain is the most dangerous enemy at sea at present'.

The Kaiser and his chancellor were informed that the final goal was to arm until Germany was strong enough to defeat the Royal Navy. Tirpitz demanded that they should make the necessary preparations to include Belgium and Holland in the German naval deployment area at the proper time. Publicly, Tirpitz at first spread the propaganda line that Germany's fleet strength would have to be sufficient to make it of interest as an alliance partner for Britain. Later he argued that the fleet would have to be sufficiently large to make a British naval attack a risk for Britain, but among close friends he explained that the 'natural and only goal' was that 'our fleet should be as strong as the British fleet'. He claimed that the high level of training of the crews and the concentration of leadership in the hands of the Kaiser would give a German fleet of that kind a chance of victory against the British who, because of their interests overseas, would never be able to concentrate their entire fleet in the North Sea. Tirpitz sought to reach the necessary level of naval armaments by proceeding step by step in a manner similar to that of the army, which forced the Reichstag to approve automatically the necesary funds (1867, 1871, 1874, 1880, 1887, 1890, 1893, 1899, 1905, 1911, 1912, 1913) and adjust its authorised strength according to available resources and the threat analysis. In this way the army was finally able to double its peacetime strength from 402,000 to 816,000 men.

In 1898 Tirpitz easily pushed the First Fleet Law through the Reichstag. This set the strength of the German fleet at nineteen line-of-battle ships and twelve armoured cruisers. Tirpitz cleverly exploited the ideology of the German bourgeoisie, which had been formed in the period after the victory over Napoleon I, when Britain was considered a model, and which consisted of nationalism, liberalism and navalism. Obtaining Reichstag approval of the Second Fleet Law in 1900, which raised the authorised strength of the fleet to thirty-eight line-of-battle ships and fourteen armoured cruisers, was more difficult; Tirpitz had to abandon his old allies, the free-traders, and form a coalition with the protectionists. Originally he had been an exponent of class reconciliation and had claimed that the fleet would promote the well-being of the workers by guaranteeing German export chances by force if necessary and would thus reconcile them with the state and social order (social imperialism). But to obtain passage of the Second Fleet Law Tirpitz joined the agrarian protectionists, who sought high foodstuff prices by stopping imports and demanded that the protests of those most seriously affected, the workers, be suppressed, by force if necessary. The Prussian finance minister, Johannes von Miquel, had brought about an alliance between the agrarians and German heavy industry in 1897–8. The industrialists believed that their sales possibilities were better on the home market than abroad; not the least attractive prospect in this respect was the extensive naval construction programme. This alliance, whose fundamental importance in determining the further development of Imperial Germany has been pointed out by Eckart Kehr, is known to German historians as the *Sammlung*. Tirpitz, who had at first sought to mobilise the representatives of social imperialism in a *Gegensammlung* of intellectuals, those involved in trade and the workers, changed course when the *Sammlung* demonstrated its determination and power in the dispute about the construction of the Mid-German Canal. As other countries reacted to German import restrictions with retaliatory duties, naval construction was carried out at the expense of trade, which it had been intended to protect and promote.

One might assume that a political constellation with the goals mentioned above would have led to bitter social conflicts. Such conflicts did indeed arise, but they were far from being as severe as might have been expected in the situation of 1900–2, in which the protective legislation was enacted. In 1891, in their Erfurt Programme, which remained in effect until 1921, the Social Democrats had offered to integrate themselves into the state and social order of Imperial Germany, not without reservations, to be sure. They shunned anything that might endanger their increasing acceptance and recognition. After 1907 even the army acknowledged this development, within limits, and in 1909 Social Democrats supported for the first time measures of a state government (in the Grand Duchy of Baden). Moreover, the economic recovery dampened the social and political conflict; after the Great Depression of 1873–94 and the latest recession (1899–1902) no one in Germany wanted to endanger the recovery by serious labour disturbances. Thus Tirpitz was able on three further occasions to induce the government to create situations at home and abroad which produced the consent of the Reichstag and other interested groups to an increase in the number of ships (1906, 1908, 1912 and a planned increase for 1917).

The 'Dreadnought leap', the change to the construction of Dreadnought-type battleships with unprecedented displacements and calibres, destroyed the financial basis of the German naval programme; the average construction costs for a major warship rose from 15.9 million to 49.5 million marks between 1890 and 1913. On the other hand, the 'Invincible leap', the removal of the armoured cruiser from its reconnaissance function to the line of battle and its continued development as a battle cruiser of the British Invincible class, permitted its actual inclusion in the squadrons of large combat ships, although it was still considered to be and treated as a cruiser. In the final period of the Fleet Laws, the authorised strength of the German high seas fleet was sixty-one heavy ships. However, the average construction costs of an armoured or battle cruiser rose from 18.9 million to 57.7 million marks between 1896 and 1912. The construction costs of other types of ships also doubled and tripled. As a result of the armaments race, which Britain entered after the 'navy scare' of 1909, both countries were caught in a rapidly escalating, unstoppable cost spiral which required a new distribution of the financial burdens among the social segments of their populations. After a hard struggle, David Lloyd George was able to achieve this goal in 1909–11. The privileged groups in Britain finally yielded to necessity. Alfred Tirpitz was unable to achieve the same thing in Germany.

In trying to carry out its naval construction programme, which was enthusiastically supported by the great majority of Germans, the Imperial German government had presented itself with an unsolvable dilemma. Although the Imperial Navy concluded in 1911, from the evidence of the exercises and war preparations of the Royal Navy, that the British would avoid a naval battle and block the shipping lanes beyond the range of the German ships, and although the bankruptcy of the German naval strategy was admitted within the navy itself, its leaders could not abandon the Dreadnought battleship and Invincible battle cruiser as its main weapons. On the one hand, the navy justified its own existence by this strategy; on the other, the crown had identified itself too closely with the naval armaments programme of 1897. It could not abandon that programme without risking a serious loss of confidence and unpredictable dangers for the constitutional system and the partners of the fundamental compromise between the people and the state on which the system was based. At the same time the naval programme began to destroy the basis of the social order, which was in turn the foundation of the fundamental compromise; in other words, everything that the armanents were intended to defend. Imperial Germany was in the process of destroying her ability to defend herself by a misplaced emphasis on her armaments programme and by progressively antagonising the other powers. It also seemed probable that the political and social structure resulting from the internal struggle over the distribution of the armaments costs would make Imperial Germany less worth defending in the eyes of many members of her armed forces. The government was confronted with an enormous crisis which was temporarily obscured by the outbreak of war in 1914 but then aggravated by the burdens of daily life in a war which Germany was losing. In the end the monarchy was overthrown not by Social Democrats but by mutinous sailors of the high seas fleet — an interesting example of the Hegelian 'cunning of history'.

Select Bibliography

H. Aubin and W. Zorn (eds.), *Handbuch der deutschen Wirtschafts- und Sozialgeschichte*, two vols., Stuttgart, 1971, 1976.

V. R. Berghahn, *Der Tirpitz-Plan. Genesis und Verfall einer innenpolitischen Krisenstrategie unter Wilhelm II.*, Düsseldorf, 1971.

W. Deist, 'Die Armee in Staat und Gesellschaft 1890–1914', in M. Stürmer (ed.), *Das kaiserliche Deutschland. Politik und Gesellschaft*, Düsseldorf, 1970, pp. 312–39.

M. Gugel, *Industrieller Aufstieg und bürgerliche Herrschaft. Sozioökonomische Interessen und politische Ziele des liberalen Bürgertums in Preussen zur Zeit des Verfassungskonflikts 1857–1867*, Cologne, 1975.

E. R. Huber, *Deutsche Verfassungsgeschichte seit 1789*, six vols., Stuttgart, 1975 to 1981.

M. Messerschmidt, 'Die Armee in Staat und Gesellschaft — Die Bismarckzeit', in Stürmer, *Deutschland* (see Deist), pp. 89–118.

—, 'Militärgeschichte im 19. Jahrhundert 1814–1890', in Militärgeschichtliches Forschungsamt (ed.), *Handbuch zur deutschen Militärgeschichte 1648–1939*, vol. 2, Munich, 1976.

—, *Militär und Politik in der Bismarckzeit und im Wilhelminischen Deutschland*, Darmstadt, 1975.

W. Petter, 'Deutsche Flottenrüstung von Wallenstein bis Tirpitz', in Militärgeschichtliches Forschungsamt, *Handbuch*, (see Messerschmidt, 'Militärgeschichte'), vol. 4, sect. VIII, 1978.

H. Rosinski, *Die deutsche Armee*, Munich, 1977.

T. Schieder and E. Deuerlein (eds.), *Reichsgründung 1870/71. Tatsachen — Kontroversen—Interpretationen*, Stuttgart, 1970.

B. F. Schulte, *Die deutsche Armee 1900–1914. Zwischen Beharren und Verändern*, Düsseldorf, 1977.

H.-U. Wehler, *Das deutsche Kaiserreich 1871–1918*, Göttingen, 1973 (transl. as *The German Empire 1871–1918*, Leamington Spa, 1985).

LOTHAR BURCHARDT

The Impact of the War Economy on the Civilian Population of Germany during the First and Second World Wars

With the application of sociological methods to historical research, the armament economy and the war economy have
attracted increasing analytical interest.* Important work — for example, the studies of the social and economic history of the First
World War financed by the Carnegie Foundation — was done in
both areas between the wars. However, this trend in research came
to a halt in Germany during the 1930s, and it was not until some
time after the Second World War that historians began to take up
similar projects again. Their interest focused on problems of organisation[1] and on the supply of raw materials, as discussed for example
by Birkenfeld and Petzina.[2] Questions were also asked about the
degree to which these areas interlocked with pressure-group interests, as the war economy as a whole was increasingly perceived as a
product of the interaction of interest groups.[3]

Comparisons between the war economies of the two wars, however, are seldom attempted; similarly, there is little interest in the
part played by the civilian population — beyond their capacity to
work and provide military reinforcements. In short, a perspective

*The German version of this essay may be found, in a considerably longer form, in
Militärgeschichtliche Mitteilungen, 15, 1974, pp. 65–97.
  Transl. from the German by Angela Davies.

on those who were, *de facto*, primarily involved is lacking. This essay cannot hope to fill this gap. It does not attempt to describe in full the complexity of the civilian experience in wartime; it can attempt only to outline the influence of the organisation of the war economy on the supply situation and, more generally, on the economic situation of the average German citizen during both World Wars. Beyond this, we shall have to enquire about the basis on which supplies to the 'average consumer' (to quote the term then in use) were made in each case.

In so far as temporal comparisons are attempted at all, the Second World War is generally considered to have been a more 'total' war than the First, not only militarily, but also in those aspects under discussion here. This assessment needs to be tested — an undertaking which can be combined with a brief survey of the factors determining the size of the burden imposed by the state on the population for the sake of the wartime economy.

We shall begin by examining the food supply situation in both World Wars, which must be seen in relation to the respective prewar conditions. In 1913, Germans consumed an average of 3,400 calories per day, which included 90 grammes of protein, 120 grammes of fat and 400 grammes of carbohydrate.[4] Initially, it must have seemed that it would not be difficult to maintain this level of consumption. Consequently, over-consumption bordering on wastefulness took place during the first months of the war, until the experts' warnings began to be heard, and the first appeals for economy were made to the public.[5]

In the months that followed, animal fodder levels proved to be too low. The reaction was a mass slaughtering of livestock, which temporarily alleviated the problem of food supplies — at the cost of a 35 per cent reduction in the stock of pigs. This was followed by a process which was repeated only too frequently during the next four years; the slaughtering led to an increase in the price of pork which in turn caused the 'Bundesrat' (Upper House) to set a maximum price for pork in November 1915. Pork thereupon, disappeared from the market, to reappear on the 'black' market (a term which became current only later) where it fetched exorbitant prices.[6]

As early as the spring of 1915, rationing was being gradually introduced in certain areas. The events described above, together with the disastrous grain harvest of 1915 and the below-average harvest which followed in 1916, were decisive in drastically increasing the level of government control over the economy (*Zwangs-bewirtschaftung*). The War Food Office (*Kriegsernährungsamt*) was created in May 1916 as a central co-ordinating authority. In the months that followed, it continued the government's attempts to bring the food situation under control. Bread had been rationed since February 1915; similar measures were soon extended to meat and further rationing measures followed rapidly.

Germany's opportunities for importing goods decreased from month to month. The extremely bad potato harvest of 1916 and the unfavourable harvests of the two following years forced the War Food Office and the Bundesrat to keep rations quite low. If the harvest of 1913 equals 100, the values for the last two wartime harvests can be calculated as shown in Table 1.[7] A shortage of labour as well as fertilisers meant that potato and grain harvests reached barely 60 per cent of peacetime levels. If we also take into account the fact that, in peacetime, Germany was unable to produce enough grain and had to import one-fifth of her grains for bread, and more than one-half of her fodder grain requirement, the wartime situation acquires additional significance.

Table 1. *Grain and potato harvests in Germany 1913, 1917 and 1918 (in million tons)*

	1913	1917	1918
Rye	12.1 = 100	7.0 = 58	8.0 = 66
Wheat	4.4 = 100	2.2 = 50	2.5 = 57
Barley	3.6 = 100	1.8 = 50	2.1 = 58
Oats	9.5 = 100	3.6 = 38	4.7 = 50
Potatoes	52.9 = 100	34.4 = 65	29.5 = 56

Under these circumstances, a level of supply that even approached that of peacetime was out of the question. Instead, substitute materials were increasingly used, especially during the last years of the war. By the end of the war, more than 11,000 different products made of such materials had appeared on the market, including 837 sorts of meatless sausage substitute alone. As early as the spring of 1916, that is before the real famine years, about 12 per cent of the food of lower-income groups consisted of these substances, which were often of rather questionable physiological value.[8]

Increasingly, however, the potato became the staple food of the people. This shift is revealed when the average food rations in the last year of the war are expressed as percentages of peacetime consumption, as can be seen in Table 2.[9] Peacetime consumption was undoubtedly higher than the subsistence minimum, which to a certain extent relativises these percentages. On the other hand, it must also be remembered that the rations officially allowed were by no means always obtainable everywhere.

Table 2. *Wartime rations of basic foods expressed as a % of peacetime consumption*

	1 July 1916 — 30 June 1917	1 July 1917 — 30 June 1918	1 July 1918 — 28 Dec. 1918
Meat	31.2	19.8	11.8
Dripping	13.9	10.5	6.7
Butter	22.0	21.3	28.1
Vegetable fats	39.0	40.5	16.6
Pulses	14.2	—	6.6
Flour	52.5	47.1	48.1
Potatoes	70.8	94.2	94.3

Even when the full official rations were available, however, they satisfied only very inadequately real calorie requirements. At the time, Waldemar Zimmermann calculated that if light physical work was done, the official ration in 1917 provided only 60.7 per cent of the needs of a person weighing 65 to 70 kilogrammes; in 1918 the figure was only 57.8 per cent. If the work undertaken was of medium strenuousness, the figures fell below the 50 per cent mark, to 49.8 per cent (1917) and 47.3 per cent (1918).[10] These statistics confirm what the average consumer knew from personal experience: that the official rations alone could not support life over longer periods of time.

The alternative was the black market. What was not available through the regular channels was on offer there in considerable quantities — at exorbitant prices which, for the lower-income groups, often approached prohibitive levels.[11]

This situation did not meet with a sympathetic reaction in conservative circles: people who had more money should be able to afford more food than others[12] — a principle which illustrates the fundamental misunderstanding of the domestic political situation which so decisively hastened the end of the Wilhelmine Reich. A contemporary liberal observer described the food situation more aptly:

'One needs only to look at the workers to recognise that they are suffering from a high degree of malnutrition, that they are starving and that — in spite of their seemingly high wages — wretchedness is written in their faces'.[13]

Supplies of clothing and other manufactured goods were by no means easier. If the level of industrial production in 1915 equals 100, the aggregate production index fell to 85 points by 1918. As this figure includes, among other things, a sharp rise in production for the war economy, it is reasonable to suggest that the reason for the decline in the overall index lies in the unfavourable development of those industries producing primarily for the civilian sector.[14] In fact, the production index fell to 76 per cent of the 1915 level for luxury foods, to 76 per cent for textiles and to 13 per cent for house construction. The 1915 level was itself already below the prewar level.

Retail prices rose accordingly. Between October 1915 and October 1918, the price of woollen materials increased by 800 to 1,700 per cent; the price of cotton materials by 900 to 1,400 per cent. The price of cotton stockings increased tenfold in the same period, and the price of suits reached more than six times the levels of October 1915, without taking into account the general decline in quality and the difficulty of obtaining supplies at all.[15] The government tried to make up for shortages, at least in part, by issuing priority vouchers and initiating house-to-house collections of textiles,[16] but with only limited success.

To enable them to fulfil their responsibilities as far as making supplies available was concerned, government authorities made use of several mechanisms which had gradually been developed during the early years of the war. As soon as a shortage became apparent, a maximum price was set to prevent overcharging.[17] In most cases, price-fixing resulted in the product disappearing from the market. In such a case, an inventory was compiled, followed by government confiscations. What was obtained in this way was supplemented by collections.[18]

Stocks of materials thus acquired were redistributed by a central authority by means of ration cards, priority vouchers and other means. As the food supply situation deteriorated, it increasingly became the custom to allow representatives of the people to co-operate with the authorities in this redistribution.[19] At the same time, requirements for scarce food and raw materials were fulfilled as far as possible with more readily available substitutes.

In addition, attempts were made to supplement stocks available inside Germany from foreign sources of supply, primarily by purchases from neutral countries. Initially this method was successful: food imports from the Netherlands and Denmark quickly exceeded prewar levels, and by 1916 they had reached several times the value of peacetime imports. Naturally they could not fill all the gaps, but they provided that quantity which 'alone made it possible to avoid serious disturbances by maintaining supplies — even if they were minimal — to the large centres of population'.[20] Subsequently the Allies, who naturally had seen what was happening, began to exert every possible pressure on Germany's neutral neighbours, with the result that exports to Germany fell off rapidly during the last two years of the war, losing their earlier significance.

The same applies to grain imports from Romania.[21] This trade, which began in the summer of 1915, had remained far below the level desired by Germany, because Romania fully exploited her favourable negotiating position and, moreover, was under strong pressure from the Allies. Her significance as a supplier of food increased only after she was occupied. Immediately after the conclusion of military operations in 1916, a 'military administration' was set up in Romania to organise the 'exploitation of the country . . . according to principles which had already been precisely laid down'.[22] As the Allies had purchased large quantities of grain in Romania, but had subsequently been unable to transport them, the German booty was considerable. Hindenburg was satisfied that, as he said in reply to a journalist's question, the occupation of the country had averted 'any danger of a food shortage'.[23]

As we know, this prediction proved to have been premature. Nevertheless, in the two years that followed, Romania made a significant, albeit involuntary, contribution to the German war economy by supplying large quantities of grain and livestock. By 31 July 1918 she had supplied Germany with more than 1.8 million tons of food and fodder alone, which represented an annual addition of 6 per cent to the German grain harvest.[24]

The occupied territories made an equally involuntary contribution to the labour sector. The majority of the prisoners and the 500,000 foreign civilian workers conscripted for labour in Germany worked in agriculture. If this reservoir of labour had not existed, the German civilian population's food supply would undoubtedly have been even smaller. In any case the situation was not particularly favourable, especially since where food was concerned, the military had absolute priority over the civilian population until the summer of 1917.[25] This policy was abandoned by Chancellor Michaelis; it reveals to what extent Germany's leaders had for a long time relied on the population's endurance as a stable element in their calculations.

For years, the permanent crisis in the food supply situation was overshadowed by ever-renewed appeals to patriotism and a willingness to make sacrifices.[26] The bad harvest of 1916 was followed by the *Kohlrübenwinter* of 1916/17, when there was little else to eat but turnips. Now, at the latest, the limits of this policy became apparent. There had already been isolated riots over the food situation in the larger towns in 1915. Initially, these lacked both central leadership and an ideological basis, and were easily defused by the promise of increased rations. In 1916 the number of riots increased; they were all focused on dissatisfaction with the general supply situation.[27]

The experience of the *Kohlrübenwinter* resulted in the morale of large sections of the population sinking even lower. A report of 3 April 1917 summarised the situation by stating that the public mood had 'become substantially more serious and depressed as a result of the present difficulties in obtaining food, and even more because of anxiety about the future'.[28] In this tense situation, the average flour ration was reduced on 15 April, and several additional allowances were decreased or abolished altogether. The labour force responded with a strike, which in Greater Berlin alone involved 300,000 workers, and quickly spread to almost all the centres of the German armaments industry.[29] At this stage, demands were still largely limited to the supply situation — for example, that food should be distributed more fairly with the aid of workers' representatives, or that the black market should be checked. At the same time, however, political undertones were becoming more and more audible.

The April strikes were brought to an end relatively quickly and without the use of force, although from this time on the strike movement never lost its momentum. Moreover, a widespread politicisation and radicalisation was now unmistakable. In 1917 workers in Leipzig had demanded 'bread, freedom, peace'; barely a year later, a handbill urged: 'Support the general strike! Join the struggle!'.[30] The question of the food supply now ranked far below political demands. At the end of this path lay the November Revolution of 1918.

The Revolution came as a shock to the entire German bourgeoisie, including Adolf Hitler, and left lasting impressions. The most important of the conclusions which Hitler drew from the events of 1918 was that, for any future war, Germany must be economically better prepared than she had been before 1914. In his view, this included securing adequate food supplies. Consequently, in September 1939 Germany was equipped with stocks of raw materials and a grain reserve of 6 million tons which under a centralised administration could compensate, *ceteris paribus*, for the import requirements of about three years. This reserve, together with the harvest of 1939, was rationed from the first day of the war, and labour and fertilisers were made available in adequate quantities.[31]

As a consequence of this policy, harvest yields were much better than those of 1914–18, although some crops did not reach prewar levels. If the bread, grain and potato harvests of 1914 equal 100, values for the First and Second World War harvests can be calculated as shown in Table 3.[32] As these figures show, at no time during the Second World War did harvest yields fall as low as the lowest levels of 1916/17. Between 1914 and 1918, average bread and fodder grain harvests were about 71 per cent of the 1914 harvest; for potatoes the figure is 79 per cent. Corresponding figures for the period between 1939 and 1943 were 88 per cent and 112 per cent respectively. In addition to this, there were imports of various sorts.[33]

Table 3.   *Germany's grain and potato harvests in the First and Second World Wars (columns 1 and 3: millions of tons; columns 2 and 4: 1914 = 100)*

Grains

	1	2	3	4	
1914	27.1 =	100	27.2 =	100	1939
1915	22.0 =	81	23.7 =	87	1940
1916	22.0 =	81	22.0 =	81	1941
1917	14.6 =	54	22.6 =	83	1942
1918	17.3 =	64	24.0 =	89	1943

Potatoes

	1	2	3	4	
1914	45.6 =	100	56.3 =	124	1939
1915	54.0 =	118	57.4 =	126	1940
1916	25.1 =	55	47.5 =	104	1941
1917	34.4 =	76	54.4 =	119	1942
1918	29.5 =	65	40.2 =	88	1943

Under these conditions, it was possible to keep the level of individual food rations substantially higher during the Second

World War than they had been during 1914–18.[34] Table 4 shows clearly that the level of supply was significantly higher during the Second World War than it had been during the First. Between 1916 and 1918, the normal flour ration could be maintained at an average level of about 92 per cent of the 1915 level; between 1939 and 1945, by contrast, the corresponding figure was 110 per cent. Average figures for meat were 100 per cent and 150 per cent, and for fat 85 per cent and 242 per cent respectively. Thus, even in 1944, rations were in general higher than those of 1917/18. However, the number of calories to which the average consumer was entitled in the first year of the Second World War was distinctly below the prewar level of 3,000, and during the winter of 1944/5 it fell finally below the long-term subsistence minimum of 1,800 calories per day.[35]

Table 4. *Standard rations of flour, meat and fat in Germany during the First and Second World Wars (columns 1 and 3: annual average expressed in grammes/week; columns 2 and 4: 1915 or 1916 = 100)*

		Flour		
	1	2	3	4
1914	—	—	1,800g = 114	1939
1915	1,575g =	100	1,688g = 107	1940
1916	1,400g =	89	1,688g = 107	1941
1917	1,540g =	98	1,688g = 107	1942
1918	1,400g =	89	1,818g = 115	1943

		Meat		
	1	2	3	4
1914	—	—	500g = 200	1939
1915	—	—	500g = 200	1940
1916	250g =	100	400g = 160	1941
1917	250g =	100	350g = 140	1942
1918	250g =	100	250g = 100	1943
			250g = 100	1944

		Fat		
	1	2	3	4
1914	—	—	270g = 270	1939
1915	—	—	270g = 270	1940
1916	100g =	100	270g = 270	1941
1917	100g =	100	206g = 206	1942
1918	70g =	70	216g = 216	1943
			219g = 219	1944

Even at this time, however, the supply situation was much better than it had been in 1917/18. Unlike what happened in the First World War, rations were delivered regularly, and people generally did not have to put up with substitutes or cancellations. Bearing in mind how strongly the population reacted to the reductions in food rations made early during the First World War,[36] it will be appreciated that the relatively favourable food situation undoubtedly had a strongly stabilising effect on the National Socialist system.

The supply of other goods was also better during the Second World War, because the civilian production sector retained a much stronger position. For example, Britain noticeably reduced civilian production immediately after the beginning of the war, and in 1942 cut it back further to 79 per cent of prewar levels. In Germany at this time it was 95 per cent of the 1938 level, and even in 1944 it was still 93 per cent.[37] As late as 1941, the net output of several industries which had no military significance continued to rise.[38] Speer's attempts to change this situation for the benefit of the armaments industry met with only partial success; as late as the fifth year of the war, more than 43 per cent of those employed in Germany were working for civilian consumption.[39]

Of course, problems of supply also existed during the Second World War. Domestic fuel, for example, was usually scarce, while supplies of textiles and shoes for the civilian population also did not nearly meet demands.[40] The relatively good production statistics conceal the real situation in so far as only a fraction of the goods produced were actually made available for normal requirements. Allied bombing raids hit a total of 1,042 towns with a population of more than 3,000 people, and in sixty-two towns, more than 50 per cent of the built-up area was destroyed.[41] These losses made it necessary, from time to time, to divert the total production of textiles and shoes to those sections of the population which had been bombed out. Above all, however, they precipitated a collapse in the supply of housing. The German building industry could not nearly keep up with the losses caused by bombing — as early as the autumn of 1944 there was a shortage of 1.4 million homes — especially as its productive capacity decreased steadily in the last years of the war. In addition, military, Party and armaments contracts made heavy demands on it.[42]

Altogether, however, and in spite of restrictions caused by the bombing, the civilian supply situation during this period was clearly better than it had been in the First World War, although the mechanisms for achieving this end had not fundamentally altered. Any changes adopted were concerned more with perfecting existing mechanisms than with the development of completely new ones. Thus the fixing of maximum prices, which had proved ineffective during the First World War, was replaced by an absolute price and wage freeze. Since this policy was enforced by the powerful resources of a police state, it met with considerable success.[43] Hitler consented to price increases in the processing of raw materials only where they would not affect the price of consumer goods.[44] Also, in 1939 Germany immediately adopted a rationing system which was an improvement on that used during the First World War. From 1916 onwards, differentiations within the system had been made according to local food preferences; in the Second World War such differentiations played a much more important part.[45] Neither these measures, nor a draconian system of penalties could completely suppress the black market, but they successfully kept it within limits until the second half of 1943. It apparently reached levels exceeding those required to meet individual needs only in the last year of the war,[46] and never even approached those of the corresponding period of the First World War.

During both wars, the authorities attempted to make the occupied areas contribute to German supplies. In the Second World War, however, the occupied areas were much more thoroughly exploited. They were made responsible for defraying the costs of the war, for supplying raw materials and, in so far as captured arms were used, the occupied countries were indirectly responsible for arming the Wehrmacht. More pertinent to the present discussion was the partial transfer of consumer goods manufacturing abroad, particularly to France.[47] This made it possible to continue meeting civilian requirements which would otherwise have been sacrificed for the sake of armaments manufacture.

Unscrupulous methods were used here, as in the exploitation of foreign food production. In his propaganda, Goebbels made it clear to the people that 'our food is not here to be eaten by the people we have conquered — they have to take the consequences of the war they forced on us'.[48] In practice, Germany's leaders did not stop there. Göring declared that a major aim of the attack on the Soviet Union was 'to obtain as much food and mineral oil as possible for Germany';[49] consideration for the Soviet population could not be allowed to prevent the realisation of these aims. Some months after the beginning of the Soviet campaign, Hitler confirmed this objective, which was also expressed in the 'Generalplan Ost' (General Plan for the East).[50] In the following years, this plan was implemented.[51] The yield was immense: by the end of the German occupation, the *Zentralhandelsgesellschaft Ost* (Central Trading Company East) alone had seized, among other things, 9.2 million tons of bread and fodder grains, that is, about five times as much as had been taken out of Romania after 1916; and in addition, 600,000 tons of meat and 3.2 million tons of potatoes.[52] These figures only partially take into account the large quantities which the Wehrmacht took for its own use.

Some works on this subject suggest that 'the "Altreich" [the area which made up Germany before 1938] did not receive any considerable quantity of goods from the occupied areas'.[53] The figures quoted above are enough to make this statement appear highly dubious. It is also contradicted by the National Socialists' frequently expressed intention of maintaining, or even increasing, German rations, if necessary at the expense of the occupied areas, and without any consideration for their standard of living.[54] In Table 5 a comparison of the food situation in Germany and the occupied areas shows that this was not an empty threat.[55] Although an exact comparison is not possible because of slight discrepancies between the figures being compared, it can be said with certainty that, between 1941 and 1944, standard rations available in the occupied areas of western and northern Europe were always only about three-quarters of rations inside Germany. The situation in Poland was clearly even worse: standard rations were never more than 60 per cent of German rations and were normally much lower.

Table 5. *Food supply in Germany and the occupied areas during the Second World War (calorific value of standard rations)*

	1941	1942	1943	1944
Germany (G)	2,445	1,928	2,078	1,981
Occupied areas (O) (excluding Poland and the Soviet Union)	1,617	1,495	1,503	1,494
Poland (P)	845	1,070	855	1,200
O expressed as a % of G	66	78	72	75
P expressed as a % of G	35	56	41	61

The situation was worst of all in the occupied Soviet territories. As early as the planning stage of Operation Barbarossa, the frequently announced intention was to let millions of 'superfluous' Russians starve to death rather than to do without Soviet-produced food for Germany.[56] Consequently, an annual average equalling two and a half times the quantity of grain that the entire Soviet Union normally exported per year in peacetime, was extracted from the occupied part of the USSR alone. Rations there were correspondingly low: children under fourteen received 400 calories per day, the average consumer 800 to 850; people doing hard labour received up to 1,900 calories per day and those doing extremely hard labour up to 2,100.[57] In other words, the only people who were at best adequately nourished were those who worked hardest — in the service of the German war economy. For years the rest of the population had to make do with rations which were far below the long-term subsistence minimum, and which were barely more than 40 per cent of those distributed in Germany at the same time. Savings made at the expense of these many millions of people were diverted to Germany or to the Wehrmacht (thus indirectly also benefiting the German people).

The argument that the Altreich was largely self-supporting in terms of food is also strikingly refuted by the fact that, as has been suggested above, a sufficient number of agricultural workers was always available during the Second World War, thus preventing the reductions in harvest yield levels that had occurred between 1915 and 1918. In fact, the amount of labour available was not only maintained at prewar levels until 1944, it was even slightly increased by the use of conscripted foreign labour.[58] As early as September 1940, 1.4 million prisoners of war and foreign workers were engaged in agriculture; barely two years later the number had risen to 2.1 million and in the summer of 1944 it was 2.6 million.[59] From 1942 onwards, 20 per cent of those engaged in agricultural work, sometimes as many as 25 per cent, had come from abroad, usually as prisoners of war or forced labourers. Foreigners employed in agriculture were considered to be good workers and their output was probably hardly less than that of their German counterparts. Therefore, if German crop figures for 1942 and subsequent years are adjusted to allow for the 20 to 25 per cent produced by foreigners, the resulting levels no longer contrast favourably with the levels between 1915 and 1918. If we also deduct the quantities of food imported from abroad, the picture is even less happy, as Table 6 shows.[60] Although reliable data are not available for all years, a rough balance which can be drawn up for the fiscal year 1942/3 at least shows the size of foreign contributions to Germany's food stocks.[61] In 1942/3, the Wehrmacht and the German civilian population consumed, among other things, 11.2 million tons of bread grains and 3.8 million tons of meat and fat. To this must be added about 0.5 million tons of bread grains and around 50,000 tons of meat and fat consumed by the foreigners working inside the Reich.[62] This gives totals of 11.7 million tons of bread grains and 3.9 million tons of meat and fat, of which 2.6 and 1.1 million tons respectively were imported from abroad — that is from the occupied territories. These calculations do not even take into account imports of fodder, which contributed significantly to the German production of meat and fat; in addition, these figures presumably do not include the amounts taken out of the occupied areas by the Wehrmacht. If it is assumed that the foreigners working in German agriculture produced about 20 per cent of German crops, these figures increase by a further 1.6 and 0.5 million tons respectively. In other words: according to these — admittedly rough — calculations, in the year 1942/3, just under 45 per cent of the bread grains, and at least 42 per cent of the meat and fat consumed in Germany and by the Wehrmacht, came from occupied territories, or were produced by foreigners working more or less involuntarily inside Germany.

Table 6. *Imports of food and fodder from abroad (in millions of tons)*

	Bread grains	Fodder grains	Meat and fat
1938/9	1.2	1.7	1.1
1939/40	1.5	0.9	0.9
1940/1	1.4	2.1	0.9
1941/2	3.0	1.3	0.9
1942/3	3.6	2.8	1.1
1943/4	3.5	1.9	0.9

Of course, an — albeit small — proportion of these quantities found its way back into the occupied territories in the form of exports, or was used to feed the foreigners working inside Germany. On the other hand, these foreigners did work which otherwise would have been an additional burden on the German people; according to Pfahlmann, foreign labour was 'one of the decisive factors in making the war possible'.[63] In addition, troops who were abroad tended largely to 'live off the country', thus improving Germany's internal food situation.

If all these factors are evaluated in the light of the questions posed at the beginning of this essay, the following results are obtained: foreign workers at times did 20 to 25 per cent of Germany's industrial labour, thus relieving the German population of this work.[64] In addition, foreign workers, both inside and outside the borders of the Reich, contributed to the feeding of the German population to an extent which, from 1941/2 onwards, was no less than 30 to 35 per cent of the total civilian consumption of bread grains, meat and fat, even after the quantities necessary for foreign workers, prisoners of war and exports had been deducted. The fact that in the Second World War there was only occasional dissatisfaction with the supply situation, and that this was insignificant compared with the strikes of 1917/18, is primarily due to these factors.

Wage and price developments also differed during the two wars. In 1914 the wage structure for workers was clearly divided according to groups of industries. The highest rates were paid in the food processing industry, followed closely by the metal, mechanical engineering and chemical industries; the lowest rates were paid in the paper and textile industries. The pay differential between the highest- and lowest-paid groups was 2.86 marks per day, or 75 per cent of the average pay in the lowest-paid group.[65]

The specific circumstances of the war economy — shortage of labour, backlogs of orders, a price boom in the armaments industry and its suppliers, a lack of raw materials for the food and textile industries — resulted in manpower requirements and profitability developing very differently from group to group. In general, the existing differential was increased, with the exception of the food processing industry which lost its leading position for the reasons mentioned above. As Table 7 shows, its place was filled, with an increased margin, by groups of industries whose products had gained in importance at the beginning of the war, and increased even further since the inception of the Hindenburg programme.[66] While wages in these industries had increased by an average of 150 per cent by September 1918, wages in the other industries mentioned above increased only by an average of 90 per cent. Consequently, by September 1918 the wage differential had increased to 6.99 marks per day, or 108 per cent of the wages of the lowest-paid group.

Table 7. *Development of average nominal industrial wages be-tween 1914 and 1918 in marks/day (March 1914 = 100)*

	March 1914	Sept. 1916	Sept. 1918
Food processing	5.69	108	150
Metals	5.54	145	234
Mechanical engineering	5.32	149	245
Chemicals	5.16	134	232
Electrical engineering	4.52	165	298
Rock, stone and related mineral products	4.68	116	188
Paper	3.93	141	240
Textiles	3.64	115	178

A similar development took place, at least to a certain extent, in social groups other than the working class. Thus almost 94 per cent of 10,000 privately employed foremen who were questioned reported an increase in salary — albeit a modest one — between the end of 1914 and the end of 1917. Two-thirds of the sample reported an increase of less than 50 per cent; only 6 per cent indicated an increase of 100 per cent or more.[67] A group of 22 per cent thus had salary increases lying between these two figures. The tripartite division into branches of industry essential to the war effort, the textile industry and a relatively large middle group, which we have already seen in wage structures, was repeated here. But salaries did not develop as dynamically as wages. Foremen were salaried employees or held permanent positions; they were therefore more strongly tied to their firms than were workers, who could choose their place of employment largely on the basis of how much they were paid. Foremen also lacked strong organisations to champion their cause in the way that the workers had the unions and the Social Democratic Party.

As always in times of inflation, state employees and those who were dependent on some other form of fixed income suffered most. Increases in their earnings were delayed, and inadequate when they came. Thus, after two years of war salaries of military officials had risen by only 15 per cent. Other civil servants with salaries of less than 2,400 marks per annum received an increase of just under 10 per cent, and those on higher salaries even less. Thus the head of one of the Reich departments was correct in stating that it was the lower officials, not the workers, who had to make the greatest economies.[68]

Those people who were dependent on state relief had a particularly hard time. At the beginning of the war, conscription, shortages of raw materials and a general lack of direction in the economy resulted in unemployment for millions, and consequently caused great hardship.[69] The families of men who had gone to war fared little better during the first few weeks of the war because the financial support for which the law provided (see Table 8) was often delayed, and sometimes was not paid at all at this early stage.[70] The levels fixed in 1888 soon proved to be too low. Before the law was amended in January 1916, a woman with three children received state support totalling 30 marks per month in winter and 27 marks per month in summer. But even before the war, the cost of feeding a worker's family of four was 34 marks per month, and by October 1915 this had risen to just under 50 marks.[71] The amendment of January 1916 increased monthly payments to 37.50 marks, but by this time, the same basket of food would have cost about 60 marks. The second increase also lagged far behind real needs: from January 1917 a woman with three children received 50 marks per month, but by October 1917 the basket of food cost almost 70 marks, and one year later the cost had risen to more than 75 marks. These calculations do not take other costs such as clothing and rent into account, nor the fact that in the second half of the war, a considerable proportion of the food allocated was not available on the open market and had to be bought, at exorbitant prices, on the black market.

Table 8. *Monthly payments laid down by law for the families of soldiers (in marks)*

	1888	Jan. 1916	Dec. 1916
Wives	12 (summer months: 9)	15	20
Children	6	7.50	10

Local authorities and/or employers supplemented state payments to a certain extent. Most towns provided a payment similar in size to the state allowance and many firms, especially large-scale enterprises which produced goods essential for the war effort and therefore made good profits, made considerable sums available for support.[72]

Nevertheless, as the data given above suggest, the income of many soldiers' families was barely enough to survive on, let alone to maintain accustomed standards of living. When the *Statistisches Reichsamt* (statistical office) established the real cost of living in April 1916, it arrived at a figure of 60 marks per head per month, even for the lowest income groups. Two years later, the corresponding figure was 80 to 90 marks.[73] The shortcomings in the public relief system hit the middle classes particularly hard because, while they received no more support than the workers, they were used to a more extravagant life-style. In addition, they felt under more of an obligation than the workers to subscribe to war loans and make other economic sacrifices. The situation was, of course, no less difficult when armaments workers with high earnings were conscripted, and their families quickly forced to adjust to the unreasonable standard of life imposed by the level of support available.

The state's prices policy contributed decisively to this development. Although maximum prices were set immediately at the beginning of the war, the government and the administration were not able to release the food which was available on the market at these prices. Official prices shown in Table 9 therefore convey an incomplete impression of actual costs.[74] The state authorities, however, were not able, and some at least were not willing, to put an end to this development. Eventually, the cost of living reached levels which workers in industries not so favourably affected by the war, and lower-grade officials, could no longer afford.[75] Even if no reliable information is available about real wages during the First World War, it is quite clear that the cost of living rose more quickly than incomes. Zimmermann has calculated that there was an increase of about 150 per cent in the average cost of living in the Reich during the war.[76] Even the wages of armaments workers only rarely achieved this sort of increase, and in all other branches of industry increases were far lower. In general, the 'real wage' indices calculated by Kuczynski (see Table 10) can be accepted, certain methodological reservations notwithstanding.[77] This seemingly relatively favourable picture of real wages deteriorates if one takes into account that it expresses *averages*: the largest increases took place in the armaments industry, while a very large percentage of wage-earners fell into groups ranging more or less below Kuczynski's index. Further, the consistently less favourable conditions among civil servants and salaried employees are not taken into account.[78]

The war hit these groups harder than it did employers and workers, and 'after their savings were exhausted, they were led to the brink of ruin'.[79]

Table 9.   *Retail prices of specific foodstuffs in Berlin, 1913–1918*
           (1913 = 100; prices for 1913 expressed in Pfennigs per
           kilogramme; for eggs, in Pfennigs per egg)

	Beef	Pork	Butter	Eggs	Wheat flour	Rye flour	Potatoes
1913	182	159	271	8	40	31	7
1916	284	216	216	338	125	139	171
1918	238	—	362	600	147	—	300
1919	291	—	507	1800	172	180	457

Table 10. *Average real wages in Germany 1914–1918, according*
           to Kuczynski

	1914	1915	1916	1917	1918
Nominal wages	100	114	138	184	234
Cost of living	100	125	165	245	304
Real wages	100	91	81	73	75

Warned by these experiences, the National Socialist leaders had made an early decision to replace flexible price ceilings with a general price and wage freeze. As this was strictly enforced and was combined with a system of state subsidies for producers, it was completely successful;[80] increases during the war were limited to 9 per cent in the wholesale price index, 12 per cent in the cost of living and 11 per cent in wages, so that real wages remained practically constant.[81]

The fact that the wage–price structure remained unchanged was not merely due to the 1939 decree which governed the wartime economy. During the First World War shortages of food and other goods had pushed up prices, and the shortage of workers had pushed up wages. During the Second World War both problems were, if not solved, then at least rendered less dangerous. This was, of course, made possible only by exploiting foreign resources, using foreign factories to satisfy the German industrialists in their pursuit of profits, and incorporating forced foreign labour into the German war economy at more or less reduced wages.

The 'principle of an economy committed to the war effort' advocated by the decrees governing the war economy could function effectively in the setting of wage and price levels only by this sort of exploitation of the occupied territories. This made it possible to do without the degree of state control which would have been unavoidable in a German war economy thrown on its own resources. Thus, even under the conditions of a 'total' war economy, Germany's political leaders were spared the conflict with industry which they had always tried to avoid, even before 1939.

Attempts were also made to make use of the experience gained in the First World War with regard to the support of the families of conscripted soldiers. As criticism had been directed firstly at the low level and, secondly, at the lack of flexibility in the payments made between 1914 and 1918, a start was made in these two areas. A system of relief was devised which provided for four different forms of assistance: the state paid rents in full; soldiers' wives received 'housekeeping money' which, in the lowest income groups, was 40 per cent of the last income received, dropping gradually to 35 per cent as income increased;[82] an allowance was paid for each child; finally, additional allowances could be applied for under special circumstances. A family of four with a middle-range income could count on state support of 70 to 80 per cent of its peacetime income; the maximum possible was 85 per cent.

Compared with provisions made during the First World War, this may appear extremely generous, even if it clearly favoured the middle- and upper-, as against the lower-income groups. These measures cost the Reich 4,000–6,000 million marks annually, a total of 27,500 million marks, which was twelve times or, in relation to the total cost of the war, three times what had been spent on support in the First World War.[83] Although this sum may seem impressive, it amounted to less than one-third of what the occupied territories were forced to pay over to Germany, in addition to the supplies discussed above.[84]

The fact that personal incomes, even in those sections of the population which depended on state support, were much higher than they had been during the First World War, while at the same time prices remained almost stable and the supply of goods was rationed, meant that a problem arose which had been completely unknown during 1914–18: large sections of the population had more money than they could spend and the excess purchasing power already mentioned was created. The imposition of a high rate of taxation was rejected by the state on psychological grounds, especially as this 'stray' purchasing power did not assume dangerous dimensions until the spring of 1944.[85] From that time on, though, a basically inflationary situation existed, which was characterised by a growing fear of inflation among the population who, as far as possible, took refuge in 'real' assets.

Another result of the generous maintenance payments made in the Second World War was that there was no real incentive for soldiers' wives to take paid work. Consequently, from 1939 on the number of women in paid employment stabilised at an average of 14.5 million, even dropping during the first years of the war, whereas it had increased by 50 per cent between 1913 and 1918.[86] Improvements in the provisions made for the population as compared with the First World War thus had a negative effect on Hitler's war efforts, but he did not dare to push the German population too far.[87] Instead he fell back even more determinedly on foreign labour and resources. For the same reason, the number of domestic servants was never substantially reduced, despite occasional protests by the workers.[88] While in Britain the number of domestic servants had fallen to one-third of prewar levels by 1943, it remained practically constant in Germany, despite the growing shortage of labour in industry.[89]

Summing up what has been said so far, significant differences, as well as similarities, become apparent in the economic situation of the average consumer in Germany during the two World Wars. In both, economic systems specific to the war situation developed; they were aimed at maximising industrial production and at making possible an optimal distribution of resources and output between the major individual areas of demand, such as the military, the Allies and the civilian population, as well as within each group. Naturally the results were, in part, very different: in 1914 the civilian population had been well, even abundantly supplied, with the result that supply levels dropped all the more abruptly in the following years, and at the end of the war lay far below the long-term subsistence minimum. The supply of consumer goods of all sorts was no better, especially as prices rose even more quickly than in the food sector. Of course, wages increased considerably at the same time, but even a continued growth in the top wages paid in the armaments industry rarely kept pace with food prices, and never with prices of consumer goods: prices and wages parted company. The process was even more marked in those branches of industry which were of less value to the war effort. The most unfavourable development took place in the real income of those on fixed incomes, whether civil servants, foremen, pensioners or people dependent on state support. From month to month, they found themselves less able to cope with rising prices, being subjected to a process of pauperisation which drove whole groups of people to the brink of economic and, only too frequently, physical ruin. The way in which the war was financed furthered this process. A collapse of morale in the wartime economy, and of belief in the state, as well as, finally, political radicalisation on a broad front, were the consequences.

In retrospect, this development may seem logical, even inevitable, but undoubtedly it was not. In fact, mistakes were made repeatedly in the planning and execution of the war economy. They were avoidable, and often enough could be remedied. However, such corrections were, as a rule, made too late, or the necessary determination to carry them through was lacking. Thus, for instance, the traditional idea that the military should have priority over the civilian population when it came to food was only very slowly replaced by the idea that both sectors had equal rights and were mutually dependent. Instead, the military was better supplied for years, while the civilian population was put off with empty catchphrases. The first warning signs were overlooked, the first criticism was ignored, or its significance was not recognised.[90] The Reich's political leadership and the supreme military command repeatedly pointed out that Germany's military situation was secure, and that 'an area extending from Arras to Mesopotamia cannot be economically crushed'.[91] In retrospect, Chancellor Michaelis justifiably regarded this 'officially encouraged and observed falsehood' as one of the most deep-seated evils of the war years.[92] Reality did not bear out official claims and encouraged a latent crisis of confidence to develop; this process was fostered by the fact that the political and social élites did not realise that 'the time for charity had passed, and that rights were being demanded in its place'.[93]

Basically, the First World War lasted much longer than the Reich's leaders could answer for on economic grounds, leaving other factors aside for the moment. The price was paid primarily by those people — the large majority of the population — who were affected by the downward movement in real wages and, beyond this, placed their material and financial resources at the service of the war. The price was also paid by the population of the areas occupied by Germany, who were integrated into the German war economy with varying degrees of compensation. Of course, in comparison with what happened later, their number was relatively low, as attempts to recruit forced labour were foiled by an international public outcry.

In view of the grave results of the Reich leadership's failures in the First World War, preparations for a war economy from the 1920s onwards were directed at avoiding similar mistakes in the future. In spite of his adherence to the 'stab in the back' legend, Hitler also adopted this view. Of course he was fond of talking about the necessity of putting 'public need before private greed',[94] but in private conversations he 'often gave us to understand that after the experience of 1918, one could not be careful enough' and that therefore special attention had to be paid to the supply of consumer goods for civilians and the maintenance of soldiers' families.[95] Consequently, the capacity for producing armaments was not exploited to the full; when, on the eve of the collapse in 1945, Speer summed up his period of office as minister for armaments and munitions he came to the conclusion that if the civilian population had been pressed at an early stage, as it had been in Britain, for example, the output figures of 1944 could have been achieved as early as 1940/1.[96] Speer had in fact attempted to introduce this sort of policy soon after taking over the ministry. After an initial period during which he seemed to be successful, a 'Führer' order was issued by which 'the manufacturing of products for the general provision of the population' was to be increased again. This decision was based on a conviction that excessive demands could not be made on the population if unrest about the food supply, together with all its possible political implications were to be avoided. This attitude was also expressed at *Gauleiter* level.[97] In general, Hitler was anxious to spare the population as much hardship as possible and to make unavoidable cuts in the most unobtrusive form. This applied even to areas in which the war economy suffered as a consequence. Thus a certain level of cultural activity was maintained throughout the entire war, after the National Socialist leadership had convinced itself that 'the population welcomes the establishment of as extensive a cultural life as possible';[98] the exemption from military service of numerous 'inspired' artists, as well as the expense, were of necessity accepted. This policy continued unrestricted until 1943, when the 'most extreme totalisation' of the war made it necessary to reduce food as well as these amenities. As far as possible, these cuts were presented as a prohibition, in response to popular demand, of something offensive.[99] For the same reasons, the collections mounted for the military and the war economy, which had been unpopular in the First World War, were limited as far as possible. Collections of jewellery, for example, were not held at all; hunters' telescopic sights were asked for as hesitantly as people's skis; a ban on the permanent waving of women's hair was lifted after popular protests, to be replaced by less obtrusive measures.[100]

Here, as in other areas, the main concern, which was even given priority over the building up of the war economy, was not to endanger the existence of the National Socialist system by making excessive demands. Unlike Wilhelmine Germany, where the stability of the system was simply taken for granted and barely given a thought, it was accorded high priority in the National Socialist state. In accordance with the experiences of 1914 to 1918, this meant attempting to protect the German civilian population from a lack of food and other goods, from excessive physical exertion and from all personal sacrifices which were avoidable by some means or other. These considerations were not motivated by a concern for public welfare as such: Hitler's intention brutally to suppress any revolution was matched by his lack of concern for Germany's fate after a lost war. For him, the people were an indispensable instrument for the implementation of his ideas, and as such — and only as such — needed to be taken care of. Under the conditions imposed by the war economy, this could not be achieved using Germany's resources alone. Therefore, the occupied areas were exploited to an extent which grossly violated international law. They provided a good fifth of all civilian workers in Germany. During the second half of the war, 35 per cent of the bread grains, meat and fat consumed in the Reich and by the Wehrmacht came from the occupied areas and were produced by their labour force; foreign firms made considerable contributions to Germany's supply of consumer goods; in addition, foreign workers produced 20 to 25 per cent of the industrial goods manufactured in the Reich. On top of this, the occupied areas paid three times what was spent on the generous support made available for German soldiers' families; only a fraction of this sum found its way back to these countries in the form of loans and other payments.

Undoubtedly, these goods and services — almost without exception obtained by coercion — were of decisive significance. The quantity of food and other goods which was available during the Second World War after the foreign share is deducted, was less, not more, than what was available from 1916 to 1918. The food supply situation deserves particular attention. Even the comparatively generous rations during the Second World War repeatedly led to popular unrest.[101] It is certainly conceivable that if rations had been reduced by 30 to 40 per cent and combined with an increase in the work load and a worse supply of goods, the result would have been much more serious disturbances.

Drawing on historical experience, the German leaders during the Second World War recognised this at an early stage. Attempts were made to overcome a potential conflict in aims between the demands of the war on the one hand, and those of the stability of the system on the other, by limiting production for the war in favour of the civilian population. As the difficulties which this produced for the war grew, the occupied areas were increasingly drawn upon to fulfil German needs. Thus, no real alternative to the Wilhelmine war economy, with the burdens that it imposed on the population, had been developed; the wartime economy, as well as the peacetime economy of the Third Reich remained relatively closely connected with economic liberalism. If a comparatively efficient war economy was nevertheless established in a state which was by no means self-sufficient, *without* plunging the civilian supply situation into a state of permanent crisis (as had been the case between 1916 and 1918), this was made possible only by exploiting the occupied areas and their population to an almost unbelievable degree.

Notes

1. See, among others, G. Thomas, in W. Birkenfeld (ed.), *Geschichte der deutschen Wehr- und Rüstungswirtschaft (1918–1943/45)*, Boppard, 1966; G. Janssen, *Das Ministerium Speer: Deutschlands Rüstung im Krieg*, Berlin/Frankfurt/Vienna, 1968; B. A. Carroll, *Design for Total War: Arms and Economics in the Third Reich*, The Hague/Paris, 1968.
2. W. Birkenfeld, *Der synthetische Treibstoff 1933–1945: Ein Beitrag zur nationalsozialistischen Wirtschafts- und Rüstungspolitik*, Göttingen, 1964; D. Petzina, *Autarkiepolitik im Dritten Reich: Der nationalsozia-*

listische Vierjahresplan, Stuttgart, 1968.
3. For example, G. D. Feldman, *Army, Industry and Labor in Germany 1914–1918*, Princeton, NJ, 1966.
4. R. Meerwarth, A. Günther, W. Zimmermann, *Die Einwirkung des Krieges auf Bevölkerungsbewegung, Einkommen und Lebenshaltung in Deutschland*, Stuttgart/Berlin/Leipzig, 1932, p. 200.
5. Generaloberst H. v. Moltke, *Erinnerungen, Briefe, Dokumente 1877–1916*, ed. E. v. Moltke, Stuttgart, 1922, p. 399; *Der Weltkrieg 1914 bis 1918*, ed. *Reichsarchiv*, vol. 9, Berlin, 1933, p. 353; *Der grosse Krieg*, no. 15(1915), p. 1,417; H. Henning, 'Der Aufbau der deutschen Kriegswirtschaft im Ersten Weltkrieg', *Wehrwissenschaftliche Rundschau*, 6(1956), p. 58.
6. A. Skalweit, *Die deutsche Kriegsernährungswirtschaft*, Stuttgart/ Berlin/Leipzig, 1927, p. 101; *Kriegsgesetze des Deutschen Reichs*, ed. K. Pannier, Supplementary no. 3, Leipzig, 1916, pp. 61ff.
7. Calculated from data in the *Statistisches Jahrbuch für das Deutsche Reich, 1919*, p. 66.
8. F. Klein (ed.), *Deutschland im Ersten Weltkrieg*, 3 vols., Berlin, 1968–70, vol. 3, p. 324; Meerwarth et al., *Einwirkung*, p. 454.
9. Meerwarth et al., *Einwirkung*, pp. 447–9, 451, 457.
10. Ibid., p. 458.
11. G. W. Schiele, in F. Felger (ed.), *Was wir vom Weltkrieg nicht wissen*, Berlin/Leipzig, 1930, pp. 421f; A. v. Batocki, in *Handbuch der Politik*, vol. 2, third ed., Berlin/Leipzig, 1920, p. 238; diary entry of 15 May 1917 by Albrecht v. Thaer (A. v. Thaer, *Generalstabsdienst an der Front und in der OHL*, ed. S. Kaehler, Göttingen, 1958, p. 121).
12. Thus the Conservative member of parliament, v. Oldenburg, at the end of January 1917, *Der große Krieg*, no. 66(1917), p. 6,242.
13. Ellinger in *Die neue Zeit* of 7 December 1917, cf. Meerwarth et al., *Einwirkung*, p. 459.
14. Data from Klein, *Deutschland*, vol. 3, pp. 301, 307ff.
15. Prices from Meerwarth et al., *Einwirkung*, pp. 421f.
16. Notification of regulations governing trade in textiles, hosiery and knitwear for civilians of 10 June 1916 (see *Kriegsgesetze*, Supplementary no. 4, pp. 223–34). For the first requisitions and price regulations on 1 February and 20 March 1916, see *Der grosse Krieg*, no. 41(1916), p. 3,928, and no. 44(1916), p. 4,170.
17. A list of wholesale and maximum prices can be found in the *Statistisches Jahrbuch, 1920*, pp. 125–7.
18. See Schiele, *Weltkrieg*, pp. 398ff.
19. Crown Prince Rupprecht of Bavaria, *In Treue fest. Mein Kriegstagebuch*, Berlin, 1929, vol. 1, p. 514; War Office Decree to the *Bundesstaaten* on ca. 13 April 1917 (*Der große Krieg*, no. 66(1917), pp. 6,682f.); W. Groener, *Lebenserinnerungen*, Göttingen, 1957, p. 363.
20. For this see the Reich ministry of the interior's memorandum on foreign trade of September 1916 (Politisches Archiv des Auswärtigen Amtes Bonn, AA I.A: Wk 18 geh. Bd. 20, Bl.144–53).
21. *Der grosse Krieg*, no. 14(1915), p. 1,371, also no. 45(1916), p. 4,309 and no. 54(1916), p. 5,114; Groener, *Lebenserinnerungen*, pp. 329–32;

Weltkrieg, ed. *Reichsarchiv*, vol. 9, pp. 344–6; Klein, *Deutschland*, vol. 3, p. 318.

22. Official WTB telegram of 2 December 1916 (*Der grosse Krieg*, no. 63(1916), pp. 5,877f.).

23. On the beginning of food deliveries from Romania under the German military administration, see ibid., p. 5,959, and no. 66(1917), p. 6,243. The phrase quoted is taken from ibid., no. 63(1916), p. 5,977.

24. *Die Ursachen des Zusammenbruchs im Jahre 1918*, Berlin, 1925, vol. 3, p. 12.

25. On the priority given to the military, see H. v. Stein, *Erlebnisse und Betrachtungen aus der Zeit des Weltkrieges*, Berlin, 1919, pp. 87f.; G. Michaelis, *Für Staat und Volk: Eine Lebensgeschichte*, Berlin, 1922, p. 286. On the feeding of the military, see Rupprecht's diary entries of 25 March, 19 April, 23 April, 3 May 1916, 9 April 1917 (Rupprecht, *Treue*, vol. 1, pp. 440, 449f., 456; vol. 2, p. 136).

26. *Der grosse Krieg*, no. 30(1915), p. 2,830; official WTB telegram of 1 August 1916 (ibid., no. 53(1916), pp. 5,056f.); letter from the supreme military command to the chancellor, 19 November 1916 (ibid., no. 61(1916), pp. 5,796f.); Groener's speech to the Central Committee of the Reichstag, 24 April 1917 (*Schulthess' Europäischer Geschichtskalender*, part 1, 1917, pp. 442ff.).

27. Rupprecht's diary entries of 29 October 1915, 8 June, 9 June, 30 October 1916 (Rupprecht, *Treue*, vol. 1, pp. 400, 478; vol. 2, p. 55); Thaer's letter of 12 February 1916 and diary entry of 15 May 1917 (Thaer, *Generalstabsdienst*, pp. 58, 121); Groener, *Lebenserinnerungen*, p. 362; Klein, *Deutschland*, vol. 2, pp. 646ff.

28. Ibid., p. 677.

29. On the strike movement of April 1917, see ibid., pp. 676ff.; *Der grosse Krieg*, no. 71(1917) to no. 72(1917).

30. Strike call in Leipzig on 16 April 1917 (Klein, *Deutschland*, vol. 2, p. 683); Spartakus handbill, Berlin, January 1918 (ibid., vol. 3, p. 146).

31. W. Tomberg, *Wehrwirtschaftliche Erkenntnisse aus fünf Kriegsjahren* (memorandum for the supreme command of the Wehrmacht, Agricultural Office, completed in November 1944). State Archives, Nuremberg, Dok. NI–7859.

32. The figures on which this calculation is based relate to the territory of the Reich as it was on 1 September 1939. For the data see Tomberg, *Erkenntnisse*.

33. Ibid. For further details see *Bilanz des Zweiten Weltkrieges: Irkenntnisse und Verpflichtungen für die Zukunft*, Oldenburg, 1953, p. 338. See also Table 6.

34. Table 4 is compiled according to figures given by Tomberg, *Erkenntnisse*, and H. Pfahlmann, *Fremdarbeiter und Kriegsgefangene in der deutschen Kriegswirtschaft 1939–1945*, Darmstadt, 1968, p. 197. See, more recently and in greater detail, K. Mack, 'Die Ernährung der deutschen Zivilbevölkerung im Zweiten Weltkrieg', unpublished typescript, Constance, 1983.

35. See *Bilanz*, p. 337. This is supplemented by R. Wagenführ, *Die deutsche Industrie im Kriege 1939–1945*, second edn., Berlin, 1963, p. 51.

36. Reports by the SD (Secret Service) of 5 April 1940 and 23 March 1942, in H. Boberach (ed.), *Meldungen aus dem Reich*, Neuwied/ Berlin, 1965, pp. 57, 242; see also pp. 94f., 111–14, 131f.
37. Wagenführ, *Industrie*, pp. 36f., 173, 191; *Bilanz*, pp. 280f.
38. Carroll, *Design*, p. 205; Wagenführ, *Industrie*, pp. 36, 50f.; A. S. Milward, *Die deutsche Kriegswirtschaft 1939–1945*, Stuttgart, 1966, pp. 31–3.
39. Wagenführ, *Industrie*, p. 158. See also, above all, Speer's speech of 6 October 1943, to the *Gauleiter* (Draft in the Bundesarchiv, R 3/1548, Bl. 26ff.; text of the speech, ibid., Bl. 63ff.); *Deutschlands Rüstung im Zweiten Weltkrieg. Hitlers Konferenzen mit Albert Speer 1942– 1945*, ed. and introd. W. A. Boelcke, Frankfurt/M., 1969, p. 88.
40. SD report of 16 March 1944, (Boberach, *Meldungen*, p. 447). Data on the output of the German clothing industry are given in Wagenführ, *Industrie*, pp. 174–6.
41. *Bilanz*, pp. 169f.
42. Wagenführ, *Industrie*, pp. 49, 56f., 93, 161.
43. Decree for the wartime economy of 4 September 1939 (*Reichsgesetz-blatt – RGBI – 1939* I, p. 1,609); F. Federau, *Der Zweite Weltkrieg. Seine Finanzierung in Deutschland*, Tübingen, 1962, pp. 24f.; *Bilanz*, pp. 318f. The official prescriptions on language in O. Oesterheld, *Die deutsche Kriegswirtschaft*, Leipzig, 1940, pp. 117ff.
44. Minutes of the conference on 13 August 1942 (Boelcke, *Hitlers Konferenzen*, p. 172).
45. First World War: Henning, 'Aufbau', p. 60. Second World War: SD report of 15 December 1939 (Boberach, *Meldungen*, p. 31); Hitler's comments of 27 July 1942 in H. Picker, *Hitlers Tischgespräche im Führerhauptquartier, 1941–1942*, new edn. by P. E. Schramm, second edn., Stuttgart, 1965, p. 485f.
46. SD report of 20 January 1944 (Boberach, *Meldungen*, pp. 475ff.).
47. Minutes of the conference of 30 September to 1 October 1943 (Boelcke, *Hitlers Konferenzen*, p. 304); a list of the goods manufactured abroad is given in Wagenführ, *Industrie*, p. 51.
48. W. A. Boelcke (ed.), *Wollt Ihr den totalen Krieg? Die geheimen Goebbels-Konferenzen 1939–1945*, Stuttgart, 1967, pp. 86f., 130; Boberach, *Meldungen*, pp. 147f.
49. Directive by Goering in June 1941 ('*Grüne Mappe*') in *Anatomie des Krieges. Neue Dokumente über die Rolle des deutschen Monopolka-pitals bei der Vorbereitung und Durchführung des Zweiten Welt-krieges*, ed. and introd. D. Eichholtz and W. Schumann, Berlin, 1969, pp. 333–5; note for the records about the meeting of secretaries of state on 2 May 1941 concerning Operation Barbarossa — see *Der Prozess gegen die Hauptkriegsverbrecher vor dem Internationalen Militärgerichtshof*, vols. 1–42, Nuremberg, 1947–9, here vol. 31, p. 84; *Wirtschaftspolitische Richtlinien für Wirtschaftsorganisation Ost, Gruppe Landwirtschaft*, of 23 May 1941 (ibid., vol. 36, pp. 135ff.).
50. Hitler on 9 November 1941 (A. Speer, *Erinnerungen*, Berlin, 1969, p. 233). On the Generalplan Ost see H. Hieber, 'Der Generalplan Ost', *Vierteljahrshefte für Zeitgeschichte*, 6(1958), pp. 281–324.

51. A. Dallin, *Deutsche Herrschaft in Rußland 1941–1945*, Düsseldorf, 1958; N. Müller, *Wehrmacht und Okkupation 1941 bis 1944*, Berlin, 1971, pp. 54ff.; *Anatomie des Krieges*, pp. 199ff.

52. *Zentralhandelsgesellschaft Ost's* sphere of activity from 17 October 1944 (*Der Prozess*, vol. 25, p. 354); further data to be found here.

53. *Bilanz*, p. 340.

54. For example, Goebbels on 21 August 1942 (Boelcke, *Goebbels-Konferenzen*, p. 273).

55. The following calculations for the occupied territories are based on *Bilanz*, p. 340; for Germany, see ibid., p. 337.

56. *Der Prozess*, vol. 29, p. 123. For the following, see Thomas, *Geschichte*, pp. 515–32.

57. Müller, *Wehrmacht*, p. 171.

58. Tomberg, *Erkenntnisse*.

59. Pfahlmann, *Fremdarbeiter*, pp. 106, 136; Wagenführ, *Industrie*, p. 46.

60. Tomberg, *Erkenntnisse*. Official figures were considerably lower. See the figures in K. Brandt, *Management in Agriculture and Food in the German-occupied and other Areas of Fortress Europe: A Study in Military Government*, Stanford, Calif., 1953, pp. 611–13.

61. These calculations are based on Tomberg, *Erkenntnisse*, and *Bilanz*; Wagenführ, *Industrie*, pp. 46, 139.

62. *Bilanz*; Pfahlmann, *Fremdarbeiter*, pp. 193–8; Boelcke, *Hitlers Konferenzen*, p. 86; *Anatomie des Krieges*, pp. 390 and 394.

63. Pfahlmann, *Fremdarbeiter*, p. 235.

64. In the summer of 1944 about 10.8 million workers were employed in industry, including 3.2 million foreigners; see Wagenführ, *Industrie*, pp. 46, 139.

65. These and the following figures from Meerwarth et al., *Einwirkung*, pp. 367f.

66. Ibid.

67. Ibid., p. 247.

68. Letter from the *Reichsmarineamt* to the Governor of Kiel of 29 June 1916. See *Militär und Innenpolitik im Weltkrieg 1914–1918*, ed. W. Deist, Düsseldorf, 1970, pp. 390f.

69. Meerwarth et al., *Einwirkung*, p. 349; Skalweit, *Kriegsernährungswirtschaft*, pp. 142ff.

70. *Gesetz betr. die Unterstützung der Familien in den Dienst eingetretener Mannschaften* (Law concerning the maintenance of the families of men in the Armed Services) of 28 February 1888 (*RGBl* 1888, p. 50), with the amendments of 21 January and 3 December 1916 (see *Kriegsgesetze*, Supplementary no. 3, pp. 14ff. and Supplementary no. 6, p. 13.). For the practical working of the law in the first months of the war, see Klein, *Deutschland*, vol. 1, p. 439; Meerwarth et al., *Einwirkung*, p. 348.

71. According to Meerwarth's figures, *Einwirkung*, p. 428. See also Skalweit, *Kriegsernährungswirtschaft*, p. 158.

72. According to its accounts and reports, BASF, for example, paid a total of almost 32 million marks. For additional information, see L. Burchardt, 'Konstanz im Ersten Weltkrieg', *Politik und Unter-*

richt, 3(1981), p. 12.

73. More precise details in *Beiträge zur Kenntnis der Lebenshaltung in vierten Kriegsjahr*, Berlin, 1918, pp. 66f.

74. A list of the maximum prices set in the war can be found in the *Statistisches Jahrbuch, 1920*, pp. 125–7. Table 8 is based on the figures in ibid., pp. 130f., and ibid., 1919, pp. 185f.

75. Meerwarth et al., *Einwirkung*, p. 444.

76. Ibid., p. 464.

77. According to J. Kuczynski, *Die Geschichte der Lage der Arbeiter unter dem Kapitalismus*, vol. 4, Berlin, 1967, p. 329, 350f.

78. For civil servants, see the list in Meerwarth et al., *Einwirkung*, p. 251.

79. Report by the Chief Commissioner of Police in Berlin of 29 October 1918, see Klein, *Deutschland*, vol. 3, p. 331.

80. See, for example the security service's report of 2 April 1942, in Boberach, *Meldungen*, pp. 252f.; notes of 23 June 1942 in Picker, *Tischgespräche*, pp. 406f.

81. *Bilanz*, pp. 318f. and pp. 280f.

82. According to Oesterheld, *Kriegswirtschaft*, pp. 129ff.

83. *Der große Krieg*, no. 62(1916), p. 5,881; L. Burchardt, *Friedenswirtschaft und Kriegsvorsorge*, Boppard, 1968, p. 8; Federau, *Weltkrieg*, pp. 59, 62.

84. Federau, *Weltkrieg*, pp. 59, 62.

85. *Bilanz*, pp. 123f.

86. Wagenführ, *Industrie*, p. 139. Figures on the work by women in Meerwarth et al., *Einwirkung*, p. 470.

87. Speer, *Erinnerungen*, p. 229.

88. Boberach, *Meldungen*, pp. 343, 347, 349, 351.

89. See figure in Speer, *Erinnerungen*, p. 549.

90. See, for example, the resolution passed by the *Kriegsausschuss für Konsumenteninteressen* (War Committee for Consumers' Interests) on 4 June 1916 (quoted in *Der grosse Krieg*, no. 49(1916), p. 4,670), but also the bread riots of 1915 and 1916. See, further, Bethmann's answer of 5 September 1916 to a petition submitted by the Social Democratic Party and the unions (ibid., no. 56(1916), p. 5,287).

91. *Der grosse Krieg*, no. 14(1915), p. 1,345; ibid., no. 38(1915), p. 3,629; the quotation is from ibid., no. 38(1915), p. 3,624.

92. Michaelis, *Staat*, p. 273.

93. Groener, *Lebenserinnerungen*, p. 130.

94. Notes of 5 and 27 July 1942 in Picker, *Tischgespräche*, pp. 440f. and 489f. Cf. para. 24 of the NSDAP's party programme of as early as 1920!

95. Speer, *Erinnerungen*, p. 229.

96. Memorandum by Speer of 27 January 1945. On this see Janssen, *Ministerium*, pp. 325–42. On the following, see Speer, *Erinnerungen*, p. 236; Boelcke, *Hitlers Konferenzen*, p. 142.

97. Minutes of the conference on 4 April 1942, ibid., p. 91. On the *Gauleiter*, see P. Hüttenberger, *Die Gauleiter*, Stuttgart, 1969, pp. 182ff.

98. Popular interest in the cultural programme: see Boberach, *Meldungen*, pp. 9f, 47f. — Hitler's and Goebbel's reactions: Picker,

Tischgespräche, pp. 406f.; Boelcke, *Goebbels-Konferenzen*, p. 33; *Bilanz*, p. 218.

99. Boelcke, *Goebbels-Konferenzen*, pp. 329–36, also pp. 343, 347; see also Boberach, *Meldungen*, pp. 336, 360, 363f., 467.
100. Boelcke, *Goebbels-Konferenzen*, pp. 39, 204f., 213; see also Boelcke, *Hitlers Konferenzen*, p. 272.
101. Boberach, *Meldungen*, pp. 64, 92f., 111–13, 146f., 161f., 176f., 230f., 242, 253, 269, 272, 393–5; Boelcke, *Hitlers Konferenzen*, p. 267.

WOLFRAM WETTE

From Kellogg to Hitler (1928–1933). German Public Opinion Concerning the Rejection or Glorification of War

1. The Briand–Kellogg Pact (1928)

On 27 August 1928 a pact renouncing war was signed in Paris.* It was named after the French foreign minister, Aristide Briand, and his American counterpart, Frank B. Kellogg. Representatives of fifteen countries solemnly declared, in the name of their peoples, that they condemned 'recourse to war for the solution of international controversies and renounce[d] it as an instrument of national policy in relations with one another' (Article 1).[1] However, the supplementary notes declaring that this did not infringe upon the 'natural right of self-defence' meant that the pact did not apply to 'defensive' wars.[2] As the criteria which qualified forceful measures as aggressive or defensive were not defined, and the question of how such a judgement was to be made was left open, the pact lacked any binding force.

*First published in *Der gerechte Krieg. Christentum, Islam, Marxismus* (Frankfurt/M., 1980), pp. 233–68; reprinted in K. Holl and W. Wette (eds), *Pazifismus in der Weimarer Republik. Beiträge zur historischen Fridensforschung* (Paderborn, 1981), pp. 149–72.
  Transl. from the German by Angela Davies.

71

During the decade that followed the First World War, several attempts were made to limit by treaty the right of nations to wage war. The Covenant of the League of Nations (1919), the Geneva Protocol (1924) and the Locarno treaties (1925) should be mentioned, as well as the resolution of 24 September 1927 by the League of Nations Assembly, declaring wars of aggression an international crime and emphasising its members' duty to settle all international disputes peacefully.[3] The Briand–Kellogg Pact was an even more far-reaching and extreme renunciation of war. Its signing marked the climax of the anti-war movement which had spread throughout the world during the 1920s as a reaction to the First World War.

If the Briand–Kellogg Pact of 1928 and its forerunners are considered in a wider historical context, it is obvious that — in spite of the omissions and inconsistencies referred to above — they represented a radical shift away from certain very well-established ideas. For many hundreds, if not for thousands of years, war had been regarded as something completely natural, decreed by fate, and therefore to be accepted as a matter of course. Since the existence of the modern state system, war had also been considered an admissable means of achieving the objectives of national policy. The pacifist movements of the nineteenth century questioned this fatalistic attitude towards war, insisting that lasting peace was possible and could be achieved providing that the right policies were pursued. However, by the first decade of the twentieth century, such movements had not had any observable effect on traditional attitudes to war.

Co-existing with this fatalistic attitude, and superimposed upon it, centuries-old theories of war existed, listing specific criteria by which it was possible to distinguish between 'just' and 'unjust' wars.[4] These theories were to some extent incorporated in international law when it was codified.[5]

The origin of such theories may perhaps be traced to a basic human need to come to terms, in a rational manner, with the phenomenon of war. Individual authors may have intended to reduce the frequency of wars, but in practice these theories were soon used to support the politics of force. If, for example, it was possible to justify a policy of war in theoretical terms by presenting it as 'just', this facilitated the demand made by a ruler and his governing élites, that his subjects risk their lives to go to war. Thus the various theories of just and unjust wars served, directly or indirectly, the political need for legitimation. They functioned as a means of domination. Their long-term effect on popular consciousness was to transform into an article of faith the idea that war would break out from time to time like a natural force and must be accepted as such.

The apologetic thesis of the 'outbreak' of war in 1914 — to take an example significant in twentieth-century German history — fits clearly into this philosophical tradition. It suggests that not political factors, but uncontrollable natural forces were at work, comparable to a volcanic eruption. Taken together with nationalist prejudices, this interpretation of the causes of the First World War goes far to explain the fact that the propaganda catch-phrase, the 'war-guilt lie', found so many receptive ears in Weimar Germany. If it was believed that everyone had 'stumbled' into war, the allocation of guilt could be understood only as a malicious anti-German denunciation.

In the Germany of the 1920s, however, there were many contrasting reactions to the war, and to the experience of a world war.[6] They ranged from glorification to rigorous moral opposition, with a great variety of attitudes between these two extremes. After the First World War, a moderate pacifism, orientated towards ideas such as the League of Nations and disarmament, was articulated more clearly than ever before. It aimed at preventing war in the short term and securing a long-term peace without, however, abandoning the popular claim, which was supported by the entire German population, for a revision of the Versailles Treaty. Throughout the 1920s ideologies with a warlike, militarist tendency competed, sometimes fiercely, with pacifist ideologies for the favour of the German people. Against this background, the signing of the Briand–Kellogg Pact must have seemed like a clear victory for the pacifist movement, and a serious defeat for those who advocated force as a means of achieving foreign policy objectives — in this case, the revision of the Versailles Treaty and the recovery of Great Power status for Germany.

The Briand–Kellogg Pact was a radical attempt to break with the apologists of war and their traditions. Thus the conviction held by those diplomats and politicians who had travelled to Paris for the signing of the treaty, that they were witnessing a moment of great historical importance, can well be understood. In his address, Briand declared that 'the event of this day fixes it as an important new date in the history of the human race'.[7] He spoke also of the symbolic significance of Gustav Stresemann's presence in Paris — an allusion to the traditional hostility between Germany and France. The signing of the Pact had provided the opportunity to receive a German foreign minister on French soil for the first time in more than a century. Not long afterwards, in the German Reichstag, Stresemann expressed his opinion that the Briand–Kellogg Pact did in fact signify the 'inauguration of a new era'.[8] In the USA there was talk of a 'revolution in human thought'.[9]

We know today that these high hopes were not fulfilled.[10] Attempts to proscribe the use of force and war as means of policy in binding international treaties, which climaxed in the Briand–Kellogg Pact, succeeded neither in promoting disarmament policies at the time, nor in preventing a Fascist Germany from unleashing the Second World War.

This raises the question as to why the solemn renunciation of war in the late 1920s was ineffective. It would be unhistorical, as well as condescending, to maintain that the politicians of the time were so naive as to believe that the age of eternal peace could be rung in with a moral condemnation of war and a formal declaration of its illegality. This sort of misjudgement of the political importance of the treaty may have occurred in individual cases, but was not the main cause of the pact's failure. Contemporary politicians were perfectly aware that the declaration made on paper still had to be translated into practical policies.[11]

The initiators of the Pact hoped that, for a start, the idea of renouncing war would receive vigorous public support in the signatory states. Briand, for example, expressed his expectation that people would gradually cease to connect ideas of 'national interest' and 'national prestige' with the idea of force. According to Briand, deliberately waging war, which had been regarded in the past as a divine right, and had survived in international ethics as a privilege of sovereignty, had at last been 'divested by law of what had been its greatest danger: its legitimacy'.[12] The objection that the Pact was not realistic because it could not be enforced was countered by Briand with the following question: 'But is it realistic to exclude moral force, including the power of public opinion, in the field of facts?'[13] This again makes it clear that the French foreign minister saw the politically significant aspect of the Pact as its effect on the masses.

Frank B. Kellogg also hoped that the moral and legal proscription of war would become effective by gaining popular acceptance in the signatory countries — by 1938 the original fifteen had been joined by a further forty-eight — and by gaining the support of leading politicians and influential journalists. In 1929 Kellogg was awarded the Nobel Peace Prize. In his address on receiving the award in Oslo on 10 December 1930, he expressed the view that over the previous ten years, statesmen had moved much closer to each other.[14] He thought that world opinion would secure peace in the future, and that none of the unsolved problems in Europe was important enough to justify a war. Kellogg seems to have believed that the contents of the Pact renouncing war, of which he had been a co-initiator, were more or less identical with 'world opinion', and that international public opinion was already a significant factor in preserving the peace. Similarly, experts on international law held that in signing the Pact, governments had acted in accordance with conceptions of law held in their respective countries.[15]

It is hardly possible to determine precisely whether or not this assessment of 'world opinion' was correct, especially as no detailed studies have yet been made of the dissemination of the idea of a renunciation of war, or of the effect of the Briand–Kellogg Pact on public opinion in the various signatory countries. Nevertheless, several observations can be made which support the proposition that the basic attitude of 'no more war' was very widespread indeed in the countries which had been involved in the First World War, suggesting that Kellogg's remarks were at least partly in tune with reality.

In his own country, the USA, public opinion in the postwar period was strongly influenced by a movement for peace and the renunciation of war which had existed there since the nineteenth century.[16] It aimed not only at the prevention of war, but also at the elimination of it as an international legal institution.[17] The anti-war movement seems to have been stronger in the USA than in any other country and the opinion that war belonged to an unenlightened, undemocratic past and had no place in a rational, modern world was widespread there.[18] The conviction that war must be forbidden ('outlawry of war') expressed in a very specific way an American belief in the power of legal and moral principles; indeed, it was part of America's sense of its political mission.[19] Thus the pact of 1928 can be regarded as a logical projection of this article of American faith. American foreign policy in the 1920s was guided by a concept of 'peaceful change' which was by no means, however, understood in purely defensive terms. It covered both economic expansion and the prevention of the further advance of anything that could be considered Communist. With regard to Europe, 'peaceful change' meant that the USA was certainly prepared eventually to settle German complaints, step by step. Unlike France, the

USA did not believe that maintaining the status quo created by the Versailles Treaty could guarantee a lasting peace.[20]

French foreign policy in the 1920s was one of 'national security' based on the provisions of the Versailles Treaty. The negotiations leading up to the Briand–Kellogg Pact reveal that France originally was not interested in a multilateral pact proscribing war. It would have preferred a limited treaty by which France and America were to renounce all wars for ever. This concern obscured the French government's intention to incorporate the USA in the French security system by a bilateral treaty. Only when it became obvious that the American government was not prepared to do this, but was aiming for a multilateral treaty, did Briand see himself as forced to co-operate.[21] If this evoked a largely positive response from the French public, it was mainly because pacifist attitudes had spread throughout France in the wake of the First World War. The veterans, in particular, who had formed associations with millions of members and a large organisational network reaching down to the smallest commune, were dominated by a deeply rooted aversion to war — although they rarely came to terms with the fact 'that their pacifism had primarily been made possible by victory'.[22] This anti-war mood, characteristic of the political climate in France during the 1920s, was combined with the feeling of inferiority *vis-à-vis* Germany. Germany's population exceeded France's by about one-third and this, taken together with Germany's economic potential, which was also estimated to be greater than that of France, was perceived as a potential threat. It strengthened the existing French obsession with the possibility of a German invasion.[23] In terms of military policy, it was reflected in their fear of taking any steps towards disarmament, considered to be against the interests of French security.[24]

In Britain too, the majority of the population was 'war-weary and demanding domestic reforms'.[25] British foreign and domestic policy-makers could not ignore this basic mood, which dominated the interwar period. The policy of appeasement, which aimed to prevent war and stabilise peace, must be seen in relation to the British population's basically pacifist attitude.[26] On the one hand, this was a result of the ideal of non-violence, which was widely proclaimed in Britain after the First World War. On the other hand, the desire for peace suited a national policy in which economic interests were of particular importance. 'Great Britain had no alternative to peace, unless she wanted to hasten the process by which she was losing her power in an international context.'[27] In 1928, the year in which the Briand–Kellogg Pact was signed, the British government made a significant decision to accept 'a standing assumption that there will be no major war within the next ten years'.[28] Subsequently, British policy — including military policy — was based on this ten-year rule. Its influence was reflected in a marked reduction in the defence budget, in a disengagement from Europe and in the policy of isolationism. Thus Britain can be cited as an example of anti-war public opinion having a practical effect on government policy.

Nothing is known about the attitude of the Soviet people towards the idea of renouncing war as it emerged in the West. Initially, the Western powers do not seem to have been interested in including the Soviet Union in the Kellogg Pact. They did not allow her to participate in the negotiations which led to the signing of the Pact. Against the will of the German government, they also prevented the Soviet Union from being one of the initial signatory powers;[29] she was not able to sign until one month later. During the 1920s the Soviet government was, in principle, extremely interested in all agreements which could contribute to the prevention of war. It was constantly seeking security from the Soviet Union's potential enemies in the West, so that internal developments could proceed without interruption. The possibility of the Western capitalist powers forming an anti-Soviet coalition was a nightmare for Soviet politicians and diplomats. The prevention of such a coalition was therefore one of the most important objectives of the Soviet Union's foreign policy.[30]

Thus, while the Soviet government signed the Briand–Kellogg Pact in September 1928, the Communist Party of the Soviet Union played a double game in that it condemned the Pact as another 'capitalist conspiracy' against the Soviet Union.[31] Nikolai Bukharin took the same line at the Sixth World Congress of the Communist International (Comintern) in the autumn of 1928 in Moscow. He suggested that the real constellations in the situation of conflict were obscured by imperialist pacifist pacts, by League of Nations' Conferences, and by the fuss being made about peace.[32] This position was in line with the Marxist–Leninist theory of war, according to which class war had shifted from the national to the international level since the Soviet Union had come into existence. It also suggested that the intensification of capitalist crises would of necessity lead to military aggression by capitalist countries against the Soviet Union. The Soviet government attempted to delay this war, which it

considered inevitable, for as long as possible, in order to improve
the position it would have at the beginning of the war.

2. Developments in Germany — Germany's 'Sonderentwicklung'

In Germany, as in Britain, France and the USA, there were
strong pacifist movements after the First World War, which were
not limited to the *Deutsche Friedensgesellschaft* (German Peace
Society)[33] and the other organisations which came together in what
was known as the *Deutsche Friedenskartell* (German Peace Cartel).
It does not do justice to the historical situation of Germany in the
1920s to limit the term 'pacifist' solely to the extreme radical
position which totally rejected military means. The right-wing alternative during the Weimar period was to regain military power by
circumventing the provisions of the Versailles Treaty, both for
national prestige and to enable the active pursuit of power politics in
the future. In this context, the Weimar coalition's foreign policy,
which was directed towards preserving the peace, must also be
called 'pacifist'. At the time, the term was certainly used in this
sense — it was not merely a term of abuse used by the nationalist
right. The German Social Democratic Party (SPD), the Catholic
Centre Party and the liberal German Democratic Party (DDP)
advocated a moderate pacifism, that is, a foreign policy of rapprochement combined with support for the League of Nations and
disarmament on the one hand, and a defensive military policy on the
other.[34] This policy was able to command the support of a majority
in parliament until 1930. Towards the end of the Weimar Republic,
however, it was attacked with increasing success by the nationalist
right which denounced the Republicans' pacifism as weak, and
spread its own power-political slogans.

The treatment accorded the Briand–Kellogg Pact in the German
Reichstag showed that not even the idea of a renunciation of war
had been accepted by all parties. In the ratification debate on 8
February 1929, 289 deputies voted for the treaty, and 127 were
against it.[35] Those against included the German Communist Party
(KPD) which opposed the Pact using the Comintern's arguments
referred to above. On the right, the German National People's
Party (DNVP), the Nazi Party (NSDAP) and the *Christlich-
Nationale Bauernpartei* (Christian National Peasants' Party) all

refused to approve the Pact. Even in the other parties, support for the Pact was dependent on certain conditions. Several speakers made it clear that they intended to use the Pact as a means of supporting German demands for a revision of the Versailles Treaty, in particular, to support the demand for disarmament of the Versailles powers. The government led by the Social Democratic Chancellor Hermann Müller also located the Briand–Kellogg Pact in the general context of a peaceful policy of gradual revision.

Although it is incomplete, the survey of public opinion in the USA, France, Britain, the Soviet Union and Germany undertaken here suggests that the idea of a renunciation of war encountered an anti-war mood which existed to varying degrees in most countries.[36] The Briand–Kellogg Pact obviously corresponded to a pacifism latent in society, even if in individual cases it was not articulated very clearly.

The following remarks are restricted to Germany where a phenomenon occurred which at first sight seems surprising. One year after the Pact was signed, the public mood changed. Nationalist ideologies with strong militarist tendencies found an increasing response in large sections of the German public. This development was directly opposed to the intentions of the Briand–Kellogg Pact, and took place in this form only in Germany. In most of the other signatory states, particularly in the Great Powers mentioned above, public opinion did not change until the second half of the 1930s, when the latent pacifism was also abandoned there, undoubtedly in reaction to the threat posed by Hitler's Germany.

The suggestion that public opinion in Germany was suddenly militarised in the late 1920s, rather than with Hitler's accession to power, is relatively new. In an understandable desire to draw a lesson from the failure of the first German Republic for the stabilisation of the parliamentary government of the Second Republic, historians after the Second World War looked primarily at the late 1920s and early 1930s to see what factors had contributed to the failure of the Weimar Republic.[37] Particular attention was paid to the anti-democratic ideas of the political right.[38] From a point of view limited to a concern with the problems of democracy' and dictatorship, the militarist ideas and mentality to which Hitler was to give organisational form seemed no more than one element in the general anti-democratic trend. They were not accorded sufficient weight as historical factors which were direct precursors of those measures introduced by Hitler's government designed to restore the nation's military capacity, both mentally and materially.

All this means that there has been a lack of studies about militarist and pacifist ideas and their development as was reflected in German public opinion between 1929 and 1933. The following remarks therefore intend to provide a certain amount of evidence to support the proposition that Germany had a *Sonderentwicklung* — a specific course of development — without suggesting a definitive answer to the difficult question of how this development is to be explained.

One current, rather apologetic, explanatory model focuses on international events. It concentrates particularly on evidence that expectations of the Briand–Kellogg Pact leading to a rapid revision of the Versailles Treaty were not fulfilled. It is true that negotiations about a reduction in Germany's reparations payments proceeded very slowly, disarmament talks stagnated and large sections of the population continued to regard themselves as discriminated against by the war guilt clause imposed by the victorious powers. The climate of public opinion in Germany was influenced indirectly by factors such as the interpretation of international events given by the nationalist parties and associations. The world-wide depression which began in 1929 led to mass unemployment in Germany, creating great economic hardship, and making the middle classes fear for their existence. The extent to which this fostered the change in attitude towards militarist policies needs to be examined in greater detail, using psychoanalytical as well as other approaches.[39] The consequences of the crisis-ridden change can be seen in the electoral successes of the right-wing parties, and in the way in which parties of the centre drifted into a nationalist course. These developments show clearly that the position which advocated a peaceful policy of revision was put on the defensive as a result of the change in mood in 1929/30, and that the call for power-political solutions to domestic and international politico-economic dilemmas found an increasing response. The nationalist parties' propaganda undoubtedly played a considerable part in this development. In addition, specific literature and films had a certain effect which was certainly significant, but difficult to measure in individual cases. These cultural products will now be discussed in more detail.

3. Literary Glorifications of War: 'Militant Nationalism'

The most radical form assumed by anti-pacifist ideas glorifying war was represented by a literary movement which should be seen as politically part of the Conservative Revolution. Its ideology has aptly been called 'Militant Nationalism';[40] aptly, because war and the nation were its focal points of reference. Its adherents were a numerically small but influential group of intellectuals. Since the beginning of the 1920s, they had been applying themselves to the subject of war in ever-new literary variations. Their productions, however, achieved mass circulation only at the end of the decade — evidence of the increase in demand for the philosophy of war these literary 'warriors' had to offer — one which today has a shocking effect.

This movement included the brothers Ernst and Friedrich Georg Jünger, Werner Beumelburg, Edwin Erich Dwinger, Franz Schauwecker, Helmut Franke, Friedrich Hielscher, Wilhelm Kleinau, Albrecht Erich Günther, Ernst von Salomon, Gerhard Günther and Wilhelm von Schramm, to mention only some of the best-known names. They were all born in the last decade of the nineteenth century and had all been to the Front in the First World War. According to their individual self-assessments, the war had proved a decisive formative experience.[41] As they rejected every form of organisation, including any binding political programme, they did not belong to any of the Conservative parties. What they had in common was a particular mentality which they were convinced it was important to preserve, even after the war.

This conviction in no way stamped them as outsiders. On the one hand, a collective memory of an inviolable 'community' of the Front was cultivated by the conservative, nationalist camp as whole. On the other, they unanimously attacked the Weimar Republic and the democratic parties which supported it, for being unheroic, unmilitant, unsoldierly, pacifist and defeatist. A nationalist and anti-democratic interpretation of the experience of war became one of the most effective of the conservative rallying cries for unity,[42] especially as the democratic left relinquished the area of military traditions, so important for the public mood, almost entirely to the political right.[43]

The large degree of unity which existed among Conservatives of the most diverse provenance in their attitudes to world war, to the experience of war and to the problem of war as such, is understandable if it is remembered that Conservatism had developed a philosophy of war since the nineteenth century. As discussed above, this philosophy saw war as a natural law, as something decreed by fate. The enlightened idea of eternal peace must therefore have seemed Utopian, something contrary to all the laws of nature. Apart from this, Conservative theory in principle evaluated war positively.[44] It was lauded as a source of the nation's strength, and as a suitable vehicle for national integration.

Literary representations of the experience of war needed only to pick out the elements of the Conservative philosophy of war which had remained constant, and bring them up to date. Of course, there were also new emphases, such as Ernst Jünger's aestheticising of war. But in general, the writers of the Conservative Revolution who had been at the Front were clearly working in the tradition discussed here, when throughout the entire Weimar period, they glorified war in their writing.

Many nationalistic veterans of the Front who were left unemployed at the end of the war and had not found, or had not wanted to find, a niche in civilian life, took an active part in the paramilitary 'Freikorps' (Free Corps) which was founded in the first years of the Weimar Republic.[45] After it was dissolved, the ex-soldiers joined the right-wing *Wehrbünde* (veterans' organisations) which succeeded it. What was produced at this time by the intellectuals among the ex-soldiers did not take the form of a political statement as such. Rather, it was a subjective and individual transformation of their experiences during the four years of the war.[46]

The politicisation of the war experience began as the economic situation stabilised from 1924 onwards, and the violent internal political conflicts of the past calmed down. During this period of stabilisation, the experience of war and the question of war guilt were no longer the focus of public discussion to the same extent as earlier. The writers of the Front found themselves in isolation for some years. But the weakening of public response did not adversely affect their production; on the contrary, it spurred them on, making them feel an almost evangelical fervour and sense of mission.[47] Subsequently, their ideology influenced the right-wing opposition parties, as well as the numerous national *Wehrverbände* (veterans' organisations) which were committed to the militant traditions. The *Wehrwolf*, the *Jungdeutsche Orden*, the *Bund Oberland*, *Bund Wiking* and other *Wehrbünde*, but above all the *Stahlhelm* provided a great deal of scope for journalistic agitation by Friedrich Georg Jünger, Schauwecker, Franke and Kleinau, and especially by Ernst Jünger, undisputed leader of the Militant Nationalists.[48] Between 1924 and 1926, they were able to use the *Stahlhelm's* journal, *Die Standarte*, as their main organ. After their break with the *Stahlhelm*, the Militant Nationalist writers attempted, albeit unsuccessfully, to unite the rest of the *Wehrbünde*. The great successes they were to have in the last period of the Weimar Republic were at first sight literary ones. But their effects were also political.

The ideology of Militant Nationalism was a cluster of irrationalisms. With some difficulty, four elements can be distinguished within it. Firstly, the personal experience of world war was idealised and transformed; secondly, war and the military tradition in general were valued highly and glorified; thirdly, Militant Nationalism was associated with a strong sense of nationalism and, finally, it demanded a state of front-line soldiers who were to be responsible for imperialistic conquests.

In marked contrast to pacifist interpretations of the war experience, nationalist writers of the Front wanted the suffering and destruction of war to be forgotten. They stridently emphasised its positive sides: 'Wir wollen das negative, bedingte, der Verwesung opfernde Teil [sic!] dieses Krieges aus unserem Gedächtnis auszumerzen versuchen, wie dies die Tendenz des Gedächtnisses immer ist — und nur das Lebendige, Große, Fortzeugende aufbehalten'.[49] ('Following natural processes, we attempt to eradicate from our memories the negative, limited aspects of this war, those which were a sacrifice to putrescence — and preserve only its living aspects, its greatness and the procreative impulses it continues to give.') This sentence alone makes it clear that, from the very beginning, the Militant Nationalists were not interested in a political, social or economic analysis of the war. What was important to them was neither verifiable evidence nor rational argument, but seeing and feeling intuitively, a transformation far removed from reality. Therefore, Militant Nationalists were not concerned about the causes of the war. In this respect they subscribed to the saying that war is the father of all things, which the widely read Oswald Spengler turned into the even catchier phrase: 'In the beginning was war'.[50] This had the status of an incontestable, eternal truth, making any further discussion of the subject superfluous. Thus it was only consistent for Ernst Jünger to argue that for an understanding of war, 'it is of secondary importance in which century, for which ideas and with which weapons the fighting is done'.[51]

Thus, when these writers wrote about war, they did not mean any particular war in a specific historical context. They meant *war as such*. Friedrich Hielscher articulated the self-conception of the Militant Nationalists in this sense. It was necessary to be 'a soldier for the sake of war', and if one could see the matter in this light, one was certain of 'the highest degree of inner peace'.[52] In the context of this aggresive philosophy of life, which has been influenced by social Darwinism, the opposition between war and peace disappeared. They became 'two sides of one and the same condition of transformation which we call life'. 'War is always present; and peace is always present. Every life proceeds by destroying other lives'.[53] Heroism was everything and humanity was nothing: 'The born warrior does not even begin to entertain humanitarian ideas; he cannot, because he is totally permeated by the fatality of war'.[54] To these literary warriors, moral, ethical or legal judgements of war seemed as absurd as did the distinction between offensive and defensive war. All this was part of a despised rational analysis, which according to A. E. Günther, only lamed the instincts:

> Natürlich ist jeder Krieg ein Verteidigungskrieg, sogar für beide Partner — sei es, dass die Lebensrechte des Werdenden gegen den erstickenden Druck des Bestehenden, sei es, dass das Lebensrecht des Bestehenden gegen die zerstörende Gewalt des Werdenden verteidigt werden: uns vermag darum diese Diskussion nur um ihres propagandistischen Wertes — um ihrer instinktlähmenden Wirkung zu interessieren.

> (Naturally every war is a defensive war — for both partners. Whether the right to life of something in the process of becoming has to be defended against the stifling pressure of the existing order, or whether the right to life of the existing order has to be defended against the destructive power of something in the process of becoming: this discussion interests us only because of its propaganda value — its effect of laming the instincts.)

For Günther, therefore, it was self-evident that the 'protection of the right to life' included aggression.[55] Elaborating on this idea, Ernst Jünger suggested that his fellow-countrymen should be proud that the rest of the world perceived them as 'one of its greatest dangers'.[56]

The 'uninhibited translation of the principles of *l'art pour l'art* to war itself',[57] which was characteristic of the ideology of Militant Nationalism, culminated in the idea that military battle, divested of all practical purposes and political aims, was one of the most noble of the arts. Wilhelm von Schramm, for example, pitied himself and others of his sort, because the First World War had been a bitter disappointment for true soldiers. Not because Germany had lost the war, but because this war had not been a war 'for the sake of the deeper idea of war', because it did not do justice to the idea of war 'as an art, as the highest and most noble style of conflict between men, as an artistic form, with its own laws, of fighting between peoples'. Instead, it was concerned only with 'purposes and practical objectives, material gain', and not with the 'solemn, elevated and bloody game' which 'since time began, has been making men of men'.[58]

Militant Nationalist writers filled thousands of pages with wisdom of this sort. They fitted perfectly into the extreme political irrationality to which the Conservative Revolution as a whole was committed.

At the same time, the socialist writer Walter Benjamin subjected the collection of essays *Krieg und Krieger*, from which many of the quotations above were taken, to precise analysis and damning criticism:

> Man soll es mit aller Bitternis aussprechen: Im Angesicht der total mobilgemachten Landschaft hat das deutsche Naturgefühl einen ungeahnten Aufschwung genommen. Die Friedensgenien, die sie so besinnlich besiedeln, sind evakuiert worden und so weit man über den Grabenrand blicken konnte, war alles Umliegende zum Gelände des deutschen Idealismus selbst geworden, jeder Granattrichter ein Problem, jeder Drahtverhau eine Autonomie, jede Explosion eine Satzung, und der Himmel darüber bei Tag die kosmische Innenseite des Stahlhelms, bei Nacht das sittliche Gesetz über ihr.

> (It should be said as bitterly as possible: in the face of this 'landscape of total mobilisation' the German feeling for nature has had an undreamed-of upsurge. The pioneers of peace, those sensuous settlers, were evacuated from these landscapes, and as far as anyone could see over the edge of the trench, the surroundings became a problem, every wire entanglement an antinomy, every barb a definition, every explosion a thesis; and by day the sky was the cosmic interior of the steel helmet and at night the moral law above.)

But the representatives of the new nationalism, who professed belief in war as a metaphysical abstraction, were not merely idealistic thinkers.

> Was sich hierunter der Maske erst des Freiwilligen im Weltkrieg, dann des Söldners im Nachkrieg, heranbildete, ist in Wahrheit der zuverlässigste faschistische Klassenkrieger, und was die Verfasser unter Nation verstehen, eine auf diesen Stand gestützte Herrscherklasse. . . .

> (What developed here, first in the guise of the World War volunteer and then in the mercenary of the *Nachkrieg* [postwar war], is in fact the dependable fascist class warrior. And what these authors mean by nation is a ruling class supported by this caste. . . .)

They were the 'war engineers of the ruling class', and as such, 'the perfect complement to the managerial functionaries in their cutaways'. 'God knows', warned Benjamin, 'their designs on leadership should be taken seriously; their threat is not ludicrous'.[59]

These were, in fact, the two roles which Militant Nationalism assumed. On the one hand, it promoted an abstract, metaphysical cult of war; on the other, it made an unmistakeable claim on behalf of the élite veterans for political domination. This claim forms the basis of what has somewhat vaguely been called the 'politicisation of the war experience'.[60] Representatives of Militant Nationalism regarded the community of the Front as the practical application of an ideal model of a national community, and considered it a suitable point of departure for Germany's political renewal. Basing their ideas on this concept of community, they developed a concrete political demand for a state made up of front-line soldiers. Its first task would be to do away with the democratic parties' policy of rapprochement, which was attacked as being 'weak'. In other words, they wanted to give up the 'unheroic' attempt to achieve a peaceful revision of the peace terms of the Versailles Treaty.

Militant Nationalism developed an almost classical ideology of militarism based on these ideas. Military conceptions of order were transferred, as emotional projections of the experience of war, on to a society living in peace, without the slightest attempt to analyse rationally the laws governing mobility in an advanced industrial society.

The idea of a state of front-line soldiers was primarily an authoritarian counter-proposal to the democractic system of Weimar. As such, it differed at least in degree from the Fascist political system implemented after 1933. But the liquidation of the hated Weimar system was only one line of attack. The projected state of front-line soldiers was also to prepare the way for military conquests. War, a heroic condition of life permanently held in esteem, had to be reinstated; not necessarily any particular war, such as a war of revenge against France or a preventive war against Poland, but simply war as such.

The writers of Militant Nationalism indulged in imperialist dreams which went far beyond those of the pre-1914 pan-Germans, and indeed matched Hitler's ideas of war in every way. As early as 1926, Friedrich Georg Jünger demanded that nationalism must tirelessly drum the imperialist idea, extended to infinity, into the German consciousness: 'Es gibt nichts Wichtigeres, nichts Dringlicheres, als den imperialistischen Willen zu beleben, zu stählen und schlagfertig zu machen. Denn jeder Kampf, der morgen oder übermorgen von uns geführt wird, geht um das Dasein. . . . Er ist Austrag über die Beherrschung der Erde.'[61] ('There is nothing more important, more pressing, than to invigorate, to harden the imperialist will everywhere, and to make it ready for battle. Because every battle which we fight tomorrow, or the day after tomorrow, will be a struggle for existence. . . . It will decide the domination of the earth!') As the nationalistic front-line soldier wanted to cast 'Germanness into a new aggressive form', for him, 'every additional screw in a machine-gun, every improvement in gas warfare was more important than the League of Nations'. It was not a matter of co-operation in the League of Nations; 'Germanness' was called upon to create the 'Imperium germanicum'.[62] Friedrich Georg Jünger was convinced that 'the nationalistic mentality is necessarily also an imperialist one'.[63]

His brother Ernst Jünger expressed his conviction that 'things look good only for a world of which we are the leaders'.[64] In his war diary, *Feuer und Blut*, he makes a plea with racist overtones for violent imperial expansion. This strikingly documents how unnecessary it is to make any distinction between fascist and militant nationalist ideas. In *Mein Kampf* Hitler wrote: 'Ein Staat, der im Zeitalter der Rassenvergiftung sich der Pflege seiner besten rassischen Elemente widmet, muß eines Tages zum Herrn der Erde werden'.[65] ('A state which at a time of general racial pollution devotes itself to cultivating its best racial elements must one day rule the earth.') Jünger wrote:

> Den Drang ins Weite und Grenzenlose, wir tragen ihn als unser germanisches Erbteil im Blut, und wir hoffen, daß es sich dereinst zu einem Imperialismus gestalten wird, der sich nicht wie jener kümmerliche von gestern auf einige Vorrechte, Grenzprovinzen und Südseeinseln richtet, sondern der wirklich aufs Ganze geht.[66]

(The yearning for wide open spaces, for infinity, is in our blood as our Germanic heritage. We hope that one day it will take the form of an imperialism that dares to go the whole way — unlike the miserable imperialism of yesterday which aimed merely to gain a few privileges, border provinces and South Sea islands.)

Without the least political substantiation, Jünger's 'overheated militarised imagination' here produced the idea of unlimited violence for its own sake.[67] Correspondingly, the vision of a Germanic world empire was expressed only very vaguely. It seemed rather like a non-essential appendage, a reluctant concession made to those who had not yet totally succumbed to political irrationalism.

4. Evidence of the Remilitarisation of German Public Opinion from 1929 Onwards

Although the ideology of Militant Nationalist writers was extreme in many ways, it was not an isolated and politically insignificant phenomenon. These writers' books, some of which had first been published years previously without attracting much attention, found a mass audience from 1929 onwards — the date can be given with relative precision.[68] This must certainly be considered evidence for a change in public mood.

Werner Beumelburg's novel of the Front, *Gruppe Bosemüller*, had an immediate print-run of 30,000 in 1930, and 65,000 was reached in 1933 (90,000 in 1935; 170,000 in 1940). His bestseller *Sperrfeuer um Deutschland* was printed in an edition of 100,000 in 1930 alone; in 1931 it reached 140,000, in 1932 150,000 and in 1933 166,000 (1935 216,000; 1938 328,000). Edwin Erich Dwinger's books were also printed in huge editions of tens of thousands. His Siberian journal, *Die Armee hinter Stacheldraht*, was published in 1929; by 1931 it had sold 27,000 copies, and by 1935 78,000. His novel *Zwischen Weiss und Rot* first appeared in 1930, and by 1932, more than 40,000 copies had been sold. Ernst Jünger's description of battle, *Feuer und Blut*, had reached its fourth edition by 1929; the fourth edition of his chronicle of trench warfare in 1918, *Das Wäldchen 125*, was printed in 1929, and the fifth in 1930 (16,000); his *Der Kampf als inneres Erlebnis* went from its fourth to its thirteenth editions between 1929 and 1933; and his book *In Stahlgewittern* also reached its thirteenth edition in 1931. In 1930 two large collections of essays edited by Ernst Jünger were published: *Krieg und Krieger* and *Das Antlitz des Welkrieges* (two volumes). The seventh and eighth editions of Franz Schauwecker's book *So war der Krieg* were published in 1929, and in 1930 it passed the 50,000 mark; after 1928, there were several new editions of his novel *Der feurige Weg*. His *Aufbruch der Nation* was published in 1930 in an edition of 30,000. Like Ernst von Salomon's books *Putsch* and *Die Verschwörer*, it was reprinted in 1933 in the Nazi series 'Das Reich im Werden'. *M.G.K.* and *Dauerfeuer*, both by the leader of the *Stahlhelm*, Franz Seldte, were published in popular editions after 1933, but had already achieved a high circulation in 1929 and 1930 (30,000). Wilhelm Michael's *Infanterist Perhobstler* had an edition of 30,000 in 1930, and Arnold Bronnen's *O.S.* 25,000. In addition to the writers mentioned here, many other authors who belonged to the Militant Nationalists or the Conservative Revolution experienced greatly increased public interest.

The group of Militant Nationalist writers contributed significantly to the flood of nationalistic war books and films which inundated Germany after 1929. The overall trend, however, was much more widely based. An analysis of the literature listed in catalogues of German books in print between 1925 and 1935 shows that a boom in books with a militarist trend and a simultaneous decline in literature with a pacifist tendency was apparent several years before Hitler came to power. The number of books concerned with 'military matters', for example, rose continuously between 1929 and 1935.[69] The large number of books published between 1930 and 1932 dealing with future wars is conspicuous (1929: 2; 1930: 12; 1931: 14; 1932: 17). The number of books which — without analysing the attitudes they express — can generally be subsumed under the heading 'World War Books', that is, books which indicate the rising level of discussion about the 1914–18 war and reminiscences of it, rose from about 200 in 1926 to about 300 in 1929 and more than 400 in 1930, dropped back to about 300 in 1931 and 1932, and then, after Hitler's accession to power, reached an absolute maximum of more than 500 titles. In 1935 public discussion of military policy stopped, and this is attributed by Hillgruber to the fact that by this time, militaristic social blueprints had largely been realised.[70]

Books on the problem of peace to which pacifist tendencies in the widest sense can be attributed experienced the opposite fate. The number of books available listed under the heading 'Peace' (a list which is certainly incomplete, but nevertheless informative) declined steadily: 35 in 1929, 30 in 1930, 25 in 1931, 23 in 1932, and only 10 in 1933. After 1933, as is generally known, pacifist literature was no longer published in Germany — it was publicly burnt instead.

In spite of the change in public mood one single anti-war book was able to maintain its position. Erich Maria Remarque's *Im Westen nichts Neues (All Quiet on the Western Front)* had a maximum edition in 1930 of 1 million in Germany, and 2 million abroad.[71] As Remarque's book was an unadorned account of everyday life during the war, and lacked any heroic pathos whatsoever, it was regarded by the nationalistic right as a massive attack on the 'honour of front-line soldiers'. Schauwecker spoke of 'the war experience of the subhuman', and F. G. Jünger expressed his contempt by describing it as a book which 'did not represent the heroic battles of the German armies, but indulged in weak complaints against the war instead'.[72] In 1932 the pacifist Carl von Ossietzky expressed his regret in the journal *Weltbühne* that Remarque's bestseller could not have an effect on politics.[73] It thus remained an 'interesting and isolated, achievement which, even though it was extremely widely read, proved unable to check nationalism in any way. According to Ossietzky, the book was a phenomenon which had swept over the people without any lasting effect. It had been picked up as a fad, read in this spirit, and then simply put down again.

The nationalistic right does not seem to have shared this view. The verbal attacks mentioned above, plus the political events of late 1930 showed that the right, strengthened by the triumphs of the Nazi Party in the September elections, was no longer prepared to stand by and watch pacifist ideas gaining influence. On the occasion of the Berlin première of the film *All Quiet on the Western Front* on 5 December 1930, turbulent demonstrations took place, organised mainly by the Nazi Party under Goebbels, *Gauleiter* (District Leader) for Berlin.[74] The showing was abandoned, and a second one had to be cancelled. A few days later, the Nazi Party arranged large public demonstrations against the film. The veterans' organisations joined in the protests. Saxony, Bavaria and Württemberg applied to the central film censorship board to withdraw the film's licence. The changed political climate is revealed by the fact that the censorship authorities complied with this request and banned further showings of the film under the pretext that it damaged Germany's image abroad. Even the Centre Party, previously one of the mainstays of the Weimar coalition, expressed its support for the ban. The chancellor, Heinrich Brüning of the Centre Party, demanded that stronger measures be taken against other pacifist films and plays as well. Brüning condemned the stand taken against the ban by Prussia's Social Democratic government as 'very dangerous as far as the impression it makes abroad is concerned'. He recommended to his own party that they should take more notice of new forms of activity ('processions, small-bore target practice, etc.').[75] The minister of the interior, Joseph Wirth, also of the Centre Party, supported the ban on the film because he thought it was necessary to 'respect certain feelings' and 'show consideration for certain dispositions'.[76] The chancellor's description of his government as a 'cabinet of front-line soldiers' is indicative of Brüning's leanings, and especially of the dominant climate of opinion in the Reichstag in 1930.[77] At his first meeting with Hitler on 6 October 1930, Brüning appealed to him 'as an old front-line soldier' to tolerate his policies. For the rest, Brüning tried to gain Hitler's support for a coalition between the Centre Party and the Nazi Party at 'Länder' (state) level.[78]

As much as literature, the cinema was a 'theatre of war' where domestic political as well as ideological conflicts were played out. After 1930 developments in the German film generally paralleled the boom in literature glorifying war. Progressive films, which were critical of social conditions and tried to communicate pacifist ideas, increasingly lost ground to authoritarian films. These 'national epics' portrayed rebels, war heros and leaders as stylised models for emulation.[79] Louis Trenker's films are typical of this type: military virtues are extrolled, and war is presented as something beyond the control of individuals which simply has to be accepted. The film historian Siegfried Kracauer has observed that 'Trenker's mountaineer was the type of man any government intent on war could rely on'.[80]

The exactness of the correlation between the flood of war books and films with a right-wing tendency and the economic crisis is striking; these cultural products found a ready audience. It can be deduced, with some plausibility, that the consumers of these cultural products no longer expected the pacifism of the system (that is, the Weimar Republic's policy of rapprochement) to achieve anything. They preferred to opt for the alternative of authoritarian and ultimately violent solutions in domestic and foreign policy. According to Prümm, during the last years of the Weimar Republic the bourgeoisie in particular adopted positions 'which defamed its positive liberal traditions as weak resentment and glorified violence and brutality as adequate political means. . . . It accepted nostalgic views which transformed the experience of war and elevated it to the normal social condition'.[81] Expressed more cautiously: the threshold of its resistance to symbolic and (later) organised and real violence was reduced.

It is not possible to establish in detail exactly who were the consumers of nationalistic war books and films. Prümm's argument that they came primarily from the bourgeoisie is plausible because, apart from the traditional right-wing voters, it was mainly the middle classes which had turned to the Nazi Party since 1930. The consumers of these cultural products included, as we know, the majority of students, 95 per cent of whom came from the middle and upper classes, and two-thirds of whom were organised in the politically right-wing students' associations. Among the 1929/30 intake of students, who had not experienced the war personally as soldiers (having been born in 1910), it became fashionable to adopt the veterans' myth *in toto*, and to idealise the war generation and its experiences of war.[82] The flood of militarism in the universities also resulted in the creation of new organisations: a *Stahlhelm* students' organisation was formed, as was a *Langemarck-Stiftung* (Langemarck Foundation) of German students. In 1930 the *Deutsche Studentenschaft* (German student body) saw its most important task as education and training in military sports.

Studies of voting behaviour between 1930 and 1933 show that after 1930 a large number of young people who had previously refused to vote as a protest, or who had been too young, voted for the Nazi Party. This reflects the historically incontestable fact that the generational conflict, characteristic of German society in the 1920s, was successfully exploited by anti-republican groups.[83] These young people, like the students, were probably consumers of nationalistic war literature. The students and youths of 1930 were the soldiers of 1939.

In the political climate described here, the political party which agitated most aggressively and determinedly against democracy, socialism and pacifism, that is, the Nazi Party, became the strongest political force in Germany within a few years. The change in public mood was only partly brought about by the Nazi Party and its auxiliary organisations, but they certainly made use of it. They could build upon, strengthen and accelerate the process of militarisation of public opinion which had already begun. Before 1933, a readiness to accept if not expressly to endorse violence had existed in society in a latent form, as a result of the dissemination of certain militarist ideologies. After rearmament was completed, this latent readiness could be activated at any time if required.[84]

5. The Power of Tradition — War Fatalism and the Claim to Great Power Status

As we have tried to show, there is much to indicate that the shift in German public opinion towards anti-pacifist and pro-militarist sentiments began as early as 1929. Thus the end of the Weimar Republic should not be seen only from the point of view of the decline of democratic government, as has normally been the case. It is necessary to trace the continuities which linked it to the causes and preconditions of the Second World War.[85] If this is done, the appointment of Hitler as chancellor on 30 January 1933 is no longer a decisive turning-point marking the beginning of a new era, as most historians have seen it. The evidence of continuity which exists in various areas of policy is reason enough at least to modify the theory of 1933 as a caesura. What remains true is that with Hitler's chancellorship, the attempt to re-establish Germany's position as a continental Great Power entered a new phase, as concrete preparations for war began.

In the seventy-five year — that is, relatively short — history of the German national state, it is striking that its beginning as well as its end were associated with a policy of war, suggesting the continuity of a policy of force directed outwards.[86] In this context, the German signature on the Briand–Kellogg Pact renouncing war seems almost out of place.

In fact, only a few years later, any traces which this treaty may have left on German public opinion were no longer visible. The hope of Briand, Kellogg and other advocates of the renunciation of war, that public opinion would prove to be a decisive factor in maintaining peace, was not fulfilled in Germany. The enormous success of nationalistic war literature indicates that precisely the opposite was the case. It allows us to see that soon after its codification, the idea of renouncing war was forgotten by large sections of the German population, or at least, had very little public appeal.

If we look for explanations of this development, we soon encounter — apart from those already discussed relating to the concrete historical situation during the last phase of the Weimar Republic — the tradition of fatalism about war described at the beginning of this essay. It clearly proved to be extremely powerful. A few newspaper headlines and an additional paragraph in the textbooks of international law were not enough to allow the idea of renouncing war to assert itself permanently against existing prejudices and articles of faith. As far as most people were concerned, and in spite of the Briand–Kellogg Pact, war remained what it had been since time immemorial — decreed by fate and a legitimate means of policy. The number of Germans who were able to distance themselves from these fatalistic traditions — on which nationalistic glorifications of war thrived — was not large enough to prevent a reversion to the politics of violence.

Notes

1. The text of the Briand–Kellogg Pact is printed in H. Wehberg, *Die Völkerbundsatzung*, third edn., Berlin, 1929, pp. 178ff.
2. For the interpretation relating to international law, see H. Wehberg, *Die Ächtung des Krieges*, Berlin, 1930; H. Wehberg, *Krieg und Eroberung im Wandel des Völkerrechts*, Frankfurt/M./ Berlin, 1953, pp. 43ff.; G. Dahm, *Völkerrecht*, vol. II, Stuttgart, 1961, pp. 347ff.; E. Berber, *Lehrbuch des Völkerrechts*, vol. III: *Kriegsrecht*, second edn., Munich, 1969, pp. 35ff.
3. For details see Dahm, *Völkerrecht*, pp. 332–47.
4. See Wehberg's survey, *Krieg*, pp. 11ff., as well as the informative article by N. H. Gibbs, T. H. Wolfe and C. D. Kernig, 'Krieg', in *Sowjetsystem und demokratische Gesellschaft. Eine vergleichende*

Enzyklopädie, vol. III, Freiburg/ Basel/ Vienna, 1969, pp. 1,026–87. For the Marxist–Leninist version of this theory, see *Gerechte und ungerechte Kriege*, by a collective of authors led by G. Rau, East Berlin, 1970. Some of the classic socialist theories justifying war are examined in W. Wette, *Kriegstheorien deutscher Sozialisten. Marx, Engels, Lassalle, Bernstein, Kautsky, Luxemburg*, Stuttgart, 1971.

5. On the legality of war in European international law, see Wehberg, *Krieg*, pp. 21ff.

6. See K. Sontheimer, *Antidemokratisches Denken in der Weimarer Republik. Die politischen Ideen des deutschen Nationalismus zwischen 1918 und 1933*, Munich, 1962, especially Ch. 5, 'Das Kriegserlebnis des Ersten Weltkrieges'.

7. Briand's address is printed in *Schulthess' Europäischer Geschichtskalender für das Jahr 1928*, pp. 502–05 (p. 504).

8. Stresemann on 2 February 1929 in the Reichstag at the first reading of the Kellogg Pact. See *Schulthess' Europäischer Geschichtskalender für das Jahr 1929*, p. 19. Stresemann had been awarded the Nobel Peace Prize in 1926, together with Briand. See A. Harttung (ed.), *Der Friedensnobelpreis. Stiftung und Verleihung. Die Reden der vier deutschen Preisträger Gustav Stresemann, Ludwig Quidde, Carl von Ossietzky, Willy Brandt*, Berlin, n.d. [1972]. Stresemann was a politician with long-term plans for the future — see M.-O. Maxelon, *Stresemann und Frankreich 1914–1929. Deutsche Politik der Ost-West-Balance*, Düsseldorf, 1972.

9. Thus Kellogg's successor as foreign secretary, on 8 August 1932. See K. Krakau, *Missionsbewußtsein und Völkerrechtsdoktrin in den Vereinigten Staaten von Amerika*, Frankfurt/M./ Berlin, 1967, p. 326.

10. The French historian Maurice Baumont judged disparagingly that the Pact was 'a theatrical victory for the idea of peace, designed to impress the imagination of the masses in their innocence': M. Baumont, *Aristide Briand: Diplomat und Idealist*, Göttingen/ Frankfurt/Zurich,- 1966, p. 74.

11. Briand, for example, who closed his address on the occasion of the signing of the Pact with a demand to allow the organisation of peace to follow its proclamation. See *Schulthess' Europäischer Geschichtskalender für das Jahr 1928*, p. 505.

12. See *Schulthess' Europäischer Geschichtskalender für das Jahr 1928*, pp. 504f.

13. On these and other weaknesses of the Pact, see Wehberg, *Krieg*, pp. 43ff., as well as Dahm, *Völkerrecht*, pp. 347ff.

14. Excerpts from Kellogg's address in Oslo in *Schulthess' Europäischer Geschichtskalender für das Jahr 1931*, pp. 342f.; see also L. E. Ellis, *Frank B. Kellogg and American Foreign Relations, 1925–1929*, New Brunswick, NJ, 1961, as well as R. H. Ferrell, 'Frank B. Kellogg', in *The American Secretaries of State and their Diplomacy*, vol XI, New York, 1963, pp. 1–135.

15. Wehberg, *Krieg*, p. 53.

16. For a survey of the groups within the American peace movement, see R. H. Ferrell, *Peace in Their Time: The Origins of the Kellogg-*

Briand Pact, New Haven, Conn., 1952, pp. 13ff.
17. Wehberg, *Ächtung*, pp. 22f.
18. This is maintained by R. N. Stromberg, *Collective Security and American Foreign Policy: From the League of Nations to NATO*, New York, 1963, pp. 55ff.
19. Krakau, *Missionsbewußtsein*, pp. 320ff., particularly p. 325.
20. W. Link, *Die amerikanische Stabilisierungspolitik in Deutschland 1921–1932*, Düsseldorf, 1970, pp. 619–23.
21. R. Gottwald, *Die deutsch-amerikanischen Beziehungen in der Ära Stresemann*, Berlin, 1965, pp. 88ff; J. Néré, *The Foreign Policy of France from 1914 to 1945*, London, 1975.
22. A. Prost, 'Les Anciens Combattants francais et l'Allemagne', in *La France et l'Allemagne 1932–1936*, Paris, 1980, pp. 131–48.
23. See J. Bariéty, *Les Relations franco-allemandes après la première guerre mondiale, 10 Novembre 1918 – 10 Janvier 1925*, Paris, 1977.
24. J.-M d'Hoop, 'Le Problème du réarmament francais jusqu' à mars 1936', in *France*, pp. 75–89.
25. P. M. Kennedy, ' "Splendid Isolation" gegen "Continental Commitment": Das Dilemma der britischen Deutschlandstrategie in der Zwischenkriegszeit', in J. Hütter et al. (eds.), *Tradition und Neubeginn*, Cologne/Bonn/Munich, 1975, pp. 156, 162.
26. See G. Niedhart, 'Friedensvorstellungen, Gewaltdiskussion und Konfliktverhalten in der britischen Labour Party 1919–1926', in W. Huber and J. Schwerdtfeger (eds.), *Frieden, Gewalt, Sozialismus: Studien zur Geschichte der sozialistischen Arbeiterbewegung*, Stuttgart, 1976, pp. 641–79; G. Niedhart, 'Appeasement: Die britische Antwort auf die Krise des Weltkrieges und des internationalen Systems vor dem Zweiten Weltkrieg', *Historische Zeitschrift*, 226 (1978), pp. 67–88 (p. 68). For the 1930s, see D. Aigner, *Das Ringen um England. Das deutsch-britische Verhältnis. Die öffentliche Meinung 1933–1939*, Munich/ Esslingen, 1969.
27. Niedhart, 'Appeasement', pp. 72, 74f.
28. Kennedy, ' "Splendid Isolation" ', p. 161.
29. Gottwald, *Beziehungen*, p. 100. M. Walsdorff, *Westorientierung und Ostpolitik. Stresemanns Rußlandpolitik in der Locarno-Ära*, Bremen, 1971, pp. 198f.
30. See among others, S. Allard, *Stalin und Hitler: Die sowjetische Außenpolitik 1930–1941*, Bern/ Munich, 1974, pp. 7ff.
31. F. A. Krummacher and H. Lange, *Krieg und Frieden. Geschichte der deutsch-sowjetischen Beziehungen*, Munich/ Esslingen, 1970, pp. 218f.
32. Minutes of the Sixth World Congress of the Communist International in Moscow, 1928, vol. 1, *Die internationale Lage und die Aufgaben der Komintern: Der Kampf gegen die imperialistische Kriegsgefahr*, Hamburg/Berlin, 1928, pp. 39f., 526, 531f.
33. See F.-K. Scheer, *Die Deutsche Friedensgesellschaft (1892–1933). Organisation — Ideologie — Politische Ziele. Ein Beitrag zur Geschichte des Pazifismus in Deutschland*, Frankfurt/M., 1981; G. Grünewald, 'Stimme der Völkerverständigung und der Humanität: Die Deutsche Friedensgesellschaft 1892–1933', *Friedensanalysen*, 10 (1979), pp. 179–200.

34. For details see W. Wette, 'Ideologien, Propaganda und Innenpolitik als Voraussetzungen der Kriegspolitik des Dritten Reiches', in Deist, Messerschmidt, Volkmann and Wette, *Ursachen und Voraussetzungen der deutschen Kriegspolitik*, Stuttgart, 1979, pp. 62–87 (= *Das Deutsche Reich und der Zweite Weltkrieg*, 1).
35. See *Verhandlungen des Reichstags, IV, Wahlperiode 1928*, vol. 423, *Stenographische Berichte*, Berlin, 1929, pp. 991–1,000 (first and second debates about the treaty renouncing war held on 2 February 1929); idem, vol. 424, pp. 1,057–80 (third debate held on 6 February 1929). An abridged version of the discussion is printed in *Schulthess' Europäischer Geschichtskalender für das Jahr 1929*, pp. 25–7.
36. This cannot be determined exactly because of a lack of individual studies.
37. The standard works by K. D. Bracher should be mentioned here: *Die Auflösung der Weimarer Republik. Eine Studie zum Problem des Machtzerfalls in der Demokratie*, fifth edn, Villingen, 1971; *Die deutsche Diktatur: Entstehung, Struktur, Folgen des Nationalsozialismus*, Cologne/Berlin, 1969; *Die Krise Europas 1917–1975*, Berlin, 1976, Ch. 'Demokratie und Antidemokratie', pp. 98–152.
38. Sontheimer, *Antidemokratisches Denken*.
39. The psychoanalytical study by K. Theweleit, *Männerphantasien*, 2 vols., Frankfurt/M., 1977/8, is stimulating. It deals with the type represented by the Freikorps soldier of the first half of the 1920s.
40. K. Prümm, *Die Literatur des Soldatischen Nationalismus der 20er Jahre (1918–1933). Gruppenideologie und Epochenproblematik*, Kronberg/Ts., 1974.
41. See Ernst Jünger's foreword to F. G. Jünger, *Aufmarsch des Nationalismus*, ed. E. Jünger, Berlin, 1928, p. xi.
42. Prümm, *Literatur*, p. v.
43. A. Rosenberg, in Kurt Kerstein (ed.), *Entstehung und Geschichte der Weimarer Republik*, thirteenth edn, Frankfurt/M., 1972, p. 94.
44. See M. Greiffenhagen, *Das Dilemma des Konservatismus in Deutschland*, Munich, 1971, pp. 258ff.; Sontheimer, *Antidemokratisches Denken*.
45. See Theweleit, *Männerphantasien*.
46. Prümm, *Literatur*, p. 38.
47. Ibid.; also H.-P. Schwarz, *Der konservative Anarchist. Politik und Zeitkritik Ernst Jüngers*, Freiburg i. Br., 1962.
48. Prümm, *Literatur*, p. 57.
49. W. v. Schramm, 'Schöpferische Kritik des Krieges', in E. Jünger (ed.), *Krieg und Krieger*, Berlin, 1930, p. 35.
50. O. Spengler, *Der Untergang des Abendlandes*, Munich, 1922, p. 448.
51. E. Jünger, *Die totale Mobilmachung*, Berlin, 1930, second edn, 1934, p. 11. (English quoted from Walter Benjamin, 'Theories of German Fascism: On the collection of essays *War and the Warrior*, edited by Ernst Jünger', *New German Critique*, 6, 17(1979), pp. 120–8 (p. 120), trans. Jerolf Wikoof.)
52. F. Hielscher, 'Die grosse Verwandlung', in Jünger, *Krieg*, p. 131.
53. Ibid., p. 129.

54. Jünger, *Krieg*, p. 63. Similarly, Jünger, *Aufmarsch*, p. 56.
55. A. Günther, 'Die Intellegenz und der Krieg', in Jünger, *Krieg*, pp. 90f.
56. Jünger, *Mobilmachung*, p. 26.
57. W. Benjamin, 'Theorien des deutschen Faschismus. Zu der Sammelschrift *Krieg und Krieger*. Hrsg. von E. Jünger', *Die Gesellschaft*, 7, 2(1930), p. 39. (English quoted from Jerolf Wikoff trans., see n. 51, p. 122.)
58. Schramm, 'Kritik', pp. 38–41.
59. Benjamin, 'Theorien', pp. 39f. (English quoted from Jerolf Wikoff trans., see n. 51, pp. 126–8.)
60. Sontheimer, *Antidemokratisches Denken*, pp. 115ff.; Prümm, *Literatur*, pp. 38ff., 186ff.
61. Jünger, *Aufmarsch*, pp. 60f.
62. Ibid., pp. 68f.
63. Ibid., pp. 63f.
64. E. Jünger, *Das Wäldchen 125. Eine Chronik aus den Grabenkämpfen 1918*, Berlin, 1925, quoted from the fourth edn., 1929, pp. 178f.
65. A. Hitler, *Mein Kampf*, Munich, 1930, p. 782.
66. E. Jünger, *Feuer und Blut. Ein kleiner Ausschnitt aus einer großen Schlacht*, Berlin, 1925, quoted from the fourth edn., 1929, p. 66.
67. Prümm, *Literatur*, pp. 208f; Schwarz, *Anarchist*, p. 59, calls Jünger a 'Gesinnungsmilitaristen' (someone with a militarist mentality).
68. The figures are taken from *Deutsches Bücherverzeichnis*, vols. 15–22. A full analysis of the size of editions of nationalist war literature published between 1929 and 1933 is difficult because, contrary to previous practice, the *Deutsches Bücherverzeichnis* for 1931–5, Leipzig, 1937, has relatively little information about the numbers of copies printed. This information was supplemented from a list of the most important war books of 1930, given by Prümm, *Literatur*, p. 75, taken from the journal ed. E. Jünger and W. Laß, *Die Kommenden. Überbündische Wochenschrift der deutschen Jugend*, 5(1930), pp. 365f.
69. The number of titles listed under the heading 'Wehr-' ('Military-') were counted.
70. A. Hillgruber, 'Militarismus am Ende der Weimarer Republik und im 'Dritten Reich" ', in *Grossmachtpolitik und Militarismus im 20.˜Jahrhundert. Drei Beiträge zum Kontinuitätsproblem*, Düsseldorf, 1974, pp. 37–51. Reprinted in A. Hillgruber, *Deutsche Grossmacht- und Weltpolitik im 19. und 20. Jahrhundert*, Düsseldorf, 1977, pp. 134–68.
71. Prümm, *Literatur*, p. 75; a list of the most important war books of 1930 is also printed here.
72. Quoted from Sontheimer, *Antidemokratisches Denken*, pp. 119f.; see also K. Rohe, *Das Reichsbanner Schwarz Rot Gold. Ein Beitrag zur Geschichte und Struktur der politischen Kampfverbände zur Zeit der Weimarer Republik*, Düsseldorf, 1966, p. 143.
73. C. von Ossietzky, 'Der Fall Remarque', *Weltbühne*, 8 (1932), pp. 549f.
74. *Schulthess' Europäischer Geschichtskalender für das Jahr 1930*, p. 243. See also S. Kracauer, *Von Caligari bis Hitler. Ein Beitrag zur Geschichte des deutschen Films*, Hamburg, 1958, p. 131; Sontheimer, *Antidemokratisches Denken*, pp. 119f.; Reimann, *Dr. Joseph Goeb-*

bels, Vienna/Munich/Zurich, 1971, pp. 149f.

75. *Die Protokolle der Reichstagsfraktion und des Fraktionsvorstandes der Deutschen Zentrumspartei 1926–1933*, ed. R. Morsey, Mainz, 1969, pp. 500ff. (from a meeting of the leaders of the parliamentary party on 12 December 1930).

76. Ibid., p. 517 (from a meeting of the parliamentary Centre Party on 20 February 1931).

77. Bracher, *Auflösung*, p. 468.

78. H. Brüning, *Memoiren 1918–1934*, Stuttgart, 1970, p. 196.

79. Kracauer, *Caligari*, pp. 152–8, 164, 171ff.

80. Ibid., p. 171.

81. Prümm, *Literatur*, pp. 70f.

82. For greater detail, see Wette, 'Ideologien', pp. 52–5; also for a bibliography.

83. H. Mommsen, 'Die Last der Vergangenheit', in J. Habermas (ed.), *Stichworte zur 'Geistigen Situation' der Zeit*, vol. 1, Frankfurt/M., 1979, p. 169.

84. In this context, see W. Wette, 'NS-Propaganda und Kriegsbereitschaft der Deutschen bis 1936', in *Francia. Forschungen zur westeuropäischen Geschichte*, vol. 5(1977), Munich, 1978, pp. 567–90.

85. For this see the volume cited in n. 34.

86. Argued by F. Fischer, *Bündnis der Eliten. Zur Kontinuität der Machtstrukturen in Deutschland 1871–1945*, Düsseldorf, 1979.

MICHAEL GEYER

The Dynamics of Military Revisionism in the Interwar Years. Military Politics between Rearmament and Diplomacy

Amidst ever more detailed descriptions of diplomatic and military affairs there is little that can help us understand the deliberate use of force in the reconstruction of European order. We know a great deal about diplomatic decision-making in every country and in every phase of nineteenth- and twentieth-century international affairs. We know quite as much about military affairs. Yet we fall short of explaining the growing readiness to use force and to make organised violence the basis of international relations. We fall short because we still labour under the venerable nineteenth-century conception that the use of force declines with progress in history or, more specifically, in industrialisation. From this it follows that war is fought only by pre-modern man. This notion of the world, of Germany, is blatantly wrong. Still, it is convenient for us to think in these terms because it makes violence appear to be a remote issue of past ages. While this approach contradicts the twentieth-century experience, our nineteenth-century conception soothes the mind.

Scholarly interpretations of the interwar years are no different in this respect. While we know a great deal about diplomatic transactions and military politics, the sources and dynamics of rearmament mostly escape us. We are far from understanding the unfolding dynamics of military affairs, either of rearmament or the use of force — unless we believe in conspiracies of greedy industrialists or in the domination of traditional élites forcibly leading a nation to war. In looking for simple answers we overestimate the power of any single group or class to coerce and manipulate whole nations. As a result we underestimate the forces behind the drive towards armament; we also underestimate the powers of resistance inherent in a process that Clausewitz characterised as producing nothing but tensions.

We may, of course, assume that the primary causes of war in the interwar years and the reasons for violence are self-evident: as they are. Yet identifying the main culprits does not relieve us from the task of trying to understand the forces behind the increasing interest in rearmament and the dynamics of this process as it interacted with domestic and foreign affairs. For if we merely identify the main actors, we reconstruct a history of villains without understanding what moves them. In fact, it is not even clear whether the actors knew what moved them; it is this which complicates our study. The limits of their comprehension are part of the phenomenon that we must analyse and understand. It is generally agreed that the officers of the Reichswehr and the Wehrmacht wished to avenge the defeat of 1918 and aimed at a remaking of the national and international order. There has been even less doubt as to the aggressive and racist intentions of Hitler. The similarities and differences between the world views of Hitler and the German military have been discussed many times. The nexus between the urge for revising the national and international order, rearmament and war is on the surface an open-and-shut case. Yet rearmament in the Third Reich followed a very twisted path, as did the decision to make war. Both responded to national and international pressures — to a point where military desire for revision first seemed triumphant, then in disarray and ultimately collapsed. After five years of strenuous rearmament some leading officers conceded that they would be unable to fight a war along professional lines and indeed wondered if they could ever fight a war again. Yet despite the obvious collapse of their strategies, the majority of the officer corps either did not care or were paralysed. At any rate, a large number of officers were ready to fight a war even without a rationale of their own.

Officers and politicians alike considered rearmament and the potential of war as part and parcel of the total complex of what has been termed revisionism already by contemporaries.[1] This concept circumscribes a set of more or less aggressive policies which were meant to alter the fragile international order and, for that matter, the domestic order(s) of Europe. While pan-European in nature, such policies were pursued most vigorously in Germany. Germany was the only country in Europe which had the resources to resist and counteract the full imposition of the Allied peace. She had both the economic muscle and the social capacity to mobilise against the imposition of a military-political and socio-economic order that reflected the designs of an internationalised security system, headed by France, and of an internationalised corporate economy, centred in the United States, rather than the perceived interests of large parts of German society. This is not to say that either one or the other was good or bad (though value judgements are mostly implied). It does say that Germany retained enough military-political strength and economic power during the interwar years to be intolerant of the imposition of order from the outside. Other nations depended on the consent of Germany, which was never forthcoming; to ask why this was so is a prerequisite for studying the practice of military revision.

For the German officer corps revision was a struggle to reconstruct an old order, which they readily identified with the Wilhelmine system, although their plans for its reconstruction remained vague and the memory of the past was remarkably diluted. The 'old order' was a myth which blended memory and desire, institutional continuities and interests. It is more accurate to say that the military searched for a different and, in their eyes, more suitable order than that imposed on them after the defeat and the military strike of 1918. They associated this 'new order' with the 'good old days' without being able to specify what they actually looked for in their military practice.

In Germany the debate about the postwar settlement involved politicians, industrialists, bureaucrats and soldiers; most of all, it involved people who, in turn, could and did influence the politicians. Revisionism became a national obsession. Popular demands for changing both the national and the international order were more often than not linked to the threat of force. Militant revisionism was one of the major factors in the demise of the Weimar Republic and it motivated the Third Reich. This is noteworthy because the turn to violence indicated that the other options of popular politics were either not available or had been defeated in political conflicts. Both answers shed light on the political and social construction of the first German republic.[2]

Revisionism was not a one-way street, however. Neither the ironclad necessities of capitalism nor the logic of a specifically

Prussian-German outlook can explain the evolution of military and militant revisionism in Germany. It was certainly not the abstract features of capitalism or of militarism that fuelled military revision and decided the direction it would take. Rather the very concrete and manifest contradictions of doing business, the organising of military forces and the retaining of political prestige shaped revisionist concerns and choices. We plead here for a concrete and material interpretation of revision, distinct from an idealistic one because present reality and past memory of military revisionists were created only in military activity, industrial production and political debate. Reference to either the necessities of capitalism or to the logic of Prussian traditionalism underestimates the great vulnerability of the predispositions and goals of the military and these arguments make them into fetishes beyond the reach of history. But political and military strategies are not a matter of eternal motivations, goals and strategies. The meaning of revision shifted, producing new challenges and opportunities as fresh struggles took shape and choices emerged. The military faction did not act as a coherent block. Its members changed their opinions. Others did the same. There was choice, uncertainty and a great deal of conflict in German politics, both before and after 1933.

Only slowly did the organisation and use of force move into the centre of revisionist politics. There was no single mechanism that inescapably led to rearmament, but there were individuals and groups who made decisions concerning rearmament and war — and who got away with as much rearmament as they were allowed to. In order to establish the exclusively military nature of rearmament, political struggles had to be fought, lost and won. Nothing happened as if pre-ordained by some metaphysical force.

Neither did these political struggles cease once rearmament became the central concern of the political scene. Rearmament would be difficult to control in the best of all possible words, let alone in the Third Reich! The process activated domestic and international tensions and caused the rearrangement and, indeed, destruction of international order in the process of accumulating weapons. In extracting material and socio-cultural resources from society, rearmament restructured politics. Both processes followed the same trajectory. Rearmament does not necessarily lead straight to war, as our liberal-utilitarian forefathers of the nineteenth century believed, but in this instance it set into motion an ever harsher and more hostile power struggle inside and outside Germany. The organisation of violence was non-productive in a more than economic sense. It destroyed order and it destroyed peaceful relations. In doing so it forced the hands of those engaged in the production of armaments and it limited the choices as to war or peace. The point to be made here is that the process of armament adds not only to the potentials of a nation, but also to the nation's liabilities. In the case of Germany we shall discover that the liabilities of rearmament quickly outgrew the assets, which forced a major reassessment of national priorities and goals in 1937 and 1938.

On this basis, therefore, we can establish the main lines of our enquiry. We will survey the following issues: firstly, the rise of a militarised revisionism with particular reference to alternatives both inside and outside the military sphere; secondly, the dynamics of rearmament and its impact on foreign affairs and, thirdly, the national and international consequences of rearmament on the intentions and military-political strategies in the Third Reich.

1. The Changing Position of Revisionism

Following the collapse of revanchist strategies immediately after the war Weimar foreign policy, in its quest for revision, concentrated more or less openly on the following demands:[3] abolition of all restrictions on national sovereignty, including an end to the military regulations of the Versailles Treaty; the guarantee of territorial integrity which implied, among other things, the end to special provisions concerning the occupation of parts of Germany and the German right to secure the sovereignty of the German nation; and the cancellation of financial and economic obligations of any kind. Sovereignty, territorial integrity and private property were the core of an amorphous set of policies that encompassed multilateral perspectives just as much as integral nationalist ones. Much has been made of secret designs behind official policy — and they did exist. But these delusions of grandeur and the petty circumvention of the Versailles Treaty only concealed the genuinely intriguing aspect of German revisionist strategy. Once Germany was unshackled, its corporate economy and military potential and the power that came with it would dominate Europe. This was the hard core of the military and industrial policies that emerged after 1924. It is quite unclear why this approach to restructuring both Germany and Europe is called moderate; that it is also called republican says more about the nature of the Weimar government than about republicanism.

Public political debate approached the same issue of revision from the vantage points of national identity and of the resurrection of Germany as a strong and powerful nation.[4] Public emotions about revision centred around defeat and revolution. These emotions reflected the loss of domestic control and security at home as much as shattered dreams of Empire. It was possible for administrative-political debate and intentions to coincide with public sentiment, but they mostly remained separate. At any rate, revision subsumed both public sentiment and military (and industrial) politics in an uneasy balance.

It was a reactionary agenda. While almost all political and social groups in the Weimar Republic supported demands for the revision of the Versailles Treaty, very few were in a position to shape that revision. Increasingly it was the conservative and radical Right who defined revision and shaped the formation of a national identity for Germany. The rising public agitation was never effectively blocked or redirected by republican groups. By 1929/30 the popular debate on the subject was identified with conservative or Right-radical causes. While it is possible to point to the money and energy devoted to preparing the German people for revision, one should also stress the inability of republican groups to develop effective alternative notions of national and international order and of political change. Both republican groups and the Left were defeated on this most vital issue. They lost the ability to structure the political debate on the organisation of national and international order. By 1929/30, their only recourse was the state — and while the Weimar state and its officials differed from conservatives and ultra-nationalists, neither were they republican. The Left's position indicated just how much they were outsiders in the Republic and how successfully they could be barred from participating in the formation of a national identity for Germany.

Partial gains were not sufficient to satisfy the German people. A growing number opposed international interdependence and any form of the reduction of statehood. It was a peculiar opposition. As a variety of nationalism, it was formed in defence of privilege and hegemony at home and abroad which were lost in 1918, rather than in resistance to subordination. It assumed the attributes of the nationalism common to European minorities while, in fact, it was a majority nationalism of the dominant groups in Germany. As such

it was not tamed by revisionist successes, but grew with them. For
the German Right, revisionism was not about the rectifying of a
grievance, but the establishment of privilege. As a result, the discrepancy between public debate and governmental politics could only
widen, because revisionist successes kept the nationalist bandwagon
rolling.

The diplomacy of revision moved more slowly than popular
demands for obvious reasons. The reconstruction of full statehood
for Germany meant a fundamental shift in the uneven balance of
power in continental Europe. Diplomats and politicians alike were
aware that the standards of 'normal' power politics in Europe —
that is, unrestrained by international agreement — sufficed to
dissolve the existing order on the continent of Europe. Whatever
the further intentions of German politicians and industrialists were,
the postwar order in Europe was built on the reduced statehood of
both Germany and the Soviet Union. This fundamental prerequisite
for European order formed in turn the intrinsic problem of revision.
Whether regaining statehood or defining political identity, Germany's revisionism always implied the reorganisation of Europe. It
was to prove of great importance that the radical Right should have
pre-empted this extremely sensitive political domain, so vital for the
future of Europe, as early as 1928/29.[5]

Military affairs accurately mirrored these tensions. On the one
hand, the military-political order of Europe was based on a disarmed Germany. Hence, the mere threat of a growing army effectively reshaped international order to a point at which maintaining
the status quo became virtually impossible. The limits for an acceptable degree of German rearmament were extremely low and had
little connection with German dreams of re-establishing a strong
army; rather, it was with the amount of stress that the existing
European order could take. Alas, this was so little that the German
military were unable to protect national sovereignty and territorial
integrity under the prevailing conditions. Of course, the military
were not the only ones capable of securing Germany and it was highly
dubious whether they had intended to do so in the first place; they
had usurped that position against little resistance. Few Germans and
remarkably few officers and politicians in other countries would
have denied Germany the right to military defence. They did not,
after all, want to cut off their own right hand.

This contradiction left Germany with a situation that was straight-
forward enough. The definition of their national security mission

was accepted or, at least, not openly challenged except by some perceptive pacifists; however, even if the military wanted only to think in terms of fulfilling a mission which could not be contested openly, they had to reorganise the European order. It seems that much effort went into obscuring these basic conditions in the past and in the present. There were certainly strong currents of Wilhelminism in addition to delusions of all kinds in the officer corps; these flourished not least because the basic issues at stake were rarely debated, let alone solved and hence can be conveniently overlooked. Sovereign statehood for Germany, the free rule of private enterprise and a compact national identity were all a danger to the European order. No wonder that the bourgeois republic never came to grips with these problems.

German officers had difficulties finding a coherent strategy for these conditions as well. Revision was not as simple as Seeckt, the first chief of the army high command, and a majority of officers would have liked. 'We have to become strong again, and as soon as we have sufficient might, we naturally take everything back that we have lost.'[6] Seeckt discovered very quickly that the main problem consisted in becoming mighty again. While he and his fellow officers did not know the prisoner's dilemma of arms control, they knew very well — at least after the occupation of the Ruhr in 1923 — how not to overstep the boundaries of a tacit European order for fear of French retaliation.[7]

Most German officers found the problems of rearmament and war — military revision — so vexing that they simply avoided thinking about its implications. While they waited for an extraordinary intervention of some kind (and eventually got the Third Reich), the top ranks of the military began to address the issue systematically after 1924. They arrived at surprising solutions, formulating these responses to the military situation in the context of the Winter War Games of 1927/8 and 1928/9 which established the basis for future rearmament. Two strains of thought can be distinguished.

Werner von Blomberg, minister of war after 1933, argued as one would expect a general staff officer to argue.[8] He recognised that Germany could not sustain any military defence against an invading French army even after the completion of a basic rearmament programme. However, he used this sound assessment to launch into a most remarkable series of suggestions and ruminations, insisting that never before in world history had 'great states suffered military rape without military resistance'. Hence, he concluded, a border militia must be established immediately along the French border just as it had been established along the Polish border some time ago. Of course, Blomberg knew very well that this border militia did not tip the balance of power between Germany and France, but in his mind the formation of such a militia at least fulfilled the 'duty of self-defence'. As such it was the only guarantee of security which Germany had. For 'what happens', he asked rhetorically, 'if France comes and rapes us despite all treaties, signatures and compromises'. Even though Blomberg was reasonably francophile, he never doubted for a second that the French would do that if they had a chance — for this was the nature of things and was not a matter of sentiment.

This argument is not unfamiliar and it is not particularly Prussian. It is usually referred to as a 'realisitic' frame of the mind in the literature on strategy. Blomberg had evaluated two war games which had made abundantly clear that Germany was militarily inferior. Given the European tradition of individual statehood, military organisation and national defence this was a most alarming situation which left Germany open to attack. It was also a situation where Blomberg's political and military reasoning failed him, because there was no military answer to the problem. In order to try to solve the issues so clearly laid out in the war games, he and many of his officers shifted, in the name of realism, from military analysis into sentiment, musing about how the world worked in principle, since reality was inscrutable. In other words, Blomberg turned from professional military analysis to ideology, because he took the problem of German security very seriously (having been charged to do so) but was unable to solve the problem within the context of professional military thinking. Quite simply, no solution was available within the confines of orthodox and professional thinking about European land warfare.

Blomberg's arguments were countered by the different logic of the 'Ministeramt' under Schleicher.[9] The Ministeramt was the main political office of the Reichswehr rather than an office of the general staff (the so-called 'Truppenamt'), even though its personnel were mostly general staff officers. The Ministeramt insisted that 'one had to have the courage to acknowledge that potentially there are political-military encounters in which the use of force was without prospect from the very beginning'. Hence, it concluded, one should act accordingly and not get involved in them. In an extension of the same logic the Ministeramt opposed the request for a border militia along the western borders, emphasising that such military measures could only increase the dangers of military conflict — sanctions against the violation of the Versailles Treaty — without commensurate gains in security or military leverage. Armament along the western border increased instability and thus actually decreased German security. Relative international stability, moreover, was the prerequisite for rearmament. Any appropriate rearmament policy had to increase German military power while maintaining international stability. In trying to walk the very narrow line between security and stability on the one hand and armament on the other, it was very obvious that the Ministeramt considered both issues as viable and soluble political issues. It suggested complex solutions to the problem of German inferiority which we cannot outline here in the necessary detail. Its principles are well known and not particularly German either. In fact, the Ministeramt pursued an arms control approach, the 'tit for tat' of the prisoner's dilemma.

Before highlighting the differences between the two points of view we must keep in mind the fact that the intentions of both factions were remarkably similar. Both aimed at the reconstruction of Germany as a major military power on the European continent and generally favoured a continental strategy, that is an alliance with the Soviet Union. Officers of both camps occasionally dreamt of an all-European alliance against the Anglo-American world. They also agreed that military force should be used 'under fortuitous military circumstances' in order to improve the position of Germany.[10] They were aggressive revisionists, having little in common with the liberal-imperialist wing in German foreign policy, who favoured integration into world markets and peaceful change in the wake of German economic growth. Unlike previous generations of officers they did understand economics and politics, but that knowledge led them to cling all the more to the primacy of power and violence. They considered the hegemony of economic affairs a temporary and corrupted state of European and world affairs. As a result, they were opposed to all attempts to overcome the tensions between states and nations by any other means except for violence.

Nevertheless, there were important differences between the two camps. Blomberg emphasised the necessity of rearmament at any price in order to meet a potential enemy with as strong a military as Germany could possibly muster under the given circumstances. He and most of his fellow officers started from the assumption that conflict was inescapable. Hence every measure for increasing the German military potential had to be taken and every effort made to prepare for war. The German general staff pleaded not only for instant unilateral rearmament, but also for the preparation for total war and scorched-earth tactics on German soil. The border militia was but one facet in a broader panoply of a total people's war against a potential invader.[11]

It is this transition from a perfectly conventional and all-European military thinking to the most extreme of plans for the preparation and the use of force which is both noteworthy and frightening. For the very ease with which concepts of a total people's war and unilateral rearmament were developed out of very conventional military standards is striking. In fact, if the German military wished to preserve their 'traditional' standards, Blomberg's stance was quite logical. Many officers, perhaps the majority, followed this line. Germany could be defended only by radically breaking apart international order and by organising all of German society in the preparation for war. To fight war at all, one had to escalate the use of force and push its organisation to the extreme. Standard military procedures of land warfare could only be maintained either by turning to irrational and ideological operational concepts or by resorting to total war. German military thinking radicalised and became irrational not simply because German officers had grandiose visions of a 'place in the sun', but because they could not carry on the ordinary business of maintaining sovereignty and territorial integrity by military force without jeopardising international and domestic order. The threshold of extremism was much lower than we might expect.

Most historians, of course, insist that it needed a 'grand conspiracy' of Prussian traditions to propel the officer corps towards such designs. They find it difficult to accept that it was very easy for officers to turn radical, and Right-radical at that, during the inter-war years. This is not a defence, rather a realisation that, under certain circumstances, professionalism and extremism go together well, so that in choosing a professional course one also accepts extremism. To ignore this link means to miss the German military condition since the collapse of instrumental warfare in the First World War. These military conditions were twofold: firstly, Germany could not defend herself without destroying international and national order; and secondly, she could not fight a war without mobilising society as a whole. The former ran counter to the postwar order, the latter to the élite status of the military profession. The two conditions together express the acute dilemma of the

German military in the interwar years.

The Ministeramt and the political leadership under Groener, himself a distinguished former chief of the general staff, resisted the turn to extremism. They considered the 'normal' military response to the German situation to be unreasonable. In the search for alternatives they deviated from a military-professional rationale and began to blend military with political approaches to rearmament, operational planning and warfare. Their attempts to fuse foreign and military policy shaped the latter half of the Weimar Republic. In their operational designs they developed an intricate system of military-political planning which in many ways resembled a deterrence system. It was based on the assumption of the primacy of a British–American economic interest in containing war in Europe rather than on the German military capability to defeat any single European army — at least for the time being. Their rearmament plans were designed to gain maximum leverage, while maintaining detente with France, which thus became a prerequisite for the rebuilding of a German army.[12]

Whatever one might think of the validity of these concepts, they show the effort that was necessary to abstain from radical solutions. None of these concepts allowed for a simple continuation of balanced professional thinking. They all necessitated the integration of military-professional approaches into a more comprehensive military-political design and depended ultimately on the international and corporate stabilisation of Europe with its hegemonic centre in the United States. The latter did not make them republican or, for that matter, peaceful. It did not even make them moderates but rather proponents of arms management and arms control. The political and military designs of the Ministeramt hinged — like most arms control arguments — on a number of prerequisites: firstly, the international economic order had to remain stable in order to provide a framework for military action; secondly, agreement had to be achieved about controlling arms on an international level; thirdly, popular fears and expectations which were reinforced within the military had to be controlled. The approach of the Ministeramt to the German security dilemma was corporate, élitist and technocratic.

After 1927/8 this latter orientation of the Ministeramt predominated over the military-professional one. However, it faced serious obstacles which were responsible for its eventual collapse. The meanderings of German disarmament policy reflect a search for rearmament and security in between growing demands for national independence in Germany and the stiff resistance of European nations to any military demands.

Chances for an international agreement on arms control were extremely slim. Still, had it been up to the arms control wing of the German military, an international agreement on arms control could have been reached.[13] Certainly it would have meant German rearmament — which arms control agreement does not imply an increase in armaments? — but it would also have meant co-operative arms management within the context of the existing political-economic order. Officers in the Ministeramt sought for a package that could somehow combine economic co-operation and German rearmament. They considered the internationalisation of infrastructure and transport policies as potential candidates for comprehensive economic co-operation with France.[14] (France had, at some point, proposed a similar initiative in respect to air traffic, but was rebuffed.) This kind of co-operation could at the same time rationalise the economic structure of both countries and monitor — through an international agency for transport and infrastructure — rapid mobilisation and troop movements. Thus a new element of security would be created in an economically beneficial way. This, in turn, would allow a more flexible approach to the revision of the military clauses of the Versailles Treaty. Mixed military-economic considerations like these were clearly on the borderline between fantasy and reality, although their frequency makes it clear that they should not be overlooked entirely. In addition, they were not much more fanciful than the ideas and negotiations concerning German-French industrial co-operation. At the same time, plans for the reorganisation of the military systems of various European nations — in the interests of compatibility — were much more serious business. Several measures were tried, though none of them was taken very far. Only in 1931 did the idea of an equalisation of military systems along the lines of a short-term military service seem to have provided a ray of hope. In Germany, the idea of a militia was thought a help to the introduction of military service and a control of the paramilitary scene. In France it could alleviate tensions over the existing short-term military service. In other words, the acceptance of a militia system eased the potential transition into a post-Versailles military order.[15]

Let us stress that these and similar projects were not greeted without suspicion. Like many arms control proposals, they were introduced in partial anticipation of the collapse of the multilateral talks on disarmament in Geneva. They were obviously ways out of the German rearmament and security dilemma. But these projects also tried to find solutions for an increasingly intractable international situation. Perhaps the surest indicator of their seriousness was the growing opposition to them from military and naval hardliners and from the nationalist Right. The resulting agitation reached a climax during the last few weeks of the Schleicher government in January 1933 when both army and navy feared that Schleicher would squander German rearmament for an international arms agreement and for welfare and work-creation policies, in the hope of saving his own career. In sum, while these initiatives should not be overestimated, they provide us with glimpses of the feasibility and the difficulties of co-operative revision.

The resistance against a co-operative reorganisation of Europe took shape very quickly. The years after 1930 were characterised by growing nationalist, unilateralist and protectionist opposition against all multilateral agreements and against co-operative arms management in particular. Although the professional military continued to make their demands for unilateral rearmament, they were the least important group in this opposition. Multilateralism was challenged by mobilised popular sentiments, on whose coat-tails unilateralists like Blomberg rode back into the military and political limelight. This is another reality of the Weimar Republic that is easily obscured, in this case by a fascination with Nazi mobilisation as yet another outlandish manifestation of the German spirit. There is nothing secret about Nazi success. Popular opposition to the international corporate order was massive and passionate. The only group that was eager to channel these sentiments without being tied down by special interests or a clearly defined social and regional base was the National Socialists. Republican and bourgeois forces were hopelessly caught by confusing republicanism with corporatism, while the Left, despite repeated attempts, was never able to expand beyond the core of the industrial working class.

The shift in popular sentiment was not immediately reflected in politics. On the contrary, it was only the outburst of radical popular politics which created an opening for more serious arms control negotiations as a last haven for élitist politics, just as it was the collapse of the postwar economic order which produced a first serious attempt to confront the issue of European order.[16]

Disarmament itself had been a debated issue for quite some time. The Preliminary Disarmament Conference (1926–30) had shown two things. Firstly, it demonstrated how difficult it was to accommodate any German rearmament without revolutionising the European order and without challenging the basic domestic compromises on foreign policy. Secondly, it had made evident in four long years that experts could negotiate forever without coming to results, if they were instructed to do so. All kinds of arms control (and a very few genuine disarmament) proposals were floated in Geneva, to be lost in the shuffle of petty diplomacy which haunts all diplomatic sideshows. No one, apart from a dedicated but tiny public, took the Preliminary Disarmament Conference seriously. It ended in the way it began — with very little notice.

Only a major initiative could have saved arms control or for that matter, an international order that was falling apart. The Geneva Disarmament Conference became the stage for this last-ditch effort to maintain some common ground rules of multilateralism in the face of economic collapse and political mobilisation against the international corporate order. It was the last major effort to maintain a semblance of international order in a fracturing world economy. Typically enough it reversed the agenda of the previous years. Political negotiations and political crisis management suddenly came to the forefront. Apart from the conferences in 1924 and 1925 which initiated the phase of multilateralism and corporate internationalism, the Geneva Disarmament Conference was the only serious conference about the political reorganisation of Europe. The shift in the disarmament agenda from technical to political negotiations was the most important aspect of the 1932 negotiations. The American secretary of state, Henry Stimson, echoed the general sentiment when he noted: 'From a general disarmament conference [the Geneva Conference] is turning into a peace conference for Europe'.[17] Peace never came. Rather the Geneva conference marked the end of an era. It failed because it neither achieved an arms control agreement (not to speak of disarmament), nor did it create a new understanding and a new consensus about European order. The conference was unable to resolve any of the contradictions which plagued Europe; rather it showed that the multilateral compromises and the corporate internationalism of industry had hopelessly fallen apart.

For the beleaguered arms control wing in Germany, this was a shattering defeat. At this point, in the summer of 1932, their policy began moving to ever more radical demands — in competition with mobilised popular opinion — and to more propagandistic policies.

Step by step, the protagonists of a multilateral course shifted towards the nationalist camp. By late 1932 the main differences between the two groups had evaporated, though the old distance between them lingered on. It was only a matter of time before unilateralist officers and popular revisionists came together and replaced the remnants of multilateralism and arms control.

The two groups did not come together easily, though. Military unilateralists tried primarily to regain military autonomy, while both the militant politicians of the Right and the radical popular revisionists changed the actual nature of military affairs. Popular revisionism was against the instrumental quality of the military élite. Thus military affairs, and even the question of war, became a matter of symbols and emotions rather than calculations on the actual use of force. Military questions were subsumed into militant politics and thus acted as a counterweight to the international economic system and its associated balance of domestic power. They were translated from the merely professional sphere to a much wider socio-political one, becoming the focal point of grievances against a relentlessly productivist order. Militant politics, which was both anti-corporatist and anti-élitist, became a central element in the social mobilisation against the international order that was imposed during the process of stabilising both the German and the international economies. Military unilateralism and militant popular revisionism were fused together by the opposition to corporate internationalism in the 1920s and have stayed together ever since. This alliance was aided by the fact that military affairs remained the only truly 'national issue' that was untouched and was, indeed, mostly neglected by an internationalised and economised politics despite the efforts of the arms control wing of the military. The neglect of military affairs in an international economic order made this into the one political arena that remained outside the predominant political-economic compromises. It was quickly occupied by all those groups who opposed not only the status quo of 1918, but also the power relations which were established by the economic stabilisation of 1924.[18] The arms control wing was never able to counter this development.

Popular and militant revisionism also opposed the corporate-multilateral approach to politics. The politics of stabilisation fragmented all political affairs — including the revision of the postwar order — into a series of ill-connected interest politics.[19] Political issues were resolved by parcelling out special issues and their respective interests. Thus, revision was scaled down into a series of individual concerns, such as Eupen-Malmedy, fortifications, the occupation of the Rhineland and diverse economic and monetary as well as military matters. Revision, like the quest for multilateral order, became a procession of discrete steps in which public concerns followed private ones. This balance also shifted in the 1930s. It was fuelled by the massive popular campaign for military preparedness (*Wiederwehrhaftmachung*) and for rearmament. These two issues became the unifying public concern that began to overwhelm the procession of interests which had shaped Weimar politics. In fact, it was the first such unifying theme of bourgeois politics in the Weimar Republic, which was otherwise unable to find a unifying national issue. The quest for rearmament and military revision blended bourgeois and popular politics. Rearmament provided a perspective for the future. It strengthened, moreover, the public domain over the competition of private interests. This development shows the effective collapse of republican and Left politics in the late Weimar Republic; they were unable to provide an alternative perspective and an alternative focus for public policy.

The failure of the Disarmament Conference in 1932 and the resultant German demands for unilateral rearmament under the pressure of popular mobilisation had immediate and far-reaching consequences for the international system. With the *de facto* collapse of the Disarmament Conference in the early summer of 1932, a central element was removed from the multilateral management of international affairs which Germany had joined during the phase of detente after 1924. As a result, Europe was thrown back on to a competitive system of nation-states. In contrast to the nineteenth century, though, this competition did not lead to a healthy and invigorating equilibrium among powers. Rather than maximising the stability and growth of all members of the European system, competition increased the inequalities among them.

The erosion of the balance of power and the collapse of a tentative multilateralism in international affairs in the early 1930s has not yet been properly understood and cannot be dealt with at any length in the present context. For our argument three points need emphasis. Firstly, while the politics of economic growth and social reorganisation were privatised and internationalised, public politics shifted into the most 'national' arenas of politics. This 'division of labour' virtually destroyed chances for inter-élite arrangements in the tradition of European diplomacy. Military affairs had assumed increasing importance — the basis for a populist reorganisation of Europe which clashed with a corporate internationalism that was neither able nor willing to deal with these popular concerns. The point here is that military affairs, together with minority issues and territorial questions, were seen as the antidote to a corporate international order and the political multilateralism that came with it. Only stabilisation made the revision of postwar order the basis for a massive popular mobilisation (as opposed to the élite revanchism of the immediate postwar years.)

Secondly, by 1932 military affairs had developed from being a matter of instrumental politics to the core of bourgeois consensus building and mobilisation in Germany. They had always been important, but never before, not even in the Wilhelmine era, had they stood in the centre of bourgeois politics. This in itself is one of the landmark transitions of the twentieth century in which bourgeois identity increasingly became defined not by industry, but by national security. The events of the interwar years were only a few steps in the transition from the nationalisation of the military before the First World War to the formation of militant national identities during the Cold War.

Finally, as military affairs became a part of bourgeois consensus and identity building, control over the preparations for and the use of force came under severe pressure. Of course, military affairs steadily gained in prominence and, hence, a unilateralist officer corps benefited also. However, the new public and popular character of rearmament and military affairs was a mixed blessing for a professional élite which insisted on its exclusive control over the preparation and the use of force. These tensions prevailed throughout the 1930s and formed much of the military politics after the multilateral and arms control wing was ousted in 1933 and unilateralist officers took charge in an alliance with National Socialists under Hitler. From 1933 on the dynamic of unilateralism and the tensions between military exclusivity and militant politics were to shape military affairs and rearmament.

2. Military Autonomy and Security

The Hitler government shifted ground very quickly. It seemingly demanded the old 'equality' and the old 'national security'. But the new military leadership under Blomberg made it abundantly clear — and the foreign office under von Neurath concurred — that it was no longer willing to negotiate armaments multilaterally. Serious efforts to negotiate an arms control agreement had been abandoned by March/April 1933. With this decision, which led to the first in a series of rearmament crises, the remaining hopes for arms control faded. The principle of unilateral rearmament replaced multilateral arms management. German rearmament was now defined as a 'permanent and monthly increasing duty for the purpose . . . of making a virtually disarmed nation ready for the defence of the Reich'.[20]

The Reichswehr leadership conceded in 1933 that 'fluctuations in the use of resources and changes of direction in the achievement of the defence of the Reich' were possible and even necessary.[21] But the same leadership also insisted that foreign political considerations could be only subsidiary and tactical. They influenced, at best, the timing of armaments measures, not the content. The shape of 'national security' was defined by national and military rather than international and political considerations.

Hitler, on the other hand, was rather more careful and cautious in this respect. He hesitated to discard a cover as convenient as arms management and the Disarmament Conference.[22] However, he quickly joined the hardliners in the military and the foreign office. Hitler was more concerned with reforming the priorities of the politics of revision than in challenging the military. Under his guidance the incremental approach to revision gave way to more calculated and long-range policies in the context of massive popular mobilisation aimed at the re-creation of a strong Germany upon the completion of rearmament. Partial political, territorial, economic and ethnic issues were now delayed in favour of successful rearmament. Partial interests and incremental procedure were subordinated to — 'co-ordinated with' would probably be the appropriate phrase — the rearmament of the Third Reich and its long-range goal of war. Setbacks in one or the other arena had to be accepted 'for the sake of the larger goal' of rearmament.[23] One can hardly overestimate the importance of this procedural shift in the revisionist agenda. With it the whole Weimar debate and the corporate internationalist approach to revision came to an end. Rearmament became the motor for revision. War became the only means of genuinely reordering Europe. Rearmament and war became the centre of future-orientated politics.

Rearmament was more than a conglomeration of intentions and

goals, though. The formation of an army is first of all an organisational process. Once it is set in motion, it is shaped by institutional-bureaucratic procedures and cannot be modified arbitrarily without chaos ensuing. Armament may be accelerated, slowed down or aborted. Taken as a whole, however, the rebuilding of an army has its own internal requirements that render political decisions inflexible. By the same token, each step in the process of rearmament may be expected to have its more or less distinct and visible political costs. While rearmament proceeds as a bureaucratic politics, it reallocates resources and reshapes the domestic and international balance of power. If the organisational logic of rearmament is abandoned, chaos will predominate; if the political and social costs of rearmament are overlooked or miscalculated, then the military-political goals of rearmament are in jeopardy.

Contrary to most other armies at the time, the Reichswehr and the Wehrmacht had a highly sophisticated system of armament planning.[24] The process of German armament was programme-rather than project-orientated and the rearmament programmes were comprehensive. The technique of comprehensive programming was initiated in 1928/9 and led to a system of overall military planning. The actual procedure consisted of a number of steps. Partial plans of offices and departments (as well as the plans of army and navy) were integrated into a master plan. The resulting draft was given an order of priorities and subdivided into yearly and, eventually, half-yearly steps which set the parameters both for the initiation and completion of individual projects. Thus 1 April and 1 October became crucial deadlines for the initiation of new projects or programmes and were generally target dates around which the whole rearmament process revolved. The microstructure of procurement was subsumed under a macrostructure of medium-range armament planning. The Reichswehr began in 1928 to plan in four-year cycles. The first of these plans, though illegal in view of the Versailles Treaty, was officially approved by the cabinet in 1929. Its implementation was checked by a special committee under the supervision of the national accounting office. A second programme was prepared from 1930 on and was implemented, according to schedule, in April 1933, that is roughly two months after the seizure of power. It was immediately accelerated and was completed in 1934. It provided a first boost to rearmament in the Third Reich. At the end of this phase Germany had a reasonably well-armed military force of twenty-one divisions (instead of seven according to the

Versailles Treaty) and a somewhat more shaky and badly armed force of thirty-nine militia formations along the eastern borders.[25]

The early completion of the second armament programme virtually forced the military back to the drawing-board in 1933. For the second armament plan ended the phase of so-called 'emergency armament' which standardised and modernised existing units and filled gaps in the twenty-one division mobilised army. Once this step in the process of rebuilding the army was completed, officers could start planning for the 'large army' about which they had fantasised for more than a decade without being able to take action. From an organisational vantage point, 1933 and 1934 were years of a major reorientation in armament planning, quite independent of the political configuration.

By the early summer of 1933 the basic domestic hurdles for building a large army had been cleared. National Socialist terror in the streets broke any domestic resistance to redistribution. Mass propaganda as well as co-option assured support for the military. On a governmental level collective decision-making as well as accounting for military expenditures were curtailed. Once these prerequisites were in place, financial negotiations could begin. In May 1933, Hitler and Schacht agreed on an eight-year fiscal coverage for rearmament measures. Schacht guaranteed a sum of up to 35 billion RM for the rebuilding of the armed forces of which a smaller part, the so-called 'Mefo Bills', were to finance non-recurring expenditures for military hardware.[26] These Mefo Bills were used as part of the eight-year armament package that was implemented after April 1934. Armament before that time (essentially the second armament programme) was financed with the help of work creation expenditures. By and large, they fit the patterns of emergency armament of the Weimar Republic.

If we take 1934 as a starting date for the new rearmament cycle, its completion could be expected for 1942. The German army, accordingly would be ready for war in the mobilisation year 1942/3. Indirect evidence leads to the further conclusion that the German army continued planning in four-year cycles and divided up the eight-year package into four-year phases.[27] According to this rough and ready bureaucratic practice the first four-year plan was designed to increase defensive armaments by stressing personnel and relatively immobile fire power. The second four years were earmarked for the strengthening of offensive capabilities primarily by improving mobility.

It is obvious that these plans did not work in the way they were supposed to. If we take the time frame of an eight-year period of rearmament, war began three to four years prematurely. We shall see below why and when these plans were altered. Here it suffices to dispel some all-too-rash conclusions. Due to the staggered build-up of the German army, the initial phase for rearmament cannot be taken as a proof of a peaceful or merely defensive (and, hence, somehow justified and conservative rather than radical and National Socialist) rearmament. The defensive armament stage was always only the first half of a programme that aimed at offensive armaments. On the other hand, of course, one cannot detect specifically aggressive intentions on the part either of Hitler or of the military in the actual build-up of the army. The first stage of rearmament was meant to provide military security for the Third Reich.

This problem has puzzled a number of historians, some for good reasons and others for less satisfactory ones. The good reason is that we have to remind ourselves that military security was always meant to be the basis for creating an offensive capability behind a 'fortress' Germany. The not so good reason is that the insistence on an intrinsically aggressive character of German armament keeps us from thinking about the implications of the first phase of armament. It is argued implicitly or explicitly, that but for the offensive 'Prussian' spirit of the Wehrmacht, there was nothing wrong with defensive armament. (Hence, the elaborate schemes designed to show the non-aggressive character of the Prussian mind.) This is very short-sighted, for it misunderstands the notion of 'military security'. We have argued in the first part of this essay that, at least under the conditions of the interwar years, military security for Germany and the existing international order were mutually exclusive — though Germany was quite safe without military security. Apart from that, we might begin to wonder what is involved in the notion of 'military security'; for the term 'security' is relatively new in military parlance. It is in fact a product of the interwar years, together with the concept of *Landesverteidigung* ('national defence').

It seems that the concept of military security was least concerned with the optimal protection of territory and society. Rather it aimed at establishing or protecting military-professional autonomy, not just in a national but also in the international environment. Military security had obviously become a safeguard for a military profession that had lost (or no longer wanted) the firm backing of the upper classes and especially of the aristocracy. The notion of military security constituted the military as a functional authority and, as such, marked a secular transition of the role of the military. It is the transition of the military from an instrument of a ruling class which controls the state to a service institution for the nation. By monopolising and identifying national security with military security, the military achieved a remarkable feat: they continued to control and to define their own service. Even more, they obliged the nation to grant the 'necessities for military security', turning upside down the relations of dependence between military and society.

In this form defensive armaments affected international order just as much as offensive ones, for the decisive element was not the character of weapons or the intentions of the officers and politicians, but the autonomy of military decision-making that is implied in the concept of military security. Unilateralism was (and is) the main expression of military autonomy and unilateralism, more than anything else, shaped the evolution of German rearmament. It was aggressive, because it was conducted autonomously and unilaterally, even if its intended goal was 'defence'.

These implications of unilateral rearmament were very well known to the German military leadership. Military attachés were most concerned about the impact of unilateral rearmament. Among them, Geyr von Schweppenburg in London belonged to the very best of his kind. Von Schweppenburg had his biases and idiosyncracies, but he and Kühlental in Paris were remarkably astute observers of German rearmament from the outside.[28] They were in a position to keep the German military leadership abreast of international developments; von Schweppenburg in particular outlined the limits and implications of unilateral rearmament. He repeatedly argued that 'gaining time was the key to the equalisation of armaments'.[29] He considered catching up and even gaining a temporary advantage over other European nations to be well within reach as long as a few basic principles were upheld. International stability was the prerequisite for rearmament. It was jeopardised, he argued, at the moment at which German rearmament could no longer be conducted in tacit concordance with Britain. Von Schweppenburg repeatedly stressed the need, if not of arms control as it was practised by the navy in the German–British naval agreement of 1935, at least of an informal understanding between Germany and other nations. He emphasised further that Britain would tolerate German rearmament only as long as it was mutually arranged or at least followed the principles of mutual information and consultation. Unilateral rearmament, on the other hand, would set into motion a most damaging escalation of diplomatic – military tensions which could pave the way for an open arms race. Between the autumn of 1933 and the spring and summer of 1934 he sent a stream of increasingly alarmed reports back to Germany in which he warned about the potentially disastrous consequences of unilateral armaments.[30] It is not atypical for his conservative style that he considered the transformation of rearmament into a popular and public issue as one of the major dangers and as one of the most uncontrollable elements of armaments.

In many ways, von Schweppenburg indicated with his reports that the arguments of the old Weimar arms control school were not entirely lost in the Third Reich. He was not the only one to do so. From Paris his colleague Kühlenthal reported in a similar way, though less effectively. In Berlin the state secretary, von Bülow, made the same point over and over again. Like the military attachés he emphasised that, apart from being dangerous, unilateral rearmament was foolish. It might achieve the opposite of what the military leadership had in mind. It was unlikely to lead to war (unless provoked), but could produce instead a permanent arms race in which the threshold for German military action was continuously raised. At the end of such an arms spiral, Bülow pointed out, 'we may be well armed . . . , but otherwise incapable of either defence or offence'.[31]

These officials, to be sure, were not 'doves'. They simply considered that the kind of armament in which the German military leadership was engaged was inefficient due to its potentially destabilising effects. They insisted that rearmament could be internationally negotiated or tolerated in unspoken élite arrangements. It seemed to them that military-political arrangements could become the equivalent of the post-1924 economic negotiations. They pleaded for the revival of power politics and diplomatic bargaining between national élites, assuming that international power politics had always provided room for the expansion of great and growing powers. Hence the prerequisite for revision was, in their mind, not so much armaments as the re-creation of a European concert. They favoured old-style power brokerage between states over unilateral rearmament.

Hitler and the National Socialists always held different notions of foreign policy from these officials. They also pursued different policy goals. The conservative military leadership, when asked, did not. Nevertheless, they insisted on their position that arms control agreements could be negotiated only as long as these agreements were consonant with their own rearmament plans. In cases of doubt they preferred a policy of *fait accompli*. In fact they sided with Hitler in their emphasis on unilateralism rather than joining the revival of conservative power politics. The quest for military autonomy through rearmament proved to be the overriding concern of the conservative and militarily orthodox leadership of the army. Their single-minded pursuit of rearmament forced them into a foreign political stance whose consequences they never grasped. They claimed that they wanted power brokerage; to nobody's surprise they achieved an arms race and an escalation of tensions that spread from Central Europe outwards. For all their concern with foreign affairs they neither understood nor really cared. Rearmament mattered.

It was one thing to demand rearmament, insist on military autonomy and to plan for a future army. It was an entirely different matter to implement these plans in the face of the blatant military weakness of Germany. The old risks of unilateralism had not vanished. Another strategic study under the new rulers showed only what the military leadership knew all along.[32] In the case of sanctions Germany was defenceless in spite of what she had gained since 1928. Hence unilateral rearmament was pursued with considerable trepidation even after a domestic agreement on rearmament made a quick start possible. International developments finally forced a decision. In the later summer of 1933, the military and Hitler together faced the alternatives of either accepting a multilateral arms control plan — the Simon Plan — as a basis for further negotiations or risking complete isolation in Geneva. Acceptance of the plan would have jeopardised the eight-year armament package and it would have necessitated the cancellation of a number of armaments contracts — tanks and heavy artillery — as well. The Reichswehr leadership was less ready than ever to make concessions.

The military drove this message home in a characteristic fashion. In September 1933 they demanded nothing less than 'force levels which were clearly above the ones of France both in terms of *matériel* as well as personnel'. They insisted that 'equality with France does not provide national security for Germany'.[33] With these demands, Germany could not but withdraw from the Disarmament Conference. On 4 October 1933 the Reichswehr minister, von Blomberg, called upon a rather more hesitant chancellor Hitler. They agreed to reject the British plan and to withdraw from the conference. To that purpose they called in the representative of the foreign office, the state secretary von Bülow, in order to discuss the procedures of German withdrawal. Both the withdrawal and the sequence of events that led to it reflect the prevalent relations of power in the German government.[34]

The only extraordinary aspect of the decision was the readiness of the German military to gamble with German security. In connection with the withdrawal from the Disarmament Conference, the mobilisation plans were put on a new footing. Blomberg ordered preparatory measures for an all-round defence against sanctions which were supervised by Ludwig Beck, the new chief of the general staff.[35] Beck implemented plans for the defence of the Reich which were only slightly different from those made in 1929. Militarily these plans made no more sense in 1933 than they had four years earlier. While the Reichswehr could now field twenty-one divisions, these still did not have sufficient ammunition and weapons to fight for more than six weeks. In spite of these calculations, under the new military leadership the army (and the navy) were ready to fight. 'The honour of the nation forces us to the defence against aggressors, even if the laurel of victory will not be ours'.[36] Militarily the situation was indeed desperate. However, German national security was in jeopardy, not owing to the military situation which had not changed since the defeat of 1918 and subsequent disarmament, but because the German military chose to gamble with rearmament.

These were tense weeks. While the military demanded and expected action, the leading officers were paralysed when it came to implementing what they had demanded. The army talked and planned tough, but acted meek. This was the initial and only leverage which Hitler possessed over the military. He acted, while the military sought to shelter from the consequences of their own demands.

These moments of military insecurity were of tremendous political consequence. Hitler filled the political vacuum which the withdrawal from the Disarmament Conference left. The military engaged in frantic mobilisation planning, some rather vague ideas about the army of the future and potential alliances schemes, and 'business as usual' in the procurement of weapons. Hitler, on the other hand, specified armament targets in order to keep open avenues of communication and potential negotiations. When the British ambassador, Sir Eric Phipps, enquired 'what the intentions of Germany were',[37] Hitler figuratively pulled an answer out of a hat.

Von Blomberg promised peaceful behaviour and junior partnership to everyone who wanted to hear, but gave no indication as to the future course of German rearmament. Hitler demanded 300,000 men and one-year military service while temporarily renouncing some heavy artillery, heavy tanks and bombers. The ruse worked. As outrageous as these demands were in view of the previous negotiations, they stuck for lack of better alternatives and were accepted, at least by Britain, as the basis for a new round of negotiations.

While Hitler's initiative calmed down the international furore, the military were irritated and infuriated by this breach of autonomy. Hilter's requirements had 'been around as considerations in the Ministry',[38] but they had not been given consideration as concrete plans. They interfered with 'planning according to German military necessities', as it was called; the bilateral negotiations continued the arms control approach which the military soundly rejected. This is not what the officers had in mind. Some, like Beck, considered it much more preferable to put the whole defensive armament package 'on the table',[39] because they were unable to understand how honest defence measures could possibly aggravate Germany's neighbours. Beck's view had distinct advantages. Since he simply could not recognise a problem with unilateral rearmament — especially a rearmament that was, as everyone could plainly see, for the defence of a militarily inferior Germany — Beck was never forced to acknowledge the army's debt to Hitler. To Beck's mind, Hitler merely confused what was perfectly reasonable to him: professional autonomy and military security.

Beck's professional logic never quite squared with international reality. We do not know what would have happened had Germany announced its plans for a defensive army. It suffices that the step-by-step announcement of rearmament led to a series of crises in foreign affairs. Stages of the long armament crisis were the spring crisis of 1933 and the October withdrawal from the Disarmament Conference that have already been discussed above. The introduction of general conscription in 1935, together with the disposition for a thirty-six division army and the occupation of the Rhineland were the next steps.

The second round of crisis was initiated by the final preparations for a new peacetime army in late 1933. The necessary plans were drafted by December of that year. The new target was an army which was to be capable of 'taking up a defensive war on several fronts with the expectation of success'.[40] To this end the army high command specified, 'as an absolute minimum',[41] a mobilised army of fifty-seven divisions which developed out of a twenty-one division peacetime army. The military leadership hoped to complete the building programme within four years of concise and consistent rearmament that left no room for 'improvisation'. They demanded a 'firm commitment' to systematic organisation and professional execution of the programme.[42]

There was, however, an old problem. While the plan for an *armée de couverture* set priorities which seemed to make military politics superfluous, the army still needed soldiers. One possibility was to leave the recruitment of soldiers to the National Socialist SA, the stormtroopers. The army leadership soundly rejected this option, which contributed to the decision to subdue the SA. Domestically, the army found little resistance to its plans at the time, though — it should be noticed — they once again had to rely on Hitler to implement their demands. Alternatively, to recruit soldiers through general conscription meant an open and visible breaching of the Versailles Treaty. This was the option which the military preferred, but they would have to face the expected reaction from abroad. For that they needed Hitler once again.

Already in December 1933 top army officials interpreted the firm commitment to rearmament as meaning 'general conscription'. They made no bones about both wanting and needing conscription at the earliest possible date, that is in the autumn of 1934. The pertinent departments of the army completed drafts of conscription laws and laid the organisational groundwork for the conscript army.[43] These plans were ready by the summer of 1934, forcing a timetable on the military leadership. If there was to be no delay in the build-up of the army, the rearmament plans of December 1933 left little flexibility. While the autumn of 1934 was the early, ideal date for the introduction of conscription, the spring of 1935 was the latest possible one. In the mobilisation half-year between October 1934 and March 1935 the 'transition period [from the old Reichswehr] to a cadre army was successfully completed';[44] the effective introduction of conscription became a necessity. Hence it was not surprising that the army high command made urgent demands and that in October 1934 Blomberg announced the army's 'intentions' of introducing military service.[45] He mentioned the spring of 1935 as the most likely date for the first recruitment orders and the autumn of that year as the time for a first levy. As we know, this is what happened;

but it proved easier to announce general conscription in a circle of officers than actually to introduce it.

Bilateral negotiations with France and Britain had made abundantly clear that general conscription was one of the most difficult areas in a potential agreement. In addition, the events in Austria during the summer of 1934 had shown that it was very difficult to keep foreign policy under control and to subordinate it to rearmament alone. The military were infuriated by the intrusion of National Socialist populism into foreign policy; they needed conscription rather than Austrian adventures. The renunciation of the Versailles Treaty — for that is the significance of conscription — was inopportune when the military wanted it most. It was delayed.

Finally, in the spring of 1935 Hitler acted, despite possible ramifications, as it was the last chance to implement general conscription without delaying the rearmament process. When the announcement came on 16 March 1935, it was a necessary and overdue measure which the military had demanded for a long time. It was certainly not an opportunistic act that followed Hitler's inscrutable sense of foreign policy. All the better, that the European nations reacted only hesitantly to the violation of the Versailles Treaty. For the military were still not ready for war — and the army high command had, once again, had their scare. Their fright, however, could not conceal the fact that it was the army which had set up the timetable for the event and which had been bitterly disappointed when it had not happened during the previous summer. It is ironic that some historians prefer to interpret military fright as an act of resistance.

The occupation of the Rhineland followed a very similar pattern. It was a last and logical step in the organisation of an *armée de couverture* and, at the same time, a first step on the way to an offensive army. The observant reader will realise that this transition should have taken place in 1938 rather than in 1936, if everything had gone according to plan. For the time being, let it suffice to point to the premature nature of the transition. Just as the previous initiatives, it developed out of 'military necessities' (Hossbach) rather than being another of Hitler's *faits accomplis*, and the military leadership were even more nervous in this case than previously. However, faltering nerves are not an indication that they had not insisted on the militarisation of the Rhineland for a long time.

In 1933/4 the plans drawn up by Blomberg and others in 1928/9 could mature. In early 1934 the general staff insisted that 'they could, for military reasons, no longer justify any further procrastination of necessary preparations' along the western borders of Germany.[46] They urged the quickest possible expansion, paramilitary training, and garrisoning of the customs service personnel along the frontiers as a preliminary measure. The formation of a border militia and fortifications were to follow.

The urgency of these demands reflected an impasse in procurement and operational planning for the enlarged twenty-one division peacetime army. Logistics had always been the weakest part of German military preparations. After the plans for an expanded army were introduced in 1933, the few logistical preparations which had been made previously no longer sufficed. As long as the army could not rely on the heavy-industrial Ruhr, the supply of weapons and ammunition was insufficient. What was worse, the endangered strategic position of Rhine and Ruhr had an impact on peacetime procurement as well. The military preferred to buy weapons in central Germany where they could support a reasonably secure industrial base. However, central Germany never had sufficient capacity to handle the flood of military orders that came with the formation of the new army. Hence, the ordnance office simply made the Ruhr part of a newly created 'enlarged central Germany'. Economically this made sense, but the protection of the Ruhr was a nightmare for operational planners. Even more worrisome was the fact that the more dependent on the Ruhr arms production became, the bigger would be the loss if the Ruhr area was occupied in the early stages of an attack.[47] There was only one way out of the dilemma — to resolve the security risk by militarising the Rhineland.

Operationally the defence of the Ruhr depended on the ability to slow down the French army along the Rhine–Black Forest line. To a large degree, the success of this operation depended on who won the race to and across the Rhine. Holding the Rhine and crossing it became one of the key operational issues in a central-European war (according to military plans, an offensive in the east required a holding operation in the west). The matter was discussed and worked out in a number of war games on all levels. The outcome of these games always pointed to the same 'sobering conclusions' that 'there was no sufficient guarantee for appearing at the Rhine, if the [German army] had to wait for a border violation by the enemy'.[48] Hence in 1935 the pertinent Fifth Section in the general staff demanded an end to the demilitarised status of the Rhineland, the strengthening of a border militia and the formation of special mobile divisions for the defence of the Rhineland. Without these prerequisites, the Fifth Section argued, a successful deployment of the German army was impossible — and if the goal of deploying an *armée de couverture* could not be achieved, any further steps towards offensive armaments and offensive deployment were in jeopardy as well.

The occupation of the Rhineland was more than just another 'military necessity'. It was at the core of procurement decisions and was of central importance for operational planning. It was the hinge on which all further steps of rearmament and operational planning depended. This hinge, the remilitarisation of the Rhineland, was placed in position at exactly the right time: at the point of transition from defensive to offensive armaments.

While rearmament and deployment planning took their course unhindered by international agreements, the officers paid a high price for their single-minded pursuit of the reconstruction of an autonomous army. While the results could be measured in more arms, they were also reflected in a growing cognitive dissonance between what the officers did, what happened and what they understood. At the end of the first phase of rearmament in 1935/6 many leading officers were disorientated and confused. Increasingly rearmament did not develop according to their designs and it produced unanticipated consequences. They began to lose control over the directions of armament which developed along its own trajectory. Initially, this loss of control was a result neither of National Socialist interference nor of a lack of information about the reaction of foreign countries. There were no major clashes between Hitler and the military until 1937/8 and the military leadership had plenty of information at hand. It was rather a loss of internal control over the armament process and a loss of conceptual clarity in charting a course for the quickly expanding army.

The demands for unilateral rearmament and for a primacy of operational planning reduced foreign policy to a matter of military ponderables and political opportunity. The military welcomed a foreign policy that served the 'point of view of national defence'[49] and, in case of doubt, insisted on it. Still counting on military factors and political opportunity in their relentless course towards unilateral rearmament, they stripped away layers of international diplomacy and turned normal state relations into military competitions. While destroying the vestiges of European order, Germany still could not live up to militarised international competition. The military continued to need diplomacy in order to minimise the risk of war. This ambivalence shaped the disposition of the German military leadership to foreign affairs. The leading officers were extremely afraid of potential wars, while they never hesitated to demand priority for armaments considerations. Officers coveted diplomatic advice while rejecting it as soon as 'military necessity' was touched. They were unable to close the gap.

The result was confusion when it came to evaluating the consequences of German rearmament or the place of a rearming Germany in international affairs. Despite plentiful information the military leadership veered from one extreme to the other. The events of 1935 serve as a good example of the vacillation of leading officers. After 16 March the foreign office remained calm and unperturbed while collecting information on what seemed to be a tense situation and a dangerously growing isolation of Germany; the military attachés agreed and did the same. The army leadership, on the other hand, became extremely alarmed. Fritsch assessed the situation as 'very serious' and suggested 'that foreign powers [only] wait for a reason in favour of a surprise attack'.[50] While he realised that other nations had taken the German coup in their stride, he interpreted the lack of immediate action as a first step in the preparation of preventive war. 'War is possible, even though it might not be likely for this year'.[51] This kind of 'worst-case' scenario is not untypical for military evaluations of foreign policy. What surprises is the quickness with which Fritsch changed his mind. While a European war was possible or even likely in April, the chances for war had all but vanished in November, though nothing very much had changed. Indeed, it was not any new insight into foreign political or, for that matter, military affairs that moved Fritsch to re-evaluate the European situation. He attributed the 'readiness [of other nations] to give in' to the 'desire for peace of the Führer' and 'to the consequences of German rearmament'.[52]

These and similar comments make one wonder whether there was any serious reasoning at all behind such comments. For the commander-in-chief not only had reduced the understanding of international relations to a matter of military affairs and of power politics, but also had not even tried to make sense of the latter. In effect, he might have come out with *any* evaluation of the foreign political situation, so fleeting were his references and so vague his interpretations. He was unable or, perhaps, unwilling to present a coherent view — even a coherent military view — of the European world.

Were this lack of comprehension a matter of Fritsch's personality, one might leave it there; for Germany was not the only country with a commander-in-chief who did not make sense. However, Fritsch was by no means the only case. The chief of the general staff, Beck, acted similarly. Having commented at some point that the current military situation in Europe was hard to understand, he concluded that international calamity was looming over Germany, and that Germany was incapable of changing these conditions in any way at all. While suggesting that minimising friction was the only sound policy, he once again found a convenient escape as far as rearmament was concerned. The situation was bad, but one could not do very much about it — except continue to rearm.[53] The same lack of foreign political guidance was also evident in the concluding remarks of the chief of the foreign armies section of the German army, Stülpnagel, to a key memorandum on Britain. After a long, thorough and well-informed analysis of the British posture towards Germany he came to a remarkable conclusion: 'Germany's military rearmament can perhaps be used in the British interest against France. On the other hand, a rapprochement of Germany and France is quite as likely. The latter would result in a catastrophic situation for Britain.'[54] Stülpnagel went on to elaborate that in the case of France turning against Britain, such an alliance should be used in order to strengthen German military power against France as well as in order to prepare Germany for an eventual show-down with France.

Statements like these are normally interpreted as examples of an enduring militaristic spirit. This is to discover military rationality where empty words and Realpolitik-al rhetoric dominate. The truth is that for Stülpnagel, Beck and Fritsch, everything was possible and nothing was sure, as long as rearmament was guaranteed: destabilisation of the European order, new alliances, coalitions with France or against France as well as with Britain or against Britain, and the cunning use of these combinations for or against one or the other. These were the options of a fake Realpolitik which used all the right words, but had lost an understanding of foreign affairs. It consisted of a dreamlike web of options and possibilities rather than of a comprehension of the driving forces and of the directions of foreign affairs. The German military leadership had a military and political vision of a strong Germany, but they did not possess the conceptual instruments to rationalise and implement this vision in the political world. Instead we find general assumptions about the Hobbesian nature of international affairs. These justified German unilateral rearmament, but neither guided the process of rearmament nor allowed for a meaningful assessment of international affairs. In the end, Blomberg's outlook of 1929 was more typical than we might have expected, and may be summarised as a combination of relentless rearmament and military ideology. The latter consisted of conventional military wisdom which had lost its integrity and its rational and utilitarian core.

It seems that something very important had happened to the organisation of violence in the military institution. The military were no longer able to establish the clean-cut instrumental rationality which had been the hallmark of the German general staff in the past. We find visions of a strong, dominant and vindicated Germany and we find relentless armaments. But the two never quite came together in a rational or instrumental plan for the use of force — a 'war-plan' in the words of Clausewitz. As a result, the military leadership were both frightened and exhilarated about the newly gained force while trying to stay abreast with rearmament in their hope for a future revision of the European order.

In fact, we may well begin to wonder whether military calculations and instrumental planning shaped the reality of rearmament or whether the military leadership did not slide along the trajectory of an ever-expanding arms race that left them breathless and confused. We might also wonder whether military revisionism was, at this point, anything more than a fig-leaf that covered the loss of direction and, even more, the loss of ability to steer the course of German rearmament. This does not take away from the offensive, even aggressive nature of German revisionism. But it raises the question as to whether the German military were in control of events or whether the erratic and unequal accumulation of weapons revealed areas of vulnerability as well as of opportunity and thus caused the mood of the military leadership to alternate between exhilaration and despair. The answer is that, while there was logic and sense in national and international development, the German military played no part in shaping it. Rather, they were themselves shaped by the dynamics of a unilateral rearmament which they had set in motion.

The German military remained wedded to rearmament and insisted, in an almost paranoid manner, on autonomy concerning armaments and operational planning. The price of such insistence was very high politically. International security collapsed, leaving rising tensions between European nations, conditions which could favour only one person in the Third Reich. Hitler successfully worked his way into armaments planning by using an increasingly strained foreign policy as leverage. The military depended on him. It must be emphasised, though, that foreign policy could be used as a lever only because the military unanimously insisted on unilateral rearmament while, at the same time, being unable to guarantee the defence of Germany. Hitler rescued the military from this dilemma. Since it was to recur with every new step in rearmament, Hitler was thus guaranteed a prominent role in military affairs.

3. Armaments and Revisions

Rearmament did not develop according to plan. Every round of unilateral rearmament produced new foreign political (and soon also domestic) crises. Each crisis was answered with a further escalation and intensification of armament. Thus, once rearmament was set into motion, it accelerated in leaps and bounds, a process that was steadied only during 1942/3, at the height of the Second World War. Acceleration of armaments was the other price the German military paid for unilateral armament, a price that soon proved too high. Von Bülow's prediction was correct; the military acquired more and more arms at an ever faster pace, but they were less and less able to fight war.

The turning-point from unilateral armament to the acceleration process arrived early. The failure of bilateral arms talks with France and Britain in April 1934 abruptly opened the question of unilateralism and security that had been avoided so far; should Germany go ahead and rearm or should she accommodate herself to the French and British demands? The answer came promptly and as expected. In May Hitler demanded 'that the 300,000-man army was to be formed by the spring of 1935'.[55] The rationale behind the new target date was simple enough. If rearmament could not be achieved in secret or under the cover of an arms control arrangement, it had to be pushed through as fast as possible. Germany thus passed into a danger zone where she was unprotected; for the diplomatic shield was gone and the military shield did not yet exist. Attaining a so-called *Risikoarmee* — risk army, *pace* Tirpitz — became the very basis for any further step in rearmament.

The sudden leap forward and the accelerated pace of rearmament created some trepidation among German officers and may go some way towards explaining their nervousness in 1934/5. Their apprehension was not without foundation. The chief of the general staff, Beck, declared that 'such a measure promotes the danger of war and is only justified in the context of foreign politics if we believe that we cannot escape conflict'.[56] This was a stern and appropriate warning, which is very often considered to be evidence of a turn against National Socialist rearmament and foreign policy. However, there was less wisdom in these sentences than one might expect. Beck spoke out against the acceleration process because he could not see the danger of unilateral rearmament in the first place. If there was no danger in creating an *armée de couverture*, why should one accelerate armament? Beck did not wish to consider that the acceleration of rearmament was a consequence of the inability to find an agreement on a much more limited arms package than the one which he and his fellow officers considered to be absolutely vital and necessary. His view of honest rearmament flagrantly contradicted the experience of the 1920s and early 1930s and the reports of military attachés and foreign office officials. Already in 1934 — and completely independently of the issue as to whether German armaments were offensive or not — Beck chased after the mirage of politically sound rearmament.

While Beck refused to see the foreign political dimensions of rearmament, he understood the organisational implications of accelerated armament very well. The new schedule favoured managerial officers in the central office of the army (*Allgemeines Heeresamt*) over the operational officers of the general staff and it put organisational designs over operational goals. Beck made his famous statement on the dangers of accelerated armament in this context. This reflected above all internal disagreements about the process of armament, which was the limit of the military's interest in the ramifications of unilateral rearmament. The eventual resolution of the conflict is revealing. The skeleton army was established, though more gradually than the central office would have liked. At the same time, it was being brought up to the strength needed by the general staff. The result was that the new army grew at a faster pace than that originally targeted; by the spring of 1935 280,000 men had been enrolled.[57] The army may not have been ready for combat at this point but at least it was under arms when general conscription was introduced.

Closer scrutiny of the sequence of events of 1934 reveals a great deal about the process of accelerated armament. It shows that Hitler, whose importance in this context has frequently been underestimated, played a key role. The military needed Hitler. They relied on him as a mediator between their interests in rearmament and the outside world. Nevertheless, Hitler neither structured the process of rearmament, nor set the targets, which were still defined by the four-year programme of December 1933. His role was to facilitate rearmament and mediate between the military and the national and international community. As such he gained influence over the pace of rearmament, because he realised more clearly than most of the officers the dangers of unilateralism. After his original intentions of finding international cover for rearmament failed, he aimed to reduce the period of vulnerability as quickly as possible. However, the decision to rearm, made jointly by the military and Hitler, had the effect of extending it.

Once the process of acceleration was set in motion in 1934, it took on its own momentum and was absorbed into military planning. At the next stage of rearmament, in the spring of 1935, the general staff offered alternative plans for further rearmament dependent on the prevailing international conditions.[58] The general staff, learning from previous armament decisions, planned for both accelerated and 'standard' armament. Barely four months later, the matter was decided on a grand scale. Rather than simply accelerating one or the other part of the programme of December 1933, the general staff came out in support of the acceleration of armaments that would allow the 'final completion of the overall programme by the autumn of 1939'.[59] Beck demanded that the German army be 'fully ready for war' by April 1940.[60]

The summer of 1935 proved a vital turning-point in prewar rearmament. It was then that the army leadership began to embrace accelerated armament as the new basis for rearmament, and 1939/40 emerged as the new target date for the completion of the overall programme. By that time Germany was to be ready for war.

The timing of this decision comes as something of a surprise. There was no major crisis that could readily explain the new acceleration of armament and it is not immediately evident what motivated the change of pace. A number of documents outline the place of the 1935 acceleration in the context of international politics. Looking back, the general staff observed:

The military-political situation during the last few years has not been altered by the current and temporary detente [*Entspannung*]. The [international] situation makes the formation of the basis for a mobilised army [*Kriegsheer*] necessary. A year ago this demand led to the decision in favour of the expansion of rearmament in the style of a mobilisation. Contrary considerations (as, for example, questions concerning the quality of armaments) had to stand back. Nothing has changed since.

The document then went on, in the same spirit, that 'the volatility of the political situation in Europe which flared up time and again' no longer allowed the luxury of steady rearmament.[61] Rearmament could no longer be stabilised. It should be recalled that in 1934 the acceleration of armament was mainly due to the intervention of Hitler, who insisted on a rapid build-up when arms control negotiations failed. The new cycle of acceleration was initiated by different expectations and by fears. Now the general staff became the main proponent of accelerated armament. They wanted more than a simple acceleration, they wanted the premature completion of offensive armament.

Support for accelerated rearmament was only a first step in a thorough restructuring of the armament programme. On 15 November 1935, the organisation branch of the general staff acknowledged the need for a major shift in armaments. In a lengthy document it argued:

The formation of a peacetime army for the present and for the future years started from the assumption that we need to create as quickly as possible the basis for a mobilised army capable of fighting a defensive war. Under the prevailing conditions and given the financial as well as technical restraints, other intentions had to stand aside. These intentions encompassed increasing offensive capabilities and increasing mobility as prerequisites for an army which is ultimately capable of fighting a decision-seeking offensive war [*entscheidungssuchender Angriffskrieg*].'[62]

The time had now arrived, the argument continued, 'to reconsider these plans which were originally targeted for 1938/9'. It conducted a sweeping review and suggested far-reaching changes. The first (operational) branch expressed its 'full agreement' with its sister branch. Quite independently, it demanded 'that in the second part of the rebuilding programme the main emphasis should be on strengthening the offensive capabilities of the army.'[63] The general staff, including Beck as its head, was determined to compress the eight-year programme into six years.

These recommendations for offensive armament spread quickly, not the least because they were once again fuelled by bureaucratic infighting — this time on the question of who controlled the offensive components of armaments, in particular the tank force. The result of these squabbles was an authoritative memorandum from the general staff at the year's end, which outlined 'considerations about the increase of the offensive capabilities of the army'.[64] It stated bluntly that the past separation of offensive and defensive armament had been too mechanical. It argued in favour of a shift in emphasis, insisting that offensive weapons like tanks could, after all, increase defensive capabilities as well. The details of the emergent bureaucratic conflict over the organisation of tank forces need not concern us here. We want only to emphasise that this recommendation of the general staff was a last step in the shift to a second cycle of rearmament whose outline had been fully accepted. How readily this was done by the majority of officers can be seen from a briefing of general staff officers in February 1936. Following orders, the chief of staff of the Seventh Division stated in an overview over the upcoming guidelines concerning the future development of the army: '[The] goal of the future build-up of the army [is the] creation of a mobilised army with the highest possible mobility [*Operationsfähigkeit*] and offensive potential [*Angriffskraft*]'.[65] The army began its planning for the offensive cycle of armament in the winter of 1935/6.

The remainder of the story is quickly told.[66] An order of 1 April 1936 set the goals for the armament cycle after October 1936. The general staff now raised the number of peacetime infantry divisions from twenty-four to thirty-six and demanded a total of forty-one army divisions; the aim was a peacetime strength of approximately 520,000 men. Six weeks later these massive demands were converted into a medium-range rearmament programme. According to the updated plans, the 1940 peacetime army was to consist of thirty-six infantry divisions, three tank divisions, one mountain division and one cavalry brigade together with much improved and increased corps and army units. The overall strength of the mobilised army was set at 102 divisional units with roughly 3.6 million men.[67] By 1 August 1936 the details of these plans were worked out. The central office presented the guidelines for the 'organisation of the peacetime and wartime army', which provided 'the basis for all future measures'.[68] The period of rapid shifts in the direction of armament came to an end. The alterations which were made after 1936 affected the pace — both in terms of retardation in 1937 and of an explosive acceleration in 1938 — but no longer the shape of the programme. An army with an offensive capability was in the making — and it was going to be ready for offensive warfare in 1939.

It should be obvious that any interpretations which consider the far-reaching political and economic changes of the Third Reich as the spontaneous reaction to a momentous crisis in 1936 are off the mark. In order to understand the causes of the developments of 1936, it is necessary to go back to the shift of opinion in favour of offensive armaments that took place during 1935. It is only appropriate that the turn to offensive armaments was accompanied by decisions on military and economic preparedness, such as the Four-Year Plan. In fact, the latter is comprehensible only in the context of decisions in favour of offensive armaments and remained subordinate to them despite its political glamour. It was not a first cause, but a subordinate function of German rearmament.

It remains unclear what motivated the premature change to offensive armaments. We have established two things so far: that no single event triggered the premature shift; and that the general staff initiated this cycle, with its far-reaching economic repercussions. But we need to know more in order to understand the process.

It is relatively easy to isolate two general factors which helped accelerate armaments. On the one hand, bureaucratic infighting fuelled the armaments process. There was always one office or one department that asked for more and faster armament; it paid to do so. Demanding more and quicker armament was the only way to control it. Bureaucratic competitiveness (backed up by military–industrial alliances that cannot be considered here) was universally considered to be disruptive, but it none the less remained a standard feature. It was the only mechanism to reconcile claims on the allocation of resources.

Yet bureaucratic competitiveness did not simply rise with the growing volume of arms contracts and with the growing power of arms contractors. Both contributed to the process, but it needed a further element, one that set armament free from the constraints of comprehensive planning and accelerated the process of rebuilding an army. The dynamics of rearmament were justified and reinforced by the collapse of international order and the growing antagonism between nations. It seems, then, that accelerated armament unfolded in a *circulus vitiosus*. It was started by unilateral rearmament which stimulated increasing international insecurity in an already volatile and desperate situation. This crisis, in turn, led back into an acceleration of armaments, which broke apart the comprehensive technocratic planning of the procurement and managerial processes in setting up an army and, as a consequence, initiated bureaucratic competitiveness as the main and guiding element in shaping rearmament. The result was a process of accelerating and intensifying rearmament which was maintained by each successive push for armaments and which, in turn, increased both inter-departmental rivalry and international tension.[69]

Resistance at home and abroad was powerless to halt the process. At home, the president of the 'Reichsbank', Schacht, and a number of industrial backers put up a fight, not against rearmament as such (as they argued in 1945), but over what predominated and who controlled rearmament and its redistributive effects. The years 1935 and 1936 were very tense, because the domestic coalition which centred around rearmament had to be renegotiated. This is the context for the Four-Year Plan clashes over 'autarky or export'. Schacht and his supporters began to agitate in favour of the reintegration of the German economy into the world market, and for a brief moment it looked as if Germany could re-forge connections with the international economy after a period of splendid isolation. They were defeated.[70] Abroad, tentative realignments also began to take shape. Very slowly other continental European nations began to increase their armament. While they did not react with sanctions, as the German military had feared, such nations did react with realignments in their domestic and international outlook. Both the tentative steps towards armament and the potential new international alliances increased the foreign political worries of the Third Reich, and also nullified much of the German rearmament, making it all the harder to catch up or, possibly, gain a slight advantage.

The military stuck to their course. They forced the rebuilding of domestic power alliances, ensured the permanent isolation of the Third Reich abroad, and did not hesitate to demand the reorganisation of German society and of international relations. Yet this determination only increased the stakes. It does not by itself explain the almost frenetic participation of the military — and of the most orthodox officers in the general staff at that; for clearly they were the ones who wanted more and faster armament at this point.

As we have seen, these orthodox officers were afraid of the growing isolation of Germany, but they were not moved by it.

International relations were calamitous, as Beck's ruminations indicated, but they were no cause for military action. As in 1933/4 they were not moved by foreign political but by military concerns. At the height of their power in Germany, they began to fear that the military goals of autonomy and revision could slip away, if they did not engage in extreme, in extraordinary, measures. They worried about the feasibility of fighting a war at the end of an eight-year rearmament period. Bülow's paradox that Germany was armed, but unable to fight, began to haunt them; for the acceleration of armament provided the necessary arms, but it also destroyed the rationale for military revision.

We know from countless studies that the use of military force was at the centre of a heated controversy between Hitler and Beck. This conflict was resolved in 1938 by a virtual *coup d'état* against the military leadership. The sordid nature of the intrigues in 1938 and their momentous consequences have coloured most subsequent research. It is only recently that historians have begun to point to the partial identity of goals between Hitler and the military leadership despite and underneath their conflicts. They have shown that the military leadership harboured their own revisionist schemes, which were very often radicalised versions of the 1914 war aims that overlapped at least partly with Hitler's grand designs.[71] Beck, like others, is not free from blame simply because he was ousted in 1938. While a convincing description of the military outlook, this interpretation is incomplete. Indeed it resembles very much those early stages of the discussions on rearmament which centred around the issue of whether there was rearmament to any significant degree or not. Just as we had to make more sense of rearmament than simply stating that it took place, we now have to understand the inner logic of military revision in order to discover both what held Hitler and the orthodox military together and what separated them.

The contentious terrain was deployment planning. Deployment plans were introduced at the same time as the transition to offensive armament.[72] Before 1935/6 the German army did not have such plans, because it considered itself too weak for any systematic deployment of forces. In 1935 a first deployment plan was worked out which was subsequently updated every year. It served to regulate and guide the potential uses of force and the potential scenarios for war. The German deployment plans differed from most other such plans; they were quite ingenious, in so far as they were drafted along the same line as the armament plans. They were growth-orientated, each plan being set up on the basis of the assumed completion of the offensive armament phase and the military capabilities at that particular time. During the so-called 'mobilisation year' the outstanding capabilities were deducted in order to arrive at the actual deployment plan for a given year. Thus the structure of the plan remained essentially unaltered, while the capabilities for force grew with every increment of rearmament — until, in 1940 or 1942, the army was ready, at least according to plan, to use its offensive capabilities in a militarily calculable fashion.

The systematic and teleological character of these deployment plans indicates the willingness of the military to subordinate all other considerations to achieving the goal of full deployment of an offensive force. They also show that the military had a very special kind of revision in mind, although they were less clear what they actually wanted in terms of the reordering of Europe. Hence the embarrassing confusion about their own and Hitler's goals which has astonished more than one historian. (The confusion should really alert them to the fact that the leading officers were very bad listeners, not caring very much about what kind of 'east' was going to be occupied as long as a war of some sort was fought.) They were however, quite clear that the manner in which the war was to be fought should be appropriate to their situation as orthodox officers of the general staff. In fact, in all conflicts between Hitler and the general staff the struggle over ways and means was much more intense than the struggle over goals. It is not that the differences between and similarities of these goals of conquest — racist reorganisation of Europe versus a Wilhelmine domination of Europe — were unimportant; rather they were never the crucial issues at any juncture, while the conflict over how to wage war remained in the centre of the debate.

The deployment plans were the tools which the military used to insist on complete control over the organisation and the use of force. The latter followed a military rationale rather than political considerations and had a very precise meaning. The use of force was dependent on the force levels which the deployment plans required after having been subject to intense scrutiny in war games, the latter being used to define the scope of military action and the necessary military strength. Force levels were defined according to military evaluations of the order of battle, morale and the leadership of other European military organisations. Of course the military never hesitated to take into consideration fortuitous political circumstances which allowed the 'premature' use of force, this being precisely defined as the use of force before a certain stage of armament was reached. For this purpose the general staff developed a set of *Sonderfälle*, special deployment plans which remained separate from the dynamic of the teleological deployment and armament planning and thus did not jeopardise the whole system.

The overriding importance of deployment plans should be evident from this summary. They provided the guidelines for the use of force on the basis of an elaborate system of war games and established the hegemony of the general staff over army organisation and procurement. They defined the limits and the possibilities for action and as such circumscribed the feasibility of revision and war according to a professional military rationale. At the same time, deployment plans were the main military check on rearmament planning. They defined the perimeters and the priorities of the armament process. Deployment planning was the nerve centre of an autonomous military.

Deployment and its rationale of professional warfare depended entirely on the ability to provide the necessary military means at the appropriate time in order to fight a war. Hence the orthodox general staff officers, more than anyone else, insisted on a very tight control of armament and pushed relentlessly for more. However German force levels, compared to other nations, remained a major problem, which increased as tensions spread outward from central Europe. At the very moment at which the deployment plans were introduced in 1935, Hitler and the military leadership began to wonder whether Germany would ever have the necessary 'edge' for fighting a war according to orthodox military expertise as it had developed in the strategic thinking of the nineteenth century. These concerns were the background for the premature turn given to offensive armament. It was punctuated by the exploration of alternative possibilities of warfare along unconventional lines which began in 1935 with the debate on a potential surprise attack against Czechoslovakia, code name *Schulung*. *Schulung* was a very odd exercise which was opposed by the general staff, even though general staff officers eventually prepared it. Opposition to it came in two ways. On the one hand, Beck protested against the exercise as 'unwarranted'. On the other hand, the general staff demanded an acceleration of armaments. The quicker rearmament was completed the surer one was of avoiding deployment without proper military backing.

The deployment debate dragged on through 1936 and 1937, while the military continued to press for more armaments. Hitler's state-ment of 5 November 1937 acted as a catalyst.[73] He questioned outright whether the military could ever be ready for their professional war and demanded the altogether more hazardous course of exploiting short-term political advantages and military windfalls. He was ready to skip carefully drafted but illusory deployment plans in favour of politically improvised warfare along the lines of those same plans. He replaced the underlying military rationale — analy-sis of the order of battle — by a hotchpotch of political and ideological considerations. Beck disagreed, as was to be expected. Forcefully he demanded more weapons and an adherence to the orthodox strategy and deployment planning, which did not allow for a surprise attack on Czechoslovakia. He also began to recog-nise the possibility that the German army would never be ready for war. His answer to Hitler's demands for political warfare placed him in a dilemma. While showing that war could not be waged in an improvised fashion, he also had to indicate that the army could not possibly fight in the orthodox military way either: resistance to war was on the increase at home and the army was not yet in a state of military preparedness. As far as potential enemies were concerned they were superior to German forces, and would most likely remain so. Neither was it very likely that one of the surrounding nations could be isolated. These were arguments that told more against orthodox strategy than against Hitler's daredevil approach. In fact, all of Beck's arguments — though not his conclusions, which insisted on the primacy of regular warfare — pointed to the fact that German armament had led into a dead end as far as the calculated and instrumental use of force was concerned.

As it turns out, Beck was isolated and not very representative of the German officer corps.[74] Still, his position is of some significance, because he had good reason to be alarmed. The dilemma which he characterised indicated a fundamental change in the waging of war. Beck faced the breakdown of instrumental warfare and thus wit-nessed one of the basic transformations of the rationale of profes-sional war. The German military were no longer able to perform the operation that was at the centre of the military profession; they were rendered incapable of aligning goals and means. They still pursued the goal of temporary superiority in a continental war, which was the prerequisite for calculated strategy, by stepping up armaments. In accelerating armament, though, they set into motion countervailing forces at home and abroad that limited their own flexibility and instrumentality.

The general staff had tried to solve one problem too many with rearmament. It had relentlessly accelerated the pace, turning from defensive to offensive armament in order to make the *entscheidungssuchende Angriffskrieg* possible within the perimeters of military rationality. In fact, it seemed, if we may recall Blomberg in 1928/9 — that rearmament was the only means of regaining the capability of fighting war according to a professional rationality of warfare. However, rearmament had paradoxical consequences. The general staff had pushed for an acceleration of armament, both to offset concerns about the feasibility of instrumental and professionally calculated warfare and to pre-empt the alternative options of either ideological war or reintegration into the world market. By succeeding with rearmament, the orthodox staff officers had, in 1938, pushed Germany to a point where she was economically and politically isolated, while her ability to fight a war along professional lines was more dubious than ever. Instrumental warfare in the grand tradition of the general staff had become a chimera by 1938. The general staff as a self-contained professional body with its own special skills — conducting war instrumentally and in a calculated fashion — faced a deadly impasse. With the collapse of instrumental rationality and professional calculability the very identity of the profession was at stake. The general staff had desperately tried to recapture a mode of warfare in which the military acted as the autonomous and decisive instrument of the state. Its officers had thought that it was only the Versailles Treaty and Germany's disarmament which kept them from recapturing that tradition. They now had to face the discovery that the national and international effects of rearmament, which they initiated, undid what they wanted to create.

While the inability to conduct an orthodox strategic campaign became increasingly evident, the options of war or peace were no longer open either. Doubts about the flexibility of the military instrument arose from very early on in the Third Reich.[75] They were most clearly expressed in the central office's guidelines for the future organisation of the army in 1936. These guidelines diagnosed the economic bottlenecks for the four years of offensive armament. They also predicted that at the end of the then-current armament phase either Germany would face demobilisation and adjustment crises or that 'following the completion of the armament phase the armed forces [would have] to be used soon'.[76] The implementation of the offensive armament programme in August 1936 had limited the freedom of choice over war and peace. Both the armed forces and Hitler had, sooner or later, to face the alternatives of either continuing to arm, with ever higher costs and ever smaller returns, or to risk a reduction of war readiness and possibly a conversion crisis. This limitation of options was the price the military paid for getting ready to fight their own war. In 1936 the price seemed reasonable and they took the chance. By 1938 it became evident that the military had forsaken one of the few options they had. While war did not become necessary, the military lost the mastery of the situation. They could not fight war according to their own professional criteria, but they could not make peace either without risking their own survival as an autonomous body — not to speak of the loss of their more daring visions of reordering Europe.

By 1938 the strategy of the military leadership was bankrupt. Despite intense and repeatedly accelerated rearmament a calculated and limited war in Europe had to be considered impossible according to an orthodox military rationale. There was little chance of isolating and limiting war to Central Europe and it was only a Central European war that could possibly be fought according to professional risk calculations. The European situation proved to be beyond military control. War threatened to expand into an all-European or even global affair which could lead only to an even greater disaster than that of 1918. After four years of intensive rearmament Germany's military position was as unprotected as ever, and rearmament had destroyed the few elements of international order that once had secured Germany. Alternatively, rearmament would swallow ever more resources and only increase the potential of domestic unrest and disquietude. Rearmament had long destroyed the bourgeois conservative consensus and it had exhausted the workers. It is at this point that Beck seriously considered the possibility of an arrangement among Great Powers — though even then he had not learnt that it was armament that was at the core of the problem of such an arrangement.

By now, however, Beck was already in a minority in the military. He was passed over. He belonged to the dwindling number of orthodox professionals in the military who insisted on complete control over strategy and operational planning. An altogether new breed of officers was ready to take over. This younger generation was not just more reckless; their operational approach was different from the older generation as well.[77] They were not interested in and were, by and large, not capable of a military analysis in the tradition of Moltke and Schlieffen with its highly deductive casuistry. Time and again, they were discovered by Beck and others who still embraced the orthodox tradition to be 'simply' maximising the use value of the available weapons. These young officers approached strategy not from the point of view of the eternal laws of strategic science, but from the point of view of weapons and their optimum use according to technical capabilities such as fire-power and speed. As Beck complained repeatedly, they never developed a coherent notion of an operation in the context of a comprehensive strategy. They were technocratic officers and not strategists — and they were more than ready to take on the challenge of fighting a war.

The German military profession arrived at a breaking-point in the late 1930s. It fell apart under the stress of the single-minded pursuit of its attempted reconstruction through rearmament. By 1938 its attempt to rebuild a professional military force that was capable of waging war in the professional tradition had run its course. Arms were amassed at great cost, but none of the goals of revision was likely to be achieved. More peaceful alternatives and even arms control orientated forms of international conduct had long been destroyed. Germany had been turned into an armed camp that could not demobilise without major social and political repercussions — and the army did not want Germany to disarm. It is at this point that Hitler took control of armament, strategy and the decisions of war and peace. Inside the military, the new generation of officers were little concerned with this change and the remaining orthodox officers had little choice but to follow Hitler out of the cul-de-sac. On their own, they knew of no other course.

The collapse of comprehensive military strategy opened up space for the politicisation and ideologisation of war. Hitler's strategic concepts and his racist and adventurist visions of reordering Europe did not make sense and were rejected in the context of orthodox strategy. They did, however, complement, justify and intertwine with the work of military technocrats with remarkable ease.

Notes

1. M. Geyer; 'Etudes in political history: Reichswehr, NSDAP, and the seizure of power', in P. D. Stachura (ed.), *The Nazi Machtergreifung*, London, 1983.
2. M. Salewski, 'Das Weimarer Revisionssyndrom', in *Aus Politik und Zeitgeschichte. Beilage zur Wochenzeitung Das Parlament* B 2/1980. See especially the essay by W. Wette in this volume.
3. J. Jacobson, *Locarno Diplomacy: Germany and the West 1925–1929*, Princeton, NJ, 1972.
4. H. Heinemann, *Die verdrängte Niederlage. Politische Öffentlichkeit und Kriegsschuldfrage in der Weimarer Republik*, Göttingen, 1983.
5. M. Geyer, 'Die Konferenz für die Herabsetzung und Beschränkung der Rüstungen und das Problem der Abrüstung', J. Becker and K. Hildebrand (eds.), *Internationale Beziehungen in der Weltwirtschaftskrise 1929–1933*, Munich, 1980.
6. The authenticity of this quote (found in G. W. F. Hallgarten, *Hitler, Reichswehr und Industrie*, Frankfurt, 1962, p. 78, n. 87) has been disputed (H. Meier-Welcker, *Seeckt*, Frankfurt, 1967, p. 473). It reflects, however, the gist of an argument which Seeckt supported repeatedly. See his contribution to the election campaign in 1930 in *Bundesarchiv-Militärarchiv* (= BA–MA), Nl Seeckt, N247/131.
7. M. Geyer, *Aufrüstung oder Sicherheit: Die Reichswehr in der Krise der Machtpolitik 1924–1936*, Wiesbaden, 1980, pp. 27–76.
8. TA 284/29 geh. Kdos. T1I, 26 March 1929, signed v. Blomberg, in BA-MA II H 597.
9. M. A. 221/29 W., 22 April 1929; ibid.
10. Memo by v. Bredow, 'Tasks of the Armed Forces' (1930), top secret, in BA-MA Nl v. Bredow N 97/9. Cf. G. Post, jun., *The Civil-Military Fabric of Weimar Foreign Policy*, Princeton, NJ, 1973, pp. 232/3.
11. Geyer, *Aufrüstung*, pp. 76–111.
12. Post, *Civil-Military Fabric*, pp. 133–58.
13. Geyer, *Aufrüstung*, pp. 121–47.
14. Diary of state secretary Schäffer, entry of 23 June 1932, in *Institut für Zeitgeschichte*, ED-93.
15. Groener was especially fond of this idea. See his interview with Associated Press (Lochner) in December 1932 in BA-MA Nl Groener N46/81, as well as his 'Entwurf zu Wehrgedanke und Weltfriede', ibid., N46/53, and his 'Frieden auf Erden. Eine wehrpolitische Betrachtung', in *Vossische Zeitung*, 228, 25 December 1932.
16. For the following argument see E. W. Bennett, *German Rearmament and the West, 1932–1933*, Princeton, NJ, 1979.
17. Henry L. Stimson Diary, entry of 6 November 1931, in Yale University Library, New Haven, Conn.
18. This aspect is largely unexplored. Protests against oppressing international conditions can be observed both in Germany and in France. While it favoured the Left in France, it favoured the Right in Ger-

many. See Geyer, 'Konferenz', pp. 201–2.

19. C. Maier, 'The two postwar eras and the conditions for stability in twentieth-century Western Europe', *American Historical Review*, 86 (1981), pp. 322–52.

20. Draft of a report to the cabinet by Major Osterkamp, April 1933, in BA-MA RH 15/v. 40.

21. Ibid.

22. G. Wollstein, *Vom Weimarer Revisionismus zu Hitler*, Bonn, 1973, pp. 31ff.

23. Foreign Minister Neurath in a conversation in 1936, according to E. Robertson, 'Zur Wiedersbesetzung des Rheinlandes 1936', *Vierteljahrshefte für Zeitgeschichte*, 10 (1962), p. 195.

24. E. W. Hansen, *Reichswehr und Industrie: Rüstungswirtschaftliche Zusammenarbeit und wirtschaftliche Mobilmachungsvorbereitungen 1923–1932*, Boppard, 1978.

25. M. Geyer, 'Das Zweite Rüstungsprogramm', *Militärgeschichtliche Mitteilungen*, 17 (1975), pp. 125–72.

26. According to a summary report of the liaison officer to the Reichs Economic Ministry, Col. Drews, 3 November 1938, in BA-MA WiVI. 104.

27. See above, p. 119.

28. Frhr. Geyr von Schweppenburg, *Erinnerungen eines Militärattaches*, Stuttgart, 1949.

29. Report 22/1 June 1934, in BA-MA RW 5/v. 404.

30. Appendix 2 to report 30/2 July 1934, ibid.

31. K. J. Müller, *Generaloberst Ludwig Beck: Studien und Dokumente zur politisch-militärischen Vorstellungswelt und Tätigkeit des Generalstabschefs des deutschen Heeres, 1933–1939*, Boppard, 1980, p. 212.

32. Sworn affidavit of Gen. Adam of 5 March 1948, in *Staatsarchiv Nuremberg* X VDB (d) Krupp no. 26.

33. RWM 404/33 VGH geh., 30 September 30 1933, in *Politisches Archiv des Auswärtigen Amtes* (= PA AA) II F Abr. 30, 8.

34. Wollstein, *Revisionismus*, and H.-J. Rautenberg, 'Deutsche Rüstungspolitik vom Beginn der Genfer Abrüstungskonferenz bis zur Wiedereinführung der allgemeinen Wehrpflicht 1932–1935', Diss. Phil., Bonn, 1973, pp. 149–65.

35. RVM 7/33 g.Kdos., RWM, 25 October 1933, in IMT vol. 34, pp. 487 ff., Doc. 140-C: 'Orders for preparations in case of sanctions against Germany'.

36. Concluding remarks during a naval exercise in 1933 by Admiral Raeder, AIIa 3878/33, g. Kdos., BA-MA II M 100/4.

37. ADAP, Series CII, 1, pp. 38–9, Doc. 23 (note of v. Neurath, 24 October 1933).

38. Ibid., p. 41, Doc. 26 (note of Frohwein, 25 October 1933).

39. Müller, *Beck*, p. 351.

40. H.-J. Rautenberg, 'Drei Dokumente zur Planung eines 300 000 Mann Friedensheeres aus dem Dezember 1933', *Militärgeschichtliche Mitteilungen*, 22 (1977), pp. 103–39; (Chef Hl. T.A. Nr. 1113/33, geh. Kdos., T2IIB, 14 December 1933, signed Beck).

41. Ibid.
42. Conference of Commanding Officers in Berlin, 21 and 22 December, 1933, ibid.
43. See the draft of a conscription law under Wehrmachtsamt Nr. 506/34, geh. Kdos., LIIb, 11 June 1934, in BA-MA II M 100/4.
44. Conference of the Commanding Officers in the Military District VII, 16 January 1935, in BA-MA RH 26-7/369.
45. Conference of Commanding Officers in the Military District VII, 10 October 1934 (report on a conference in Berlin), in BA-MA RH 26-7/333.
46. ADAP, Series CII,2, Doc. 452, pp. 802 ff.
47. M. Geyer, 'Zum Einfluß der nationalsozialistischen Rüstungspolitik auf das Ruhrgebiet', *Rheinische Vierteljahrsblätter*, 45 (1981), pp. 201–64.
48. Fifth Section, General Staff, Nr. 378/36, g.Kdos., 14 February 1936, in BA-MA II HH 593/3.
49. F. Hossbach, *Zwischen Wehrmacht und Hitler*, Wolfenbüttel, 2nd ed., 1965, pp. 82 ff.
50. Conference of Commanding Officers, n. d. (24 April 1935?), in BA-MA RH 26-7/369.
51. Report of a Conference on 25 November 1935, (Ia Seventh Division 3625/35, g. Kdos., 27 November 1935), ibid.
52. Ibid.
53. See Beck's Critique of a military political study (ca. 1935), in Müller, *Beck*, pp. 444ff.
54. Chief T3 (Foreign Armies), The position of Great Britain, memo of 12 November 1934, in BA-MA RW 5/v. 405.
55. Talk of Major Ochsner before the War Academy, 20 November 1936, top secret, in BA-MA H 1/324.
56. Müller, *Beck*, p. 351.
57. Rautenberg, 'Rüstungspolitik', p. 312.
58. TA/T2, note concerning proposal of the Central Office for a 36 division army, 21 March 1935, in BA-MA II H 652/2.
59. Note of Beck concerning the second phase of rearmament (7 July 1935), in Müller, *Beck*, pp. 457–9.
60. Ibid.
61. Second Section, General Staff, 9 July 1935, in BA-MA II H 652/2.
62. Note of the Second Section, General Staff, 15 November 1935, ibid.
63. First Section, General Staff, 2547/35, g. Kdos., 23 November 1935, (signed v. Manstein), ibid.
64. Memo of O.Qu.I/ Second Section, Nr. 2655/35, g. Kdos., 30 December 1935, (signed Beck), in BA-MA II H 662.
65. Conference of the First General Staff Officers of the Seventh Division, 10 February 1936, in BA-MA RH 26-7/369.
66. W. Deist, *The Wehrmacht and German Rearmament*, London, 1981, pp. 36–53.
67. W. Deist et al., *Ursachen und Voraussetzungen der deutschen Kriegspolitik*, Stuttgart, 1979, p. 439.
68. AHA 1790/36 AHA Ia, 1 August 1936, in BA-MA RH 15/v.9.
69. For a similar analysis see Müller, *Beck*, and Deist, *Wehrmacht*.

70. A more detailed discussion in F. Forstmeier and H.-E. Volkmann, (eds.), *Wirtschaft und Rüstung am Vorabend des Zweiten Weltkrieges*, Düsseldorf, 1975.
71. M. Messerschmidt, 'Das Verhältnis von Wehrmacht und NS-Staat und die Frage der Traditionsbildung', in *Aus Politik und Zeitgeschichte. Beilage zu der Wochenzeitung Das Parlament*, B 17/ 1981.
72. The following summarises the argument of Geyer, *Aufrüstrung*, pp. 417–37. For Schulung see Müller, *Beck*, pp. 227–31. Donald Shearer III, Mill Valley, Calif., is in the process of putting together a detailed account of operational planning and war-gaming for the period. He has collected hitherto unknown material on early deployment planning in the Third Reich, especially on 1935.
73. The Hossbach summary of Hitler's remarks on 5 November 1937, in IMT, vol. 25, pp. 403 ff., Doc. 386-PS.
74. Müller, *Beck*, pp. 272–311.
75. See above n. 69 and the discussion of the Document in Deist. et. al., *Ursachen*, pp. 434–6.
76. Ibid.
77. See my essay on 'The German Practice of War, 1914–1945', in the second ed. of *Makers of Modern Strategy*, Princeton, NJ, forthcoming.

JOST DÜLFFER

Determinants of German Naval Policy, 1920–1939

1.

The writing of naval history,[1] like the navy itself, does not have a long tradition in Germany.[2] For a long time, naval historiography in Germany remained in some ways subordinate to its subject, its task being to create as soon as possible a tradition for the navy similar to that of the army. For this reason, only a few independent historians were able to write well-researched studies in the field of naval history during the years between the wars.[3] The statement of Kurt Assmann, the director of the historical department in the navy high command (OKM) during that period, concerning Admiral Raeder's influence on his department, gives us a good idea of the limitations and pressures under which historians in this field were forced to operate. It also sheds much light on the value of official works on the history of the war at sea between 1914 and 1918.[4] Assmann relates:

His [Raeder's] main wish was that our work present the great achievements of the navy and the men who had led it to the German people in a favourable light. . . . The retired wartime admirals often used their contacts with him to influence the writing of history as they wished to see it. . . . In one of the arguments I had with him, I became so angry that I dared to make

Transl. from the German by Dean S. McMurry.

152

the bold observation: 'Sir, I am convinced that it is a matter of indifference to you what we write, as long as the old admirals don't give you any trouble!' For a moment Raeder was speechless; a storm seemed to be gathering. Then he laughed and said: 'Well, it really can't be quite that bad'. I became even bolder and answered: 'But it is, just as bad as I said!' After that I had the upper hand for a while, but only until Raeder's next evening with his old comrades!

Even though the influence of the 'old boys' on the naval chief was probably exaggerated in this anecdote to make it more amusing, the subordination of naval historiography to the official line is obvious. After 1945 this situation was no longer possible, but efforts to help 'the navy' (whatever may have been meant by this general term for various views and interests) continued to play an important role, even without institutional influence. Raeder's memoirs, which were based largely on reports submitted by the former departmental experts of the navy high command and were given a uniform style (primarily by Admiral Förste), are the most conspicuous example of this tendency.[5] Despite all the achievements of naval historiography, only in recent years has there been a discernible trend towards combining naval history with general history, to move from a concern with problems of methodology to new levels of knowledge and thus to topics quite different from those found in earlier naval history.[6] This may not make the resulting insights more certain — the lack of certainty is a common problem of all social sciences — but the perspectives it leads to encompass completely new areas compared with previous naval history.

In this respect we should mention the works of two authors who, with differing results, have each attempted to apply this new approach to naval history. Carl-Axel Gemzell has used the instrument of organisation sociology and attempted to determine the conditions under which, primarily in the strategic thinking of the navy, innovations were developed between 1888 and 1940.[7] In contrast to the traditional argument that they were the almost automatic results of international political developments and the strategic situation, Gemzell advances the thesis that the internal problems of a bureaucratic organisation (generation conflicts, competitive thinking, striving for promotion and other factors) played an important role, often in a striking combination with strategic or construction innovations. The question of the relative significance of these two

levels arises. Gemzell's conclusion is determined by his methodological starting-point. To make a somewhat simplified observation
which cannot do justice to the wealth of material researched or the
abundance of new insights in his work, Gemzell places the major
emphasis on the internal naval causes of innovation.

Volker R. Berghahn approaches the naval construction programme of the Wilhelmine era from an entirely different perspective.[8] A large number of different levels of analysis can be found in
his work, two of which the author himself considers to be of
especial importance and which can be expressed concisely but
somewhat simplistically by the sentence: 'The Tirpitz Plan had as its
purpose the construction of a fleet against the parliament [Reichs-
tag] and against England'. To rephrase this observation for our
purposes, we can say that the naval construction programme had
two primary functions. On the one hand, it was intended to protect
the only half-constitutional political system by generating enthusiasm for the fleet rather than for social or political reforms; on the
other hand, it was intended to provide the chance of a military
victory against the then-strongest fleet in the world. In this way, it
was hoped, Germany would acquire a position which would enable
it, in the long run, to inherit the British Empire. Berghahn also
considers the question of the relative significance of foreign policy
and domestic political factors, concluding that they constituted a
complex tangle of interrelated cause and effect which can scarcely be
separated. In this respect the two levels are thus of equal importance. Berghahn has more recently attempted to solve the methodological problem by using other approaches, principally by taking
as his starting-point the internal difficulties of the German social
and political system (autism, the primacy of maintaining the system)
which, however, cannot be discussed in detail here.[9]

2.

In the following pages, in a continuation or perhaps
extension of the two methodological starting-points mentioned
above, we shall attempt to evaluate the relative influence of various
factors on the development of the German navy and above all on the
fleet, the foundation of its political power.[10] Within this frame of
reference it may be useful firstly to present the various levels of
analysis. The choice of these levels may well seem arbitrary, but

they should suffice to provide an adequate explanation of actual naval policy even though we shall not attempt to distinguish them systematically from each other.

Level 1: Conflicts within the navy and decision alternatives
These were always present to some degree, since no organisation can function without constant compromise between conflicting interests or opinions. Here we need to consider only those differences which acquired a decisive importance for the general development of German naval policy; four of them are especially significant.

Firstly, the internal consolidation of the navy after the First World War. This was a period when naval personnel consisted largely of members of the Ehrhardt and Loewenfeld marine brigades. Because of their comparatively radical mentality, which was focused on land warfare and was often extremely anti-republican, they constituted a serious threat to the main line of naval policy under Behncke and Zenker, which was directed towards an early re-establishment of a German naval presence at sea, domestic political restraint and a (temporarily) reduced role of Germany in international affairs. Their influence was to prove significant until 1925, at least, and probably until the end of 1927; the former Freikorps leader, von Loewenfeld, occupied a key position in the naval leadership until that time.[11]

Secondly, we should mention the Wegener controversy, which Gemzell describes.[12] The main points at issue were whether naval strategic thinking had really been world-wide in scope and whether the importance of naval bases had been and should now be generally accepted in the relatively small German navy of the 1920s. This controversy also reflected indirectly the question as to how far the navy should develop new strategic concepts and, more importantly, make its influence felt in domestic politics or whether it should be content for the time being with a relatively modest position in the state.

Thirdly, Raeder's promotion to commander-in-chief in 1928 provided long-term discipline and unity within the navy and prevented conflicts from becoming public. Whereas, to put it somewhat simply, the principle had been accepted until then that a certain disregard for the state and its laws could be tolerated provided that it served the interests of the navy, Raeder now established clear lines of responsibility. Moreover, he was able to demand and obtain within the navy an at least minimal recognition of the existing political order. As, however, this recognition was based on a certain authoritarian view of the state in general, in which a strong order was preferred to weakness or to none at all, Raeder was able, using his undisputed authority, to steer the navy safely through the changes of 1933 to a secure position within the National Socialist state.

Finally, with the beginning of large-scale naval construction after 1937, two possible paths of development became clear: long-term, to build a navy centred round the creation of a complete battle fleet or, in the short term, to aim at creating a basis for the waging of an effective war at sea. The alternatives for realising the second possibility were a submarine fleet (advocated by Dönitz) or a cruiser fleet with a core of 'Panzerschiffe' (armoured cruisers) as advocated by Heye. Neither possibility was rejected in principle but, contrary to Raeder's intentions, only the construction of the battle fleet, the Z-Plan, was actively pursued.

Level 2: Domestic power relationships
During the Weimar period the main factor here was the budgetary power of the Reichstag,[13] which, together with the general economic situation, had a great effect on naval development. The aftermath of the First World War, together with limited funds, did not permit continuous construction of warships until after 1925. Within the navy the phase of a middle-term construction programme was reached after 1927. Until then funds had been approved without any real difficulty, but the status crisis in the navy, new armaments demands — the Panzerschiff A — and a shift in the structure of domestic political power — the formation of the Müller government — combined to slow down warship construction. The basic plan was not changed by this interlude, but prior to 1932 the time-scale had to be extended several times. The substitute construction plan advanced by the navy and finally passed by the Reichstag as part of the 1931 budget was intended to make naval armaments independent of that body, but it was a decision that contained the seeds of future conflicts. After 1932 the Reichstag ceased to be a limiting factor. Schleicher's basic decision to strive for a limited rearmament met with a divided reaction in the navy, but Hitler's coming to power produced a complete change in the relationship between the navy and the government. For a few months the defence minister, von Blomberg, was able to exert a restraining influence on the wishes of the navy, comparable to that which Groener had exerted earlier. Then, however, Hitler became

the decisive factor in naval planning. In the course of time the dependence was completely reversed. After 1935 Hitler began to push for faster naval rearmament. The naval command was able to take advantage of this favourable situation only with considerable effort. Thus it is not surprising that Hitler, in part against the wishes of the navy, exerted a decisive influence on naval planning through the battleship concept of the Z-Plan, or that he pushed for an acceleration of rearmament, which the naval command regarded with extreme scepticism.

It should be noted here that pressure groups other than those already mentioned did not exert any influence on naval rearmament during the period under consideration. One can speak of a naval-industrial complex from the mid-1920s to the mid-1930s only in the sense that the navy leaders sought to advance their goals by arguing that their programmes would create jobs in depressed industries. From the beginning of rearmament, the navy financed a considerable part of the necessary investment in order to accelerate the expansion of industrial capacity. Motivated by considerations of military policy, it also guaranteed the profits of private industries which, therefore, did not need to form lobbies. By the late 1930s, however, this relationship was largely reversed. The firms involved were not especially interested in being harnessed completely to the naval rearmament programme. Raeder did not go so far as to nationalise the reluctant companies, but he did threaten to place their planning under stronger state control.

Level 3: Foreign policy determinants
Here we must distinguish between the role of the navy in German foreign policy as a whole and the general effect of foreign policy on naval construction. Within the framework of German defence planning, the navy always had a certain role as a potential means of applying military force. Early in 1929 it became a subject of international discussion as a result of the construction of the Panzerschiff A and from then on was a factor that influenced Germany's relations with Britain, France and even the United States. Whenever the German government showed a tendency to use questions as to the number and construction of the Panzerschiffe as a means of obtaining concessions in military armaments or questions of financing, the navy was only partially successful in countering such policies.

In Hitler's foreign policy programme the navy acquired a new significance. An essential part of Hitler's programme was the securing of planned conquests on the Continent through temporary renunciation of competition for world power status with Britain. Although the incompatibility of this goal with British efforts to achieve a 'general settlement' to preserve peace in Europe was obvious, the Anglo-German naval agreement of 1935 could be seen as representing a first step towards an alliance of the two 'Germanic nations'. Hitler, however, had begun to have doubts about the possibility of realising this concept even before the agreement was signed. Earlier than expected, the two strongest sea powers, Britain and the United States, demonstrated their determination not to accept German expansion on the continent passively. Whereas the agreement with Britain already had the purpose of obtaining international acceptance of the rapidly expanding German navy, as early as 1937 Hitler was aiming at preparing for a future world conflict with the sea powers after achieving a hegemony in Europe. The Z-Plan, which envisioned a large fleet after about 1944, was an expression of this intention.

Doubtless the most important factor in the effects of foreign policy on naval armaments was the Treaty of Versailles. Its limitations on the German navy were to be decisive for the following fifteen years. The navy was given neither the possibility of concentrating on the construction of one or two classes of ships nor of constructing a 'normal' fleet. The hope of separate naval negotiations with the victorious sea powers remained subordinate to a foreign policy which gave priority to the army. Only in 1932 did the general revisionist line lead to the prospect of a mutual agreement to relax the restrictive naval clauses of Versailles, but this door was closed the following year by the hard line taken by the foreign minister, von Neurath, and the defence minister, von Blomberg. Within the framework of his British policy Hitler exercised restraint in questions of naval armaments until the beginning of 1935, but the naval agreement ratified the unilateral termination of all previous armaments limitations in at least one area, allied with the acceptance of new obligations. Although the German navy leaders were critical of the limiting of the German fleet to 35 per cent of the British navy, this limitation did not impose any substantial reduction on middle-term armaments goals. The naval negotiations, which were continued until 1939, had no influence on real naval construction.

Level 4: The international naval power system[14]
This system is closely connected with level 3. The first attempt to

establish multilateral naval armaments limitations for the five greatest sea powers — Britain, the United States, Japan, France and Italy
— was made at the Washington conference of 1921–2. This not very
successful undertaking served as a yardstick for the German navy,
as its comparatively lenient conditions showed where other states
were prepared to set their limits. For this reason the wish to
participate in the concert of the five sea powers was of great importance in German naval thinking. Prestige was also an important factor; in the eyes of the navy, Germany's inclusion in the
sea-power system would be, for the time being, an acceptable
compensation for its own weakness. The Washington limitations
presented an excellent negotiating argument for German revisionist
aims. Moreover, the concept of a 'normal' fleet, as accepted in
Washington in 1922, with its core of battleships and heavy cruisers,
became the standard for the fleets of the participating states as well
as for Germany. As maximum limits had been agreed upon, the
participating states sought to expand their fleets accordingly. The
so-called 'Washington cruiser' was as much a sign of the pressure produced by this system as was the continued dominance of the battleship mentality. Similarly, the Washington limits help to explain the
lack of any inclination in the German navy to place the main emphasis of naval rearmament on special classes such as cruisers, submarines or aircraft carriers.

With the disintegration of the order established by the Washington Conference, the naval construction programmes of the various
states were increasingly determined by the plans of other countries.
The construction of the German Panzerschiffe after 1928 was a major factor in increasing the pace of the naval armaments race. France
reacted to the three 10,000-ton German ships and their 28-centi-
metre guns with two 26,000-ton ships with 33-centimetre guns.
Italy followed in 1934–5 with two 35,000-ton battleships, while
Japan was not prepared to recognise even these limits. The
50,000-ton German type-H battleships envisioned as the centre of
the Z-Plan fleet could be considered as a further development of this
attitude. However, such an interpretation is rather superficial compared with a political motivation for demanding and realising certain technical plans. In Germany at least other motives were
primarily responsible for the increase in the construction of large
ships. There were of course differences in individual parts of the
fleet construction programme. Below the level of policy and
military-strategic planning there was the adjustment of the fighting

abilities of the various fleets according to the strength, number and composition of potential enemies. It is not necessary however, to examine this development here.

Level 5: The system-stabilising effect of naval construction

As in the Tirpitz period, the German navy remained convinced of the close connection between naval construction and 'national strength', whatever may have been understood by that term. The fleet was believed both to express and to strengthen national unity. For admirals such as von Trotha, Michaelis and Behncke these views remained the guiding principles for a new attempt to establish Germany as a sea power at some future point.[15] Of course the revolution and the Kapp-Putsch in 1918–20 had produced precisely the opposite result — a profound distrust in almost all political groups of anyone wearing a blue uniform. The second naval crisis (1927–8), with its revelations of the somewhat scandalous activities of Captain Lohmann; and the discussion about the Panzerschiffe, again made the navy a centre of domestic controversy.[16] The political obtuseness of the navy and the different attitudes of the political parties in the naval armaments question led to a government crisis which, however, was only the expression and not the real cause of domestic political differences.

In 1933 Hitler realised the goal of national unity and uniformity in a sense quite acceptable to the navy leadership; as a result fear of populist tendencies declined. As expected, the 'government of national concentration' resumed naval construction after a brief hesitation.

As this was done without much publicity, however, it could not be used to aid the promotion of social integration. In Raeder's opinion only the completion of the Z-Plan fleet would have had such an effect; only then would Germany have been able confidently to base its foreign policy on a strong fleet. Raeder did fear that the extreme pace of rearmament in the years 1937 to 1939, which led to a deterioration in working conditions, would produce new social tensions, whose essential cause was thus the naval programme itself. We shall present Hitler's views on this subject later.

To summarise: we have considered five determinants of German naval policy — factors within the navy itself, domestic politics, foreign policy, the sea-power system and the stability of the domestic system. Opinions may differ about the precise distinctions between these levels, and additional motives may also be shown to have been important in naval planning. However, simply to total the determining factors cannot produce many insights if the question of their relative importance is left unanswered; the combinations of these factors must be analysed. That is the purpose of the third section of this essay; one that will eliminate the temptation to which many historians so easily succumb when they develop new insights on only one level and then proceed to generalisations or even definitive explanations of events.

3.

In this section we shall attempt to classify the various determinants according to their importance, with the proviso that, if we describe one factor as being dominant in a given period, this does not imply that others were insignificant. In some instances there was a special department in the navy high command with institutional responsibility for gathering the relevant information. We can speak only of a relative dominance of certain elements which were decisive for the shaping of naval policy, above all in the area of ship construction. The levels and determinants should not be considered in isolation, but rather as exerting a reciprocal influence on each other in a variety of ways. This can be demonstrated for the categories used here if we attempt to answer the question: is foreign policy really *foreign* policy?[17] To concentrate only on the major arguments, we must dispense with an analysis of such feedback processes here. There is room for only one example: Chancellor Brüning supported the navy whenever he could, and the navy's relationship with him was rather good (therefore, domestic policy), but this relationship was part of Brüning's foreign policy plans. For him naval rearmament was undoubtedly important as a distant objective, but in the short term it had value as an excellent means of obtaining concessions from the other powers. This situation contained the seeds of possible long-term conflict between the navy and the chancellor, although Brüning's efforts to cultivate good relations with the navy covered up this disagreement. Apart from reasons of foreign policy, Brüning's decision to use the navy question as a bargaining point in international negotiations was determined, above all, by his domestic political dependence on Schleicher and Hindenburg, for whom the army, not the navy, was more important.

The first phase of German naval policy after the First World War was decisively influenced by the consolidation of the domestic political scene and lasted from about 1920 to 1925. Personnel changes in all ranks were extremely frequent; radical brigade members often occupied important positions but withdrew when they found themselves unable to realise their aims in the navy. The same was true of a number of commissioned and non-commissioned officers and men who could find no suitable field of activity in the reduced navy of the early 1920s and who thought too much emphasis was being placed on trivial details. The gap between the reality of a daily routine and the future perspectives of a new sea power was too great for them. In addition, new criteria for personnel selection had to be established and, above all, new principles of training based on the experience of the collapse of 1918 had to be developed.

This situation was also closely connected with the diminished influence and prestige of the navy at home, but this, we believe, was a secondary factor. After 1920 some of the old ships were again placed in service. Because of the financial situation and the widespread distrust of the navy, only the construction of a light cruiser could be considered as a new project. New ships would certainly have accelerated the internal consolidation of the navy, but they could hardly have covered up its difficulties. Similarly, in the field of technology, Germany could have gone beyond the limitations of Versailles in the early 1920s, but it seems probable that the price for such a step would have been a deeper domestic crisis.

The second phase covered the period from 1925 to 1927 when, after the internal consolidation of the navy had been largely completed, the dependence on the Reichstag, which was still not taken quite seriously, was the most important factor.[18] The navy cleverly expanded its new construction programme step by step, but in this period its leaders became so self-confident that they often regarded the financial limitations imposed by the Reichstag as a nuisance. As the question of constructing new battleships became more pressing, the armaments limitations of the Versailles Treaty also became more burdensome. In these years the navy leaders constantly expected that, as a result of repeated attempts, the limitations imposed by foreign policy considerations would soon be removed; initially, therefore, they gave the construction of new battleships a low priority. The Panzerschiff was a military technical compromise, a result of the continuing tonnage limits, but it was also intended as a means to achieve revision in the future.[19]

In the third phase, from 1928 to 1932, Raeder's authoritarian leadership prevented the development of any more critical, alternative policies within the navy itself. On the other hand, the domestic political question of the status of the navy, which occasionally seemed more of an existence crisis, became more serious. At the end of 1928, Raeder observed: 'For everyone, even favourably disposed groups, the navy has become a red flag'.[20] The linear projection of accelerated ship construction for the future suffered a sharp break. Every appropriation for a Panzerschiff led to a bitter debate in the Reichstag; the Reichswehr leaders therefore preferred to slow down the realisation of their plans;[21] this also seemed advisable because of the economic crisis, which made it increasingly difficult to obtain approval of new budgets without cuts. In 1931, with deepening domestic conflicts, the leader of the SPD faction in the Reichstag, Otto Wels, even exaggerated the importance of the Panzerschiff issue to the point of describing the alternative as either toleration of the navy programme or creation of a 'fascist dictatorship' in Germany. The navy leaders still hoped for a relaxation of the existing limitations for their new ships but, because of the delay made necessary by domestic political considerations, this question was not urgent at the time. In the autumn of 1932, however, Panzerschiff C was begun reluctantly, essentially within the previous limits. Because this ship generally corresponded to the Versailles limits, but not to the Washington agreements, the navy acquired a means of exerting pressure on the formation of German foreign policy. It was applied effectively when Panzerschiff C was at first postponed until 1933 and then rescheduled for early completion.

The fourth phase extended from the spring of 1932 until the beginning of 1933. The foreign policy constraints on German naval policy discussed above did not change, but the political dependence of the navy at home did. Basing his overall calculations on domestic, economic and foreign policy factors, Schleicher also determined the course of German naval policy and decided to carry out a 'reconstruction' (*Umbau*) of the Reichswehr.[22] This marked a turning away from Versailles; the resulting real changes were, however, quite modest. As Schleicher's plans mainly affected the army, all the navy could do was to attempt to obtain an adequate piece of the pie for itself. Schleicher's domestically motivated decision was, however, a more decisive change than the actual armaments themselves.

In **the fifth phase**, from 1933 to 1935 and beyond, we must make a distinction already implied in discussing the Schleicher period. Although naval policy became extremely dependent on Hitler, there were differences of opinion between the naval leadership and the chancellor as to which factors should determine further developments. Hitler showed consideration for the navy as an independent power factor, if at all, only until the autumn of 1933. Thereafter, his views on foreign policy, especially with respect to Britain, guided the course of future naval expansion. Domestic political obstacles, such as the economic and financial crisis which had been so important in the recent past, no longer played a significant role. At the end of 1933 and the beginning of 1934 there was considerable uncertainty among navy leaders about available funds, but this was primarily a question of planning. In Hitler's view, even more than in that of the navy, the point at issue was to make full use of the abundant resources, since at that time more labour, raw materials and funds were available than could readily be used.

The navy accepted Hilter's wishes both as the only decisive criterion in naval construction and as necessary for reasons of foreign policy. Thus the theses of the *de facto* determination of naval policy by domestic political factors[23] or by foreign policy considerations can be both defended.[24] The navy leaders were inclined to assume that Hitler shared their views and to attribute differences to 'higher' political considerations which they did not understand. One difference resulted from the fact that, although he was aware of its weakness, Raeder still regarded the sea-power system as a major revision problem; for Hitler only the bilateral relations with Britain were important. This situation remained unchanged until the beginning of the London naval negotiations; in their guidelines for the negotiations the navy leaders expressed scepticism about the prospects of bilateral negotiations. They concentrated more on the approaching conference of the Washington powers.[25] As, however, Hitler's main concern was not to alienate his desired ally, Britain, by going his own way on questions of naval armaments, he tolerated violations of the Versailles limits only to a certain extent. This led to some strange compromises, which were detrimental to the navy's interests. Moreover, Hitler was especially concerned that all new ships which violated the Versailles limits should not be finished until after Britain's attitude towards the German alliance plans had become clear. The development of the 35 per cent formula was a compromise between Hitler and the navy leaders. For the chancellor Britain was the only important factor, whereas the navy continued to concentrate on the international sea power system.

To summarise: few of the domestic political obstacles which had obstructed attempts to increase naval armaments earlier were still present in the period 1933 to 1935. The remaining limitations, which could not be completely ignored for foreign policy reasons, did not significantly hinder the continued expansion of the navy. As, however, the Second World War broke out in 1939, the size and composition of the fleet at that point were still essentially a result of the decisions of this phase.

In **the sixth phase** from 1935 to 1937, following the naval agreement with Britain, the limitations on naval construction for foreign policy reasons largely disappeared. Measures already prepared beforehand could now be carried out or continued in the open. Certainly the navy regarded the new agreement and the expected supplementary agreement as a strait-jacket which greatly reduced its development possibilities. However, since naval thinking had had the idea of a 'normal fleet' as its goal since the end of the 1920s, it cannot be argued that alternative solutions were blocked by the agreement. Fleet construction at maximum capacity in all categories was guaranteed until at least 1940; only the extent of the obligations entered into for the years thereafter gave cause for concern. Nevertheless, the navy's own ideas, which qualitatively went far beyond the previous limitations, were realised. Rearmament for the armed forces as a whole, but especially for the navy, was pushed through at maximum speed, even though the first signs began to appear that the country's economic situation, together with shortages of labour and certain raw materials for armaments, would not permit the continuation of such a pace.

In **the seventh phase**, from 1937 until the outbreak of war in 1939, the gap between Hilter's view of the determinants and that of the OKM became even larger, although the navy was unaware of this development. It is possible that Raeder grasped the implications of the construction programme better than his fellow officers, but I do not know of any direct evidence which would permit a definitive judgement in this question. The navy was now able to disregard all remaining international agreements. The extent, time and possible political consequences of such an action were noted carefully, but this had only a minimum effect on planning, as Hitler always decided to increase the number and size of the ships, regardless of treaty obligations. The navy leaders now found themselves under a new form of domestic political pressure; Hitler demanded the construction of a large fleet more rapidly and of a different kind than the one desired by OKM.[26] This situation became apparent as early as the middle of 1937, but its connection with a change in foreign policy was first made expressly clear to the navy in May 1938. The navy now had to be ready as soon as possible for military action against Britain. Raeder made two suggestions which completely discarded previous planning: at the end of 1937 he offered to speed up submarine construction, which could serve as a weapon against Britain.[27] Hitler accepted this suggestion as a supplementary measure to the large warships, but the increased submarine construction was not even begun. The same thing happened to the cruiser fleet built around Panzerschiffe, which Heye, the first staff officer at the Admiralty, suggested in the summer of 1938. In November, Hitler agreed to this proposal but insisted on the priority of 'his' battleships, which required a much longer construction time. As a result, and because of the lack of shipbuilding capacity, the Panzerschiffe were eventually relegated to a lower priority in the Z-Plan.

How can Hitler's insistence on his own views be explained? Was he producing the wrong weapons, which would be ready far too late, or were his plans based on calculations other than simple hostility towards Britain, the main factor in the thinking of the navy leaders? The second possibility is most probably correct: the 35 per cent fleet, strengthened by the construction of more submarines, would suffice, in Hitler's view, to keep Britain from interfering with his policy of conquest on the Continent.[28] The decline of Britain's world empire would make such a decision unavoidable and perhaps finally force the island state into an alliance with Germany. Otherwise — almost in accordance with Tirpitz's risk theory — the 35 per cent fleet would have to be able, together with the air force, to clear the way for continental expansion by driving Britain from the Continent without, however, destroying her. Only after such wars in eastern and western Europe could the war between the continents for world domination take place. For such a war Hitler needed the Z-Plan fleet and thus demanded that its main components be ready by 1944. It did not even occur to the navy's leaders to plan 'beyond Britain', which they considered the main enemy.

Moreover, a new, restrictive domestic factor had to be considered in the naval construction plans. From 1937 to 1939 the branches of the armed forces were engaged in a bitter struggle with each other and with various civilian departments for raw materials and labour, as other programmes were also constantly expanding. The navy, however, had the highest growth rate. The simple realisation of the initial plan proved unfeasible, but it remained the basic guideline until the outbreak of war in 1939. In addition to constant delays in armaments programmes, this resulted in a worsening of working conditions and, at least in certain branches, the beginnings of labour unrest. For the navy itself the competition for scarce raw materials and labour at home became decisive; this situation was aggravated by the fear of causing social disintegration as the result of the rapid pace of rearmament, which the navy did not want.[29] The navy leaders were thus caught in a dilemma between Hitler's demands for more armaments and these new pressures. To solve this problem, they relied increasingly on Hitler's ideologically justified omnipotence. The Führer did indeed favour the navy but, until the beginning of the war, his interference did not produce any basic change in the armaments programmes.

The question remains as to why Hitler pushed the German political and social system into such a crisis by insisting on the simultaneous realisation of all armaments plans. Would a slower rearmament pace not have been advantageous, even from his point of view? This was impossible for two reasons. Firstly, the sea powers opposed German expansion in Europe much sooner than Hitler had originally expected. If the 'living space in the east' was to be conquered before they could interfere, Germany would have to act quickly, as time was on the side of the sea powers and only new German conquests on the continent of Europe could guarantee access to new raw materials and other resources. For this reason it was necessary, in addition to the Blitzkrieg weapons, to develop important naval weapons for the following stage. Secondly, the growing gap between the necessary military *potential* and German armaments *possibilities* also supported this argument. The spreading dissatisfaction with working conditions — compulsory work for more than 1 million people, up to sixty working hours a week — could not be assuaged much longer by such measures of social integration as military pomp, great civil construction projects, increased German power on the international stage and the successes of the revision policy. In Hitler's eyes everything pointed to war in the near future; first a Blitzkrieg against Poland, which would, however, have to be followed by further campaigns to gain new sources of raw materials and secure Germany's military-strategic position. The fact that Hitler gave priority to naval armaments in 1939, although they would not be available for five years, shows that he was thinking beyond a continental war, even one against the Soviet Union and/or France. For him naval construction in this last phase of the interwar period was determined by a complex mixture of domestic political crisis strategy and expansion aiming at world domination, whereas the navy leaders continued to concentrate on Britain and the limited German armaments production capacity.

Our study has shown both the unsatisfactory nature of attempting to examine German naval policy through parallel levels of analysis, and the inadequacy of stressing the simultaneous importance of all the factors involved. By analysing the relative importance of the main determinants in seven phases of German naval policy between the wars, we have obtained more precise results than would have been possible by a simple assertion of the primacy of either domestic or foreign policy.

Notes

1. The following essay is based on a paper presented at the Militärge-schichtliches Forschungsamt, Freiburg i. Br., on 13 December 1973. Since its first publication it has been revised and the notes have been amplified. For a comprehensive overview of the current state of research see K.W. Bird, *German Naval History. A Guide to the Literature*, New York/London, 1985.
2. Precursors like the Hanseatic League, the Prussian Navy, the fleet founded by the 1848 National Assembly or offshoots like the development of the Austro-Hungarian navy were of no importance in comparison with the 'Reich-centredness' which emerged with the creation of the North German Confederation of 1867. The former have only recently received some attention in: W. Hubatsch et al., *Die erste deutsche Flotte 1848–1853*, Herford/Bonn, 1981; Deutsches Marineinstitut/Deutsche Marine-Akademie (eds.), *Die deutsche Marine. Historisches Selbstverständnis und Standortbestimmung*, Herford/Bonn, 1983.
3. See above all E. Kehr, *Battleship Building and Party Politics in Germany*, Chicago, 1973.
4. K. Assmann, 'Großadmiral Dr.h.c. Raeder und der Zweite Welt-

krieg', in *Marine-Rundschau*, 58 (1961), pp. 3–17, ibid., p. 8.

5. E. Raeder, *Mein Leben*, 2 vols., Tübingen, 1956/57. There are various materials and documents on this in Bundesarchiv-Militärarchiv Freiburg i.Br. (BA-MA) Nachlaß Admiral Förste (N 328).

6. J. Dülffer, 'Marinegeschichte in Deutschland', in *Neue Politische Literatur*, 17 (1972), pp. 101–10, as well as Bird, passim.

7. C.A. Gemzell, *Organization, Conflict and Innovation. A Study of German Naval Strategic Planning 1888–1940*, Lund, 1973; important groundwork relating to this systematic analysis was done in idem., *Raeder, Hitler und Skandinavien. Der Kampf für einen maritimen Operationsplan*, Lund, 1965.

8. V.R. Berghahn, *Der Tirpitz-Plan. Genesis und Verfall einer innenpolitischen Krisenstrategie unter Wilhelm II*, Düsseldorf, 1971. B's hypotheses were extensively discussed in H. Schottelius/W. Deist (eds.), *Marine und Marinepolitik im Kaiserlichen Deusschland 1871–1914*, Düsseldorf, 1972. See also W. Petter, 'Deutsche Flottenrüstung von Wallenstein bis Tirpitz', in *Handbuch zur deutschen Militärgeschichte 1648–1939*, part VIII, *Deutsche Marinegeschichte der Neuzeit*, Munich, 1978, pp. 13–262, ibid., pp. 154ff.

9. V.R. Berghahn, *Rüstung und Machtpolitik am Vorabend des Ersten Weltkrieges*, Düsseldorf, 1973; idem, *Germany and the Approach of War in 1914*, London, 1973.

10. Detailed references for what follows have been deleted. They may be found in my study: *Weimar, Hitler und die Marine. Reichspolitik und Flottenbau 1920–1939*, Düsseldorf, 1973. See generally M. Salewski, 'Marineleitung und politische Führung 1931–1935', in: *MGM*, 10 (1971), pp. 113–58; idem, *Die deutsche Seekriegsleitung 1935–1945*, 3 vols., Munich, 1970–5.

11. This view was opposed by E. Wegener in *Marine-Forum*, 50 (1975), pp. 160–2, and 51 (1976), pp. 21–3.

12. Gemzell, *Organisation*, pp. 215ff., 266ff. (On W. Wegener's book from 1929).

13. W. Wacker, *Der Bau des Panzerschiffes 'A' und der Reichstag*, Tübingen, 1959; K.W. Bird, *Weimar. The German Officer Corps and the Rise of National Socialism*, Amsterdam, 1976.

14. S. W. Roskill, *Naval Policy between the Wars*, 2 vols., London, 1969, 1976.

15. W. Rahn, *Reischsmarine und Landesverteidigung 1919–1928. Konzeption und Führung der Marine in der Weimarer Republik*, Munich, 1976; Bird, *Weimar*, pp. 40ff.

16. Rahn, *Reichsmarine*, pp. 96ff.; M. Geyer, *Aufrüstung oder Sicherheit. Die Reichswehr und die Krise der Machtpolitik*, Wiesbaden, 1980.

17. E. Krippendorff, 'Ist Außenpolitik *Außen*politik?', in *Politische Vierteljahresschrift*, 4 (1963), pp. 243ff.

18. Bird, *Weimar*, pp. 137ff.

19. Slightly divergent interpretation in Rahn, *Reichsmarine*, pp. 233ff.; idem, 'Marinerüstung und Innenpolitik einer parlamentarischen Demokratie — das Beispiel des Panzerschiffes A 1928', in *Die deutsche Marine*, pp. 53–72.

170 The German Military in the Age of Total War

20. Raeder to Levetzow, 31.10.1928, BA-MA N 239/7/31; see generally: G. Granier, *Magnus von Levetzow. Seeoffizier, Monarchist und Wegbereiter Hitlers. Lebensweg und ausgewählte Dokumente*, Boppard/Rh., 1982.
21. The role of Reichswehr Minister Groener, who supported the Panzerschiff project for his own reasons (which differed from Raeder's) has been illuminated by: Geyer, *Aufrüstung*; W. Deist, 'Die Aufrüstung der Wehrmacht', in *Das Deutsche Reich und der Zweite Weltkrieg*, vol. I, *Ursachen und Voraussetzungen der deutschen Kriegspolitik*, Stuttgart, 1979, pp. 371–534; ibid., pp. 382ff.
22. On this see especially Geyer, *Aufrüstung*, pp. 286ff.
23. I.e. through Hitler's power politics.
24. I.e. through the policy which Hitler adopted towards Britain. On the question of this thinking in terms of 'primacies', see J. Dülffer, 'Der Finfluß des Auslandes auf die nationalsozialistische Politik', in E. Forndran, F. Golczewski and D. Riesenberger (eds.), *Innen- und Außenpolitik unter nationalsozialistischer Bedrohung. Determinanten internationaler Beziehungen in historischen Fallstudien*, Opladen, 1977, pp. 295–314; ibid., pp. 295f.
25. *Akten zur deutschen auswärtigen Politik 1918–1945. Serie C: 1933–1937*, vol. IV, Göttingen 1974, No. 100 (23.5.1935); see also Salewski, *Marineleitung*, pp. 138f.
26. Not so Salewski, *Seekriegsleitung*, vol. 1, passim.
27. A IV 5719 geh. v. 5.11.1937, BA-MA M 1424/31263; SK 352/37 geh., Ibid., Slg. Raeder 3.
28. J. Henke, *England in Hitlers politischem Kalkül 1935–1939*, Boppard, 1973.
29. T. W. Mason, *Arbeiterklasse und Volksgemeinschaft. Dokumente und Materialien zur deutschen Arbeiterpolitik 1936–1939*, Opladen, 1975, pp. 100ff.

ROLF-DIETER MÜLLER

World Power Status through the Use of Poison Gas? German Preparations for Chemical Warfare, 1919–1945

Frequent discoveries of poison gas ammunition from the Second World War and the current discussion about the danger of a chemical arms race on German territory have recently drawn the attention of the public to historical developments that had been largely forgotten.[1] While conventional warfare studies have become so numerous that it is almost impossible to keep up with new publications in that area, German preparations for chemical warfare between 1919 and 1945 have been ignored in historical studies published in Germany since the Second World War. Occasional references in Anglo-American literature, usually based on an evaluation of contemporary intelligence reports, hardly do justice to the specifically German aspects of the subject.[2] The recently published work of the East German historian Olaf Groehler is also inadequate, among other reasons because the author avoids politically sensitive topics such as the co-operation between Germany and the Soviet Union in the 1920s.[3] In contrast to the years after the First World War, German experts and officers involved in the development of chemical weapons during the Weimar Republic and the Third Reich have tried to avoid publicity and to conceal their work.[4]

The world-wide condemnation of chemical warfare since the

Transl. from the German by Dean S. McMurry.

1920s, the prohibition of preparations for it imposed on Germany by the Treaty of Versailles and the fact that chemical weapons were not used in the Second World War go far to explain the lack of works on this subject. Above all, the subject of poison gas has extremely negative associations because the Third Reich practised gas 'warfare' against millions of defenceless victims in its concentration and extermination camps.

An analysis of German preparations for the use of poison gas between 1919 and 1945 shows a hubris in certain military circles, who were supported by branches of the chemical industry and who wanted to give their country's leaders an instrument which seemed to many officers, industrialists and other advocates of gas warfare a most promising weapon in the struggle for world domination. Basing their planning on the concept of total war, they were determined to place the most radical form of industrialised warfare in the service of an aggressive striving for world power status. Compared with conventional weapons, this form of warfare seemed to offer maximum destruction of the enemy's manpower for a minimum expenditure of personnel and materials. Because of the leading position of the German chemical industry in the world at that time and the country's plentiful supply and suitable raw materials, chemical ammunition was considered a typically German weapon.

Indeed, the development and first use of the lethal poison gas must be considered a German contribution to industrialised warfare during the First World War. The anticipated success failed to materialise, however, as the opposing powers quickly caught up. Both sides limited the use of poison gas to the battlefield, sparing the civilian population less for humanitarian reasons than because of the prohibitive costs of protective equipment, decontamination materials, and so on. In the autumn of 1918 the German military authorities even considered using chemical ammunition against demonstrators and rioters in Germany but finally decided against it.[5] The total amount of chemical ammunition used by all nations involved in the war was about 100,000 tons. Approximately 1 million soldiers suffered gas poisoning; between 65,000 and 90,000 died as a direct result.[6]

After the armistice at the end of 1918, the German army still had a large arsenal of gas weapons, which the military leaders planned to use in the event of a resumption of hostilities.[7] The immediate problem was, however, to maintain Germany's technical superiority, particularly in the production of the 'king of poison gases', mustard gas, and to prevent the surrender of facilities and reserve stocks to the victors. In order to evade the restrictions of the peace treaty, an 'accident', which destroyed the most important facilities or made it impossible to enter them for years, was staged at Breloh, the gas testing area near Hamburg in northern Germany.

Dr Hugo Stoltzenberg, who was to become a key figure in the development of German chemical weapons, was chosen to direct the clean-up, which lasted until the mid-1920s and cost many lives.[8] In the following years Stoltzenberg tried, with the help of the military authorities, to establish a new industrial base for the production of chemical weapons. This was necessary because IG–Farben, the most important producer and lobbyist during the First World War, was subject to international controls and the old factories were located primarily in the demilitarised Rhineland. Stoltzenberg had been an assistant of Professor Fritz Haber, who received the Nobel Prize for chemistry in 1918.[9] Haber, who had been on the list of war criminals, stopped doing research with poison gas but continued to play an important role as a go-between for poison gas contracts at home and abroad. The third member of this trio was Colonel Max Bauer who, as Ludendorff's right-hand man, had been a leading advocate of chemical warfare during the First World War.[10] After the Kapp-Putsch in 1920 Bauer travelled about the world as a professional military adviser and agent for a 'reactionary international'. He advertised German expertise in gas warfare in Turkey, Spain and other countries and prepared the way for Stoltzenberg.

Spain, who was suffering heavy casualties in her war against the Rif-Kabyles in Morocco, became one of Stoltzenberg's first customers. With the support of the German armed forces leadership Stoltzenberg pushed out the French competition and supplied the Spanish with poison gas from Germany and from factories he constructed near Madrid and in North Africa near Mellila. Chemical ammunition thus found a new application as an effective weapon in the hands of European colonial powers against poorly trained and equipped native troops, for example when used by the British in the border areas of Afghanistan.[11] But German military leaders were also determined to use it against the victors of the First World War. The army high command (*Heeresleitung*) under General Hans von Seeckt believed it could start a 'war of liberation' in the very near future.[12]

When the French occupation of the Ruhr at the beginning of 1923 subjected this policy to a premature test, it soon became clear that a trial of strength with the old enemy, with either conventional or chemical weapons, could not yet be risked with any chance of success.[13] At a conference with representatives of the army ordnance department Stoltzenberg suggested the reactivation of the remaining secret stocks of wartime chemical weapons stored at Breloh.[14] In addition, he was able to offer his factory then under construction in Hamburg which, he claimed, would be able to produce 6 tons of asphyxiating gas (green-cross marking) and the same amount of mustard gas per day within three months after receipt of an order, as well as 6 tons per day of blue-cross shell-gas after an additional six months. That was hardly more than one-tenth of German production in 1918.

As a long-term solution it was decided to build a new, large plant for the production of phosgene and mustard gas at Gräfenhainichen, near Halle in central Germany. The plant was to be chlorine factory equipped for the secret production of mustard gas and with loading facilities for a capacity of 7,000 tons per year, more than Germany had produced during the First World War. In addition, contacts were made with the Soviet government in order to have additional production potential, beyond the reach of the Entente, in case of war. The situation certainly seemed favourable. Moscow had already made known its strong interest in political as well as economic co-operation with Germany. In the bilateral negotiations concerning a military component for the Treaty of Rapallo, which had been going on since early 1923, the Soviet side made the delivery of German chemical warfare technology the *conditio sine qua non* for closer relations.[15]

In the summer of 1923 Stoltzenberg travelled to the Soviet Union on behalf of the army ordnance department to find a suitable factory for the joint production of poison gas. He found what he was looking for in Trotsk near Samara on the lower Volga. Representatives of the 'Society for the Promotion of Industrial Enterprises' (Gefu), a cover name of the Reichswehr for its illegal armaments production activities abroad, were able to start negotiations with the leading Soviet chemical warfare experts as early as 27 September 1923.[16] Agreement was reached on the establishment of the 'Rusk Germanskaja Fabrika Bersol' for the production of phosgene and mustard gas as well as the construction of loading facilities capable of producing more than 1 million artillery shells. With these shells alone the Reichswehr would have been able, in the event of war, to more than double its stock of legal, conventional artillery ammunition with poison gas shells produced in Russia.

While in other Western industrialised countries the proponents of chemical warfare were losing ground and governments as well as parliaments were demanding more international agreements to prevent chemical warfare,[17] Germany obviously regarded gas as the weapon of the future. At the same time as the efforts of the American government áchieved a breakthrough with the signing of the Geneva chemical warfare protocol in 1925, there was a real boom in German military publications advocating chemical warfare.[18] When comparing the future significance of the modern weapons systems, that is tank, aeroplane and gas, there was a clear consensus of opinion that a future war would be marked by the massive use of chemical weapons;[19] the use of aeroplanes and gas attacks on civilian populations would also have far-reaching consequences for the conduct of war. The advocates of gas warfare all over the world described the gas bomb as the 'most humane' weapon. The German experts disagreed only on the question of whether the most important enemy would be France, because of the political constellation, or the USA because of her highly developed chemical industry. Since the Reichswehr's war plans were still defensive and based on the safe area of central Germany between the Weser and Oder rivers, where a serious lack of production plants for trinitrotoluene (TNT) had to be considered, the main gas weapon, mustard gas, presented excellent possibilities as a terrain barrier and in guerrilla warfare.[20]

In the mid-1920s the practical preparations for chemical warfare underwent a basic change: from hectic improvisation and illusory grant projects to long-term, systematic rearmament.[21] The causes of this change were to be found in domestic politics as well as foreign policy. Stresemann's policy of detente in the West removed the immediate danger of war and seemed to promise a long period of peace. Prohibited and dangerous armaments, particularly chemical weapons, constituted a permanent danger for this policy, as any disclosure about them would completely discredit it. Under pressure from the political leadership, the Reichswehr was forced to find better ways of concealing embarrassing projects and to liquidate the ones most likely to be exposed. This affected mainly Stoltzenberg's large project in Gräfenhainichen and Trotsk.

In both cases the Reichswehr decided to terminate its projects with Stoltzenberg, not only because of alleged technical and financial shortcomings but also because of massive intervention by the powerful IG–Farben concern.[22] The large-scale production of chlorine in Gräfenhainichen endangered the dominant market position of the concern, whose own facilities were operating at only 75 per cent capacity. There was also the danger that the Allied Control Commission might unmask the plant in Gräfenhainichen as the first stage of illegal poison gas production and, as punishment, subject the whole German chemical industry to closer supervision and regulation. Stoltzenberg's activities abroad did not directly affect the interests of the concern, but the possibility cannot be excluded that the IG–Farben management wanted to prevent a competitor from gaining a strong position in possible future markets.

In any case, IG–Farben's petitions to the Reich chancellery and the foreign ministry were successful; the army high command reached a settlement with Stoltzenberg and severed its relations with him. The project in Trotsk was abandoned and the half-completed facility was turned over the Russians. Gräfenhainichen was dismantled. Stoltzenberg was ruined financially; his firm was dissolved. This necessitated placing the production of poison gas on a new basis. Until the end of 1925, the high command had assumed that they would be able to store a large supply of mustard gas in Germany and that this would be sufficient, together with the production at home and abroad, to cover the foreseeable requirements for gas troops, aeroplanes and artillery.[23] In mid-1926, however, a stock analysis by the logistics staff showed this assumption to be completely unfounded: 'Whereas all large states are making preparations for chemical warfare, all plants for the production of poison gas in Germany are destroyed or scattered'. In the safe area of central Germany, only the factory of the small firm Heyden near Dresden was ready to produce at most 2 tons of phosgene per day.[24]

The Reichswehr leadership devised three ways to improve the situation. On the military level they attempted to block all efforts of the Geneva disarmament conference to place the German chemical industry, as *potentiel de guerre*, under international supervision in order to enforce the prohibition of gas warfare.[25] As in the production sector this also prepared the way for closer co-operation with the large chemical concerns. The planned construction of small plants capable of expansion was quickly sacrificed to this development. Experts from the artillery department had demanded that decentralised depots of raw materials and equipment should be prepared in peacetime to 'permit the quick replacement of one factory with another in the event of loss'. At a conference on 24 April 1928 Captain Thomas, later head of the office of economy and armaments of the armed forces high command (OKW) and therefore one of the leading men in the Third Reich, pointed out that 'all further measures are dependent on consultation with the heads of the main branches of the chemical industry'.[26]

In addition, efforts were also increased to improve the necessary technical facilities. Notwithstanding all controls and prohibitions, the Reichswehr promoted poison gas research at scientific and suitable state institutions. Experiences and research results were compared at annual meetings; the head of the army ordnance department repeatedly pointed out the great importance of such work. Since other countries had not made any great progress in this area, it was necessary 'to develop and utilise the types of poison gas we have to produce the maximum possible effect with the smallest possible amount'.[27] He described the main areas of poison gas research as firstly, improving the utilisation and effectiveness of existing types of poison gas, secondly, determining the simplest production processes with the highest output and thirdly, research to discover or develop new kinds of poison gas.

Without practical field testing, scientific research and laboratory work were of little value to the military. This consideration made a continuation of the Reichswehr's work in the Soviet Union advisable. Both the Soviet and the German sides wanted to develop basic principles for the optimal use of chemical weapons and to test new gases, equipment and tactics.[28] The main consideration was the possible use of aeroplanes for strategic gas attacks outside the combat area. As early as 1927 German specialists using German aeroplanes carried out tests twenty miles from Moscow under an agreement with the Red Army, continuing tests conducted in Germany in 1925 under the cover of 'pest control'. The training area was called Ukhtomskaja, from which the name of the new joint project was also derived.

'Tomka' was an especially designed gas test area on the Volga near the earlier Stoltzenberg factory. At the beginning of 1928 the first group of twenty-eight German experts was sent to Volsk. After tiring, tedious work they finished the necessary facilities in the unspoilt forest. Supplies, vehicles, four field howitzers and four aeroplanes were brought from Germany. For the poison gas tests the Soviet authorities had cleared a large area of villages and inhabitants, but apparently not with absolute thoroughness. When the

German military attaché Köstring observed the release of gas during an exercise and protested that Soviet civilians were still in the area, the Soviet officer in charge merely remarked: 'When they smell the gas, they'll clear out.'[29] The annual tests lasted nine months and were concerned primarily with the use of mustard gas in various forms. The aim was, among other things, to practise laying down effective terrain obstacles by using gas. Mustard gas and diphosgene were supplied for the tests by the Soviet Union, presumably from the plant in Trotsk. Occasionally other types of gas were used.

The tests were preceded by thorough preparations in scientific institutions in Germany. Trials of different ways of using gas were supplemented by test series involving animals, especially horses and dogs. The German specialists in Tomka were supported by numerous Soviet scientists and officers. Results were often exchanged and were sent to Berlin every month. Top-ranking officers of the Reichswehr and the Red Army, for example the Soviet chief of staff, Tuchachevskij, were able to observe the progress of the work at first hand. The close relations with the Soviet Union were of decisive importance for the Reichswehr and not merely in the area of testing and developing gas weapons; under existing circumstances the Soviet Union was considered the only dependable supplier of raw materials and weapons, especially of poison gas, in the event of German involvement in military hostilities.[30] As Germany was not equipped to use poison gas in the first phase of a military conflict and did not expect its use by an enemy, gas production in Germany was restricted to planning. A production capacity of 500 tons per month was considered a desirable goal. The manufacture of gas masks and similar protective equipment for the army was, on the other hand, legal and presented merely a financial problem. The improvement of civil defence against gas weapons, which was promoted by the military, also made very slow progress. All things considered, Germany was still far from being prepared for chemical warfare.

It is therefore not surprising that conventional weapons were given a clear priority in the armaments plans of the Reichswehr. This did not, however, reduce the enormous significance attributed to poison gas. At the beginning of the 1930s arguments in favour of poison gas again played an important role in the discussions of German military theorists. They hoped Germany would be able to conquer enemy industrial centres, for example in Polish Upper Silesia and the Czechoslovakian armaments industry in Bohemia, with a fast, mobile shock army in case of war and would thus be able to expand her inadequate armaments base. To capture the necessary facilities undamaged, a recognised military expert suggested in all seriousness the use of poison gas: 'Nowadays, with highly developed technology, several thousand people are always dispensable'.[31] The army ordnance department described preparations for the mass production of at least one gas for offensive purposes as the most urgent task.[32] Concurrently, systematic training in gas warfare was begun within the framework of courses for the artillery department.[33] The advantages of chemical warfare were explained to the students; the conclusion stated: 'Poison gas will, therefore, also be used in future wars in spite of all the slander against it, if one may use that expression for a thing, just as firearms were accepted all over the world in spite of the protests of the knights'.[34] Germany was in unusually good position to profit from this development, as she had the best chemical industry and could make up for her inferiority in conventional weapons with poison gas.

However, the indispensable tests in Tomka were halted as early as 1932. Political reasons were not the only factor in this development. As the Red Army now wanted to conduct field tests involving large-scale use of poison gas and its own production was not sufficient for this purpose, the Reichswehr was asked to have a large, efficient company produce poison gas in Germany; in this connection the Russians were thinking primarily of IG–Farben.[35] The leading Soviet negotiator for the Tomka programme in 1933 explained that Germany could not wage a war without the 'big business' of the chemical industry and for that reason IG–Farben must be included in the practical war preparations. In making this suggestion the Russians were certainly not motivated solely by a concern for German welfare. As a precondition for the conclusion of an agreement they demanded technical assistance from IG–Farben for the production of various chemical components of poison gas in the Soviet Union. Moreover, they sought a joint development of a new poison gas for both armies which would be more potent and faster-acting than mustard gas. Although German research had not produced any spectacular new innovations in chemical warfare since the First World War, the Russians repeatedly expressed the belief that Berlin already had more modern types of poison gas at its disposal and was withholding them from its Soviet partner. This mistrust may have been caused by several incidents in which Red Army officers had not been permitted to participate in German gas warfare manoeuvres; the German defence minister had denied the Russians unrestricted access to German gas warfare preparations as early as 1927 because 'after all, they might be our enemy some day'.[36]

In Tomka itself the Red Army had begun to enlarge the test area for its own needs in 1931. This may have given additional impetus to German plans to reduce gradually the tests in Tomka and transfer them to Germany, mainly for financial reasons.[37] On the other hand, the artillery department pointed out that further progress in the area of chemical warfare was dependent on exercises with real poison gas. Under existing conditions such exercises could be carried out only in Tomka. Tests and exercises involving the use of poison gas over large areas in Germany itself were impossible even after the National Socialist assumption of power and the ensuing increased militarisation of the country.

It is, therefore, understandable that the mutual German–Soviet interest in gas warfare survived longer than that in testing tanks and aeroplanes.[38] In several conversations with German representatives, Tuchachevskij stated that he was prepared to continue the gas tests in spite of the increasingly tense political relations between the two countries.[39] In his function as chief of staff of the army ordnance department, Lieutenant-Colonel Thomas visited the Soviet Union in September 1933 as one of the last German officers involved in the test programme and was able to see for himself the enormous economic resources to which Germany would have access if she continued her good relations with that country.[40] In a report on this trip the ordnance department stated again that it was strongly interested in continuing the Tomka tests.[41] But before the agreement reached in the complicated negotiations between Tuchachevskij and the German military attaché in Moscow in the spring of 1933 on future German tests in Tomka could be carried out, the man whose government German military leaders hoped would start a rapid and unlimited rearmament decided to stop the gas tests on Soviet soil in the summer of 1933. Adolf Hitler, who, as a corporal on the Western Front in the spring of 1918, had himself been a gas casualty, ordered an end to gas tests in Soviet Union.[42] The Germans left Tomka, the stocks of gas stored there were destroyed and all the equipment was sent back to Germany. An order of the defence minister of 21 July 1933 stated that future chemical tests were to be conducted only in Germany.[43] However, efforts of the artillery department to reactivate the earlier gas testing area in Breloh failed because of the minister's objections.

Can this obvious restraint be adequately explained as simply a result of Hitler's subjective aversions or even of a basically different concept of war? Hardly, for as late as May 1933 a secret German memorandum on the air force build-up was approved at the highest level;[44] it envisioned the surprise, large-scale use of high explosive, incendiary *and* gas bombs against the civilian population of enemy cities, an idea of the Italian air war theoretician Douhet, to terrorise the population of the enemy and force him to abandon the fight. Hitler's dilatory attitude was probably due mainly to the fact that, for ideological and diplomatic reasons, he did not want to ally himself with Stalin and make the initial German rearmament dependent on the discretion and goodwill of the Soviet regime. Such an alliance policy, which Seeckt, who was now retired, again called for in a widely-read booklet at this time, was also controversial in military circles.[45] Even before Hitler came to power an increasing number of Germans had come to regard the Soviet Union as the main enemy in a future war and rejected Seeckt's views. Instead of exposing herself to the 'poisonous influence' of Bolshevism and giving the Soviet Union aid, a policy of questionable value for Germany, these circles argued that it would make more sense for Germany to develop and produce the weapons she needed on her own and use them in the struggle with France and the Soviet Union to regain her former power status.[46]

In the intensive rearmament programme which was begun after Hitler's coming to power, the responsible military officers tried repeatedly to persuade the political leadership to give more weight to gas warfare. At the conclusion of a chemical warfare exercise for the army high command, the newly organised department of gas troops summed up these ideas in an urgent memorandum of 19 June 1934.[47] It was pointed out that 'the use of poison gas must be expected at the very start of a war'. Therefore it was necessary to abandon all improvisations and start large-scale preparations for gas production.

Whether the Führer *wants* to use chemical weapons in the coming war or not depends perhaps on political and other considerations. But there can be no doubt that he must be given the possibility of using them by careful preparations in peacetime and that his future freedom of decision must not be restricted by some omission in war preparations.

At the moment Germany was not in a position to use poison gas in even a very limited way because there had been no opportunity since the last tests in Tomka in 1931 to advance '*scientific research* in the development of new types of poison gas by indispensable *practical tests*'.

Small-scale tests at the training area near Munster were suggested as a crash programme; weapons, ammunition and other equipment for the use of poison gas were to be developed to the point of field readiness, and production preparations were to be speeded up as much as possible. The question of when soldiers should first practise the use of real poison gas would be decided later. Such tests were at any rate necessary to obtain usable information for an appropriate organisation, arming and equipping of the gas troops. Although all training in the use of gas weapons had been strictly forbidden, at least the use of gas for training should now be allowed.

This programme was approved by the OKH and its success was evaluated a year later.[48] As part of a large-scale test series new methods of rendering areas unusable or impassable by means of poison gas were tried out. The air force agreed to cooperate and to conduct spraying tests. New types of the familiar blue-cross and mustard gas were examined by the gas office of the army ordnance deparment (WaPrw 9) in co-operation with the army gas laboratory in Berlin-Spandau as well as the army experiment station Raubkammer near Munster. Thus a continuation of the earlier tests in Tomka was guaranteed.

In the production sector German plans concentrated first on mustard gas and tear gas. By March 1936 a total of 1,300 tons were available, temporarily stored at individual factories in central Germany.[49] The supply of chemical shells and bombs was kept as low as possible, since the expected progress in the development of new kinds of poison gas and equipment for using it might render large stocks obsolete. It was planned to use the newly organised gas troops ('Nebeltruppe') to support the gas bombardments of the artillery and the dropping of gas bombs by the air force with spray equipment and rockets.[50]

At a gas demonstration in Munster on 25 November 1935 the commander-in-chief of the army was persuaded that the chemical weapons were ready for combat and could be introduced in large numbers. Plans presented by the department of gas troops four weeks later envisioned, in spite of all remaining shortcomings, the formation and outfitting of special gas warfare units.[51] Further preparations for chemical warfare were to be masked with the pretext 'that we must be able to pay back in kind an enemy who violates the Geneva Protocol of 1925. We support the use of this argument that we have to be able to retaliate because the training frees us from all limitations'. A gas regiment was to be set up for every army corps, with a second and third battery as gas and decontamination units.

The justification for German chemical rearmament, as well as the related technical and organisational measures, differed little from that of other Great Powers at the time. As far as production capacity was concerned, German plans were based on levels reached at the end of the First World War (30 tons per day).[52] But this certainly did not make poison gas a decisive weapon in any future war. The Army Section–General Duties Branch (*Allgemeines Heeresamt*) criticised the reports from WaPrw 9 for being too concerned with tactical questions and not drawing any clear conclusions about possible present and future use of poison gas. The military leaders, especially, demanded the development of an effective attack gas 'which will kill unprotected persons or have a quick effect on the skin of persons wearing masks'.[53] The Italian Abyssinian campaign demonstrated the decisive effects poison gas could achieve.[54] This was typical of the new type of colonial war as practised after the First World War by the British, French, Spanish and Japanese; only conventional poison gas was used. Comparable results could not be expected against a modern army trained for gas warfare. But as early as 1936 IG–Farben had developed a new poison gas of a type which had been repeatedly demanded by military leaders and against which there was no protection, the extremely effective nerve gas Tabun, which remained a German monopoly until 1945. In retrospect, some experts assume that its use would have enabled Hitler to win the Second World War.[55] Mass production, however, required seven more years of development. Even the handling of this dangerous gas created so many problems that none of the few persons aware of its existence expected it to be ready for use in the field at an early date.

The further development of new kinds of poison gas and chemical weapons as a whole received less and less attention within the total rearmament of the Third Reich. Hitler's memorandum of August 1936 with its requirement that the German armed forces be ready for a war within four years resulted in an acceleration of war preparations and an increasing number of economic bottlenecks, which forced the regime to set strict priorities in the armaments programme. The necessity of creating a completely new air force, building up the navy to approximately the level of other Great Powers and greatly enlarging the army, in addition to developing many new weapons and munitions and organising a new, larger military infrastructure within the shortest possible time presented almost insurmountable obstacles.[56] In the early stages of the armaments race with her potential enemies Germany could not, with her limited resources, achieve a lead in conventional and chemical weapons at the same time. Moreover, poison gas — of which mustard gas was the type most frequently used — was not capable of a decisive effect on the battlefield but led rather to the danger of drawn-out trench warfare, as in 1914–18. The German leaders were aware that Germany could not afford a long war of attrition; on the other hand the gas weapon retained its value as a deterrent against an enemy who might in desperation resort to chemical warfare. Advocates of gas warfare were, of course, also found among the military leaders of the other Great Powers, but for them, much more than for the Germans, gas was mainly a weapon of deterrence or retaliation. They were aware of the strength and resourcefulness of the German chemical industry and also, as the First World War had shown, how unscrupulous the German leaders could be. For these reasons they were not attracted to the idea of a first use of chemical weapons or of deliberately starting a chemical war. The situation in Germany was quite different. A powerful lobby, which consisted mainly of spokesmen for large chemical firms, who expected to receive a major share of the resulting contracts, and of individual army officers, who wanted to win the coming war for Germany, promoted the intensive development of chemical weapons.

The decisive initiative came from the industry. During a conference of the military economic staff on questions related to poison gas on 11 November 1936 IG–Farben made its first move.[57] A representative of the trust took up the old arguments from the First World War and persuaded the officers present that mustard gas and tear gas could be produced in any quantity desired, as the raw materials were readily available. The army should therefore draw the correct tactical conclusions and not waste poison gas by relying primarily on expensive shells and bombs but rather 'spread or drop it from aeroplanes in simple containers (of paper etc.)'. It was agreed to build up a supply within four years that would be sufficient to conduct a chemical war for three months and to develop a production capacity of 6,150 tons per month for further needs.

The strategy of IG–Farben was clearly aimed at a quantitative German superiority in conventional types of poison gas, primarily mustard gas. The idea of striving for a qualitative superiority with the help of Tabun was not in the interest of the firm until the new gas was ready for production and combat use. Neither was it really profitable to build so-called stand-by plants which would be put into operation only after the outbreak of a war in which chemical weapons were used. If the trust wished to become involved in the production of poison gas on a large scale, and it seemed determined to do so, a continuous, consistent demand would have to be created which could be justified on military grounds only if a large-scale offensive use of poison gas were planned at the outset of a war.

From the beginning support could be expected from the military experts concerned, as they untiringly promoted the idea of gas warfare to members of the general staff. In a position paper Lieutenant-Colonel Ochsner, department chief of the Nebeltruppe, pointed out that success through surprise, as had been achieved in 1915, would not be possible in the future.[58] Decisive results could be obtained only if either a new kind of poison gas able to penetrate any kind of protective clothing were developed and used, or if a new method of attack could be employed. Numerous efforts were being made in the first area but Tabun, the most promising gas, could still be produced only in laboratories and had failed its first field test. Germany would therefore have to concentrate on the second area. Ochsner advocated using poison gas in large quantities for a surprise attack and then, after the first strike, in continuous and uninterrupted attacks. In this way Germany could hope to defeat the enemy, as long as it had not developed its gas protection and, above all, the necessary discipline to withstand a gas attack. The enemy would inevitably suffer so many gas casualties within a few days that its medical facilities would be overloaded and supplies of anti-gas clothing and equipment would be exhausted. The most important aspect of chemical warfare would then become obvious: the psychological effect. Even the best troops would finally lose their nerve if they were exposed to enemy gas without sufficient protection.

IG–Farben supported these ideas with a memorandum of its own.[59] This claimed that mustard gas, the old type of gas normally used in land warfare, could even *determine* the outcome of a war if it were used against the enemy's civilian population. While high explosive and incendiary bombs caused relatively limited and easily repaired damage, mustard gas, with its

> unpredictable and mysterious effects, could cause lasting panic and completely paralyse life in contaminated cities. It creates such fear among the population that work and transportation would be halted for a long time. Gas victims would fill the hospitals and medical decontamination supplies would be exhausted. Emergency and decontamination measures are far more costly for the enemy than the use of poison gas for the attacker. If necessary, the civilian population can live for a while in the cellars of houses destroyed by bombs or fire, but not if poison gas makes every door-handle, every fence, every paving stone a weapon of the enemy.

The possibility that the German population might be similarly affected and demoralised by enemy retaliation in the form of gas attacks was rejected with the remark that a morally strong, highly disciplined and technically equipped people would remain steadfast and that in this respect Germany was extremely well prepared. In conclusion IG–Farben asserted that 'chemical weapons are the weapons of superior intelligence and superior technical-scientific thinking. As such they are able to play a decisive role for Germany at the Front as well as against the enemy hinterland'.[60]

In July 1938 at Göring's suggestion, Carl Krauch, a director of IG–Farben, submitted a detailed plan to accelerate the expansion of German output of militarily important raw materials used in the production of poison gas.[61] On the basis of the production level already achieved, (700 tons of mustard gas per month) an expansion to 9,300 tons per month was to be carried out within four years. This was slightly more than envisaged in the Entente programme for 1919 (8,300 tons per month). Krauch's further plans aimed at a maximum production capacity of 19,300 tons per month by 1945. A ration of 1:2 between poison gas and conventional explosives was to be achieved. In this connection Krauch also suggested the formation of a 'chemical officer corps'.[62] Trained personnel from the universities and the chemical industry were to be kept together in the armed forces and used in special units.

> In the officer chemical corps the leaders will develop who will ensure that the value and use of chemical weapons are properly

appreciated at the highest military command levels. In the course of the next few years a military organisation will be created which will only be possible in Germany and which will guarantee that the superior German chemical weapons will also be used appropriately.

Krauch also promised that the industry would be able to guarantee the absolute technical superiority of German production facilities if the leaders 'accept the value of chemical weapons and begin to make full use of existing possibilities'.

In reality, of course, IG–Farben was simply not in a position to assume the role Krauch had described. For almost twenty years the trust had produced no poison gas for military purposes; it sought to remedy this lack of experience by appointing Stoltzenberg director of the planned chemical weapons factories. Stoltzenberg, however, rejected the offer; he did not want to give up his hard-won independence and subordinate himself to his biggest competitor. To promote the German lead in chemical warfare, he was only prepared to support Krauch with several memoranda containing practical suggestions for new uses of chemical weapons.[63] In any case, he would have been a poor choice, as the army ordnance department still distrusted him and attempted to impede his activities in Spain, Yugoslavia and Brazil. Relations between IG–Farben and the army ordnance department were characterised by considerable tension; the military tried to maintain the idea of a decentralised powder, explosives and gas production organised around medium-sized enterprises. IG–Farben was able to base its opposition to these plans not only on Göring's protection and his instructions to Krauch but also on its domination of the market for the most important primary products. For example, it was in vain that the military demanded an impartial distribution agency for sulphuric acid, as it was common knowledge that most explosives factories obtaining their sulphuric acid from IG–Farben did not always receive as much as they ordered.[64]

In the end the army ordnance department lost its struggle with chemical big business; this defeat also settled the question of the autonomy of military armaments policy. At a conference on 17 February 1939 both sides agreed to work together more closely and to include IG–Farben in the production cartel under the direction of the army ordnance department.[65] In the mean time, Göring had appointed Krauch as 'plenipotentiary for special questions of chemical production', but the available resources were not sufficient to enable the expansion plans in numerous areas to be completed on schedule. Synthetic fuel production, rubber and light metals for new tanks and aeroplanes consumed all available resources. Poison gas was given a lower priority.[66] Since war was imminent, Krauch had drawn up a short-term plan with a production capacity of 7,800 tons per month as its goal. The essential basic chemicals were available, but not the quantities of steel and iron necessary for construction of the production facilities. In October 1938 only 50 per cent of the necessary cement was delivered; in January 1939 the armed forces reduced Krauch's steel allocation by 30 per cent. The extension of the West Wall had been given the highest priority.

Krauch's protest took the form of a warning in the form of a memorandum to all interested parties. On 13 January 1939 Göring discussed the situation with the department of Nebeltruppe.[67] At that time the supply of poison gas amounted to 2,900 tons and production capacity was 515 tons per month. The disparity between these figures and Krauch's grandiose plans was obvious; there was even a danger that the existing mustard gas factories would have to close down in the summer because a shortage of iron prevented the procuring of the necessary storage containers. In spite of Göring's support, the precarious situation could not be significantly improved, but this did not discourage the gas-warfare lobbyists. Shortly before the outbreak of war, Colonel Ochsner, now the newly appointed inspector of the Nebeltruppe, reformulated with greater precision his previous suggestions for conducting an offensive with chemical weapons.[68] He referred to a letter from Krauch of 20 June 1939 in which the latter informed the military leadership that the large-scale mustard gas programme could still be carried out in spite of the reservations of the army weapons office: '*If the political and military leaders view chemical weapons as a means to achieve a quick military decision*, it is still possible now to carry out the large-scale poison gas programme outlined in the memorandum by giving priority in the mobilisation preparations to the use of this weapon'. Ochsner accepted the ideas of the Krauch group and combined them with his own views already cited above. Uninterrupted large-scale attacks were, according to these plans, to be carried out not only against enemy armies but also against the civilian population. Ochsner expected a psychological effect from the use of poison gas, for 'the stupid and hysterical earlier propaganda of the League of Nations has also influenced world opinion in this question in such a way that panic is inevitable'. With an eye to the approaching struggle with Britain, Ochsner suggested planned, daily attacks using every kind of poison gas: 'There can be no doubt that a city such as London could be terrorised in this way that enormous pressure would be exerted on the enemy government'. The 'material destruction and psychological effect' of poison gas made 'its regular use as part of an overall plan and not only as deterrent or retaliation absolutely essential. Determined leaders will know how to justify its use politically to our own people and to the world'. Krauch supported this effort with a new long-term, large-scale programme in August 1939.[69] He argued that Germany could not catch up with the Western powers in high-explosive munitions production, an area where they had built up a lead in the course of almost two decades. On the other hand, Germany was in a significantly better position in chemical weapons. In proportion to the labour and raw materials used, an incomparably greater effect could be achieved in this area than with other types of weapons. 'Chemistry is definitely the weapon of the poor man, but it can achieve decisive results only if it is used unexpectedly at the beginning of a war and to an extent considered completely impossible by the enemy'. If the military leaders were prepared to appoint a man with full dictatorial powers to deal with technical production problems (and here Krauch probably meant himself), it would be possible to reach a production capacity of 22,000 tons per month by 1 January 1944. However, the National Socialist leaders could not wait so long to start their war, nor did they intend to. Hitler himself still had an especial interest in an arrangement with Britain which would free him in the west for his planned conquest of 'Lebensraum' in the east. Accepting the ideas of the 'gas war' lobby would make such an agreement impossible. For this reason Hitler agreed at the beginning of the war to declare officially his intention to refrain from a first use of poison gas, after the Western powers had already made similar declarations.[70] Secretly, however, he gave instructions to continue the preparations for gas warfare but did not decide on a particular programme. The responsible departments then attempted to determine the possibilities of obtaining raw materials and production facilities and to agree on a production programme.[71] The demand of the army general staff that production of all kinds of mustard gas be expanded as much as possible served as a guideline. The navy saw a possibility of using mustard gas in attacks on enemy merchant vessels to make food shipments inedible so that 'workers who have to unload the ships in the harbour will refuse to go on board because of the danger of being contaminated'.[72] The army wanted to use large quantities of mustard gas in the area in front of the West Wall if necessary to stop a French attack from the Maginot Line.[73] After new calculations Krauch's projection was reduced from 19,000 tons per month to 15,000 or 16,000. On 1 October 1939 Colonel Ochsner reported to Halder, chief of the general staff, on the results of the conversations and compared the projected goals for mustard gas production with the figures from the First World War to provide a yardstick for evaluation (see Table below).[74]

Projected goals for mustard gas production (in tons per month)

	Germany	France	Britain	USA
Annual* production 1918	7,038	—	—	—
Maximum production 1918	1,000	510	3,000	6,000
Production after 1.11.39	900	—	—	—
Expansion goal	15,000	—	—	—

* *Total* production for 1918

After the defeat of Poland, the German armed forces no longer needed to plan for a defensive use of poison gas in the West. A new possibility was discussed, the large-scale use of poison gas to destroy the French army.[75] But the necessary German quantitative and qualitative superiority could be achieved only after the autumn of 1940. The long-range rocket for gas attacks on London would not be available for three or four years.[76]

The gas weapon was therefore not ready for a decisive strike, as Krauch and Ochsner had planned, in Hitler's approaching offensive in the west. Further preparations were made with the goal of having an adequate supply of gas available in case the offensive failed or the Allies began using chemical weapons. Hitler did not agree to the proposed decreased expansion of gas production to 12,000 tons per month and accepted it as only temporary, since otherwise the already difficult situation in the powder and explosives industries would have deteriorated even further. Production was to be increased to 15,000 tons as soon as iron and steel supplies permitted. Hitler also wanted to build the new Tabun factory as soon as possible and to achieve production of 1,000 tons of the gas per month; he set the spring of 1941 as a deadline. In a conference of the agencies involved in carrying out these plans on 15 November 1939, it was assumed that this gas would probably be used only in the 'final battle'. Tabun was thus a kind of 'life assurance'.[77]

After Krauch had received a promise from Göring of a considerable increase of the iron and steel quota for his programme on 28 November 1939, the expansion could be started as planned.[78] In the preparations for the attack in the west, which was postponed several times, the general staff considered chemical weapons in a dilatory fashion and was mainly interested in the use of smokescreens to overcome the French fortifications.[79] It was calculated that the available supply of poison gas would suffice for an attack on a front of, at most, 50 kilometres; a large scale attack could not be planned before 1 October 1940 and could then be repeated only once.[80] Many German soldiers were not issued with gas masks and other protective equipment, and there was little protection for the civilian population.[81] In spite of all the assistance Krauch was receiving, his planning experienced repeated delays. According to the report prepared by Göring four weeks before the start of the campaign in the west, the following development of production could be expected (the figures show tons of poison gas per month):[82]

1 April 1940	1,860
1 October 1940	3,860
1 April 1941	8,060
1 October 1941	9,060

The new Tabun factory in Dyhernfurth on the Oder was supposed to produce 6,000 tons per month after 1 April 1942. Krauch requested an order that all available capacity should be utilised immediately and that the necessary resources should be provided to achieve a total supply of 94,300 tons of poison gas by 1 October 1941. This would certainly have given Germany the possibility of conducting an offensive gas war. At that moment, however, everything seemed to be working against these plans. Germany could have achieved total supplies of 14,632 tons of poison gas by 1 April 1941, but the production rate would have tended to decline. In any case the unexpectedly rapid victory over France made the use of gas superfluous. The euphoria of this victory achieved by conventional weapons kept the National Socialist leaders from using gas during the Battle of Britain in the autumn of 1940. An order from the OKW of 24 August 1940 forbade all branches of the armed forces to use poison gas.[83] Even the use of gas as a retaliation was made subject to Hitler's approval. A gas offensive may have seemed a particularly attractive possibility at this time, for the incendiary and high explosive bombs could not defeat Britain who, moreover, had no real possibility of retaliating after a gas attack. From a military point of view, however, this was inadvisable; the use of gas bombs would not suffice to force the surrender of the British government and the gas used would prove a serious embarassment to a German invasion; adequate protective clothing and equipment for the invaders was lacking.[84] On the other hand, British air attacks on German cities, even with a comparatively small number of planes, greatly alarmed the National Socialist leaders. Unlike Ochsner, Krauch and other advisers, Hitler and his inner circle had not been sure of the ability of the German population to withstand the hardships of war during the past months, and after the victory over France they wanted to maintain public optimism. In this respect even small-scale British retaliatory gas attacks could have had a devastating effect. In reports on the morale of the population compiled by the security police, the frequently encountered fear that the British would in desperation resort to a gas war was noted with concern. According to widespread rumours the British had dropped leaflets with the following message: 'There are eight of us and we come every night. If you come with Stukas, we'll come with gas!'[85] In fact the British government tried carefully to avoid any hint of possible retaliatory measures against a German first use of gas and stated publicly that they abhorred the idea of using gas and would never be the first to use it.[86] Although Hitler also decided not to use gas, this decision was probably influenced by his plans to attack the Soviet Union. The hope of a quick victory in the east would be dimmed by the risks and problems of a war with chemical weapons.

After all, it was known that the Soviet Union had been preparing intensively for a gas war for years and had good production facilities and an excellent civil defence programme. The German general staff seriously expected a Soviet first use of gas and therefore intensified their gas defence measures.[87] A pamphlet intended to warn soldiers on the Eastern Front about the cunning tactics of the Red Army stressed especially poison gas and bacteria.[88] Hitler noted with relief that Stalin did not resort to chemical warfare after the start of the war in the east.[89]

Little is known about the decision-making process on the Soviet side, but there can be no doubt that the Soviet leaders were considering using chemical weapons. The invading troops pushing deep into

Soviet territory were practically unequipped for gas warfare; because of the catastrophic transport situation, they would have been unable to ship enough chemical weapons and protective equipment from Germany to the Front. The Nebeltruppe were engaged in supporting the field artillery with their rocket launchers and conventional ammunition. However, the Red Army certainly lost a considerable portion of its chemical protective equipment in the bloody battles of the summer of 1941; new units did not even have enough conventional weapons. Reeling from the German attacks and its own losses, it did not have the high morale and discipline necessary for chemical warfare. We can also assume that at least the older Soviet officers were as averse to using poison gas as their counterparts in the Western armies; it was the Russian army which had suffered the greatest losses from gas in the First World War. Above all, however, the plan to launch a counter-offensive to drive the German troops from Soviet soil must have played an important role. In such an offensive, the use of chemical weapons would only have created obstacles.

Thus the warring nations confined themselves to watching their enemies mistrustfully. The British cabinet reacted to reports that the Germans planned to use gas on the Eastern Front by threatening retaliation.[90] Goebbels, who was very worried about the war-weariness of the German people, attempted to counter reports of a planned Bolshevik gas attack with threats of retaliation. In reality he was happy that the discussion of this sensitive subject quickly died down.[91] After the gigantic encirclement battle near Kiev, the Soviet campaign seemed almost over; the German high command ordered the gas warfare programme to be stopped and preparations continued only in the air force.[92]

Moreover, the German gas war lobbyists had not succeeded during the previous months in defending their expansion programme against the requirements of other programmes and projects.[93] The crisis in German armaments production in the second half of 1941 forced them repeatedly to reduce their production. Even the high-priority project in Dyhernfurth suffered. Since the spring of 1941 IG–Farben had concentrated all its efforts on starting the technically very difficult mass production of Tabun.[94] The commander-in-chief of the army himself was still pressing for a completion of the work in the summer of 1941 in order to be able to start at least partial production. But in November the armaments office in Breslau suddenly ordered the transfer of all labourers from

Dyhernfurth to complete the IG–Farben plant in Hydebreck and increase the production of synthetic fuel, which had achieved priority since German troops had failed to reach the Caucasian oilfields. This made it impossible to complete the buildings of Dyhernfurth before winter. Although director Ambros of IG–Farben, the poison gas expert of the trust, succeeded in obtaining the cancellation of this order, precious time had been lost in the construction of the Dyhernfurth plant.

It was no accident that the German leaders became more interested in poison gas at the end of 1941. The failure of the German attack on Moscow and the impending entry of the United States into the war caused the armaments minister, Todt, to call upon Hitler to conclude peace.[95] Hitler himself conceded to his disheartened advisers that a balance of forces apparently prevailed on the Eastern Front and that now Germany hardly had a chance of victory.[96] The confusion of the highest leaders gave the advocates of gas war an opportunity to try again to promote their ideas. The army ordnance department informed Hitler at the beginning of December 1941 of the progress in the development of nerve gases.[97] Work on the gas Trilon 83 (Tabun) had been completed; the plant in Dyhernfurth, with a production capability of 1,000 tons per month, could probably be put into operation in the spring of 1942. The newly developed gas Trilon 46 (Sarin), six times as deadly as Tabun, was to be produced at first in an experimental plant at the rate of 100 tons per month. This quantity was sufficient for a possible use against selected targets while other types of gas would be available for other tasks in a gas war. The department concluded:

> Neither captured documents nor other intelligence sources contain any indication that the use of these or similar gases with the same effects is to be expected from the enemy. This means that Germany is clearly superior in the area of gas warfare, and this superiority must be maintained, as requested, by the construction of an experimental facility.

This was a final plea for the offensive use of poison gas which, however, was obviously not accepted by Hilter or the military leaders. The chief of the army general staff noted in his diary on 8 January 1942: 'Colonel Ochsner is trying to talk to me into a gas war against the Russians'.[98] This plan had nothing to do with deterrence or preventive action for, in spite of intensive efforts, no clear evidence had been found that Germany's enemies had decided to use gas.[99] As had been the case earlier, Ochsner was by no means alone; rather he was a 'military spokesman for like-minded groups in the chemical industry and the armaments agencies'.[100] On the industry side, the office of economic expansion under Krauch's direction had already drawn up a new summary of its plans and on 6 November 1941 described the expansion of poison gas production capacity to 9,400 tons per month as a matter of top priority.[101] As real production figures had reached their lowest level since the start of the war, considerable efforts would have been necessary to achieve that goal. Although the chief of army armaments and the reserve army, Fromm, issued the appropriate order on 19 January 1942, the situation had hardly improved by the ensuing spring.[102] The army ordnance department reported on 27 March 1942 that available capacity was not sufficient 'to meet the requirements for starting a gas war. Expansion or building of additional capacity was stopped as a result of the restrictions placed on construction in 1941. The expansion of new capacity or the change to gas munitions will require one to two years'.[103] Even the prevailing shortage of ethylene oxide caused by the increased use of glycol for anti-freezing agents forced a production stop which crippled about one-third of available capacity.[104] But the original stockpiling goals could still be met. There were now about 30,000 tons of gas in shells and 10,000 tons in storage ready for possible use.[105]

When the German forces began their summer offensive in 1942, the use of gas was no longer being seriously considered. Nevertheless, Stalin seems to have expected the worst and pressed the British government to repeat their threat of retaliation.[106] Churchill's public declaration that a German gas attack on the Eastern Front would be answered by British gas attacks against Germany caused great uneasiness among the German population.[107] Hitler reacted with a demand that Speer maintain German superiority in gas warfare whatever the cost, in order to be prepared for all possible developments.[108]

Speer, however, could not make any encouraging promises.[109] Resources were not available to expand chemical weapons productions capacity, and production of the 'secret weapon', Tabun, was started in September 1942 with only one-tenth of the planned capacity. Hitler was not satisfied and ordered that by the following spring a capacity of 7,000 tons per month must be achieved. To carry out this order a special group 'K' was set up in the armaments supply office to check production constantly. Krauch who, in agreement with Speer, took over full responsibility for the munitions programme and was finally able to eliminate the army ordnance department, named the IG–Farben director Ambros as a member of the group and secured the influence of the trust in this area, too.[110] The completion and expansion of the plant at Dyhernfurth received absolute priority, as only a qualitative superiority was still considered possible and all hopes were placed in the new nerve gases. By the end of 1942 the production *capacity* for all chemical weapons reached 9,450 tons per month, which exceeded Hitler's instructions.[111] But because of the catastrophic raw materials situation, real production had sunk to the lowest level of the entire war (273 tons in December 1942). Compared to that of its enemies, Germany's position became progressively worse. While Germany produced a total of 70,000 tons of poison gas by 1945, the United States had achieved a production of 146,000 tons and Britain 35,000 tons. Soviet production figures are not known, but it can be assumed that they were not lower than those of Germany. The growing Allied air superiority reduced the German chances of a successful strategic use of poison gas, especially as, because of inadequate air defences, it had to be assumed that the greater part of the German population would be exposed to massive retaliation.

In any case the Allies did not consider using gas. When the American forces arrived in Europe, they brought several thousand tons of gas with them to be prepared if Germany introduced chemical weapons, but their commanders were instructed to use gas only on orders from the president.[112] Nevertheless, American soldiers, as the result of an accident, became the first gas casualties of the war. When German aircraft bombed a US freighter with a cargo of poison gas in the harbour at Bari, 83 sailors were killed and 534 severely injured by escaping gas; more than 1,000 civilians were killed.[113]

The British government also continued to regard poison gas as a weapon to be used only in response to a German first use. However, in order to forestall expected German reprisals, the British planned in such a case to 'drench German cities with gas on the largest possible scale'.[114] In contrast to the Allied position, Hitler was again pressed, after the débâcle of Stalingrad, to use gas offensively, and this time not only by the earlier advocates of such weapons but also by his closest companions such as Goebbels, Bormann and Ley. In the spring of 1943 he enquired repeatedly about the progress of chemical weapons and summoned Ambros and Speer to a conference on 15 May 1943 to discuss the suggestion to use poison gas on the Eastern Front.[115]

Asked about the possibilities open to the enemy, Ambros stated that they could produce more mustard gas because they had better access to ethylene. Hitler was not satisfied with this answer because he was primarily interested in the new nerve gases. To Hitler's great disappointment, Ambros pointed out that, contrary to claims made in earlier memoranda by Krauch and Ochsner, it was not certain that Germany had a monopoly in this area. The basic information about Tabun and the newly developed, much more deadly Sarin had been published more than forty years before. If these gases were used, the enemy would be able to produce much larger quantities than Germany. Ambros' remarks should not be considered a rejection of continued production of chemical weapons or their use. The strategy of IG–Farben was aimed at obtaining large orders as well as funds for further expansion of production facilities. This tactic was in accord with previous gas warfare plans, the creation of large reserves and sufficient production capacity to be able to achieve success with a single, massive strike. On the other hand, we must consider that, after the catastrophe of Stalingrad, the IG–Farben management surely no longer believed in a victorious end to the war. To persuade the political and military leadership into a gas war would certainly have led to the destruction of the IG–Farben plants by Allied bombers. But perfecting the new gas weapons would give the trust a valuable dowry for a postwar arrangement with its former American partners. As a result of the conference, Hitler ordered that production of Tabun be doubled, to 2,000 tons per month, by the end of 1944; production of Sarin was to be quintupled from 100 to 500 tons per month.[116] Total poison gas production capacity was to be raised to 12,950 tons per month. The use of chemical weapons was considered a 'means to achieve a final victory'.

Hitler's appointment of his former personal physician, Professor Brandt, as special commissioner for gas defence was another indication that he was at this time actually considering an offensive with chemical weapons. Brandt was ordered to have 60 million primitive anti-gas respirators (*Volksgasmasken*) produced and to complete arrangements for the protection of the civilian population. However, it is extremely doubtful that a 'final victory' could have been achieved by using gas, particularly nerve gas, as has been recently asserted.[117] The available German delivery systems might have been sufficient to cover the Fronts; at most long-range rockets could have been used to attack London, but this would not have been a decisive blow against the armies of the enemy powers or their morale and superior armaments potential. The only certain result would have been a devastating retaliation by enemy bomber fleets against the small number of gas factories, supply dumps and loading facilities, as well as against German positions from which the gas attack had been started and related approach routes. At the beginning of 1944, in expectation of the Allied invasion and the collapse of the Eastern Front, the German leadership became more interested in the use of gas. In spite of the increased enemy air attacks, which caused considerable disruption in the production of basic materials and equipment, those in charge of gas production were called upon to do everything to make up the time lost as a result of the lack of labourers, building materials, equipment and raw materials.[118]

Hitler told the Romanian Marshal Antonescu that, because of the lack of effective protective equipment, the use of the new poison gases could not be considered for the time being.[119] If, however, this condition could be met, he would then 'attack London and other cities within a certain radius. . . . In any case Germany was well prepared in this area, too. After all, it was the country where chemistry had been developed and had better gas and explosives than the enemy'.

The Allied landings in Normandy offered, from the German point of view, an especially interesting target for a gas attack; the British were so confident that they left their protective equipment at home. The soldiers in the beachheads did not even have gas masks.[120] However, on the day before the invasion, Ambros mentioned serious difficulties and shortages in a report on the state of German gas production.[121] The supplies of mustard gas (27,000 tons) and Tabun (8,500 tons) were certainly not impressive and the important factories were without any protection against air attack. It is not surprising that Hitler was disappointed by the lack of progress and informed Speer that he intended to entrust Himmler with the task.[122] IG–Farben succeeded in retaining control of the production sector, but responsibility for testing was given to the SS. Himmler's henchmen went to work in their own way. Dr Rascher, an SS staff doctor and special protégé of the 'Reichsführer SS', had already suggested trying poison gas intended for combat use on concentration camp prisoners in 1942.[123] The effects had previously been observed only in tests with animals or as a result of accidents. As groups of prisoners were to be executed anyway, Rascher was of the opinion that they should also be used for experiments; this suggestion was actually put into practice in the concentration camps Sachsenhausen and Natzweiler.[124] In 1944 the SS was also interested in the development of new ways to employ poison gas, for example, a gas pistol for assassinations. One plan had as its goal the improvement of air defences by igniting gas-saturated air to create a wall of flames.[125]

Another secret suggestion was aimed at the use of bacteria to disrupt the enemy supply system.[126] There were serious reasons for developing this last alternative; the British government had sought to make up for the less developed state of its chemical industry through considerable efforts in the area of bacteriological warfare. The anthrax bomb was ready for use in the summer of 1944.[127] In reaction to the German use of V-weapons, Churchill ordered a study of the possibilities of conducting a chemical and bacteriological war against Germany. The ideas developed by the joint planning staff in this regard were similar to those of the corresponding groups in Germany.[128] After consideration of all advantages and disadvantages, the use of chemical weapons was rejected, but biological weapons were not used only because of the lack of time. The thoughts of the SS leaders were similar; although the possibility of biological warfare was considered, the idea of using bacteria was not pursued further. In a position paper Himmler's personal staff recommended: 'Just as with gas warfare, it will be better if no one starts it'.[129]

However, the gas war lobby remained active, although the poorly equipped German troops had much more need of smokescreen protection against enemy fighter-bombers. But the tactics of smokescreening, which to the great surprise of the Germans had been employed very effectively by the British and Americans in Italy and France, had been neglected by the German army during the past several years. After Ambros had submitted a new gas programme on 1 August 1944, Goebbels and Ley pressed Hitler to permit the use of the chemical 'secret weapon', at least on the Eastern Front. But Speer replied to Hitler's questions by referring to technical production problems, difficulties in obtaining the necessary raw materials and, indirectly, to the superiority of the enemy in this area. He also hoped to obtain the support of OKW by suggesting to Hitler a halting of gas production in favour of powder and explosives.[130] However, Keitel rejected this proposal, as he believed that 'if we really want to do it', it ought to be possible to maintain the most important parts of the gas production programme. He felt that a complete stop would eliminate gas as a usable weapon, because since no one would seriously consider using a weapon for which there were no replacements after available supplies had been exhausted. Although he doubted Speer's information, he had no choice but to proceed according to the suggestions of the armaments minister.[131] Hitler also gave his consent but demanded that all means be employed to bring production of the most important materials up to an acceptable level. At a conference afterwards in the armaments ministry Professor Brandt explained this decision in two respects: in Tabun, Germany had at its disposal a new kind of gas which alone would probably be able to counter effectively a possible mass use of poison gas by the enemy and force him to stop using chemical weapons; the same was especially true of Sarin, 'the accelerated production of which can decide the war'.[132]

It seems that Hitler kept both possibilities open until his death. Living in constant fear that the Allies could gas him in his Führer bunker, he had even more protective equipment installed. However, on 4 February 1945 he ordered that all supplies of poison gas be removed in time to prevent their falling into enemy hands.[133] It was, though, forbidden to destroy gas supplies; the secondary effects might be misunderstood by the enemy or could even provide a pretext for retaliation. The evacuation measures were given top priority in allocating scarce transportation space. The most important production facilities for nerve gas were also supposed to be moved to central Germany in this way.[134]

In the confusion of the German collapse dramatic and unexpected developments often occurred in spite of all organisational precautions. Several plants and storage facilities could not be evacuated in time and were involved in the fighting.[135] A direct order was issued prohibiting the marking of gas, chemical ammunition and chemical weapons plants in danger of being captured by the enemy with warning signs.[136] Moreover, on 2 April 1945 Hitler ordered the most modern types of gas to be removed and stored in barges on the Elbe and the Danube to prevent their being lost through sudden enemy attacks.[137] On 8 April during the removal of about 20,000 tons of chemical ammunition from an important supply depot in central Germany, for which the civilian population of the area was also pressed into service, enemy fighter bombers attacked the loading station and poison gas escaped. At least four people were killed and the countryside was contaminated for about 20 kilometres around.[138]

In Berlin there were no clear ideas regarding the further use of poison gas. In April 1945 the Wehrmacht operations staff concerned itself with stopping the risky transfers of chemical weapons and ending preparations for chemical warfare in an orderly way. The main aim was to avoid giving the enemy any pretext for starting a large-scale gas war against the parts of Germany still under Berlin's control, with their high population density and numerous refugees.[139] The suggestion was made, therefore, to inform neutral countries that Germany did not intend to use poison gas. In addition, the enemy was to be given the positions of the supply depots, in order to avoid further incidents. Keitel's previous orders forbidding such actions were confirmed by Hitler after these suggestions had been explained to him on 16 April 1945.[140] Hitler rejected any attempt to contact the Western powers. Already surrounded by Soviet troops in his bunker in Berlin in an atmosphere dominated by the impending end of his world, Hitler no longer considered the protection of the German population worthy of his attention.

The use of poison gas could have given him the possibility of dying in a last blaze of destruction. By 31 December 1944, shortly before the complete breakdown of production, 63,166 tons of poison gas had been produced; 16,365 tons were in storage containers, the rest in shells and bombs.[141] The use of these weapons would not have reversed the course of the war, but it would have made possible the carrying out of Hitler's 'scorched earth' order and the collective suicide he desired, which could not be realised with conventional weapons and a bureaucracy which was no longer under Berlin's complete control. The fact that Hitler did not use every means to achieve this end may have been due to the irrational hope that a way out of his situation could still be found; for example, an arrangement with the British and the Americans. The use of poison gas would have closed this door and guaranteed the immediate destruction of the remainder of Germany that he still controlled. In the last few days before Hitler's suicide, when he had to abandon even these hopes, there was no longer any possibility of destroying the German people along with himself.

Different conclusions can be drawn from the German experience with poison gas between 1919 and 1945. On the one hand, it seems to offer a model case of working deterrence: although before 1939 the entire world was persuaded that the next war would involve the use of chemical weapons, with all their accompanying horrors, and all warring nations at least considered for a time the idea of a gas offensive, the chemical-biological disaster did not take place. Even the assumption of their own technical or quantitative superiority did not cause the countries involved to use poison gas. On the other hand, an analysis of developments reveals a shocking unscrupulousness, especially but not exclusively in Germany, on the part of politicians, military leaders and industrialists. In the final analysis the decision about a possible first use'of poison gas was dependent on unpredictable factors and individuals. That even a psychopath such as Hitler, with his dictatorial powers, resisted the arguments of a powerful military-industrial lobby is therefore no reason for optimism about the present or future. The Federal Republic of Germany has indeed renounced even the possession of poison gas, but an enormous number of chemical weapons are still to be found on the territory of the two German states: underground in the form of gas left from both World Wars, above ground in the chemical arsenals of the Super Powers.[142]

Notes

1. Revised and extended version of an article first published in *Militärgeschichtliche Mitteilungen*, 27 (1980), pp. 25–54 — Most of the following documents cited are now published by H. G. Brauch/R. D. Müller, *Chemische Kriegführung — Chemische Abrüstung. Dokumente und Kommentare. 1: Dokumente aus deutschen und amerikanischen Archiven*, Berlin, 1984.
2. See, for example, S.M. Herch, *Chemical and Biological Warfare*, London, 1968; F.J. Brown, *Chemical Warfare. A Study in Restraints*, New Jersey, 1968, esp. pp. 230ff., as well as the publication by the British television commentators R. Harris and J. Paxman, *A Higher Form of Killing*, London, 1982.
3. O. Groehler, *Der lautlose Tod*, Berlin (-East), 1978; published in a condensed version as 'Vorbereitungen für die chemische Kriegführung durch die deutsche Armee zwischen erstem und zweitem Weltkrieg', in *Revue Internationale d'Histoire Militaire*, 43(1979), pp. 167–180. This also applies to K.-H. Ludwig, 'Anmerkungen zur Vorgeschichte der Giftgas-Überreste aus dem 2.Weltkrieg', in *Technikgeschichte*, 46(1979), pp. 321–6.
4. See, for example, the account by the former departmental head in the

Heereswaffenamt Lt. Gen. ret. Dipl. Ing. Erich Schneider, 'Technik und Waffenentwicklung im Kriege', in *Bilanz des Zweiten Welt-krieges. Erkenntnisse und Verpflichtungen für die Zukunft*, Olden-burg 1953, pp. 223–47, here pp. 233f. On the writings after the First World War see the survey by A.M. Prentiss, 'Chemical Warfare Bibliography', in ibid., *Chemicals in War*, New York, 1937, pp. 703–29, and v. Tempelhoff, 'Der chemische Krieg im Spiegel des neuen ausländischen Schrifttums', in *Wissen und Wehr*, 17 (1936), pp. 252–67, 306–11.
War see the survey by A.M. Prentiss, 'Chemical Warfare Bibliogra-phy', in ibid., *Chemicals in War*, New York, 1937, pp. 703–29, and v.Tempelhoff, 'Der chemische Krieg im Spiegel des neuen aus-ländischen Schrifttums', in *Wissen und Wehr*, 17(1936), pp. 252–67, 306–11.

5. See E.-H. Schmidt, *Heimatheer und Revolution 1918*, Stuttgart, 1981, pp. 226–9.

6. On the figures see K. Justrow and H. G. Mehl, 'Gasmunition und hergestellte Kampfstoffmengen im Weltkrieg 1914/1918, (Mittel-mächte und Alliierte)', in R. Hanslian (ed.), *Der chemische Krieg*, vol. 1, Berlin, 1937, pp. 48–76, and the critical comments in Harris and Paxman, *A Higher Form*, p.51. On the history of chemical weapons during the First World War see also U. Trumpener, 'The Road to Ypres: The Beginnings of Gas Warfare in World War I', in *Journal of Modern History*, 47(1975), pp. 460–80; *The Problem of Chemical and Biological Warfare*, vol. I, *The Rise of CB Weapons*, Stockholm/New York, 1971; and Groehler, *Der lautlose Tod*, pp. 24ff.

7. Truppen-Departement Nr. 512/1.19 A 10 II. Ang.-Betrf., Report by TD-Director with the Kriegsminister of 22.1.1919 (Bundesar-chiv-Militärarchiv, hereafter: BA-MA, RH 12-4/v.38).

8. See the forthcoming study by R. Kunz and R.-D. Müller, *Giftgas für Deutschland und die Welt. Die Geschichte der Chemischen Fabrik Dr. Hugo Stoltzenberg.*

9. See also K. Lohs, 'Fritz Haber und der chemische Krieg', in *Zeit-schrift für Militärgeschichte*, 10 (1971), pp. 432–45.

10. On his biography see A. Vogt, *Oberst Max Bauer. Generalstabsof-fizier im Zwielicht. 1869–1929*, Osnabrück, 1974.

11. See Harris and Paxman, *A Higher Form*, pp. 61f.

12. R.-D. Müller, *Das Tor zur Weltmacht. Die Bedeutung der Sowjet-union für die deutsche Wirtschafts- und Rüstungspolitik zwischen den Weltkriegen (1919–1939)*, Boppard, 1984.

13. Ibid., pp. 110ff.

14. File note of meeting by *Inspektion* 4 of 26/27.1.1923 (BA-MA, RH 12-4/v.38).

15. See 'Ganz geheime Aufzeichnung des Deutschen Botschafters in Mos-kau vom 29.7.1923', (Politisches Archiv des Auswärtigen Amtes, here-after: PA, Botschaft Moskau, Akten betr.Mission Heller/Morsbach).

16. Protocol of meeting of 27.9.1923, in *Akten zur deutschen auswärtigen Politik 1918–1945*. Serie B: 1925-1933. Bd. 2/2, Nr. 107, Anl. C.

17. See the survey in *The Problem of Chemical and Biological Warfare*,

pp. 231ff.

18. See, for instance, R. Hanslian, *Der chemische Krieg*, Berlin, 1925, which became a standard work and went into its second edition as early as 1927.

19. See *Militär-Wochenblatt*, 110 (1925/26), and *Wissen und Wehr*, 7(1926).

20. See also M. Geyer, *Aufrüstung oder Sicherheit. Die Reichswehr in der Krise der Machtpolitik 1924–1936*, Düsseldorf, 1980, pp. 98f.

21. Ibid., pp. 114ff., as well as E.W. Hansen, *Reichswehr und Industrie*, Boppard, 1978, pp.114ff. and K.Nuß, *Militär und Wiederaufrüstung in der Weimarer Republik*, Berlin (-East), 1977.

22. See the correspondence with the Reich Chancellory of March/May 1925 (BA, R 43 I/420).

23. See the file notes of meeting of 18.1.1924 and 5.1.1926 (BA-MA, RH 12-4/v.38).

24. Abschrift.H.Wa.A.Nr.256/26,gKdos, "z" – oral report by the *Waffenamt (Nachschubstab)* given on 24.4.1926 at the *Truppenamt*, concerning the possibility of gearing German industry towards armaments production (BA-MA, RH 12-4/v.38).

25. Copy of Truppenamt Nr.547.29 V.H.III,gKdos, Hammerstein's comments of 28.11.1929 (BA-MA, II H 474).

26. Reichswehrministerium-Heer-Inspektion der Artillerie.Nr.492.28,gKdos, In 4 IV — file note of the meeting on 24.4.1928 (BA-MA, RH 12-4/v.38).

27. Minutes of the annual meeting of the scientific staff on 25.4.1931 (BA-MA, RH 12-4/v.37).

28. See for the following the reports by the *Gaskampferprobungsstelle der Reichswehr in der UdSSR* (Tomka), 1931–33 (BA-MA,RH 12-4/v.55) and the draft of a picture volume on Tomka by L.v.Sicherer, the former head of the station (BA-MA,MSg 2/782).

29. *General Ernst Köstring. Der militärische Mittler zwischen dem Deutschen Reich und der Sowjetunion 1921–1941*, edited by H.Teske, Frankfurt a.M., 1965, p. 49.

30. Mar. Ltg. B. St. Nr. 3560/30, gKdos, "Z" of 28.1.1930 (BA-MA, RH 8/v. 904). On the decision to postpone the preparations for production see Wehramt Nr. 1083/29, gKdos, "z"-Organisations-Kriegsspiel - Betr.Gaskampfstoffe -, letter of 6.12.1929 (BA-MA, RH 8/v.1007).

31. A.Caspary, *Wirtschafts-Strategie und Kriegführung*, Berlin, 1932,p.158.

32. H.Wa.A.Nr.30/31 Pl.WaPrwS. — Schreiben v.26.5.1931 — Betr.: Vorbereitung für Kampfstoffherstellung (BA-MA, RH 9/v.940a).

33. See the Reichswehr Ministry decree of 30.10.1933: 'Aufgaben und Organisation der Heeres-Gasschutz-Lehrgänge' (Institut für Zeitgeschichte, hereafter: IfZ, MA-479, pp. 956–63).

34. Talk by Major Ochsner on 'Chemische Kampfmittel und Nebelstoffe in neuzeitlichen Heeren', on 23.11.1931, given to weapons instructors (BA-MA, II H 483/2).

35. Meeting on To.-Programm on 17.10.1932 (BA-MA, RH 12-4/v.54).

36. Notes on a conversation between Stresemann, the Foreign Office and the Reichswehr leadership of 18.5.1927 (PA,Osec-Büro des Staatssekretärs, Bd.4).

37. Memo of January 1932 (BA-MA, RH 12-4/v.55).
38. See on this H.-J. Rautenberg, 'Deutsche Rüstungspolitik vom Beginn der Genfer Abrüstungskoferenz bis zur Wiedereinführung der allgemeinen Wehrpflicht 1932–1935', Bonn, PhD thesis 1973, pp. 204–11.
39. Deutsche Botschaft Moskau.Der Militärattaché Nr.142/33 - Report for Chef des Truppenamts of 16.5.1933 — Betreff:Versuche in To (BA-MA, RH 12-4/v.54).
40. See his later description: G.Thomas, 'Gedanken und Ereignisse', in *Schweizer Monatshefte*, 25(1945), p. 258.
41. Quoted in ADAP (see note 16), Ser.C:1933-1937, Bd.1/2, S.463, fn. 10.
42. See A.Hitler, *Mein Kampf*, Munich, 1939, pp. 220f.
43. Minister-Amt Nr. 241/33, gKdos, W.IIa — Order issued to Wehramt of 21.7.1933 (BA-MA, RH 12-4/v.54).
44. B.Heimann and J.Schunke, 'Eine geheime Denkschrift zur Luftkriegskonzeption Hitler-Deutschlands vom Mai 1933', in *Zeitschrift für Militärgeschichte*, 3(1964), pp. 72–84.
45. H.v.Seeckt, *Deutschland zwischen Ost und West*, Hamburg, 1933.
46. F. Immanuel, *Der große Zukunftskrieg — keine Phantasie*, Berlin, 1932.
47. In 4 Nr. 3317/34, gKdos, In 4 IVa – Betr.:Vorbereitung für Kampfstoffverwendung – of 19.6.1934 (BA-MA, II H 474).
48. See the notes for the speech by the Artillery Inspector with the Oberbefehlshaber des Heeres and the Chef des Generalstabes des Heeres on 25.9.1935 (BA-MA, II H 474).
49. WaPrw 9 Anl.zu Nr.388/35, gKdos, (BA-MA, II H 474).
50. On the history of the contingents see H.Rielau, *Geschichte der Nebeltruppe*, Cologne, 1965, and J.Emde, *Die Nebelwerfer*, Friedberg, 1979.
51. Der Inspekteur der Artillerie Nr. 1210/35, gKdos, In 4 IVc - memorandum for AHA of 16.12.1935 — Vorbereitung für den chemischen Krieg (BA-MA,II H 474).
52. Anl.zu WaPrw 9615/35,gKdos - file note, n.d., (BA-MA, II H 474).
53. AHA K 1a/In 4 IVa-108/36, gKdos - Memo for Generalstab des Heeres vom 6.3.1936 (BA-MA, II H 474).
54. See also W.Volkart, 'Die Gaswaffe im italienisch-abessinischen Krieg 1935/36', in *Allgemeine Schweizerische Militär-Zeitschrift*, 116 (1950), pp. 744-750, 799-816, 870-887, and 117 (1951), pp. 47-60, 99-110.
55. Harris and Paxman, *A Higher Form*, p. 86.
56. See also W.Deist, *The Wehrmacht and German Rearmament*, London, 1981.
57. In 9 Nr.809/36, gKdos - Note of WStb discussion on chemical Warfare problems of 11.11.1936 (BA-MA,III H 269).
58. AHA Nr. 590/37, gKdos, In 9 Ia, draft (BA-MA,II H 474).
59. Surveys relating to questions of chemical warfare, January, July, August 1938 (Dok. NI-8917) (BA, R 25/133).
60. Bemerkungen über den grundsätzlichen Wert der chemischen Waffe of 25.7.1938, ibid.
61. Zusammenfassung der Ausbaumöglichkeiten der Pulver, Sprengstoffe und chemischen Kampfstoffe in Rahmen der deutschen Chemiewirtschaft of 13.8.1938, ibid.
62. Reichsstelle für Wirtschaftsausbau, Abt.F, Vorschläge zur Nutzbar-

machung der deutschen Chemie für die Landesverteidigung.Bildung eines Chemiker-Offizierkorps, 21.7.1938, ibid. On the politics of the IG-Farben see also J.Borkin, *Die unheilige Allianz der I.G.Farben*, Frankfurt a.M., 1979, pp. 55ff. (transl. as *Crime and Punishment of I.G. Farben*, New York, 1978).

63. Gedanken eines Kampfstofftechnikers zur Strategie und Taktik der Gaswaffe (Dr Hugo Stoltzenberg), January 1938 (BA,R 25/133.)

64. WRo IIa, 66b 1161, file note of a discussion in the *Heereswaffenamt* on 26.2.1937 (BA-MA, Wi/VIII.2).

65. *Anatomie des Krieges*, Berlin (-East) 1969, Dok.No.87, pp. 201–3.

66. On the following see also the review of the question to be found in a memorandum by the Reichsamt für Wirtschaftsausbau of 21.4.1942: Zur Entwicklung des Pulver-, Sprengstoff-, K-Stoff- und Vorprodukten-Programms seit 1937 (BA,R 25/191).

67. In 9 Nr. 25/39, gKdos,- file note of the discussion with the ObdL on 13.1.1939 (BA-MA, III H 269).

68. Allgemeines Heeresamt Nr. 486/39, gKdos, In 9 Ia — Memorandum for GenStdH 1.Abt. - Betr.:Verwendung von chem.Kampfstoffen im Kriege, 28.6.1939 (BA-MA, III H 269).

69. Reichsstelle für Wirtschaftsausbau: K'stoff-Großprogramm (langfristig), August 1939 (BA, R 25/143).

70. On the preparations for chemical warfare in Great Britain see P. Harris, 'British Preparations for Offensive Chemical Warfare, 1935–1939', in *Journal of the Royal United Services Institute*, 125 (1980), No. 2., pp. 56–62. On the situation at the beginning of war see Brown, *Chemical Warfare*, pp. 230f.

71. See copy, dated 4.9.1939/Gr. of letter of 3.9.1939 to Major General Thomas-Betr.: K'Stoff, In 9 Nr. 659/39, gKdos; discussion with Thomas (WStb) on 5.9.1939, OKH (BdE) K7b AHA/In 9 IIa Nr.688/39, gKdos; letter to top military authorities of 17.9.1939 concerning the results of discussion on 8.9.1939 at In 9 (BA-MA, III H 269); moreover RoIII(a), file note of meeting of *Chemie-Arbeitsstab* on 5.9.39 concerning raw materials for new chemical warfare programme (BA-MA, Wi/VIII.2).

72. See Einzelheiten über K-stoff-Arten u.K-stoff-Fertigung nach dem gegenwärtigen Stand (Sept.1939) (BA-MA, Wi/VIII.2).

73. See Groehler, *Der lautlose Tod*, pp. 191f., as well as Generaloberst Halder, *Kriegstagebuch* vol. 1, Stuttgart, 1962, pp. 85, 93f.

74. AHA Nr. 800/39, gKdos, In 9 — Vortrag vor dem Herrn Chef des GenStdH am 1.10.1939 (BA-MA, III H 269).

75. See Groehler, *Der lautlose Tod*, p. 195.

76. Halder, *Kriegstagebuch*, p. 85 (26.9.1939).

77. Pl.Lummitzsch, file note of a discussion with General Thomas on 15.11.39 concerning the finalisation of the new plan to expand chemical warfare production (BA-MA, WiIF5/717); see also Halder, *Kriegstagebuch*, p. 145 (21.12.1939).

78. See Memorandum by the Reichsamt für Wirtschaftsausbau of 21.4.42, p. 7; Chef in 9 Nr. 899/38g Kdos, meeting General Thomas on 15.12.1939 (BA-MA,III H 269); OKW/WiRüAmt/Ro 3009/39 g.K.,

Pulver-, Sprengstoff- und Kampfstoff-Herstellung, 12.12.1939 (BA-MA,RH 8/v.1022); OKH/BdE Nr.2650/39, gKdos, letter to *Feldzeugkommandos* of 12.9.1939 (BA-MA,Wi/IF5.365).

79. Halder, *Kriegstagebuch*, pp. 175f. (30.1.1940).
80. Ibid., p. 220 (5.3.1940).
81. Ibid., p. 226 (22.4.1940); see also Brown, *Chemical Warfare*, p. 239.
82. Planung und Lage auf dem K'Stoff-Gobiet, 16.4.1940 (BA,R 25/190). (Mathematical errors have been corrected by the author.)
83. OKW/WFST/Abt.L (Chef) Nr. 00665/40gKdos, Anweisung betr. Bestimmungen zur Einschränkung von Kampfhandlungen, *Kriegstagebuch des Oberkommandos der Wechrmacht (Wehrmachtführungsstab) 1940–1945*, vol. I, Frankfurt a.M., 1965, p. 970.
84. Brown, *Chemical Warfare*, p. 244.
85. *Meldungen aus dem Reich*, edited by H. Boberach, Neuwied/Berlin 1965, p. 81 (No. 100 of 27.6.1940).
86. References in C.O.S. (42) 70(0), 21.3.1942, War Cabinet. Chiefs of Staff Committee. Chemical Warfare. Note by Secretary (Public Record Office, hereafter: PRO, CAB 80/61).
87. OKH/Chef der Heeresrüstung u.BdE/Stab Rüst.IIa Nr. 1587/41,-gKdos, letter to OKW/WiRüAmt betr.Gaskriegsvorbereitungen of 17.6.1941 (BA-MA, Wi/IF5.120 T.1); see also Groehler, *Der lautlose Tod*, pp. 214ff.
88. AOK Norwegen Ia/Ic, Merkblatt vom Juni 1941 (BA-MA, RW 39/20).
89. *Adolf Hitlers Monologe im Führerhauptquartier 1941-1944*, Hamburg, 1980, p. 93 (17./18.10.1941).
90. See note 86.
91. Goebbels' diary, entries of 26.7. and 22.8.1941 (BA, NL 118/90). At this time, rumours and worries re-emerged among the German population about possible gas attacks by the British; see *Meldungen aus dem Reich*, pp. 171f. (21.8.1941).
92. *Kriegstagebuch des Oberkommandos der Wehrmacht* (see note 83), pp. 1045–7. In view of the general military situation, the OKW no longer expected the use of gas on the Eastern front. Ibid., p. 1051.
93. See OKW/WiRüAmt/Ro(IIIc) Nr. 1822/40,gKdos, letter concerning Chlor- und K- Stoffanlagen of 7.9.1940 (BA-MA,Wi/IF5.255); see also Übersicht des Reichsamtes für Wirtschaftsausbau über Pulver und Sprengstoffe für Wehrmachtzwecke of 22.1.1940 (BA, R 25/190).
94. On the following see the account given by the I.G.Farbenindustrie A.G. in their note to OKW/WiRüAmt, 22.11.1941 (BA-MA, Wi/IF5.208).
95. See R.-D. Müller, 'Das Scheitern der wirtschaftlichen "Blitzkriegstrategie" ', in *Das Deutsche Reich und der Zweite Weltkrieg*, vol. IV, Stuttgart, 1983, p. 1023.
96. Halder, *Kriegstagebuch*, vol. 3, p. 295 (19.11.1941).
97. WaA/WaStab, file note for the Führer und Obersten Befehlshaber der Wehrmacht, 2.12.1941 (BA-MA, RH 2/v.929).
98. Halder, *Kriegstagebuch*, vol. 3, p. 376 (8.1.1942).
99. See OKH/GenStdH/Gen d Nbl Tr Nr.300/42geh., Mitteilungen über Gaskriegsvorbereitungen im Ausland N.15, 20.2.1942 (BA-MA, RL 2

II/106); ibid., also reports on investigations into alleged use of chemical warfare by the Russians; see also Mitteilungen No. 18 of 16.8.1942 (IfZ, MA-329, p. 2964–75).

100. Groehler, *Der lautlose Tod*, p. 223.
101. Überblick des Reichsamtes für Wirtschaftsausbau of 21.4.1942, p. 4. A list detailing available production capacities up to 14.11.1941 may be found in BA-MA, Wi/IF5.255.
102. Groehler, *Der lautlose Tod*, p. 223.
103. Ibid., p. 226.
104. Memorandum by Reichsamtes für Wirtschaftsausbau: Lage auf dem K-Stoff-Gebiet, Stand 15.5.1942 (BA R 25/191).
105. List of Reichsamt für Wirtschaftsausbau of 6.7.1942 (BA, R 25/191).
106. C.O.S. (42) 96(0), 13.4.1942, War Cabinet, Chiefs of Staff Committee, Chemical Warfare, Report (PRO,CAB 80/62). See also Groehler, *Der lautose Tod*, pp. 206ff.
107. *Meldungen aus dem Reich*, No. 284 of 14.5.1942 (BA, R 58).
108. *Deutschlands Rüstung im Zweiten Weltkrieg*, edited by W.A. Boelcke, Frankfurt a.M., 1969, p. 159 (23 – 5.7.1942).
109. Memorandum by Ministeramt [Speer] relating to a discussion with Hitler of 24.7.1942 (BA, R 25/191).
110. Note by Dr Ritter, Reichsamt für Wirtschaftsausbau of 20.7.1942 (BA, R 25/191).
111. Memo of Reichsamt für Wirtschaftsausbau of 1.12.1942: Die Lage auf dem K-Stoffgebiet (BA, R 25/191).
112. The Joint Chiefs of Staff Washington, Memorandum for the Secretary, British Joint Staff. Mission, 11.1.1943 (PRO, CAB 80/39). On the preparations for chemical warfare by the Americans see L.P. Brophy et al., *United States Army in World War II. Chemical Warfare Service*, Washington, 1959.
113. Harris and Paxman, *A Higher Form*, pp. 144ff.
114. C.O.S. (43) 66, 27.2.1943, War Cabinet. Chiefs of Staff Committee. Chemical Warfare. Minute by Prime Minister (PRO, CAB 80/39).
115. On the developments see the Memorandum by Ambros 'Die Lage auf dem Kampfstoffgebiet. Auszug aus dem Vortrag im Führerhauptquartier am 15.Mai 1943 mit einer Gegenüberstellung der Situation vom 1.März 1944' (BA, R 3/1894). At the same time there were again rumours among the German population about an impending gas war. See *Meldungen aus dem Reich*, No. 381 of 6.5.1943 (BA, R 58).
116. File note of a discussion with GB Bau on 26.5.1943 relating to the expansion of Dyhernfurth (BA-MA, Wi/IF5.238). On the general situation in this field see also Groehler: *Der lautlose Tod* (note 3), p. 256.
117. See note 55.
118. Memorandum by Ambros: 'Die deutsche K-Stoff-Produktion', 1.2.1944 (BA R 3/1894).
119. *Staatsmänner und Diplomaten bei Hitler*, edited by A. Hillgruber, vol. II, Frankfurt a.M., 1970, p. 403.
120. Harris and Paxman, *A Higher Form*, p. 85.
121. RLA/PSV/PS 592/44 g.Rs.,Stand der K-Stoff-Fertigung und Ausbau-Planung, 5.6.1944 (BA, R 3/1894).

122. See also Borkin, *Die unheilige Allianz*, p. 123; A. Speer, *Der Sklavenstaat*, Stuttgart, 1981, pp. 282f.
123. Note by Dr Sigmund Rascher to the Reichsführer SS of 9.8.1942 (IfZ, MA-295, S.70574).
124. Harris and Paxman, *A Higher Form*, pp. 81ff.
125. Correspondence between RSHA/Pers.Stab and Westf.-Anhalt. Sprengstoff A.G., Oktober/Dezember 1944 (IfZ, MA-292, S. 8106-17).
126. Note by SS-Sturmbannführer Mehlstäubl to the Reichsführer SS of 27.9.1944 (IfZ, MA-292).
127. Harris and Paxman, *A Higher Form*, pp. 97ff. Apart from Britain, Japan was also interested in the production of biological weapons; see R. Gomer et al., 'Japan's Biological Weapons: 1930-1945', in *Bulletin of the Atomic Scientists*, 37 (1981) no. 8, pp. 43–53.
128. Harris and Paxman, *A Higher Form*, pp. 152ff.
129. Reichsführer SS/Pers.Stab to SS-Sturmbannführer Mehlstäubl, 17.11.1944 (IfZ, MA-292).
130. Speer to Keitel, 11.10.1944 (BA, R 3/1734).
131. See the inquiry by WFSt/Org (IVa) with the Speer Ministry of 20.11. 1944 (BA, R 3/1894).
132. Rüstungslieferungsamt/Amtsgruppe PS Nr. 1099/44, file note on discussion with Staatsrat Dr. Schieber on 2.11.1944 (BA, R 3/1894).
133. OKW/WFSt/Org.Nr.001250/45,gKdos, Order of 4.2.1942 concerning preparations for gas warfare (BA-MA, RW 4/v.720).
134. Letter of Reichsamt für Wirtschaftsausbau betr.Bauprogramm Geilenberg of 4.1.1945 (BA, R 25/76); WFSt/Qu./OrgF-priority telex of 16.2.1945 (BA-MA, RW 4/v.720).
135. WFSt/Qu.1 Nr.003046/45,gKdos, Note concerning the Air Force's chemical warfare depots at Frankenberg, 29.3.1945; GenStdH/GenQu/Abt.I/Gr.Mun.Nr.I/03345/45,gKdos, Report for Chef OKW of 14.4.1945 (BA-MA, RW 4/v.720).
136. Chef OKW/WFSt/Org(IVa)Nr.909/45,gKdos, Order relating to defensive measures to be taken against enemy action against chemical warfare installations of 30.3.1945 (BA-MA, RW 4/v.720).
137. Chef OKW/WFSt/Org(IVa)Nr.941/45,gKdos, Order relating to the securing of chemical warfare munitions against loss through sudden enemy advances of 2.4.1945 (BA-MA, RW 4/v.720).
138. WFSt/Qu.1 (Trsp.) Nr. 01269/45, gKdos, Note of 8.4.1945 (BA-MA, RW 4/v.720).
139. WFSt/Org(F) Nr.003631/45,gKdos,Note of report on K-Stoff-Munition of 15.4.1945 (BA-MA, RW 4/v.720).
140. Ibid. marginal notes by Keitel.
141. According to list by WaIRü (Mun6/Ixe)(BA-MA, RW 4/v.720) and OKH/ChefHRüst u. BdE,Nr.10/45,gKdos.,Produktionsmeldung für Dezember 1944 (BA, R 3/1948).
142. On the topicality of these problems see H.G. Brauch, *Der chemische Alptraum*, Berlin/Bonn, 1982.

KLAUS A. MAIER

Total War and German Air Doctrine before the Second World War

In 1915 the Italian General Emilio Douhet proposed that his government should destroy Vienna by an air attack of 500 bombers and so end the war without any longer sacrificing the blood of Italian soldiers on the Isonzo battlefield. As we know, Vienna escaped this fate. Whereas she was never under large-scale air attack, London was not so lucky.

In the spring of 1917 the German supreme army headquarters believed that British morale had been shaken by the recent military successes of the central powers. As a result it decided to support the initiation of unrestricted submarine warfare, which would affect both British life and the war effort, with an air offensive against major British towns, especially London. The main purpose of these raids, which were carried out by Bombergeschwader 3, was to attack British morale and reduce it to a point where the British government would have to surrender.

After the war the British committee of enquiry into breaches of the laws of war wanted certain German air officers, who had taken part in these raids, brought to trial as war criminals according to Art. 227 of the Treaty of Versailles. Against this suggestion the Air Council circulated a memorandum for the urgent consideration of the cabinet. It contained the following argument:

... the present situation makes it necessary to emphasize the peculiar reverberation of such contemplated prosecutions upon the RAF. These German officers and men are to be tried in time of peace before a court exclusively composed of their ex-enemies for acts which do not differ from those ordered to be carried out by the Royal Air Force upon German towns. The orders given included directions to bomb German towns (where any military objective was situated), to destroy the industrial activities there by bombings during the day, and to weaken the morale of the civilian inhabitants (and thereby their 'will to win') by persistent bomb attacks which would both destroy life (civilian and otherwise) and should, if possible, originate a conflagration which should reduce to ashes the whole town and thereby delete a whole centre of industrial activity.[1]

These few remarks on air strategy in the First World War demonstrate how even then war had degenerated into total war.

Total war, with its roots in the mass conscription armies of the French Revolution, reached its ultimate form with the technological innovation of aircraft. Air forces made it possible to bomb the civil population as well as war production deep behind the front-lines held by the armed forces.

In its absolute form total war has three main consequences. Firstly, not only a nation's armed forces but also the whole nation are exposed to attack. Secondly, this is why not only the armed forces but also the nation must mobilise for war. Thirdly, because total mobilisation cannot be managed only when war occurs, but must be organised in peacetime also, the distinction between peace and war eventually becomes muted. Thus the often-quoted formula of Clausewitz, that war is only the continuation of policy by different means is reversed: peace has become the continuation of war by different means.

During the interwar period no government or general staff formulated a national strategy along this abstract approach of total war and total mobilisation. But elements of total war were inherent in the air doctrines of nearly all the major European powers. The protagonists of an independent air force especially tended towards a doctrine of total war, the very *raison d'être* of this new force. Attempts to limit air war by international agreement failed, because the conflicting national interests and divergent concepts for the use of air power could not be reconciled.[2]

There are aspects of the German situation in particular that are of special interest. In Germany the necessity of preparing the nation for a future war, a total war, coincided with the traditional interests of the old social and political élites, who wanted to stop all socio-political movements in German society, and halt the effects that originated from the industrial revolution. German society failed to reform itself according to the requirements of a modern industrial state. Total war and total mobilisation, the old social élites hoped, would provide further support for the restoration of their position in German society. They felt that in a state mobilising for total war they could intimidate others and prosecute democratic movements for sabotage of an all-out national effort.[3] There were also extremists among the protagonists of total war, who believed that war is the fate of humankind and that a society mobilising for war was realising a law of nature.

The affinity of this conception of total war and total mobilisation with National Socialist ideology is evident. In fact, this affinity paved the way for an entente between an essential portion of the German military establishment and the Nazi regime. With Göring as air minister and commander-in-chief of the Luftwaffe the connection between the Luftwaffe and Nazi regime is a striking one. It might be supposed, therefore, that from this connection a 'total war' ideology dominated German air war doctrine. However, Nazi Germany never built up a strategic air force comparable to British Bomber Command or the US Army Air Force; the dominant role of the Luftwaffe was a tactical one.

This view of the Luftwaffe as a tactical force must not lead us to overlook either the strategic aspects or the elements of 'total war' contained in the German concept of air warfare,[4] which was interdependent with and influenced by the aggressive policy of the Nazi regime.

As early as 1926 the Reichswehr compiled 'directives for the conduct of operative air actions'.[5] These attacks by units of the airforce should be used to destroy enemy morale by an initial blow against urban and industrial centres and also against food supplies. Such was the strategic thinking of the Luftwaffe leadership when Hitler came to power and started the overall rearmament.

In May 1933 General Milch, then state secretary for aviation, presented Göring with a study written by Dr Knauss, director of the Lufthansa and later commandant of the Air War Academy in Berlin Gatow. In his study Knauss feared that German rearmament might provoke preventive war by France and Poland. To deter these powers Knauss proposed an air force of four-engined bombers, each with a total bombload of 2,000 kg, including high explosive incendiary and gas bombs. In the event of a war Knauss wanted this air fleet to be directed against vital enemy centres of war production, transportation and, last but not least, against the population of large cities. Concerning the effectiveness of such raids he argued:

> Terror-bombing of enemy capitals or an air offensive against industrial areas will produce moral collapse so much earlier, the weaker national cohesion is, the more the urban masses follow materialistic interests and the more these masses are divided by socio-political tension and political controversy.[6]

In March 1935 Göring announced to the world the existence of his Luftwaffe. Not one single aircraft out of a total of 2,500 machines — of which only 800 were combat-ready — met the requirements demanded by the Knauss study. Not only financial and technological difficulties, lack of raw materials and skilled labour but also lack of sound management and of clear direction had produced an air force in which quantity prevailed over quality and whose fighting power in war games proved 'completely insufficient' for a two-front war with Germany's immediate neighbours.

But these shortcomings did not deter Hitler in March 1935 from introducing the Luftwaffe as an instrument of political pressure. He announced to the British foreign minister, Sir John Simon, that the Luftwaffe had already reached parity with the RAF and very soon would equal the French Armée de l'Air.

In comparison with Knauss, Major-General Wever, the chief of the Luftwaffe general staff, advocated a more moderate conception of air war. In his inauguration address to the Air War Academy in November 1935 he set air priorities as close co-operation with the army and navy against the enemy's armed forces; by also demanding that the Luftwaffe must aim at halting enemy war production, Wever added a secondary strategic role to the primary tactical function.[7]

This line also followed an official instruction entitled *Luftkriegführung*, first published in 1935, which not only concentrated on air attacks against the armed forces but also demanded offensive actions to paralyse the morale of an enemy's civil population. Although terror-bombing was minimised by this instruction, in October 1936 Major Deichmann, chief of the operations section of the Luftwaffe general staff, concluded a lecture on 'principles for the operative conduct of the air war' by saying that he had indeed confined himself to speaking about air attack on war production, but that the Luftwaffe must equally provide ways and means by which it could strike at the morale of an enemy's civilian population.[8]

During the second half of the 1930s Hitler's aggressive foreign policy underwent a fundamental change. He had originally hoped to conquer 'Lebensraum' (living space) for the German people in the east, i.e. in parts of the Soviet Union, either in alliance with Britain or at least with her standing aside. He now realised that the British government was trying to halt his drive to the east by containing Nazi foreign policy within a general European peace settlement. From that time Hitler's ambitions faced the risk of a major European war against Britain and her allies; it is also undoubtedly the reason why Hitler, refusing to give up his long-cherished Lebensraum dream, had to mobilise German resources as fast as possible. He had to wage a succession of short wars before the Western powers were prepared to intervene successfully. Timing became all important.

Hitler's Blitzkrieg concept, which he once described as 'applying military force and thereby taking big risks', became also the guiding rule for further German air armament. In April 1937, Göring ordered a final stop to the development of the two four-engined bombers, the Junkers Ju 89 and the Dornier Do 19. Because he calculated that the German aircraft industry could produce two and a half twin-engined bombers instead of one four-engined aircraft, Göring once again gave quantity precedence over quality. He thus committed the Luftwaffe to a medium-range air force which, with its Heinkel He 111, Junkers Ju 86 and Dornier Do 17, proved unfit for a long-range strategic air offensive against Britain. With dive bombers like the Junkers Ju 87 and with the 'speed bomber' the Ju 88, the Luftwaffe tried to compensate for the lack of bomb-load capacity and defensive armament until a four-engined bomber would be available. The Heinkel He 177, the only four-engined bomber whose development Göring ordered to continue, later turned out to be a total failure.

Hitler's decision to intervene in the Spanish Civil War on the side of General Franco's party was welcomed by Göring as an opportunity to test his Blitzkriegs Luftwaffe under combat conditions. Owing to Franco's lack of heavy weapons, the Legion Condor was engaged mainly in close air support operations. Under its chief of staff and last commander, Wolfram Freiherr von Richthofen, the Legion developed a very effective tactical method for this sort of air action, but it was also engaged in strategic air operations. According to a report written during the summer of 1938 the Legion had attacked the following objectives: the enemy air force; units of war production; government quarters and the civilian population; supplies and transportation; troops in transit and those in the front line.

Concerning the attacks on civilians, it was reported that the population had been impressed and terrorised by successive air attacks, especially in those towns where the air defence measures had been proved inadequate. In general, the reports ascribed the collapse of morale to the lack of discipline and organisation among Spanish workers.[9] The destruction of the small town of Guernica in April 1937 is even now considered by many to be a 'masterpiece' of terror bombing. According to entries in the personal diary of von Richthofen, who ordered the raid, Guernica was attacked because it was an important centre of communications in the rear of the retreating Basque army.[10] The bombload used by the Legion Condor consisted of two-thirds high explosive and one-third incendiary bombs, the mixture the Legion called *Generalstabsmischung* (General Staff mixture), because it had proved very effective in previous attacks on towns and villages which, it was presumed, contained enemy headquarters.

Beyond its character as a hitherto unthinkable air operation, we must suppose that von Richthofen welcomed the probable effect of the Guernica raid on the morale of the government and population in Bilbao, for the Germans were by that time extremely eager to attack the Spanish Atlantic ports. Indignation and dismay caused by the air raid were world-wide, finding an eternal figuration in the famous painting executed by Pablo Picasso for the Spanish pavilion at the Paris International Exhibition of 1937. Above all, the Guernica raid shocked public opinion and Parliament in Britain — whose population now had to become acquainted with the knowledge that Britain could no longer consider herself as a safely isolated island off the north-west coast of the European continent. The British considered Guernica to be the Luftwaffe's opening chords to a total war in the air.

This widespread fear of the German air menace prevented the British political and military leadership from making a clear-headed analysis and realistic evaluation of the Luftwaffe's real striking power in a strategic war in the air. It thus had a fatal effect on British foreign policy, above all during the Czech crisis in the autumn of 1938. On 28 September of that year, when the crisis was at its peak, the military intelligence section of the British war office (MI5) circulated a warning that at the very moment that Britain declared war on Germany, the Luftwaffe would attack London.[11] Chamberlain shared this view, justifying his policy which led to the bloodless British defeat at Munich by reference to the German air threat. A cabinet paper reports Chamberlain's impressions as follows:

> . . . he had flown up the river over London. He had imagined a German bomber flying the same course, he had asked himself what degree of protection they could afford for the thousands of homes which he had seen stretched out below him and he had felt that we were in no position to justify waging a war today.[12]

Ironically, it was the inability of the Luftwaffe to hope for any decisive results from an air offensive against Britain that caused Göring to warn Hitler against going too far at Munich; after Munich the Luftwaffe, of which Göring had ordered a five-fold increase by 1942, considered its chances in an all-out air offensive against British supplies and war production to be very poor. But in the reports after Munich we also find a surprising amount of argument concerning the Luftwaffe's role as a deterrent force and, if needed, as a terror weapon.

In May 1939 the intelligence section of the Luftwaffe general staff believed that the Third Reich was the only state that had advanced to a conception of total air war in both offensive and defensive respects. Following on from this, the intelligence section pointed out that during the Czech crisis, the Luftwaffe had been able to exert enormous political pressure; thus it did not have to prove its real striking power in actual combat. It was also believed that the Western powers, because of their democratic constitutions and parliamentary systems, were able to be less flexible in their political and military decision-making processes than was the authoritarian German Führer state. This prejudice led to the hazardous prophecy that although the Western powers were bound by treaties and promises to Eastern Europe, a conflict in this region could be localised.[13]

A three-day staff manoeuvre by Luftwaffe Fleet 2, which was earmarked for wartime air operations against Britain, gave clear indications of the technical and tactical shortcomings of the Luftwaffe for such operations. The fleet commander, General Felmy, criticised chiefly the slow progress in tactical training caused by the rapid expansion of the Luftwaffe. His report concluded that a strategic air offensive against Britain could not be launched until 1942 when the Luftwaffe would possess long-range bombers or when the Wehrmacht had captured forward air bases in the Netherlands or France. But if war with Britain should occur before this time, Felmy wanted the Luftwaffe to attack London and other British population centres in a pure terror-bombing offensive.

Felmy's anticipation of the decisive results of such an offensive, like the anticipation of the intelligence section, rested upon the experience gained during the Czech crisis. The digging of slit trenches in public parks and the handing out of gas masks in London in September 1938 was seen by Felmy as an indication of a high degree of war hysteria in Britain — in contrast to the situation in Germany. He proposed to exploit this hysteria in case of war.[14]

Felmy was supported by a study by the army high command, which proposed chemical warfare by the Luftwaffe 'on a very large scale'. The army high command pretended that stupid and unrealistic propaganda by the League of Nations had influenced world opinion to a point where panic had become inevitable: 'It is beyond any doubt that a city like London can be struck with such fear that the government would be subject to enormous pressure'.[15]

The operations section of the Luftwaffe general staff was less optimistic about the political results to be obtained by terror-bombing London, but it too hoped that the continuous bombing of industrial centres, even by small units, would eventually lead to a collapse of morale in large areas of Britain.

On 22 August 1939 Hitler told his Wehrmacht commanders that the attack on Poland would be solely a matter of nerve. He said: 'I have always taken big risks. And also now I run a big risk'.[16] Four days later he wrote to Mussolini:

As neither France nor Britain can achieve any decisive successes in the West, and as Germany, as a result of the agreement with Russia, will have all her forces free in the East after the defeat of Poland, and as air supremacy is undoubtedly on our side, I do not shrink from solving the Eastern question even at the risk of complications in the West.[17]

Among these three factors in Hitler's calculations of risks — Western unpreparedness for war, the Stalin–Hitler pact and German air supremacy — air power was of twofold importance. By its considerable tactical skill and experience in launching surprise air attacks and close air back-up operations, the Luftwaffe would be able to support a short campaign in Poland. A *fait accompli* in Poland before the Western powers could complete deployment in the west would, Hitler hoped, prevent these powers from declaring war at all.

More important than this tactical role for the Luftwaffe in Hitler's calculation of risks was its image as a deterrent force, gained through years of producing fear and political intimidation by its actions as well as through German propaganda. Hitler's view that the Western powers would once again shrink from going to war, as they had done in 1938, was shared by the larger part of the Luftwaffe's command. In the eyes of these men, intoxicated by the Nazi ideology of a total war, deterrence by the Luftwaffe rested not only upon its lead in strategic striking power, admittedly limited, but also upon the political structure of the Reich. The German state with its Volksgemeinschaft, its totalitarian peoples' society, seemed to be better mobilised for a total war in the air or on the ground, than did the Western democracies.

When Hitler initiated hostilities in September 1939, he had at his disposal a Luftwaffe that had become the force best suited for his Blitzkrieg strategy of short continental campaigns. On 3 September 1939 Britain and France declared war on Germany; as a deterrent force the Luftwaffe had failed. In the short term the Luftwaffe could and did meet the demands of a Blitzkrieg policy. But with the Battle of Britain, the failure of the Russian campaign and the entrance of the United States into the war, the Luftwaffe faced challenges that it was not equipped to meet.

Notes

1. Public Record Office (PRO) London, Cab 24/98. J. Kuropka, *Image und Intervention: Innere Lage Deutschlands und britische Beeinflussungsstrategien in der Entscheidungsphase des Ersten Weltkrieges*, Berlin/Munich, 1978, pp. 244ff.
2. D. C. Watt, 'Restraints on war in the air before 1945', in M. Howard (ed.), *Restraints on War: Studies in the Limitation of Armed Conflict*,

Oxford, 1979, pp. 57ff.

3. H.-U. Wehler, 'Der Verfall der deutschen Kriegstheorie: Vom "Absoluten" zum "Totalen" Krieg oder von Clausewitz zu Ludendorff', in U. v. Gersdorff (ed.), *Geschichte und Militärgeschichte: Wege der Forschung*, Frankfurt/M., 1974, pp. 273ff.

4. See the author's detailed examination of the interrelationship between the tactical and strategic elements in the German air war concept before the Second World War, 'Totaler Krieg und operativer Luftkrieg', in K. Maier, H. Rohde, B. Stegemann and H. Umbreit, *Die Errichtung der Hegemonie auf dem europäischen Kontinent (Das Deutsche Reich und der Zweite Weltkrieg*, vol. 2), Stuttgart, 1979, pp. 43ff.

5. *Bundesarchiv-Militärarchiv* (BA-MA) Freiburg i. B., Lw 106/11.

6. B. Heimann and J. Schunke, 'Eine geheime Denkschrift zur Luftkriegskonzeption Hitler-Deutschlands vom Mai 1933', *Zeitschrift für Militärgeschichte*, 3(1964), pp. 72ff.

7. Publ. in *Die Luftwaffe. Militärwissenschaftliche Aufsatzsammlung*, ed. *Reichsminister der Luftfahrt und Oberbefehlshaber der Luftwaffe*, 1(1936) part 1, pp. 5ff.

8. K.-H. Völker, *Dokumente und Dokumentarfotos zur Geschichte der deutschen Luftwaffe*, 198, Stuttgart, 1968.

9. BA-MA, RL 7/57.

10. Partly publ. in K. Maier, *Guernica, 26.4.1937. Die deutsche Intervention in Spanien und der 'Fall Guernica'*, Freiburg, 1975, pp. 75ff.

11. F. H. Hinsley et al., *British Intelligence in the Second World War: Its Influence on Strategy and Operations*, vol. 1, London, 1979, p. 82.

12. U. Bialer, *The Shadow of the Bomber: The Fear of Air Attack and British Politics 1932–1939*, London, 1980, p. 157.

13. BA-MA, RL 2/535.

14. BA-MA, RL 7/42.

15. BA-MA, RH 12-9.

16. Akten zur Deutschen Auswärtigen Politik (ADAP), D, VII, Nr. 192f.

17. ADAP, DL. VII, Nr. 307.

BERND WEGNER

'My Honour is Loyalty.' The SS as a Military Factor in Hitler's Germany

On 19 July 1943 the English author J. B. Priestley explained to the British public in a BBC broadcast how one should imagine the Armed SS (*Waffen-SS*):

> ... the élite of the Nazi thugs and butchers, young men carefully and deliberately brutalised to make them eager and willing to knock and mow down anyone. And these men are no normal soldiers; strictly speaking, they aren't soldiers at all, even though they may often fight at the Front. They are heavily armed police troops trained to protect the Nazi regime against revolts, in Germany or elsewhere, or, if necessary, against mutinies in the German armed forces. They are the hard core of Nazism, the Praetorian Guard of this last, insane empire.[1]

What makes Priestley's judgement interesting even today is that it anticipated the picture of the Waffen-SS presented in historical literature since that time: the Waffen-SS as the Praetorian Guard and élite of the National Socialist system, its function as a police troop for the internal protection of the regime, its role as a counterweight to the Wehrmacht, which was never considered completely loyal and last, but not least, its shocking amorality. Most studies have stressed the role of the Waffen-SS as a terror instrument and

Transl. from the German by Dean S. McMurry.

neglected its military significance. However, a highly apologetic literature has developed which concerns itself exclusively with the military role of the Waffen-SS. Its achievements on the battlefield are isolated from the context of the history of the SS and National Socialism and presented as it were in an historical vacuum. In this way members of the Waffen-SS appear to have been 'just like other soldiers'.[2] Their achievements and sacrifices are described as the results of timeless military virtues and skills.

The actual history of the Waffen-SS was indeed as varied and contradictory as the picture of it to be found in historical texts.[3] Towards the end of the Second World War, in addition to units of the German army, navy and air force, no fewer than thirty-eight divisions and eighteen army corps of the Waffen-SS surrendered. More than 800,000 men had by then served in its ranks; 20 to 25 per cent had been killed. Under the operational command of the army, SS units had fought since the beginning of the war on all fronts with the exception of North Africa, and had frequently played a critical role in decisive battles. Names such as Rostov, Kharkov, Demyansk, Kursk and Cherkassy, Caen and Falaise are closely associated with important offensive and defensive successes of Waffen-SS divisions.[4] More than 400 officers of the Waffen-SS were awarded the Knight's Cross; several of them even commanded armies and army groups towards the end of the war.

Although these facts may seem to indicate that the Waffen-SS was a 'normal' military organisation, an entirely different picture emerges when we consider its origins. The first armed units were organised from the political organisation of the protection squads (*Schutzstaffeln*) after the National Socialists came to power in 1933. The SS as such had existed since 1925. After Heinrich Himmler's appointment as its leader (Reichsführer SS) in 1929, it had developed more and more into the party police of the National Socialist movement. This political background also influenced the early history of the SS *soldiers*. It was no accident that they were organised at a time when the position of the National Socialists, which was still by no means unchallenged, had to be strengthened by reliable armed formations. This connection is most easily seen in the SS Death's Head (*Totenkopf*) units in charge of external security at the concentration camps until they were incorporated into the Waffen-SS, as it was called from then on, shortly after the outbreak of the war. Although the Death's Head units had rudimentary military features, they were not a military organisation, nor were they considered as such, as is made clear by an order issued in 1936 by their leader, Theodor Eicke, a man who thoroughly detested both the professional military and the bourgeois world. Eicke explained: 'We don't carry weapons to look like the army but rather to use them when the Führer and the movement are in danger'.[5]

The SS *Verfügungstruppe* (special duty troops), the most important precursor of the Waffen-SS, were not originally a military organisation, rather they were first formed in 1933–4 under the revealing name *Politische Bereitschaften* (political ready reserves) by the regional SS commands, that is they were decentralised and organised independently of the state. Only the later *Leibstandarte SS Adolf Hitler* was formed on Hitler's direct order in March 1933 as his personal guard, also without any constitutional basis. The internal political function of the new units became clear in June 1934 when part of the *Verfügungstruppe*, primarily the *Leibstandarte*, were used in the liquidation of the *Sturmabteilung* (SA) leadership. Moreover, all of Hitler's relevant decrees before the war clearly confirm that the SS *Verfügungstruppe* were intended to be the Führer's personal instrument 'for special internal political tasks'.[6] A possible military use at the Front in the event of war is always mentioned in these documents as a secondary possibility. Also, Himmler's nomination as Chief of the German Police in June 1936 appeared to confirm that the SS and its militarised units were to be orientated towards a primarily domestic function. Finally, we should remember that even during the war the Waffen-SS never quite lost the character of an instrument for combating enemies within: the staffs of the concentration camps were organisationally part of the Waffen-SS. Units and formations of the Waffen-SS were used behind the front as part of 'anti-guerrilla actions' and assigned, in limited numbers to be sure, to *Einsatzgruppen* (action groups) of the security police and the security service. There they became instruments of National Socialist mass annihilation policies.

This brief description permits us to draw a first conclusion: in the short history of the Waffen-SS, military, political and even police functions were closely intertwined. The extent and kind of this interrelationship seem typical of the historical peculiarity of the Waffen-SS. In the following pages we will attempt to define this reciprocal relationship between its military and political elements more precisely.

The elimination of the SA as a political power factor in the summer of 1934 was the first decisive breakthrough in the development of the SS from an internal party security force to, as it were, the omnipresent police organisation of National Socialist rule. The SS, which was raised to the level of an 'independent organisation within the NSDAP' the following month, was able to expand its influence considerably in almost all areas of German society by the end of the decade. In the area of internal security the Reichsführer SS achieved, through the SS security service, the concentration camps and the gradual takeover of the police apparatus, a monopoly within a very short time. But the SS was also increasingly able to influence cultural policies and even historical research (for example through its own research organisation in pre- and early history) as well as the economy and foreign policy.[7] In this expansion of the 'Black Order' into all areas of society, the role of the Waffen-SS was at first modest and rather inconspicuous. At the beginning of 1935 the total SS strength was over 200,000, but the *Verfügungstruppe* numbered barely 5,000; another 2,000 men served in the Death's Head units. Nevertheless, in the autumn of 1934 the first serious tensions developed between the SS and the army high command (*Heeresleitung*). The primary cause of these tensions, which were to dominate the relationship between the army leaders and the leadership of the SS until the collapse of the regime, was the far-reaching military ambitions of the SS.[8]

The negotiations between the two sides in the autumn and winter of 1934 give one a first impression of these ambitions. After the elimination of the SA, when rumours were circulating that the *Leibstandarte* would be expanded to a modern infantry regiment and that the SS was receiving weapons to equip its own division, the defence minister (later war minister) von Blomberg felt it necessary to issue a directive clarifying the relationship between the army and the SS. This directive of 24 September 1934, which had been agreed upon with the Reichsführer SS, was also intended to reassure those army officers who feared that the SS, like the SA, could become a threat to the armed forces.[9] Accordingly, the decrees stressed the *political* rather than the military character of the SS as a whole, which made military training and equipment superfluous. There was, however, one exception: the SS *Verfügungstruppe* were permitted, with express reference to their 'special internal tasks', to form a total of three regiments and several smaller units. The formation of additional units and the question of organising them into a division was to require the agreement of the defence minister. In the event of war, according to the directive, the SS units were to be placed at the disposal of the armed forces, which were also responsible for their combat training in peacetime.

Although Blomberg's order may seem quite restrictive in certain details, its significance for the further development of the SS *Verfügungstruppe* lay in the fact that in it the armed forces, in official usage collectively referred to as the 'nation's sole bearers of arms', recognised for the first time the existence of an additional 'bearer'. This recognition even meant that service in the SS *Verfügungstruppe* was accepted as military service and pay and order of rank were adjusted to correspond to the system in the armed forces. The fact that the formation of an SS division and its operational use at the Front remained an open possibility eventually proved to be no less important. Indeed, Himmler used this and other ambiguous parts of Blomberg's directive as a starting-point in his negotiations with the army leaders during the following months; the positions of both sides were in themselves not entirely free of contradictions. For example, while the army leadership tried to limit the possible serious consequences of the ending of its military monopoly by the SS, neither did it wish to renounce the advantages of having additional military units at its disposal without bearing the costs of running them. The situation was even more delicate for the SS leadership, as its goal was to let the *Verfügungstruppe* acquire the technical potential and training of the army without appearing too openly as its rival. Above all, however, the SS militarised units were not to become a simple appendage of the army; Himmler feared, with good reason, that under such circumstances they would gradually be lost to the SS both ideologically and politically. In his negotiations with the army he therefore denied all military ambitions, while at the same time seeking its assistance in the military training and equipping of his *Verfügungstruppe*.[10]

Such an attitude did not exactly reduce the army general staff's distrust of the SS; the negotiations produced no real results. Himmler's demand that the SS be permitted to have its own artillery, a decisive precondition for the formation of an SS division, was especially unacceptable to the army leaders. (The SS *Verfügungstruppe* did not receive its first artillery regiment until the summer of 1939.) The army also refused to recognise service in the SS Death's Head units or SS *Junkerschulen* (officer training schools) as the equivalent of military service and did not even want to grant

Himmler's request for a regular exchange of officers and training personnel between the SS units and itself. In spite of this extremely reserved attitude of the army leaders, the fact that Himmler attempted to realise such demands in the autumn of 1934 is significant. It shows that even at this early date he was very interested in a further development of his armed units along professional military lines.

How persistent this interest was can be seen in the development of the *Verfügungstruppe* and Death's Head units in the following years. For example, in spite of the resistance of the army, the *Verfügungstruppe* was almost able to triple its strength within four years (1935–8). The Death's Head units, which were not subject to any limitations by the armed forces, more than quadrupled. Thus by the end of 1938 the SS had no fewer than 23,000 men under arms, a small number compared to the following years, but more than anyone had expected in the autumn of 1934.[11] The growth of expenditure for the militarised units was even more dramatic. Outlay for the improvement of their infrastructure (barracks, equipment, weapons and so on) rose almost twice as fast as personnel costs. All these figures would have been considerably higher if the finance minister had not drastically cut the budgets submitted by the SS leadership.[12] The expansion of the armed SS units was accompanied by a reorganisation. The battalions of the Death's Head units and the *Verfügungstruppe* were expanded to form regiments. Towards the end of 1937 each of the organisations consisted of three regiments and several smaller units; each received a fourth regiment after the annexation of Austria. After August 1936 the military training of the SS soldiers was organised and co-ordinated by an 'inspector of the special duty troops' (*Inspekteur der SS-Verfügungstruppe*), a former Reichswehr general with an office similar to a division staff. Two SS officer candidate schools (*Junkerschulen*) trained officers for the *Verfügungstruppe* in one-year courses. With an enrolment of about 300 cadets, the schools passed out each year more SS officers than the militarised units required. This 'over-production' of officers after 1934–5 was certainly not unintentional and was another indication of the long-term interest of the SS leaders in the creation of their own efficient, broadly based military force which would at least equal the best army units. Consequently the training and education of the SS officer cadets concentrated primarily on the requirements of the military profession. Instruction at the academies consisted mainly of military subjects and practical weapons and combat training, similar to the officer academies of the army.[13] Although ideological indoctrination also played a significant role, it had less importance as a special subject than as part of the attempt to create an SS mentality with the ultimate aim of producing a specifically National Socialist type of professional soldier.

According to Blomberg's order of 24 September 1934, the young SS officers trained in this way should have been assigned to the SS *Verfügungstruppe*. As, however, the academies produced many more officers than were required, more and more of them were transferred to other branches of the SS or the police after finishing their courses. In 1937, for example, only 24 per cent of the academy graduates returned to the *Verfügungstruppe*, whereas 40 per cent served as police officers, 12 per cent in the SS high command, 10 per cent in the Death's Head units or the concentration camps, 4 per cent in the security service and 7 per cent in the regional staffs of the general SS.[14] The transfer of fully militarily trained SS officers to non-military branches of the SS and the police had two primary aims: firstly, it was intended to create, quietly and inconspicuously, officer reserves not included in the quota of the *Verfügungstruppe* and outside the sphere of authority of the Wehrmacht; secondly, it was well suited to strengthening the contacts between the various branches of the SS and the police and thus preserving the unity of the SS as a whole; this, in Himmler's view, was an essential ingredient in its struggle for political power.

The success of the SS in making its armed units into a 'second bearer of arms' was reflected in Hitler's decree of 17 August 1938.[15] It had been Himmler's policy since 1934 gradually to free the *Verfügungstruppe* from the limitations placed on them by the army, and Hitler himself now gave this policy his approval. Although it is certainly an exaggeration to describe the decree of August 1938 as the 'birth certificate of the SS',[16] it did emphasise the military role of the SS much more strongly than had Blomberg's directive of September 1934.

Two points are important here. Firstly, in the directive of 1934 the formation of the *Verfügungstruppe* was justified by explicit reference to their special internal tasks; there was no mention of the SS being an independent military force. In his negotiations with the army high command, as we have seen, Himmler also refrained from making such a demand. But the situation in August 1938 was quite different. The war preparations had entered a decisive phase, and the

SS now had a significant armed force at its disposal, whether the army high command liked it or not. The balance of political power between the SS and the army leadership had shifted. Whereas the SS had been able to expand its power constantly, in 1938 the army leaders were facing their most difficult crisis. With the removal of its commander-in-chief, General von Fritsch, who had fallen victim to an intrigue in which the SS was involved, and the resignation of its chief of staff, General Beck, during the Sudeten Crisis in August, the army lost two of its most determined opponents of the SS. Hitler's decree of August 1938 shows that Himmler certainly understood how to take advantage of the opportunity of the moment. In the document, which was based on a draft by the Reichsführer SS, the internal function of the militarised units was mentioned again but, a year before the outbreak of the war, this very general reference had little more than formal significance. Far more important was the fact that mention was made of the prospect of using the *Verfügungstruppe* as mobile troops at the Front during wartime. Indeed the SS units were completely integrated into the mobilisation plans of the army in 1938–9; they also participated in the German annexations of the Sudetenland and Austria. In the conflict with the army, the balance had obviously shifted in favour of the SS. The question was no longer *whether* the 'asphalt soldiers' would be used as a single unit at the Front during wartime but only *how* they should be employed. The army high command wanted to combine them as far as possible with the army; Himmler's goal, on the other hand, was to build up a separate SS 'army' which would be connected only very loosely with the regular army, if at all. After the outbreak of the war a compromise was reached. The front units of the Waffen-SS were placed under the operational command of the respective army units, but in personnel and disciplinary matters as well as training, replacements and military justice, they remained attached to the SS.

The second point is that Hitler's August 1938 decree contained another far-reaching decision, which was supplemented by a further enactment of 18 May 1939.[17] This permitted the SS to use the hitherto non-military Death's Head units in military functions. In the event of war, it was planned to turn the guarding of the concentration camps over to older members of the general SS. The Death's Head units thus made available were to provide replacements for the *Verfügungstruppe* and also to form the core of new units. For this so-called 'reinforcement of the SS Death's Head units' the SS was to be allowed to recruit an additional 25,000 men, primarily from the ranks of the general SS. Together with the already existing Death's Head units, this produced a second 'SS army' of about 40,000 men within a few months, as it were a replacement army for the *Verfügungstruppe*, with which it was combined in November 1939 to form the Waffen-SS.

This complete transformation of the Death's Head units into a semi-military instrument is the last of a number of examples which show the determination of the SS leadership to build up a qualitatively and quantitatively significant military apparatus of their own in spite of the resistance of the armed forces. Thus the use of the Waffen-SS at the Front and its rapid growth after 1939 cannot be interpreted simply as the results of the necessities of war; rather these developments were the logical consequence of a policy pursued since 1934. However, the war and the decreasing political influence of the army leadership, the main opponent of all SS military aspirations, created extremely favourable conditions for the realisation of that policy. Precisely how favourable is shown by the fact that the total strength of all Waffen-SS units increased by twenty-six times to almost 600,000 men in the five and a half years between early 1939 and the middle of 1944. Compared to 1935 this meant a growth of eighty-fivefold within less than ten years. Thus the war proved to be not the cause but rather a necessary condition for the transformation of the Waffen-SS from an élite Praetorian Guard into a supranational mass army. Because of the extent of this process, which we have already indicated, and its momentum, the numerical expansion also led to far-reaching structural changes in the SS forces.

How was the rapid growth of the Waffen-SS during the war possible after all previous attempts to obtain more volunteers for the SS *Verfügungstruppe* had failed owing to the veto of the armed forces leaders? The SS had three ways of reaching its goals: firstly, it tried to obtain an increase of its quota of conscripts through negotiations with the armed forces high command, which was responsible for the allocation of persons liable for military service. Before 1941 the SS quota was not quite 1 per cent and until that year the negotiations were not very satisfactory; the armed forces needed every man and were not prepared to increase the SS quota.

A second way was to recruit as many volunteers as possible for the Waffen-SS regardless of the quota set by the armed forces. The excess call-ups of course had to be disguised or concealed from the armed forces. This method could be used only to a limited extent and for a short time.

The third way, and in the long run the most successful, for the SS to fill its growing personnel requirements was to tap sources of recruits beyond the borders of the Reich and *ipso facto* beyond the reach of the German armed forces. Possible sources were the millions of Germans living in south-eastern Europe and the Baltic states as well as non-Germans, so-called 'Germanic' volunteers, from the countries occupied by or allied with Germany in western and northern Europe. In the spring of 1940 the first regiments, comprising about 600 'Germanic' volunteers altogether, were formed. This was the first step towards the transformation of the Waffen-SS into a multinational army in which the proportion of German nationals amounted to only about 40 per cent by the end of the war.[18]

This change in the ethnic make-up of the Waffen-SS gave rise to a number of practical and fundamental problems, which cannot be discussed in detail here. Different political expectations of the foreign and so-called *Volksdeutsche* (ethnic German) volunteers, language and motivation difficulties, national or regional conflicts, prejudices and sensitivities, ideological differences and different standards of military training — all resulted in a previously un-known heterogeneity in the Waffen-SS and completely changed its character. In addition to these particular problems, which affected primarily the *Volksdeutsche*, the accelerated expansion of the Waffen-SS produced a large number of very general difficulties which, in their total effect, threatened its inner structure and even endangered its ideological *raison d'être*.

Among the most serious of such wartime developments was the gradual weakening of the voluntary principle. The Waffen-SS never became a conscript army; the idea of the voluntary obligation of the SS man was much too important a part of its self-image as an élite 'order' to permit that. In the totalitarian Volksgemeinschaft, the national-racial community of the Third Reich, however, there were numerous opportunities to exert more or less massive pressure on young people to 'volunteer' for the Waffen-SS. With Himmler's silent consent and without any regard to the protests of the armed forces, SS recruiting offices made increasing use of such opportuni-ties after the outbreak of war. For example, some regiments of the general SS ordered their members to volunteer for the Waffen-SS under threat of punishment if they failed to do so. Members of the Hitler Youth were often prevented from returning home after attending a recruiting programme of the Waffen-SS until they had 'volunteered'. Young men waiting to be called to the armed forces were required to explain why they had not volunteered for the Waffen-SS; occasionally they received special delivery letters in the middle of the night informing them that it was the personal wish of their Führer Adolf Hitler that they join 'his' service. After 1942 these and even more direct methods became the rule.[19]

The *de facto* abandoning of the voluntary principle and the accepting of a growing number of foreigners with very different ideological motivations tended in the long run to dilute the idea of the Waffen-SS as an 'ideological order'. With the loss of this essential foundation and its reduction to an almost exclusively military role, the Waffen-SS was in danger of becoming what Himmler wanted to avoid at any price — a 'fourth branch of the Wehrmacht', in addition to the army, the navy and the air force.

Forced recruiting, poor quality replacements and a shortened training period contributed to the increasing loss of the military-élite quality of the Waffen-SS, which Himmler regarded as a dangerous development. A considerable increase in the formerly very unusual cases of desertion was one symptom of this development, as was the fact that newly organised units of the Waffen-SS occasionally failed in battle, whereas others fought extremely well. One indication of the extreme disparity in performance is the fact that, of all the Knight's Crosses awarded to members of the Waffen-SS, 90 per cent were distributed between less than one-third of the divisions. These differences became more pronounced the longer the war lasted, in the second half of which only a small part of the Waffen-SS was made up of the élite armoured divisions in the tradition of the prewar SS, which formed the backbone of the German forces on the defensive. Poorly equipped and trained divisions, with fighting ability that was at best average, had become more typical of the general picture. In short, with the wave of new formations in 1943, if not before, the Waffen-SS as a whole ceased to be a military élite.

The high casualties suffered by the Waffen-SS were not the least important cause of this development. By the end of 1943 50,000 of its men had been killed, more than double the total strength of the Waffen-SS a year before the outbreak of the war. Most affected by these losses were the prewar militia — the *Leibstandarte*, *Das Reich*,

Totenkopf and *Wiking*. Thus it was the best soldiers of the prewar years from the *Verfügungstruppe* or the Death's Head units who suffered the highest casualties. Because they received preferential treatment in the allocation of personnel and new equipment, these divisions continued to belong to the élite of the German armed forces until the end of the war. As 'fire brigades' they were in almost constant combat on the Eastern, Western and Southern Fronts and established the legendary but, because of numerous atrocities, notorious reputation of the Waffen-SS.[20]

This reputation was purchased at an extremely high price, especially among the officers. According to available but rather incomplete sources, losses among officers amounted to 5 per cent of the total casualties, twice as high as their actual percentage strength.[21] Taken in conjunction with the hasty formation of more and more new SS divisions and army corps and the resulting need for more officers and trained personnel, these losses give us an approximate picture of the shortage of leader cadres in the Waffen-SS. We must also remember that it was primarily ethnic Germans from other countries or foreign volunteers who were recruited for the new units; according to Himmler, however, only about 10 per cent of the required leadership personnel could be provided by these groups.[22] Consequently, German cadres had to be utilised, a method which not only aggravated the lack of leadership cadres in the SS as a whole but also created considerable friction within the units concerned.

The rapid expansion of the Waffen-SS and the simultaneous high losses accelerated the structural change in the ranks of the higher officers. In mid-1944, for example, of all the generals and higher staff officers of the Waffen-SS fewer than half had been on active duty in SS armed units before the war. The result was to undermine the ideological cohesiveness of the senior officers, who in any case differed greatly in social origin and education.[23] In short, and in spite of its military successes, the expansion of the Waffen-SS led to the loss of its distinctive political and ideological make-up. This occurred among the mass of foreigners, *Volksdeutsche* and forced recruits who served in it as well as in its leadership groups. As a whole it did remain a ready instrument of National Socialist policies of conquest and annihilation, but in reality the differences between the front units of the army and those of the Waffen-SS gradually disappeared. The central SS departments endeavoured to stop this development through more political indoctrination and similar measures but achieved no decisive success because of the exigencies of the war.

The structural changes in the military units of the SS were accompanied by changes in the high command, which was thoroughly reorganised and enlarged in 1939–40 in order to cope with the greater complexity and volume of tasks entrusted to them.[24] Although this reorganisation was inevitable, it created a number of persistent problems which were aggravated by the pressures of the war and personnel shortages. Examples can be found in the many conflicts of authority between various old and new departments which, without any clear hierarchy, were all concerned in one way or another with the Waffen-SS: the *SS-Hauptamt* (main office) for personnel data, recruiting, reserves and ideological indoctrination; the *SS-Führungshauptamt* (leadership main office) for military operations, equipment and training; the SS personnel office for officer's personnel files and appointments; the SS high court for all legal questions and the administration of military justice in the SS units. In practice these areas of responsibility were often much less clearly defined than this list indicates. For example, the *SS-Führungshauptamt* had its own personnel office and an office for ideological indoctrination — a situation that was the cause of a feud with the main personnel office and the *SS-Hauptamt* that lasted for years.[25] Such conflicts prevented any real co-operation among the offices concerned, especially in cases where it was urgently necessary; agreement was never reached, for example, in the very important question of what level of growth was both possible and necessary for the armed SS. Instead, the *SS-Hauptamt* attempted to recruit the greatest number of soldiers as quickly as possible, whereas the *SS-Führungshauptamt* sought, usually in vain, to slow the pace of recruiting because of equipment shortages and the very limited training capacity.

It was typical of Himmler's style of leadership that he usually did not attempt to defuse such conflicts of authority and collisions of interest at an early stage by clear, final decisions. Instead, when a conflict became serious, he confined himself to making a one-time decision which was generally determined less by practical organisational considerations than by the ability of individual SS departments to influence him. Such a decision-making process was, on the one hand, typical of the National Socialist leadership principle of avoiding clear, long-range decisions and strengthening the authority of leaders at various levels by encouraging competition among subordinate organs.[26] On the other hand, there were obviously numerous real difficulties which made the SS apparatus increasingly difficult to control. Himmler accumulated so many offices during the war years and his activities became so varied that he could no longer keep track of them.[27] In this situation he became more dependent on his department heads who, for their part, were competing with each other for his favour and doing everything in their power to shield their respective departments from critical outside eyes. Such mutual distrust was certainly not merely a result of personality conflicts; to a considerable extent it was an integral part of the SS leadership structure. In this respect the lack of administrative routine and know-how was as significant as the fact that the central SS departments never had time for continuous development. Himmler's inclination to interfere constantly in the organisational structure of his main departments only strengthened the tendency of the responsible administrative heads to expand their own domains at the expense of other departments. The situation was made more difficult by the fact that, apart from decisions made by Himmler himself, established forms for resolving conflicts in the SS leadership were generally lacking. Under normal circumstances all these factors would probably have been less important, but they prevented the central SS bureaucracy from coping effectively with the demands of the war and an overly ambitious expansion programme. The extent to which this situation impaired the ability of the Waffen-SS to function may be shown by a single example: in the summer of 1942, when Himmler wanted to know the strength of his Waffen-SS, the *SS-Wirtschafts- und Verwaltungshauptamt* (economic and administrative main office) informed him that the number was 270,000 men, the *SS-Führungshauptamt* gave a figure of 220,000 and the *SS-Hauptamt* was not able to provide any information at all.[28]

Why then did the SS leadership pursue such a gigantic expansion of the Waffen-SS if that goal presented so many risks and problems? What was the purpose of this over-hasty attempt to establish a mass army when a more modest programme combined with efforts to maintain the status of an ideological and military élite would have been closer to the original SS ideals? A plausible answer to this question is possible only with reference to the postwar plans of the SS. We can assume that Himmler had a direct personal interest in the two main German war aims, the establishment of a colonial *imperium* in eastern Poland and the Soviet Union and the expansion of Germany into a 'Greater German Empire' through close association with and domination of its western and northern European neighbours. Himmler's statements of this period and the role of the SS in German occupation policy leave no doubt that the SS leadership was determined to become the driving force in the so-called 'new European order' after the war.[29] By seeking to obtain the greatest possible influence on occupation policy, the SS leaders were attempting to decide in advance and in their favour the expected redistribution of offices and responsibilities after the war.

In this situation a strong and omnipresent Waffen-SS was the best guarantee of the consolidation and expansion of SS power. The necessary massive build-up of the Waffen-SS could, as the prewar years had demonstrated, be achieved only under wartime conditions. With this fact in mind, both Himmler and, especially, the chief of the SS central recruiting office, Gottlob Berger, were interested in expanding the Waffen-SS as rapidly as possible during the war. The expansion programme had the additional objective of giving the SS a large number of armed units for the postwar period. Even at an early stage of the war Berger wanted to retain the Death's Head division as well as the SS police division (*Polizeidivision*) after the conclusion of the campaign in the west, even in the event of an extensive demobilisation of the army.[30] A few months later Himmler issued an order that required his personal approval for the discharge of each individual SS officer in case of a demobilisation.[31] In November 1941 he demanded that the Waffen-SS have a peacetime strength of 100,000 men. Together with the normal police and the security police this would result in a 'state defence corps' (*Staatsschutzkorps*) of around 400,000 men.[32] In the summer of 1944 he spoke of twelve armoured divisions and an additional thirty European divisions to be at the disposal of the SS after the war, more than the entire number mobilised during the entire war.[33]

Although Himmler's plans for the postwar period were grandiose, they were not unrealistic (apart from the very important assumption that Germany would win the war), for if Germany had been victorious, the SS could have based its claims to a military role not only on the Waffen-SS but also on the potential of its members who had served in the Wehrmacht. At the end of 1942 there were some 120,000 of them, including approximately 8,000 reserve officers. The SS leadership had good reason to hope that the return of this large number of militarily trained and experienced soldiers to the general SS in the postwar period would make possible a militarisation of the entire organisation and thus a general elimination of the difference between the Waffen- and the 'civilian' SS. This goal is also indicated by the fact that the SS leaders worked out early plans for making *every* SS officer an officer of the army reserve after the war or for eliminating differentials in service ranks and pay resulting from different standards of training and promotion in the Waffen-SS, the general SS and the police.[34]

However, even these were not the limits of Himmler's ambitions to make the SS into a first-class military force. As we have seen, he had earlier perceived the possibility of using the military potential of the neighbouring 'Germanic' states. By very intensive recruiting the SS did succeed, mainly after the attack on the Soviet Union, in attracting some tens of thousands of volunteers from these potential soldiers, but the number never amounted to more than a very small proportion of the population fit for military service in the countries concerned. For this reason, and in a typical combination of military and political considerations, the SS leadership developed as early as the winter of 1942 the plan to form pan-Germanic armed forces on the basis of universal conscription in those countries.[35] These armed forces were to be under the supervision and command of the SS (Hitler appears to have approved this idea) without, however, being a part of it. The reason for this strange organisation was quite simple: the SS wanted to create a mass military base without renouncing its own later reorganisation as a voluntary and select 'order'. This aim also explains why, even during the war, the distinction was made in the Waffen-SS between soldiers actually fit for the SS and their units (so-called SS divisions) and those soldiers who only met the less demanding fitness requirements of the army and who formed the so-called 'volunteer divisions'. While the first group were regarded as destined to form the basis of an ideologically pure postwar Waffen-SS, the volunteer divisions were to form the core of the pan-Germanic army mentioned above. Proof of the seriousness of Himmler's intentions was his attempt to organise a model 'Germanic' SS tank corps (III SS Panzerkorps) in the spring of 1943.[36]

This brief essay provides a comparatively precise definition of the relationship between military and political factors that was typical of the Waffen-SS. There can be no doubt that, apart from the first few months of its existence, the Waffen-SS was a military organisation intended for military tasks. Thus Priestley's description of its members as, strictly speaking, 'no soldiers at all' was mistaken. However, what made the Waffen-SS unusual from an historical point of view was that it was much *more* than a simple military organisation. In contrast to the armed forces and their role as the legitimate military instruments of the state, the Waffen-SS, though supported by the state, was the military instrument of the National Socialist movement. Its military achievements, indeed its whole existence, were thus inseparably connected with the political goals of the SS, the establishment of a new racial and ideological order in Europe. The military activities of the SS, its concentration camps, its policy of deportation and mass annihilation, its occupation and economic policies were all different expressions of a single political will, although the individual soldier in the Waffen-SS may not have been aware of this fact. The destruction of the National Socialist regime and its vanguard, the SS, thus also meant the end of the Waffen-SS, although not of the German military tradition.

Notes

1. J.B. Priestley, 'Macht es Montag' ['Make it on Monday'], radio talk on 19.7.1943. (National Archives, Washington D.C.: Microfilm Series T-175/roll 56/–1669). Quotation (including title) here transl. from a German version of the original English transcript.
2. Thus the title of a book by one of the best-known generals of the Waffen-SS, P. Hausser, *Soldaten wie andere auch. Der Weg der Waffen-SS*, Osnabrück, 1966.
3. A survey of the older literature is given by K.O. Paetel, 'Der Schwarze Orden. Zur Literatur über die SS', in *Neue Politische Literatur*, (1958), pp. 263ff. as well as in R. Koehl, 'The Character of the Nazi SS', in *Journal of Modern History*, 34 (1962), pp. 275ff. For the more recent literature see B. Wegner, 'Die Garde des "Führers" und die "Feuerwehr" der Ostfront. Zur neueren Literatur über die Waffen-SS', in *Militärgeschichtliche Mitteilungen*, 23 (1978), pp. 210–36.
4. On the most important campaigns of the Waffen-SS see F. Duprat,

Les Campagnes de la Waffen-SS, 2 vols., Paris 1972, 1973.

5. Order by Th. Eicke of 6.4.1936, Ziff. 5 (National Archives: Microfilm Series T-175/roll 96/ — 6458ff.)

6. Thus, for instance, in the directives of the Reich Defence Minister of 24.9.1934 (Bundesarchiv – Militärarchiv: H 1/323), printed in Hausser, *Soldaten* pp. 232ff.

7. A colourful survey of the great variety of the SS activities can be found in H. Höhne, *Der Orden unter dem Totenkopf. Die Geschichte der SS*, Gütersloh, 1967. Overview also in B. Wegner, 'The Aristocracy of Nazism. The Role of the SS in Nationalsocialist Germany', in H.W. Koch (ed.), *Aspects of the Third Reich*, London, 1985.

8. On the struggles between the Army and the SS in the 1930s see also K.-J. Müller, *Das Heer und Hitler. Armee und nationalsozialistisches Regime, 1933 bis 1940*, Stuttgart, 1969, pp. 147ff., and B. Wegner, *Hitlers Politische Soldaten: die Waffen-SS 1933–1945. Studien zu Leitbild, Struktur und Funktion einer nationalsozialistischen Elite*, Paderborn, 1982, pp. 84ff., 113ff. (To be published in English by Basil Blackwell, Oxford, at a later date.)

9. See note 6 above.

10. An excellent illustration of this is to be found in a number of documents on these proceedings which have meanwhile been published. See also K.-J. Müller, *General Ludwig Beck. Studien und Dokumente zur politisch-militärischen Vorstellungswelt und Tätigkeit des Generalstabschefs des deutschen Heeres 1933–1938*, Boppard a.Rh., 1980, pp. 372ff. (Doss. 14a–d).

11. See Wegner, *Politische Soldaten*, p. 104 (Tables 2 and 3).

12. Ibid., pp. 105ff.

13. Ibid., p. 160 (Table 7). See also the account by the former *Junkerschulen* commander which contains many details, but barely lives up to the minimum standards of scholarship: R. Schulze-Kossens, *Militärischer Führernachwuchs der Waffen-SS. Die Junkerschulen*, Osnabrück, 1982.

14. Wegner, *Politische Soldaten*, p. 142 (Table 6).

15. Hitler's decree of 17.8.1938 (Bundesarchiv: NA 19/neu 1652), printed in Hausser, *Soldaten*, pp. 252ff. (doc. 6).

16. Höhne, *Orden*, p. 414.

17. Hitler's decree of 18.5.1939 (Bundesarchiv: R 2/12 172a).

18. On the recruitment policy of the Waffen-SS see especially G.H. Stein, *Geschichte der Waffen-SS*, Düsseldorf, 1967, pp. 31ff., 39ff., and 87ff.; see also G. Rempel, 'Gottlob Berger and Waffen-SS Recruitment, 1939–1945', in *Militärgeschichtliche Mitteilungen*, 27 (1980), pp. 107–22.

19. Detailed references in Wegner, *Politische Soldaten*, pp. 273ff.

20. A critical appraisal of the military achievements of the Waffen-SS is offered above all by Stein, *Geschichte*, and with reference to the individual divisions, by J.J. Weingartner, *Hitler's Guard. The Story of the Leibstandarte SS Adolf Hitler, 1933–1945*, London/Amsterdam 1974; see also C. W. Sydnor, jr., *Soldiers of Destruction. The SS Death's Head Division, 1933–1945*, Princeton, 1977.

21. This, at least, applies to the first half of the war; see also 'Zusammen-

stellung der Verluste der Waffen-SS', n.d., possibly Spring 1942 (National Archives: Microfilm Series T-175/roll 106/ — 9348f.).

22. Speech by Himmler on 28.1.1944 (National Archives: Microfilm Series T-175/roll 94/ — 4800f.).

23. More detailed, Wegner, *Politische Soldaten*, pp. 207–59, and idem, 'Das Führerkorps der Waffen-SS im Kriege', in H.H. Hofmann (ed.), *Das Deutsche Offizierkorps 1860–1960*, Boppard a.Rh., 1980, pp. 327–50. For the prewar years see the comprehensive study by G.C. Boehnert, unfortunately as yet unpublished, 'A Sociography of the SS Officer Corps, 1925–1939', Ph.D. thesis, London, 1977.

24. A good survey of the organisational development of the Reichsführung-SS is given by H. Buchheim, 'Die SS — das Herrschaftsinstrument', in H. Buchheim et al., *Anatomie des SS-Staates*, Olten/Freiburg i.Br., 1965, vol. I, pp. 239ff.

25. Further details in: Wegner, *Politische Soldaten*, pp. 195ff. and 269ff.

26. On this controversial issue, see also generally: P. Hüttenberger, 'Nationalsozialistische Polykratie', in *Geschichte und Gesellschaft*, 2 (1976), pp. 417–42, as well as the anthology by G. Hirschfeld/L. Kettenacker (eds.), *The 'Führer State': Myth and Reality. Studies on the Structure and Politics of the Third Reich*, Stuttgart, 1981.

27. In October 1939 Himmler was appointed "Reichskommissar für die Festigung deutschen Volkstums", in August 1943 he became Reich Minister of the Interior. Following the destruction of the Military Intelligence Service (*Abwehr*) he commanded from February 1944 the only secret service organisation in the Reich. After the July 1944 Plot he was also put in charge of the Reserve Army. He also became *Chef der Heeresrüstung*, commanded the anti-partisan units and the newly formed *Volksgrenadier* Division. Finally he supervised the POW Administration.

28. On the correspondence in question see National Archives: Microfilm Series T-175/roll 33/ — 2226ff.

29. On this see also the forthcoming contribution by H. Umbreit in *Das Deutsche Reich und der Zweite Weltkrieg*, edited by Militärgeschichtliches Forschungsamt, vol. 5: *Strukturen der Kontinentalherrschaft*, Stuttgart (ca. 1986).

30. Berger to the Reichsführer-SS, 3.7.1940 (National Archives: Microfilm Series T-175/roll 104/ — 6156).

31. Order by Himmler of 17.3.1941 (National Archives: Microfilm Series T-175/roll 189/ — 7601).

32. W.D. Noack, 'Sind Offiziere der Waffen-SS berechtigt, Dienstgrade der Wehrmacht zu verwenden?', in *Das Militärarchiv im Bundesarchiv*, part 7 (Nov. 1965), pp. 13f.

33. Speech by Himmler on 3.8.1944, at Posen, printed in *Vierteljahreshefte für Zeitgeschichte*, 1 (1953), esp. p. 393.

34. On this see above all a *Denkschrift* by the Chef des SS-Personalhauptamtes of 30.8.1940: 'Vorschläge für die Vorbereitungen zum Wiederaufbau der Schutzstaffel nach Beendigung des Krieges in personeller Hinsicht.' (Bundesarchiv: NS 19 / neu 414).

35. Further details, and references in B. Wegner, 'Auf dem Wege zur

pangermanischen Armee. Dokumente zur Entstehungsgeschichte des III. (germanischen) SS-Panzerkorps', in *Militärgeschichtliche Mitteilungen*, 28 (1980), pp. 101–36.
36. See also ibid.

GERHARD SCHREIBER

The Mediterranean in Hitler's Strategy in 1940. 'Programme' and Military Planning

Any attempt to define the role of the Mediterranean in German strategy in the period between the cease-fire with France and the invasion of the Soviet Union should be prefaced by two considerations, which should be constantly borne in mind when assessing the views and plans of the Germans between June 1940 and June 1941.[*]

On the one hand, reference should be made to Hitler's 'Programme'. This was the term he used expressly to describe[1] his political ideas.[2] Although formulated in his mind in 1919, once put into writing, of course, his Programme did not represent an inflexible sequence of political and military campaigns for arriving at world domination. In fact, where the interpretation of Hitlerian policy is concerned, the term 'Programme' and its adjective 'programmic' should be used — in Andreas Hillgruber's sense — rather as heuristic aids, where the point of departure should be the sum of all demonstrable motives and objectives.[3] Furthermore, in the case of Hitler's Programme, it should be stated that, throughout, the main thrust[4] of the content is closely linked with the need to provide Germany with 'Lebensraum' or living space — space that would be won by the conquest of European Russia.[5] At the same time, it recognised the Mediterranean as a zone of Italian influence,

[*]The German original of this article appeared in *Militärgeschichtliche Mitteilungen*, 28(1980), pp. 69–99.
Transl. from the German by Marianne Howarth.

so that this area did not represent an objective, as such, in Hitler's strategy.[6] This is an important factor in the evaluation and historical categorisation of the operation of the war, as conceived by German Chiefs of Staff for this area in the summer of 1940.

On the other hand, it should be stressed that after the victory in the West, Hitler was recognised as a political and military leader.[7] This fact was falsified, after the defeat of 1945, by some German generals seeking to prove[8] that Hitler's strategic incompetence had to some extent hindered their chances of victory.[9]

Without in any way wishing to discharge the élite members of the political, military and economic leadership of their historical responsibility,[10] it can be stated that German strategy at that time was exclusively Hitler's strategy. The various advisers, advisory groups and chiefs of staff were left increasingly behind in the wake of their Führer's long-term objectives — although it would be too far-reaching an exegesis of Hitler to describe them as a *quantité négligeable*. Taken as a whole, these objectives provide the only relevant frame of reference within which there is a historical place for every measure considered as a possible solution for the political and military dilemma in which the Germans found themselves. Thus, the question of the significance of the Mediterranean in German strategy requires us first to review the objectives Hitler actually pursued from 1940. Together with an outline of the most important operational and military plans there will then be an analysis of whether and to what extent these plans can shed some light on the connection between actual German strategy in 1940 and the Programme.

As early as 5 November 1937, during a discussion with the leaders of the Wehrmacht in the Reichskanzlei, Hitler outlined the purely instrumental function of the Mediterranean in the realisation of his foreign policy concept.[11] Given the diversion strategy ploy outlined at that time, the German–Italian Steel Pact of 22 May 1939[12] and German endeavours to persuade Mussolini to enter the war in August 1939[13] must also be taken into account. All in all, it can be established that until the summer of 1940 Hitler's prime concern was to exert strategic pressure on Britain and France via the Mediterranean. As it then began to emerge that the sensational successes of the Wehrmacht would not spell an end to the war but would actually lead to a deeper involvement in it, something of a reappraisal seems to have taken place in Hitler's attitude to the Mediterranean.[14] However, when a strictly limited operation by the

Wehrmacht in this area was considered, that did not imply a change in the objective itself. This development, which may be discerned from June 1940 onwards, was encouraged by the fact that when Italy entered the war the Mediterranean became an area of operation for the Axis powers.[15] The changed situation in Europe also meant that Spain moved closer to Germany, and this opened up additional perspectives for German foreign policy from June 1940.[16]

All the same, the initial German response to the new situation was somewhat cautious.[17] This may well be explained by Hitler's confident expectation, following the fall of France, of reaching agreement with Britain on the 'basis of the division of the world'.[18] Although this may not be a literal quotation of Hitler's words,[19] it does express the dominant conviction shared by his closest advisers concerning his subsequent political intentions. This historical analysis of Hitler's policy up to 31 July 1940 does not actually require concrete statements on the details of such a 'plan of division' to have been made.[20] Nothing was actually written down at the time. In any case, the Secretary of State, von Weizsäcker, could hardly have assumed that it would be sufficient grounds for an Anglo-German agreement for the British to withdraw from the mainland of Europe and leave it to the Germans.[21] Of prime importance here is the fact that an agreement with Britain actually *was* an aim. Early German thoughts on how to increase military pressure on London by adding the Mediterranean to German strategy in the war of supplies against the British Isles, did not conflict with the envisaged compromise. Instead, they were intended to force the British into accepting that compromise, if necessary.[22] Finally, and the available sources permit little reasonable doubt on this, all moves by the German political leadership in the weeks between May and July 1940 must be interpreted in the light of Hitler's repeatedly stated intention: that as soon as an agreement with Britain was reached,[23] he would devote himself to his real objective — the Soviet Union. Originally advanced by Gerhard L. Weinberg in 1953,[24] this aspect of research has been qualified subsequently, but also in general confirmed.[25] To repeat the details here would be superfluous, but the facts will be summarised to assist an appropriate evaluation of German strategy in the Mediterranean. From them it emerges that before the victory in the west Hitler had already expressed his resolve to attack the Soviet Union as soon as possible.

For example, Weizsäcker noted on 23 May 1940 that, whether London was ready for peace immediately or whether a German air offensive would be required to force peace, there would probably be a 'further reckoning' in the East. He spoke of the 'East, where there is a space [*Raum*] and fluid frontiers', of a new order which the German Reich would establish there — as in the rest of Europe — and with which the 'other continents' would have to come to terms.[26] Even leaving aside the fact that the 'first reckoning' had already taken place, in Poland, other statements by the Secretary of State suggest that he understood the direction of German intentions. The Balkans and south-eastern Europe cannot have been the targets of the military action he meant.[27] Certainly, the situation in the south-east could have been used to justify a resolution of basic 'Eastern problems' — and Weizsäcker spoke of them; the dynamics that the war itself was beginning to develop did not escape him. All the same, his remarks contain no indication that the proposed measures were considered particularly urgent. There was no feeling of being under campaign pressure at that time, even though the secretary of state was fully acquainted with the pragmatic actions of Soviet policy. Moreover, his note does not imply anything to suggest that this proposed 'further reckoning' was reactive in character. On the contrary, the diction seems to indicate that Weizsäcker knew what was at stake, namely the conflict with the Soviet Union — that is, an undertaking planned long in advance, motivated by ideology and power politics.

On 2 June 1940 Hitler is said to have informed some of his escort to *Heeresgruppe A* in Charleville that, after the anticipated peace with Britain, he would at last 'be able to concentrate on [his] major and real task: the conflict with Bolshevism'.[28] However, this piece of information given by General von Sodenstern fourteen years after the event contradicts a statement made by Lieutenant-Colonel i. G. Böhme. According to this statement, on 25 June, in the Führer headquarters at Bruly-le-Pêche, Hitler did describe the struggle with the East as Germany's remaining task; but he also said that he might only 'take it on in ten years', and that it was entirely possible he might even have to leave it to his successor.[29]

There is certainly room to doubt Sodenstern's information, because fourteen years is a long time where human memory is concerned. But one should not seek to confirm one's reservations about Sodenstern's account by uncritically accepting Böhme's information, which is also merely a personal recollection[30] — and furthermore, one first voiced twenty-six years after the event. The fact that Sodenstern's recollection corresponds with statements made by sources closer in time to the event counts in his favour, which cannot be said for Böhme. For instance, on 30 June Weizsäcker informed the chief of the army general staff that in Hitler's view there would probably be a need for a further show of German military strength, after which London should probably be ready to make concessions and leave Berlin 'the rear clear for the East'. Feelings of being under threat did not feature in this context either, as the secretary of state's subsequent statements prove, even though these are brought forward time and again. If one believes Weizsäcker, Hitler was perfectly happy with the Soviet Union's mode of behaviour,[31] and at the very same time was contemplating aggression against it in the near future. Nevertheless, the 'English Question . . . and the Eastern Question' were already the main focus of the operational statements of the General Staff on 3 July 1940. Thus, in these quarters, preliminary thought was being given to the 'military attack on Russia' even before Hitler gave formal orders for an operation of this kind.[32]

For an analysis of Hitler's strategy in the second half of 1940, it is possible, therefore, to establish that Hitler clearly regarded the victory in the West with an eye to the East. Further, it should be pointed out that despite some unresolved questions in German-Soviet relations and the pragmatic exploitation of the war situation by the Soviet Union,[33] there was no acute threat then to vital German interests, nor was there a serious fear of one on the part of the Germans.[34] It must also be borne in mind that until approximately mid-July (and this can be substantiated), Hitler was expecting the early conclusion of an Anglo-German agreement, which would have eliminated definitively a military danger to Germany in the West.

This means that Moscow's chances of applying pressure on Berlin in the event of continuing Anglo-German hostility — the view put forward by proponents of the preventive war thesis — would have disappeared. Thus it also becomes clear that Hitler was intending to commence his attack on the Soviet Union under conditions which would have rendered his subsequent argument in justification of the Eastern campaign (namely, that it was a question of attacking London via Moscow) just as baseless as the alleged need[35] (in view of the British refusal to take up his peace offer) to 're-neutralise' the United States of America.[36] Originally, therefore, Hitler considered war with the Soviet Union in a situation in which he undoubtedly would not have been under pressure to campaign. Only one causal motive can be singled out for his intention: the idea, outlined in his Programme, of gaining Lebensraum in the East.[37] When analysing Hitler's decision of 31 July 1940, we must remember that he was working on the realisation of the core of his racial-ideological Programme at a time when he was also expecting a clear rear to the West.[38]

Let us now turn to the military concept following the cease-fire with France. In his study dated 30 June 1940 of the possibilities available to him of 'Continuing the War against Britain', the chief of the Wehrmacht command,[39] General (as he later became) Jodl, first included the Mediterranean as a theatre of war for the Wehrmacht in German operational planning.[40] In the course of time, these early considerations formed the conceptual framework for most of the later ideas on a German war operation in the Mediterranean, but they should be seen at that period in the context of the peace compromise Hitler sought with Britain.[41] Unlike the view held from the end of August — especially by the German Navy — the Mediterranean remained an ancillary theatre of war for Jodl. He regarded it simply as a further set of ways and means of making the British ready for peace. His priorities remained the war of supplies[42] and the preparations for the invasion of Britain.[43] Apart from that, Jodl was convinced that any 'extension of the war at the periphery' could be mounted only in collaboration with those states with an interest in the break-up of the British Empire. In his view, these included Italy, Spain, Japan and the Soviet Union. He also thought support against Britain from Arab countries was a possibility. However, he rejected direct and comprehensive action on the part of the Wehrmacht in the Mediterranean. His idea was that the Italians and the Spanish should fight for the main operational objectives in this area — Gibraltar and Suez — with limited German support.[44] With this conceptual foundation as its base, a swiftly-formed 'Reconnaissance Staff Gibraltar' began, as early as July 1940, to review the chances of a successful military operation against the Rock.[45] Almost simultaneously, on 16 July 1940, Hitler signed 'Directive No. 16: On Preparations for a Landing Operation against England'.[46] At the same time, though, questions of a central African colonial empire and Atlantic bases for Germany were being discussed further.[47] Finally, among other ideas broached in conversation, Hitler even suggested 'constructing a front hostile to Britain from the North Cape to Morocco'. But in all of this, the only factor to emerge clearly — an established research finding — is his disinclination to launch a direct attack on Britain. Hitler was convinced that the destruction of the British Empire would be of benefit only to the Americans and the Japanese, and not to the Germans[48] — at least not at that stage. This restraint on the British question was well known in political and military circles and in the summer of 1940 it was interpreted, in the German Foreign Office[49] and in the navy high command,[50] as a sign of lingering German reluctance to succeed to the British Empire at that stage.

Whatever Hitler's own attitude, it is indisputable that he saw the basis for achieving his global objectives,[51] not in the destruction of the British Empire, but in the construction of a German continental empire, for which obtaining Lebensraum in the East was a *sine qua non*.[52] Along these lines, he noted in August 1941: 'What India was for Britain, the Eastern Raum will be for us'.[53] And again in September 1942: 'The colonies we shall obtain all over the world will not compare with the East!'[54] This long-term power-political objective was founded on Hitler's racial ideology and therefore, in connection with this, Hitler's decision-making in July 1940 will be considered before turning detailed attention to plans for a German war operation. This is because their place in Hitlerian strategy can be identified only in direct relation to the answer to the question of whether or not, in July 1940, Hitler reached a 'decision' — a final decision, never reversed — on aggression towards the Soviet Union.

In July 1940, appropriately described as the 'real turning-point of the Second World War',[55] Hitler's appraisal of the situation entered a phase in which the United States and the Soviet Union were increasingly cited as an explanation of the continuing British will to resist.[56] As already indicated, there had been a relative deterioration in the situation for the German Reich in July, as a result of British resistance and the growing determination of the American President, Roosevelt, to commit himself unreservedly to London.[57] All the same, there can be absolutely no doubt that when Hitler was initiating the preparations for the military solution of the so-called Russian problem, he did so because he wanted to follow his pro-grammic motivation, and not because he had to as a result of some objective constraint or other.

It should be remembered, moreover, that there were no 'indi-cations' to suggest 'Russian activity' against Germany.[58] Certainly, alongside Halder's note that the 'Russians are afraid of compro-mising themselves with regard to us and do not want a war', and the observation that Stalin was demonstrating a 'pleasing rejection' of

Britain, there is also a note that on the Soviet side there was a 'call [for] war against Germany'. It is very unlikely that an entry of this kind was an expression of concern about the Soviet Union, because almost invariably the Germans underestimated Soviet military strength. An attack on the Soviet Union did seem something of a risk, however, since it would create a war on two fronts. So what Halder's diaries actually express — apart from speculative suspicion arising from the ideological clash of the National Socialist and Soviet regimes — is a fundamental lack of confidence about the possibility of regulating relations between Berlin and Moscow peacefully and permanently. On reading the remarks for 21 July, one gains the strong impression that even then, priority was being given[59] to the military solution in the East, over other attempts to break the dilemma of the German war operation.

A number of models which have been put forward to explain Hitler's turn against the Soviet Union could lead one falsely to assume that constraints of a power-political nature in German–Soviet relations were the primary cause of the change in direction of Hitler's policy. In reality, though, the sources, even all together, illuminate only some aspects of political development. They do not in fact negate Hitler's decision to turn his attention to the objective he had always aimed for, even under conditions which he had originally sought to avoid. In no way, though, do they explain the reason for this decision. On this point it can be fundamentally established that a very clear distinction must be drawn between the appraisals of the situation undertaken in Hitler's circle but which did not always reflect his view, and the factors Hitler himself claimed to perceive. In any case, the arguments he advanced in July not only fitted in easily with his programmic considerations, but also tended to camouflage them,[60] which could have been of great psychological and propaganda advantage.

All the same, some officers seem to have realised what really lay behind the discussions in July 1940 on the continuation of the war. This is indicated by some significant remarks, such as that made by the chief of the operations department of the *Seekriegsleitung* (director of the war at sea), Rear Admiral Fricke. On 28 July, in his *Betrachtungen über Russland* (Observations on Russia), he remarked laconically that the 'chronic danger' of Bolshevism must be 'removed somehow or other'.[61] On 29 July, Jodl told his chief of the civil defence department in the Wehrmacht command, General (as he later became) Warlimont, and three other officers on this staff, of

Hitler's determination to remove the threat Fricke had inveighed against 'once and for all'.[62] Since Jodl, in revealing this information, was contravening one of Hitler's orders, there can be no doubt that he was convinced of the seriousness of the intent.[63] He countered the objections of his subordinates, who pointed out the risk of a war on two fronts, with the statement that there could be no discussion of 'the Führer's decisions'. Further, it must be emphasised that Jodl did not seek to explain Hitler's deviation from previous strategic principles by reference to political or military constraints, but rather as follows: 'The Führer is afraid that after a victory over England, the mood of the people will no longer enable him to start a new war against Russia'.[64] Even if this is not a literal quotation, the tone of this statement of Jodl's shows once again that in the summer of 1940, Hitler was envisaging war with the Soviet Union solely because he wanted war as a matter of principle, and thought the time was right. In direct consequence of the 'briefing situation' of 29 July, Warlimont was set to work on the *Befehl 'Aufbau Ost'* (Command Preparations East), by means of which preparations were to be initiated without delay for the transport, deployment and accommodation of the mass of the army and Luftwaffe, in the somewhat inaccessible communication network of the occupied territories in the west of Poland.[65] Only by disregarding the connection between Jodl's information and the *Aufbau Ost* order is it possible to sustain the illusion that the latter does not express an intention to attack the Soviet Union, and that it really referred to 'setting up this newly-occupied Polish territory as a future border area, by expanding the railways, roads, troop accommodation, airports, etc.'.[66] After it then emerged that the attack on the Soviet Union could not take place in the autumn of 1940, but only in the spring of 1941, all time constraints on the preparations for aggression were lifted. Large-scale troop movements that were too premature were ruled out on camouflage grounds, as the *Aufbau Ost* order also stated. All the same, the theoretical and practical arrangements for the organisation of the campaign, and the planning of the operations intended, started in the summer of 1940 and were not halted at any time up to June 1941.[67]

It was during Hitler's conversation with Brauchitsch, Jodl, Keitel and Raeder on 31 July 1940,[68] the main focus of which was primarily Operation Sea Lion, that the 'decision' to 'smash' the Soviet Union in May 1941 was finally taken. Hitler was reckoning on a campaign of five months' duration, the objective of which was

obviously not meant to be a conventional victory but the 'destruction of the life force of Russia'.[69] In itself, this choice of words
should have alerted his audience to the fact that no normal war was
imminent,[70] but rather 'the most terrible war of conquest, enslavement and destruction known to modern history'.[71] Hitler was
preparing to implement his racial-ideological programme.

This decision of 31 July represented a decisive step on 'Hitler's
way towards "his" war'.[72] Repeated attempts have been made to
call it into question, both where its character is concerned and in
terms of what it says about the nature of the Second World War,[73]
even though events before and political and military deliberations
afterwards show that Hitler had definitively decided upon an attack
on the Soviet Union.[74] This does not mean that he was later unable
to make detours or to adjust the timing: it is well known that Hitler
remained flexible on tactical questions until well into the war.
Finally, in order to arrive at a proper assessment of Hitlerian
strategy, it is necessary to bear both of the following in mind: his
ability to adapt his policy to constraints and his ideologically-
founded long-term aims, which were described as inalienable. A
review of this kind shows, and especially for the second half of
1940, that the decision of 31 July meant what it is said.

However, one cannot interpret Hitler's decision-making in the
summer of 1940 in a relevant way, if the historical development is
broken down into the individual stages of a foreign policy process
of action and reaction, without also asking questions about the
long-term origins of certain actions, and where they were supposed
to lead to and why. If the questions whence and whither are kept in
sight as questions about the history of the Third Reich, this history
becomes — with a little give and take — a documentation of Hitler's
programmic desires. The surviving documents make it quite clear
that, to make the attack on the Soviet Union an *idée fixe* for Hitler,
there was no need for his entourage to 'have a word in his ear'.[75]
Only by ignoring the ideological character of Hitlerian policy is it
possible to dismiss his political manoeuvres and military preparations from May 1940 as a simple reaction to Stalin's behaviour.[76]

Furthermore, it is entirely proper to have reservations about the
argument that in the 'time between 31 July and 5 December 1940
. . . an interest in the military plans of the OKW [Wehrmacht high
command] and the OKH [army high command] for a campaign
against the Soviet Union' on Hitler's part cannot 'be proved'.[77]
There are in fact numerous pieces of evidence to prove Hitler's

'interest' either directly or indirectly. For example, on 10 August and 15 September he took a close and intensive interest in Soviet battle strength in connection with a plan of attack.[78] At a meeting with Raeder on 6 September he discussed the most propitious point in time for aggression in the East. On that occasion, Hitler promised to make the OKW take into account the ideas of the commander-in-chief of the German navy (ObdM) with regard to setting the date, which proves at least that he was informed about and indirectly involved with the planning process.[79] It has been established, moreover, that he had direct influence on the drafting of the *Aufbau Ost* order, the camouflaging of military measures directed against the Soviet Union.[80] Finally, on 4 November, when he was obviously talking to various members of the military about the Eastern campaign, he gave orders to continue doing everything 'to be ready for the grand reckoning' with the Soviet Union. Similarly, work proceeded on the 'Preparations East'.[81]

To summarise: on 31 July 1940, Hitler set in motion a process by means of which — and in accordance with his Programme – he sought to make Germany the 'master of Europe and the Balkans', while at the same time wanting to rob Britain both of her last potential ally on the Continent and of hope of support from the United States. In his view, the defeat of the Soviet Union would necessarily lead to an increase in the political power of Japan, thus affecting American security interests, in consequence of which it would no longer be possible for the United States to ally herself in Europe. All in all, for Hitler at the end of July 1940, the war had taken on a global dimension.[82]

To return now to the Mediterranean, it becomes clear that its role in the German war operations of June and July 1940 was seen in the light of the peace compromise sought with Britain. It is with this in mind that one must interpret Hitler's readiness, expressed on 16 June to Vigon, the Spanish chief of the general staff, to engage in military action on the southern European front, given certain circumstances.[83] The same applies to his conversation on 1 July with Alfieri, the Italian ambassador, in which he offered the engagement of a portion of the German Luftwaffe in the Eastern Mediterranean.[84]

German interest in direct influence on developments in this area increased on 3 July, [85] when the British fleet attacked French naval forces in Mediterranean ports. A few days later, on 7 July, Hitler repeated his offer of military support for Italy in a conversation with Ciano. He was exaggerating when he claimed that his staffs had 'already seriously considered' the capture of Gibraltar, but on this occasion he did cite to the Italian foreign minister the central condition for realising intentions of this kind — namely, Franco's agreement![86]

In fact the Generalissimo's reservations about a military escapade while the defeat of Britain was not yet assured, together with Mussolini's negative attitude (which can be explained by his endeavours for national independence), acted as a barrier which Hitler had to overcome before he could send his armies to the Mediterranean. The use of force did not enter into it, simply because it was too risky. Given the position adopted by Washington and London on the Spanish question, Berlin did not even have at its disposal any effective means of applying pressure. A snub to Italy was ruled out *per se*. The only possible option was the diplomatic route. But taking this course meant seeking agreement not only with Madrid and Rome but also with Vichy, because otherwise there was a fear that the French territories in North Africa — still, then, loyal to Pétain — might actually fall. This would have given the British enormous advantages, and would also have presented the Italian troops with a second front. It was important to bear all these interactions in mind as soon as the eastern and western Mediterranean became areas of operation for the Wehrmacht. However, it soon emerged that any other attempt to balance French, Italian and Spanish interests with one another could meet with success only if Berlin made binding assurances to Vichy on peace conditions. In this respect, Hitler was particularly unwilling to commit himself in any way. However, as this fact came to light only later, the preliminary military studies for the capture of Gibraltar continued, as did those for the support of the Italian forces by German Panzer and Luftwaffe units.[87]

It emerges from Jodl's studies of 30 June that initial plans for a German war operation in the Mediterranean were begun without the pressure of any particular deadline. After 31 July, the preliminary studies concerned were unmistakably geared to the dictates of the Eastern campaign Hitler was now envisaging.[88] It does not seem that this changed in any way until the beginning of 1941, when the Mediterranean area acquired a new strategic quality for the German war operation, as a result of Italian military defeats. Whatever may have been going on in the political arena, operational planning was not affected; it was not interrupted at any time, and the actions proposed were meant to be completed by the spring of 1941.

Since 7 August, the Army group in the Civil Defence Department had been studying the material problems which a Wehrmacht engagement in the Mediterranean was likely to imply. This staff had already expressed its view on similar problems on 30 July, and on 31 July Jodl had proposed sending a Panzer corps to North Africa. The cancellation of Operation Sea Lion, already suspected then, was of relevance in this connection, which is why army, Luftwaffe and navy were jointly considering, in a special working group, the conditions for the capture of Gibraltar.[89]

In the context of these investigations, Warlimont agreed on 8 August to the deployment of German troops in North Africa, remarking that they could be spared until the spring of 1941 if there was not to be a landing in Britain. In so far as one could decide on a dual action, that is, an attack on Gibraltar and the Suez Canal, he thought it possible that the British position in the Mediterranean could be defeated in the winter.[90] A few days later, on 13 August, there was a review of the situation by Jodl, which Keitel outlined to Hitler on the same day. Here much emphasis was placed on breaking the British 'will to resist' by the spring of 1941.[91]

At first sight one could assume that both Jodl and Warlimont were bearing in mind the possibility, mentioned on 21, 30 and 31 July, of not mounting Operation Sea Lion until the spring of 1941.[92] However, this cannot be the case, simply because Hitler had taken a negative line towards such proposals on 31 July; and besides that, it was not until 17 September that the invasion was postponed 'indefinitely'. Then from 12 October, it was included in the calculations as an operational possibility for the spring of 1941;[93] but the two generals could not have suspected any of this in August. On the other hand they did know, from 29 July, that if the landing was not to take place in 1940, Hitler was intending to turn against the Soviet Union — on 31 July he named the precise date for his aggression — so that the 'Luftwaffe, steeled by recent successes in the East [could be] fully available against Britain by the autumn of 1941 at the latest'.[94] This information from Warlimont makes clear what was concerning him and Jodl at that time. Now under considerable pressure of time, they were still trying to obtain something which had seemed theirs for the asking in May and June: a clear rear to the West for the attack on the East, which was why the British 'will to resist' had to be broken by a war operation on the periphery.

In the following weeks, the military staffs drew up operational plans for a German war operation in the Mediterranean. On 13

August, Hitler agreed to a four-phase operation to take Gibraltar, on the assumption that this would meet with Franco's consent.[95] This ran as follows:

1. Binding agreements with General Franco to the effect that with completely camouflaged German participation, Spain would secure the defence against a British advance or a British landing in Gibraltar zone;
2. Surprise attack by strong German Luftwaffe units from the port of Bordeaux on the British fleet in the port of Gibraltar, simultaneous transfer of Stukas and coastal batteries to Spain;
3. Destruction of the harbour port and dispersal of the British fleet by Stukas and coastal batteries;
4. Taking the Rock by land attack and sea attack if possible; in this event, unconditional recognition of Spanish supreme command, but a guarantee that in practice the conduct of the operation would remain in German hands, via the medium of the German commander.

It was on this basis that the 'Operational Plan for the Attack on Gibraltar' was drawn up.[96] At the same time, Hitler was ready to participate in a parallel Italian offensive against Egypt with a modern Panzer brigade.[97] In this context, the organisational department in the German Army High Command reckoned that it would take six weeks to put together the men and materials for a rapid corps for action in North Africa. Of course, this did not mean that they would be actually ready to fight by then.[98] But it can be established that, at a time when the Italians were making the start of their North African offensive directly dependent upon the German landing in Britain,[99] Hitler was urging Wehrmacht participation in the advance on the Suez Canal. Not only did he consider such an operation appropriate for completely 'wresting' from the British their 'power position in the Mediterranean', but also he could see that this was a way of establishing very favourable conditions for the Axis powers' war at sea operations.[100] This thinking also fits in with Hitler's basic attitude at that time, which was either to use military pressure to force London to compromise before the attack started in the East; or to lie low until the victory over the Soviet Union would have robbed Britain of her 'continental sword'.

In the course of these deliberations, the Atlantic also became the focus of German strategy, as the islands there increased in importance as a way of guaranteeing the immediate Front area during the

Eastern campaign. The *Seekriegsleitung* (Skl.), which had clearly
recognised the dangers arising in this area for the various German
war operations that had been co-ordinated with one another, and
referring both to Hitler's statements of 31 July and the civil defence
department's ideas about support for the Italian offensive against
Egypt, remarked in this connection:

> In the view of the Skl., there can be no doubt that British
> preparations for an occupation of the islands are in hand. How-
> ever, actually taking them is something the British are only likely
> to consider in the event of an enforced surrender of Gibraltar and
> of Spain and/or Portugal entering the war. If Gibraltar is lost, an
> immediate British occupation of the islands must be regarded as a
> strategic essential for Britain. Consequently, in the context of
> deliberations about Spain and/or Germany taking Gibraltar, it is
> necessary to consider whether the Canary Islands are adequately
> prepared to defend themselves prior to that event, or at least to
> consider a simultaneous occupation of those islands by German
> troops.[101]

When the danger of a coalition between London and Washington
increased with the so-called Destroyer Agreement,[102] the Skl. again
called for an occupation of the Canaries and the Azores. Raeder was
also concerned about Dakar and north-west Africa.[103] On 6 September he approached Hitler on these problems.[104] In fact, the
invasion of Britain had not yet been officially postponed, but the
commander-in-chief of the navy was already firmly assuming it
would be. He laid particular emphasis on the fact that expelling the
British from the Mediterranean was a decisive strategic measure for
the German war operation. Its success would strengthen the position of the 'central powers in south-eastern Europe, Asia Minor,
Arabia, Egypt and in Africa'. Raeder was counting on access to
limitless supplies of raw materials and was anticipating an advantageous 'point of departure for further actions' against the British
Empire. As in the West, where the conquest of Gibraltar implied an
extension of the German war operation to include the Atlantic
islands, so in the East there was an extension of plans to include the
Indian area. The German navy even thought in terms of threatening
India, and assumed the integration of the Sudan, Egypt and the
Arab territories in the German–Italian economic area.

After Raeder's address, Hitler first expressed his intention of
forestalling the British and the Americans by occupying the Azores,

the Canaries and the Cape Verde Islands. In this context he was probably concerned about protecting his south-western flank and the Atlantic fore-field in view of the attack on the Soviet Union. The civil defence department in the *Wehrmachtführungsstab* was now directed to assemble the documents required for this kind of undertaking.[105] On 22 September an initial study was also presented by the Navy Group which, though subsequently reworked in various ways, then served generally as a basis for further detailed investigations regarding an occupation of the islands in the Atlantic.[106] In the German army high command, attention was also turned to the eventuality of American troops landing in West Africa and on the Atlantic islands. In this connection, Halder approached the German navy with various questions, the response to which (on 10 September) was that these kinds of operations presented 'no problem' to the American forces. In fact, even in the event of a British defeat, there would be no difficulties for the Americans in maintaining the west coast of Africa as an important strategic position for the 'Anglo-Saxon world'.[107]

All in all, in September 1940, the protagonists of a peripheral strategy suggested concentrating German operations in three areas, independently of the continued war of supplies against Britain. They were, firstly, the Near and Middle East as the target of a German–Italian offensive, which would have a profound effect on the African and Indian areas; secondly, the Iberian peninsula, where the capture of Gibraltar would necessarily affect Spain and Portugal; and thirdly, the immediate Atlantic Front area of Europe and West Africa, which raised the question of the role France would play in German strategy.

In August and September 1940, there was no progress worth mentioning in the political or military arenas — especially where the co-ordination of the German–Italian war operation was concerned, which was essential for German intentions. However, the attack mounted by British and Free (anti-Vichy) French troops on Dakar[108] — Operation Menace, 23–25 September — heralded some movement in the rather static situation within the Four Power construct of Berlin–Madrid–Rome–Vichy.[109] As a direct result of French Equatorial Africa going over to General de Gaulle's movement, a more conciliatory attitude on the part of Germany towards the Pétain administration was discernible in August. The German side recognised that French Morocco, Algeria and Tunisia were at risk. In this situation the *Seekriegsleitung* was particularly insistent that everything should be done to strengthen Vichy's influence in French overseas territories.[110] But the relationship between Germany and France was also reviewed benevolently in the Wehrmacht high command.[111] It was only the German army leadership that apparently continued to remain sceptical.[112]

The OKM (German navy high command) feared an Anglo-American advance into the West and North African areas in September. This could have led to incalculable dangers for Italy, so German 'airborne troops and aerial combat forces' were to be transferred to Casablanca to strengthen the French defence. However, the navy leadership was even considering a fundamental revision of Franco–German relations. On this subject the *Seekriegsleitung* commented:

> In pursuing the fundamental war aim of annihilating the British will to fight, and the exclusion of Britain from the European area, it seems to the Skl. that the moment has arrived for joining with the French to secure the African colonial empire and its vital sources of supply for Europe. With a joint war effort against Britain which, once final peace conditions have been established for France (problems of Italian territorial claims must be resolved), is regarded as completely within the bounds of possibility, there is a large likelihood in Skl.'s view of forcing Britain out of the Central African area (by occupying Freetown) and thus to deliver a severe blow to its organisation of supplies (escort traffic from the South Atlantic — South America, South Africa). The realisation of the great operational objective in the Mediterranean — the expulsion of Britain from the Mediterranean — can be greatly facilitated![113]

Thus, within the German navy, it was assumed that a rapprochement with Vichy was almost axiomatic and, following the entry of the United States into the war, it was expected that 'all European countries would join together in the struggle against the Anglo-Saxon Empire',[114] which basically meant nothing other than a conceptual anticipation of the 'war of the continents', reviewed again in 1941!

As far as joining forces with France was concerned, Jodl, Raeder and Warlimont were all more or less of the same opinion. Although aware that their thinking could jeopardise the 'objectives of the war' as pursued to that point, they still wanted to persuade Hitler to adopt the course they proposed.[115] Raeder explained the German navy's views, referred to above, to Hitler on 26 September and in doing so argued 'above and beyond the concerns of his own department'.[116]

Naturally, the Mediterranean was at the centre of statements made by the ObdM, which now urged that the situation in this area should be dealt with in the winter of 1940. On this point, it should be noted that both the 'foreign armies west' department and the German military attaché in Washington, General von Boetticher, reported in August and September 1940 that a well-equipped American army would not be ready for action on the European continent before the middle of 1942.[117] At that time Raeder saw things differently; at least, he stressed again the need to secure the Canary Islands, and he underlined once more the strategic significance which would attach to the capture of Gibraltar and the taking of the Suez Canal. Apart from that, Raeder mentioned the possibility of advancing from Egypt via Palestine and Syria through to Turkey, a concept which he used to formulate the navy high command's alternative to Hitler's strategy. This stated that Ankara in German hands would put a 'completely different complexion' on the 'problem of Russia'. In general, the Soviet Union had a 'basic fear of Germany'; on this point the Grand Admiral agreed with both Hitler and Weizsäcker. He even thought that 'the need for an attack on R.[ussia] from the North' would be questionable, following the implementation of the operations he proposed.

Hitler largely agreed with the ObdM's observations. The fact that, at that particular time, he was tending to follow the plan of his foreign minister (von Ribbentrop)[118] for an anti-British alliance system (now known to history as the *Kontinentalblock*)[119] probably played a decisive role here. The problem of the USA seemed temporarily to dominate in Hitler's strategic calculations when he turned his attention to this interim solution. However, it cannot be stressed clearly enough that the basic intention of aggression against the Soviet Union was varied exclusively and solely for tactical reasons.[120]

Hitler's central objective — based on power politics and racial ideology — remained unchanged. In analysing Hitler's readiness to consider this Realpolitik alliance conception of Ribbentrop's, there is a general impression that he permitted an attempt — without an option — which was actually set in motion in tandem with the preparations for the military solution in the East, but which, significantly, did not place these in jeopardy at any time. Not that this should cast doubt on the seriousness of political actions at that time — at least as far as the rationale of the interim solution mentioned above is concerned — but rather it should be pointed out that Hitler had not in any way made up his mind in favour of the *Kontinentalblock*.

On 27 September 1940, one day after Raeder's address, Germany, Italy and Japan signed the Triple Alliance,[121] which can be seen in political and historical terms as within the framework of Ribbentrop's *Kontinentalblock* policy. For the *Seekriegsleitung*, it was a direct incentive for extensive 'observations on the question of Japan in the Triple Alliance'. This came to the conclusion that Tokyo had first to be steered towards the 'common war objective of the Triple Alliance powers, the downfall of the Anglo-Saxon coalition'. Should any Japanese activities otherwise lead to an early American entry into the war, Germany could easily allow for this, since 'in so far as the naval war operation is affected by it, the sum of the advantages' would outweigh 'that of the disadvantages'.[122] This study highlighted once again the real difference between Hitler's strategic concept and that of the German naval leadership. Both had the international power position of the German Reich as their objective — although its nature was perceived very differently. The German navy followed a strategy designed to serve overseas objectives, and in this the Mediterranean had inevitably to assume special importance. In the OKM, it was believed that the problem of the Soviet Union which the political leadership had brought to the fore could be resolved via London and Washington, because the open questions in German–Soviet relations would sort themselves out following the anticipated victory against the democracies. On the other hand, as already indicated, Hitler's intention was to take the German continental empire route to world power, and the key to this was the Soviet Union. In this context, once the peace compromise he sought with Britain seemed to remain an illusion, Hitler was primarily interested in a stable southern flank, but not in the conquest of the Mediterranean, which would have claimed numerous forces without bringing any serious progress in deciding the war. Correspondingly, in Hitler's view, the *Kontinentalblock* project (which at first sight seems to suggest that he was falling in with the naval leadership's strategic course) actually served only to obtain a clear rear in the West, even if — though only for a short time — that did mean closer co-operation with Stalin.

The diplomatic offensive to realise this intention began on 4 October, with the meeting of Hitler and Mussolini at the Brenner

Pass.[123] On this occasion too, Hitler explained the British will to resist as relying on London's hopes of Washington and Moscow. In terms of the threat thesis, it is interesting that neither he nor Mussolini identified any serious threats to German interests from Soviet policy, although at that time Hitler did express his doubts on the possible success of the attempt to drive Stalin back 'to India or at least the Indian Ocean'. This again confirms that it was not his pragmatic policy of improvements in position that, in the summer of 1940, led Hitler to bring the so-called Russian question into play.

It was entirely in accordance with this that he emphasised, in a conversation with various members of the military on 14 September, that people in the Soviet Union were disappointed by the low German losses in the Western campaign.[124] This fact had worked to Germany's advantage, in so far as it had 'already put a brake on Russia's assault on Finland and the Balkans as a result'.[125] Against this background, he was able to regard future developments 'with some peace of mind',[126] and would not regard a certain amount of tension, for which one would have to allow in the future, as a tragedy.[127] Thus, although Hitler more or less ruled out a threat to Germany from the Soviet Union, he still required his military chiefs to prepare for a war with her.[128] Nor did he change the date — May 1941. Where the threat from the Soviet Union was concerned, this did not feature in his arguments as a whole until after the event, when his statements were characterised first by propaganda in justification, and later by the construction of myths.[129]

However, the focus of the discussion at the Brenner Pass was the intention of 'bringing France and Spain and in this way' constructing 'a continental coalition against Britain'. The solution to the problem — and the two dictators agreed on this — could only be found in a 'grandiose deception', which would have to be primarily at France's expense. As a result, on 20 October, Hitler set off on a round trip, during which he intended to initiate the 'counter-march of Europe against the Western democracies'.[130] But the meetings with Laval (the French deputy prime minister) in Montoire, on 22 October,[131] with Franco in Hendaye on 23 October,[132] and with Pétain, again in Montoire, on 24 October,[133] produced no concrete results. Balancing the interests of the individual states in the form of the 'deception' also seemed to be very difficult. When Hitler went to meet Mussolini directly after these discussions, therefore, he intended not only to prevent the Italian attack on Greece after all,[134] but also to dispose of Italian resentment about Franco-German collaboration and Spain's entry into the war.[135] By the time of his arrival in Florence, it was too late. The aggression against Greece could be delayed no longer. Hitler was annoyed, but under the circumstances he refrained from any criticism of Mussolini. He even offered him a division each of airborne and parachute troops to enable Crete to be protected against a British invasion.[136]

As to the fate of the *Kontinentalblock*, it needs only to be said that the smaller western European version failed by, at the latest, December 1940. However, this date is based on Hitler's appraisal of the situation, not on the objective conditions for realising this intention. By contrast, the major *Kontinentalblock* (which would have led to an interim solution in Hitler's political calculations as a result of including Moscow in Berlin's anti-British alliance system) had been *de facto* abandoned after Molotov's visit to Berlin of 12 and 13 November 1940. But with all such attempts to fix dates, it must be remembered that at the end of October, Hitler had already displayed a tendency to reject his foreign minister's ideas, and once again to accord the 'primacy of the Eastern policy' top priority in German politics.[137]

The military plans for a Mediterranean war operation had hardly progressed to fruition by the day of the Italian assault on Greece. After 28 October, it emerged that the Wehrmacht engagement in North Africa was threatening to become more uncertain than ever. Hitler obviously had little appetite for military co-operation with Mussolini. On the German side, consideration was now being given to an advance to the Aegean from Bulgaria, as an alternative to a Libyan engagement. In addition, Hitler was insisting on the capture of Gibraltar, in which only the Spaniards, not the Italians, were now to participate. Furthermore, he was still toying with the idea of occupying the Atlantic islands — and possibly also Portugal. Here, his general concern — easily recognisable as such — was for stabilisation measures for the German–Italian war operation, not for strategic decision-making in this area.

This could not satisfy the protagonists of the peripheral strategy, because they wanted a good deal more. Warlimont, who was primarily concerned to avoid a war on two fronts, as has been shown, therefore expressed his reservations about the war operation envisaged in the Eastern Mediterranean on 1 November. But Jodl, who in August was still fixated on breaking the British 'will to resist' before the start of the Eastern campaign, was once more operating as Hitler's mouthpiece. He referred to the anticipated stabilisation effect that the fall of Gibraltar would produce, and in any case the proposals for the mining of the Suez Canal and attacks by the German Luftwaffe on the British Alexandrian squadron were unaffected.[138] This concept must have been completely unsatisfactory for the *Seekriegsleitung*, who saw in the Mediterranean an alternative to the war objective of the Soviet Union, and thus went even further than Warlimont's ideas. All in all, the events of the last weeks had prevented the development of a clear command situation for the Mediterranean, with a corresponding definition of the main points. In Hitler's conversations with the OKW, the OKH and the OKL (Luftwaffe high command) on 4 November, it did at least become clear how — in the light of the change in circumstances since 28 October — the political leadership saw the further plans for Wehrmacht action in this area. Hitler now wanted to dispense with the transfer of a Panzer unit to Libya. Quite realistically, he no longer believed that the Italian troops would continue their offensive against Egypt in the foreseeable future. On the other hand, his interest in massive support for Italy in Greece had grown, because since the British landings on Crete and Lemnos he was afraid that incalculable risks could arise there for the Axis powers. Concern about the Romanian oilfields and Turkey particularly worried Hitler. However, he continued to reject the advance to the Suez Canal via Turkey (Anatolia) and Syria, which cropped up in different ways in conversation. Since the end of October, the prime mover for such an operation had been Major-General (as he was then) Paulus, senior quartermaster 1 on the general staff of the German army. But Halder and Brauchitsch also adopted a favourable stance on this question.

On 4 November, Hitler also expressed his further intentions concerning Gibraltar, the Canaries and the Cape Verde Islands. The precondition for any actions in this connection was still Franco's readiness to enter the war. Should it come to an occupation of the Azores, it would be justified to the Portuguese as a preventive measure. To deter Lisbon from supporting London in any way, from even attempting to do so, Portugal would have to be threatened with an invasion by German troops. Directly after the conclusion of operations in the Western Mediterranean, German troops and artillery were to be stationed in North Africa (Ceuta), and the leadership of the entire operation of defending the Straits of Gibraltar would have to be in German hands.

In the *Seekriegsleitung*, whose chief had been informed of Hitler's views by Jodl on 4 November, feeling was now running against the occupation of the Canary Islands, and warnings were being issued against providing the British with an excuse — the invasion of Portugal — for taking military possession of the Azores. Basically, though, following the information from the Wehrmacht high command, all these questions were too significant from the navy's perspective to leave them at that. As a result, the problems associated with them were raised again during Raeder's next review of the situation with Hitler.[139] This conversation of 4 November confirmed once again that plans for a German war operation in the Mediterranean were at a dead end.

The indecisiveness characteristic of crises was also eventually reflected in Directive No. 18, which Hitler signed on 12 November.[140] On the same day he was conducting his first conversation with Molotov.[141]

Directive No. 18 set out the guidelines for the 'preparatory measures of the high command for future war operations'.[142] Substantially, the predominant considerations were those on Wehrmacht engagement on Spanish and Portuguese territory. On a purely formal level, though, the prime concern was the problem of France. In the context of the co-operation now being sought with the French against the British, France, for the time being, was not to be regarded as a warring ally. Of course, France would have 'to tolerate, and where required, support German war measures by mounting its own means of defence'. On the subject of the defence of colonial possessions against the British and the supporters of General de Gaulle's movement, the idea that it might come to the 'participation of France in the war against Britain in full measure' was not ruled out. The intervention of German troops in Spain and Portugal, now described as Operation Felix, was designed on the one hand to assist in the capture of Gibraltar (under discussion since 30 June), and on the other hand to rule out a situation where the British established themselves anywhere on the Iberian peninsula, or on the Spanish or Portuguese Atlantic islands. Hitler now wanted Spanish support in the defence of the Canaries; he regarded the occupation of the Cape Verde islands as worth striving for; and the OKW commissioned a study of a landing both in the Azores and Madeira. Nothing had changed in the conditions for German troop engagement in Libya.

The directive also mentioned military operations in the Balkans; since 4 November, these had been perceived as flank protection for the campaign against the Soviet Union,[143] and were to start out from Bulgaria, with possession of the Greek mainland to the north of the Aegean Sea. On the problem of the USSR and the directive stated specifically:

> Political discussion aimed at clarifying Russia's attitude in the coming period have been initiated. Regardless of the outcome of these discussions, all orders given orally for preparations for the East are to be continued. Directives will follow as soon as the basic outlines of the Army's operational plan have been communicated to and approved by me.

Hitler's interest in the military preparations for aggression against the Soviet Union in the period before 5 December can hardly be demonstrated more strikingly than by this directive. Molotov had scarcely departed when Hitler admitted that he had not been expecting very much from his visit. He did not even consider a 'marriage of convenience' possible between Germany and the Soviet Union. In consequence of the new situation, which confirmed the old state of affairs, the 'command posts' in the East were to be completed with 'all haste', and Hitler intended to set up permanent headquarters in East Prussia.[144] In strict line with these measures, Weizsäcker, who had not initially wanted to rule out a German–Soviet accord directly after the discussions in November,[145] noted on 17 November: 'People are saying that no order can be created in Europe without liquidating Russia'.[146]

In the meantime — as a direct result of the conversation between Fricke and Jodl on 4 November and also prompted by the negative effects which the Italian venture into the Balkans had brought about for the North African theatre of war — the *Seekriegsleitung* had produced a comprehensive review of the situation in the Mediterranean,[147] which served as a basis for Raeder's situation report to Hitler on 14 November.[148]

By way of introduction, the ObdM stated that a development 'decisive for the war' was looming in the Mediterranean, and that this had become possible because of the cancellation of Sea Lion, the military failure of the Axis partners, and American aid and assistance for Britain. In consequence, the British 'will to resist' had already hardened noticeably. However, Raeder undermined the force of his own arguments when he stressed that, because the British still lacked the strength for an offensive, the situation was not actually a cause for concern. Seen in this light, his wish was not to remove an acute and precarious situation, but to take preventive military action, designed to avoid a serious danger for the Axis powers in the Mediterranean. There seemed to be unmistakable signs of this, which is why the Skl. urged counter-measures. The aim of the measures proposed by the ObdM was to drive the British out of the Western and Eastern Mediterranean. That went well beyond Hitler's known intentions, which is why Raeder also sought to make his proposal attractive by referring to the alleged 'decisive significance for the war' which a victory against Britain, and its attendant effects on the African and Asian countries, would imply.[149] On this occasion he repeated his view that Germany would have to respond to the Americans and British joining forces, by setting up a European community of states and taking possession of the African area. The naval leadership had visions of the cotton, copper, oil and foodstuffs of all kinds which a large German-controlled European/African economic area could provide.

In addition, attention was focused on those aspects which affected the security of the German position in the Balkans, as well as questions of Asia Minor, Egypt, Arabia and the Sudan. The attack on the British colonial empire in East Africa and the threat to India represented long-term objectives in a plan which sought the capture of the entire Mediterranean by the Axis powers. The conquest of Gibraltar, the securing of French North Africa against insurrection movements, and the occupation of the Greek mainland were the conditions for achieving this.

Hitler was able to agree to some of Raeder's ideas, because at that time he was considering an autonomous Wehrmacht operation to secure Greece for German interests in about three month's time. But he did reject the Grand Admiral's renewed proposal to attack the Suez Canal from the East. Views were also divided on the question of whether it was sensible and necessary to occupy the Atlantic islands. The OKM had now become very sceptical on this matter, whereas the *Seekriegsleitung* was fundamentally in favour of effectively securing the Canaries. Raeder urged caution on the Portuguese question, in order not to provoke the Americans or the British into occupying the Azores, Angola and the Cape Verde Islands. Of course, arguments of this kind cannot have cut much ice with Hitler, simply because he assumed that the Anglo-Saxons would react to the German advance in Spain by landing on the Azores anyway. He cited another reason that was both revealing and forward-looking for his interest in this group of islands: the Azores would permit him 'to attack America, assuming it entered the war, with a modern Messerschmidt type with a range of 12,600 kilometres, thus compelling it to build up its very inadequate air defences instead of aiding Britain'.[150] So, despite the ObdM's objections, investigations into the defence capabilities of these islands were to, and did, commence without delay.[151]

The last but, in the context of Hitler's strategy, the most important item for discussion was devoted to the problem of the Soviet Union. One day after Hitler's second talk with Molotov, Raeder knew that Hitler still wanted to wage a conflict with her. The Grand Admiral refrained on 14 November — as he had done on 26 September — from indicating alternatives. He was not opposed basically to Hitler's plans for aggression, but simply suggested a 'postponement until after the victory over Britain'. Raeder probably also did not want an immediate conflict with the Soviet Union because, as long as the struggle with Britain was going on, the Navy needed the eastern Baltic as a training and exercise area.[152] This was, in a sense, a specific departmental justification for the basic demand that before the start of a 'spring campaign' against the Soviet Union, 'England' would have to be 'run to ground'.[153]

Thus it is possible to establish for the middle of November that Hitler had completely reverted to the line he had been taking between May and July — that is, he wanted an early military solution to be pushed forward in the East. In the weeks to follow, efforts were now intensified to persuade Spain to enter the war, but these were no longer influenced by the idea of a peace compromise in the West, as they had been. Instead, they were now primarily designed — against the background of threatened confrontation with the United States — to serve the purpose of safeguarding the Mediterranean and north-west African areas against any Anglo-Saxon advance, in view of the Eastern campaign. Alongside this there was also, naturally, another objective — to stabilise the Italian position.[154]

Consequently, plans for the capture of Gibraltar and the defence of the facing North African coast came to the forefront of military preparations for intervention in the Mediterranean. The greatest significance was attached to them, for the purposes of political and military stability in all of north-western Africa. However, once again, the realisation of this kind of objective came up against difficulties, not in the military, but in the political sphere. Thus the conversations Hitler had with the Spanish Foreign Minister, Serrano Suñer, on 18 and 19 November, again failed to result in a concrete agreement that Franco would enter the war.[155] Actually, Hitler seems to have been content with an agreement that entry into the war had not been ruled out. At any rate, he appeared remarkably confident, despite the slowly-growing threat of time being short. In fact, the period allowed for the Balkans operation, which was supposed both to give direct support to Italy and to protect the flank of the Eastern campaign, was clashing with the period allowed for Operation Felix. As it would have been very difficult for the Luftwaffe to support both actions at the same time,[156] the capture of Gibraltar had to be completed before beginning Operation Marita, code-name for the capture of the 'north coast of the Aegean — and if this proves necessary — the whole of the Greek mainland'.[157] To make matters more difficult still, it emerged from the preliminary studies for Felix that the need, on the one hand, for extensive camouflage of the operation, and the idea, on the other, of mounting it as a Blitzkrieg, were mutually incompatible. If conditions of strict secrecy were observed, which also implied camouflaging troop movements on French territory, this meant that thirty-two to thirty-eight days had to be allowed in the plans from the crossing of the Spanish border to the attack on Gibraltar.[158] To reduce this period to a minimum of twenty-five days, Hitler agreed to the suggestion of conducting as many movements in France as possible during the preparatory phase of the operation, even if these could not be camouflaged.[159] The intention was then to dispatch to Spain on 6 December the advance parties for Operation Felix, which had to be completed by the spring of 1941 at all costs.[160]

On 5 December, Admiral Canaris set off for Madrid via Bordeaux, where he briefed the army liaison mission which had been assembled for Gibraltar. On 7 December, the day of his arrival in the Spanish capital, he had a meeting with Franco.[161] At this time, the draft of Hitler's Directive No. 19, relating to Felix, had just been completed. Its implementation depended on the agreement of the Spanish head of state. He alone would decide whether — as planned in the directive — Hitler could give orders for the 'aero approach into Spain' from 10 January, or not.[162]

A discussion had taken place on 5 December between Hitler, Brauchitsch, Halder, Jodl and Keitel,[163] in the course of which Hitler talked in very optimistic terms on Spain's entry into the war.[164] He emphasised again that Wehrmacht intervention would essentially be confined to the Western Mediterranean. Participation in the Italian offensive against Egypt was ruled out for the time being. He intended only to give the Italians direct support for a limited period, in the shape of the Luftwaffe units already intended for transfer to southern Italy. They had to attack the British fleet and the Suez Canal by the spring of 1941. Hitler made Operation Marita, which the army high command had meanwhile included in its plans for a date immediately after the snow had melted, dependent on further political developments in the Balkans. In doing so, he did not want to exclude the possibility that it might not be actually mounted after all. Leaving this consideration aside, its preparations were to be advanced so that orders for the military operations could be given at any time from the beginning of March. Hitler had definitively abandoned Operation Sea Lion. And in this connection, he left no room to doubt — as was also the case in July — that in his view the 'decision on European hegemony' would and must be made 'in the struggle against Russia'.[165] The mounting of Operation Otto (the code-name at the time for the military preparations for the assault on the Soviet Union), was therefore still to be scheduled for the end of May 1941.[166] With this date in mind, Hitler, on that same 5 December 1940, worked out the following proposed dates for the German war operation in the Mediterranean:

1. Air war against the British fleet in the Eastern Mediterranean from 15 December onwards;
2. Attack on Gibraltar, start beginning of February, end four weeks later;
3. Operations against Greece, start beginning of March, ending — given favourable conditions — end of March, perhaps not until end of April.[167]

If Hitler's prognoses about Franco's attitude had come true, this way it still would have been possible to secure north-western and West Africa, that is, the area which formed the 'strategic flank of the entire Front' for various German military interests.[168] However, Hitler and his generals knew from 8 December that Admiral Canaris' mission had failed. Franco refused to enter the war at this stage, basing his refusal primarily on the economic weakness of his import-dependent country. But Canaris cited another reason for Spain's caution: the Caudillo had 'clearly given to understand that Spain could enter the war only when Britain was on the very brink of collapse'.[169] It is true that Franco later hotly disputed these statements of the Admiral's,[170] but it seems reasonably that his vacillation in the second half of 1940 basically served one purpose: that of avoiding Mussolini's mistake of entering the war too soon. Hitler apparently perceived this, because on 10 December he decided: 'Operation Felix will not be carried out, because the political prerequisites are no longer present'.[171]

Thus, German military planning concerning the Mediterranean had temporarily become obsolete, because a viable basis could not be established on which to implement it. This weighed particularly heavily, because just at this time Berlin was fearful that the insurrection movement in the French colonies would spread to French possessions in North Africa. The Germans definitely believed that General Weygand, the delegate general of the Pétain government there, was capable of establishing a counter-government. Hitler now ordered a study of the 'most extreme consequences' in this event. The result was the preparation of the operation known as Attila, which sought to respond to the secession of the North African territories from Vichy by taking possession of the as yet unoccupied areas of France.[172] At the same time, the idea was to try and bring the French 'home fleet and those parts of the French air force located at domestic airports' under German control. Should this fail, they should at least be prevented from 'going over to the enemy side'.[173]

The *Seekriegsleitung*, which had cherished such great hopes of a German war operation in the Mediterranean and of Franco-German co-operation, displayed a distinctly resigned reaction to these changed circumstances. Disappointment was widespread, as a comment on this point in the war diary of 12 December shows;[174] and an analysis of the 'main problems of the current situation' of 20 December remarked, with a sense of disillusionment, that the 'expulsion' of the British fleet from the Mediterranean which had been regarded as 'decisive for the war' could not now be achieved.[175] Furthermore, the stamina of the Italian people had become questionable; and apart from that, there was evidence of a 'danger to German and thus also to European interests in the African area'. All in all, Germany would have to assume that the 'hope of deciding the war in the Mediterranean' would not be fulfilled.

These and other thoughts, taken from the review of the situation of 20 December, were voiced again by Raeder in his address on 27 December.[176] Hitler now seemed to subscribe, in the main, to the

ObdM's view. In the meantime there was further mention of actions in support of Italy in Tripolitania, as a concrete request for assistance from Rome had been made on 19 December. Mussolini asked that a German Panzer division should be dispatched to Tripoli, in order to be able to mount an active defence of the colony once again. The Italians also hoped for war materials to equip ten divisions at this time. They were in special need of artillery, lorries and anti-aircraft and anti-tank cannon.[177]

On 27 December, Raeder and Hitler agreed that capturing Gibraltar would be desirable. But as long as Franco withheld his consent, Operation Felix could not be carried out. However, after this briefing on the situation, Hitler did agree to try once more for Spain's entry into the war. He clearly set great store, after all, in arriving at a stabilisation of the situation in North Africa before the start of the Eastern campaign. In the course of his remarks, Raeder again expressed 'severe reservations about Barbarossa before the downfall of Britain'. In response, Hitler's attitude demonstrated his firm conviction that the only promising route to London was via Moscow: first and foremost, 'the last continental opponent must be eliminated under all circumstances before he could get to grips with Britain'.[178] In this context, it can be no surprise that in December he began, in his arguments, to labour increasingly those allegedly objective reasons which were meant to render the attack on the Soviet Union plausible.

Only one day after this conversation between Raeder and Hitler, General Marras, the Italian military attaché in Berlin, expressly emphasised to the chief of the OKW the extremely precarious position the Italian units in the Balkans found themselves in. Relief could, of course, be provided by a single regiment of German mountain troops. In the North African theatre, he regarded Cyrenaica as lost, and Italian North Africa would probably not hold without German support. Significantly, the Italian attaché laid most emphasis on the effect on morale that the mere appearance of a few German troops could have on the Italians, as well as on the British.[179] On 3 January Rome knew that Hitler was fundamentally prepared to divert Panzer troops to Libya, and one mountain division to Albania. Furthermore, Italy would receive arms and equipment from stocks captured by the Germans.[180] Though hampered by winter storms, preparations for Operation Marita likewise proceeded.[181] In addition, the flying units of the Tenth Flying Corps had meanwhile arrived in Upper Italy.[182] All the same, this did not imply that a final decision had been made on the engagement of German troops in Albania and Libya.[183]

It was during his meeting with representatives of the OKW and the high commands of the three branches of the Wehrmacht on 9 January that Hitler first announced his determination to put together a Panzer unit for Libya immediately.[184] Following meetings with Mussolini on 19 and 20 January, agreement was finally reached that, from 15 February onwards, German troops should be transferred to North Africa.[185] The Wehrmacht mission in Albania, which Hitler had already presented as questionable on 9 January, was, however, abandoned on 15 February, because the Italian front in this area had stabilised itself in the meantime.[186]

Further items for discussion on 9 January related to Operation Attila, although it was assumed it would become superfluous with the commencement of Marita. In view of the burdens the Eastern campaign would inevitably impose on the Wehrmacht, but also as a result of political conditions, Hitler ordered Operation Felix to be called off as well.[187] In fact, he vacillated on this questions for a few weeks more until at last, following the inconclusive meeting between Franco and Mussolini on 12 February, the subject of Spain's entry into the war had to be shelved for the foreseeable future.[188] The German side had to recognise generally that as a result of the Wehrmacht's incapacity for military action, evident since the victory in the West — at least regarding the continuation of the war in quest of a decisive outcome — and of the unmistakable British will to resist, as well as the weaknesses displayed by Fascist Italy, it was increasingly difficult to achieve the power-political wishes of the Third Reich *vis-à-vis* Spain and Vichy France.

To some extent, it was as a result of this stagnation that Hitler went definitely on to the offensive on 9 January 1941. In so doing, the Eastern operation provided the strategic frame of reference for all discussions. Since July 1940, the central elements of his general argument had changed no more than the Eastern operation itself. In connection with this, Hitler was in a light-hearted mood concerning the success obtained to that point by his policy of aggression. On his own admission, this policy was in pursuit of one single principle: 'crushing the most important enemy positions in order to come one step further forward'. In this sense, 'Russia must now be crushed'.[189] There was something else that was striking: nothing of a reactive nature could be discerned which could have been used for the fall-back position of the preventive war, for example. Once again Hitler's remarks show that he was acting with a deliberate objective in mind and not opportunistically, without an objective. Of course, the time factor played a role for him, especially against the background of the international developments after July 1940. This fact has been pointed out repeatedly and verified through research. However, all the actions that can be related to this must be interpreted in the light of Hitler's unshakeable determination to wage aggression against the Soviet Union, as planned in his Programme. This was the real objective — and developments in the summer and autumn of 1940 demonstrate this in a significant way — and Hitler's political actions must be subsumed under this objective. But he had already decided, in July 1940, to take this decisive step as quickly as possible, in order to arrive at the main purpose of his power-political calculations, via the 'destruction of the life force of Russia'. In doing so, he did not pause to reflect upon the previous German experience of exploiting conquered Eastern territories in the First World War. Very like his programmic writing, *Mein Kampf*, it was stated in 1941 that:

the vast Russian area contains immeasurable riches. Germany must rule it economically and politically, but not annex it. Thus, Germany will have all the possibilities for waging war in the future even against continents, it could not be defeated by anyone any more. If this operation were to be carried out, Europe would hold its breath.[190]

The engagement of the Wehrmacht in the Mediterranean could not offer an alternative to a perspective of this kind and indeed, in the final analysis, the thinking outlined here (on the subject of a German war operation in this area) only goes to show once again that at no time before June 1941 did Hitler consider comprehensive and lasting action there. It was primarily a matter of making Great Britain ready for peace by means of a peripheral war operation, and thus to round off the success in the West, so as then to be able to turn his attention to the East under programmic conditions. Thus it was only one, though a very significant one, incidental action in Hitler's strategy, which of course could not be mounted at the right time. German plans for the Mediterranean area were linked with aggression in the East, indirectly to begin with, but increasingly directly after the Italian assault on Greece and the subsequent resulting instability in the Balkans. Then, with the Italian barrier to the penetration of German troops in Mussolini's sphere of influence removed, Hitler signed Directive No. 22 on 11 January 1941, on 'assistance by German forces in the fighting in the Mediterranean'. This stated that its sole intention was assistance required by Italy 'on strategic, political and psychological grounds',[191] but the so-called strategic grounds now included the military security of the southern flank of Operation Barbarossa. If the Italian military situation had made Wehrmacht intervention in the Balkans seem a necessity, the commitment to the Eastern campaign in the concrete situation after October 1940 made it virtually indispensable, as indeed became clear in the first few days of November. Seen like this, everything that was considered on the German side at the time can be classed as support, stabilisation or securities, not as an operation to determine the outcome *per se*. Without wishing to lose oneself in that limitless area of 'would-have-been' history, it seems necessary here to pass a few basic comments on the ever-controversial answer to the question as to whether a victory over Britain in the Mediterranean would have decided the war. It should first of all be stated that, as both Rome and Berlin knew, the Mediterranean did have an extraordinary significance for London, though not a vital one. It can also be stated with certainty that its loss would not have broken the British will to continue the war, because it was not the possession of this area, but rather the connections with the Dominions and, in particular, the support from the USA, that were the essential prerequisites for Britain's ability to survive.[192] Therefore, if the expulsion of the British from the Mediterranean area would not have led to a turning-point in the war, in the same way it is extremely questionable whether the Axis powers would have succeeded in obtaining from it the advantages hoped for by the *Seekriegsleitung*. At any rate, the connections, on the one hand, with the countries with raw materials, and with the oil reserves in the Middle East, and the possibilities, on the other hand, for protection available to the Axis powers, do not suggest this to be the case. Viewed in this light, it can be assumed as likely that if Hitler had taken the route to the Mediterranean on the premise that it was an alternative to his own strategic concept, one way or another he would have found himself confronted by the same situation as had developed after the victory in the West in 1940: that is, the impossibility of achieving a victory decisive for the outcome of the war, and the certain knowledge that time was working against him.

Notes

1. See J. Thies, *Architekt der Weltherrschaft. Die "Endziele" Hitlers*, Düsseldorf, 1976.
2. H. Picker, *Tischgespräche im Führerhauptquartier*. Completely revised and extended new edition, Stuttgart, 1976, pp. 57f., 21 July 1941.
3. See K. Hildebrand, *Das Dritte Reich*, Munich/Vienna, 1979, pp. 168–80; A. Hillgruber, 'Hitler's Strategy and Politics in the Second World War', in *Politics and Strategy in the Second World War. Germany, Great Britain, the Soviet Union and the United States*, Manhattan/Kansas, 1976, pp. 23–30, here pp. 23f.; W. Deist, M. Messerschmidt, H. E. Volkmann and W. Wette, *Ursachen und Voraussetzungen der deutschen Kriegspolitik*, Stuttgart, 1979, pp. 536–47.
4. The contents of Hitler's Programme are most clearly expounded in *Hitlers Zweites Buch. Ein Dokument aus dem Jahr 1928*, G.L. Weinberg (ed.), Stuttgart, 1961; on the realisation of the Programme, see K. Hildebrand, 'Hitlers "Programm" und seine Realisierung 1939–1942', in *Kriegsbeginn 1939. Entfesselung oder Ausbruch des Zweiten Weltkrieges?*, G. Niedhart (ed.), Darmstadt, 1976, pp. 178–224.
5. A. Hillgruber, 'Die "Endlösung" und das deutsche Ostimperium als Kernstück des rassenideologischen Programms des Nationalsozialismus', in *Hitler, Deutschland und die Mächte, Material on the Foreign Policy of the Third Reich*, edited by M. Funke, Düsseldorf, 1976, pp. 94–114; E. Jäckel, *Hitlers Weltanschauung. Entwurf einer Herrschaft*, Tübingen, 1969, pp. 29–57; cf., for a direct reference *Adolf Hitler. Monologe im Führerhauptquartier 1941–1944. Die Aufzeichnungen Heinrich Heims*, edited by W. Jochmann, Hamburg, 1980, pp. 294, 330f.
6. For selected works on German–Italian relations 1933–40 see M. Funke, *Sanktionen und Kanonen. Hitler, Mussolini und der Internationale Abessinienkonflikt 1934–1936*, Düsseldorf, 1970; J. Petersen, *Hitler–Mussolini. Die Entstehung der Achse Berlin–Rome 1933–36*, Tübingen, 1973; F. Siebert, *Italiens Weg in den Zweiten Weltkrieg*, Frankfurt-am-Main/Bonn, 1962; G. Schreiber, *Revisionismus und Weltmachtstreben. Marineführung und deutsch-italienische Beziehungen 1919 bis 1944*, Stuttgart, 1978.
7. See A. Hillgruber, 'Grundzüge der nationalsozialistischen Außenpolitik 1933–1945', in *Saeculum*, 24 (1973), pp. 328–45, here p. 338.
8. See for example F. Halder, *Hitler als Feldherr*, Munich, 1949.
9. See S. Haffner, *Anmerkungen zu Hitler*, Munich, 1978, pp. 87–90.
10. See Deist, note 3 above, *Ursachen* etc., in particular pp. 703–16.
11. See Schreiber, *Revisionismus*, pp. 111f.
12. See E. D'Auria, *L'Italia contemporanea dal primo al secondo dopoguerra*, Rome, 1979, pp. 273f.; M. Toscano, *The Origins of the Pact of Steel*, Baltimore, 1967.
13. For the Italian reaction, see G. Bocca, *Storia d'Italia nella guerra fascista 1940–1943*, Rome, 3rd ed., Bari, 1973, pp. 57–65.
14. See A. Hillgruber, 'Politik und Strategie Hitlers im Mittelmeerraum', in idem, *Deutsche Großmacht- und Weltpolitik im 19. und 20. Jahr-*

hundert, Düsseldorf, 1977, pp. 276–95, here pp. 276f.

15. Studied in detail in F. Bandini, *Tecnica della sconfitta. Storia dei quaranti giorni che predettero e seguirono l'entrata dell'Italia in guerra*, 2nd ed., Milan, 1964, pp. 613–722; D.M. Smith, *Mussolini's Roman Empire*, London/New York, 1976, pp. 202–35.

16. See D.S. Detwiler, *Hitler, Franco und Gibraltar. Die Frage des spanischen Eintritts in den Zweiten Weltkrieg*, Wiesbaden, 1962, pp. 22–5.

17. O. Dankelmann, *Franco zwischen Hitler und den Westmächten*, Berlin (East), 1970, pp. 107f.

18. Generaloberst Halder, *Kriegstagebuch. Tägliche Aufzeichnungen des Chefs des Generalstabes des Heeres 1939–1942*, vol. 1. *Vom Polenfeldzung bis zum Ende der Westoffensive (14.8.1939–30.6.1940)*, Stuttgart, 1962, p. 308, for 21 May 1940.

19. See B. Martin, *Friedensinitiativen und Machtpolitik im Zweiten Weltkrieg 1939–1942*, Düsseldorf, 1974, pp. 243f.

20. See, for an opposing view, B. Stegemann, 'Hitlers Ziele im ersten Kriegsjahr 1939/40. Ein Betrag zur Quellenkritik', in *Militärgeschichtliche Mitteilungen*, 27 (1980), p. 97.

21. See *Die Weizsäcker-Papiere 1933–1950*, edited by L.E. Hill, Frankfurtam-Main/Berlin/Vienna, 1974, p. 204, for 23 May 1940.

22. J.C. Fest, *Hitler, eine Biographie*, Frankfurt-am-Main/Berlin/Vienna, 1973, pp. 871f.

23. On the subject of Great Britain see J. Henke, *England in Hitlers politischem Kalkül 1935–1939*, Boppard-am-Rhein, 1973, esp. pp. 303–10.

24. For an early study of this difficult area, see the study by G.L. Weinberg, 'Der deutsche Entschluß zum Angriff auf die Sowjetunion', in *VfZG (Vierteljahrshefte für Zeitgeschichte)*, 1 (1953), pp. 301–18; see also the critique by H.-G. Seraphim and A. Hillgruber, 'Hitlers Entschluß zum Angriff auf die Sowjetunion' in *VfZG*, 2 (1954), pp. 240–54.

25. See Hildebrand, *Das Dritte Reich*, pp. 61f.; A. Hillgruber, *Deutschlands Rolle in der Vorgeschichte der beiden Weltkriege*, 2nd ed., Göttingen, 1979, pp. 103–7.

26. *Weizsäcker-Papiere*, pp. 204f.

27. For a different interpretation, see Stegemann, 'Hitlers Ziele', p. 98.

28. Sodenstern's statement, based on his recollections, was first published in K. Klee, *Das Unternehmen 'Seelöwe'. Die geplante deutsche Landung in England*, Göttingen/Berlin/Frankfurt-am-Main, 1958, p. 189; see also W. Ansel, *Hitler confronts England*, 2nd ed., Durham NC, 1960, pp. 107f.

29. H. Böhme, *Der deutsch-französische Waffenstillstand im Zweiten Weltkrieg*, part 1, *Entstehung und Grundlagen des Waffenstillstandes von 1940*, Stuttgart, 1966, p. 79.

30. Stegemann, 'Hitlers Ziele', pp. 97f.

31. Halder, *Kriegstagebuch*, p. 375.

32. Ibid., here vol. 2, *Von der geplanten Landung in England bis zum Beginn des Ostfeldzuges (1.7.1940–21.6.1941)*, Stuttgart, 1963, p. 6; Hillgruber, *Deutschlands Rolle*, pp. 106f., deals directly with this subject.

33. See A. Hillgruber, *Sowjetische Außenpolitik im Zweiten Weltkrieg*,

Düsseldorf, 1979, pp. 51–67.

34. See Seraphim and Hillgruber, 'Hitlers Entschluß', p. 231; Weinberg, 'Der deutsche Entschluß', pp. 305–18; for a partially opposed treatment, see S. Allard, *Stalin und Hitler. Die sowjetische Außenpolitik 1930–1941*, Berne/Munich, 1974, pp. 208–14.

35. On Hitler's peace offer of 19 July 1940, see Martin, *Friedensinitiativen*, pp. 301–36.

36. See S. Friedländer, *Auftakt zum Untergang, Hitler und die Vereinigten Staaten von Amerika 1939–1941*, Stuttgart/Berlin/Cologne/Mainz, 1965, pp. 70–3; A. Hillgruber, 'Der Faktor Amerika in Hitlers Strategie 1938–1941', in *Nationalsozialistische Außenpolitik*, edited by W. Michalka, Darmstadt, 1978, pp. 493–525, here pp. 512f.

37. On this problem see C. Streit, *Keine Kameraden. Die Wehrmacht und die sowjetischen Kriegsgefangenen 1941–1945*, Stuttgart, 1978, pp. 25–66.

38. Significantly, the adherents of the preventive war thesis omit from their interpretations the actualisation of the Eastern campaign at the time that peace overtures were being made to Great Britain; see P.W. Fabry, *Die Sowjetunion und das Dritte Reich. Eine dokumentierte Geschichte der deutsch-sowjetischen Beziehungen 1933–1941*, Stuttgart, 1971, pp. 155–94, 425f.

39. Renamed the *Wehrmachtführungsstab* from 8 August 1940.

40. Published in *Dokumente zum Unternehmen 'Seelöwe'. Die geplante deutsche Landung in England 1940*, edited by K. Klee, Göttingen/Zurich/Frankfurt-am-Main, 1959, pp. 298f.; for earlier considerations of this kind within the German navy, see Schreiber, *Revisionismus*, pp. 201–38.

41. See W. Ansel, *Hitler and the Middle Sea*, Durham, NC, 1972, pp. 8–12; A. Hillgruber, *Hitlers Strategie, Politik und Kriegführung 1940–41*, Frankfurt-am-Main, 1965, pp. 157f.

42. See L. Gruchmann, 'Die "verpaßten strategischen Chancen" der Achsenmächte im Mittelmeerraum 1940/41', in *VfZG*, 18 (1970), pp. 456–75, here pp. 460ff.

43. See K.A. Maier, H. Rohde, B. Stegemann and H. Umbreit, *Die Errichtung der Hegemonie auf dem europäischen Kontinent*, Stuttgart, 1979, pp. 368–74.

44. *Dokumente*, pp. 299f.

45. On the military and technical details see C.B. Burdick, *Germany's Military Strategy and Spain in World War II*, Syracuse/New York, 1968, pp. 18–28.

46. *Hitlers Weisungen für die Kriegführung 1939–1945. Dokumente des Oberkommandos der Wehrmacht*, edited by W. Hubatsch, Munich, 1965, pp. 71–5.

47. Hillgruber, *Hitlers Strategie*, pp. 244f.; *Lagevorträge des Oberbefehlshabers der Kriegsmarine vor Hitler 1939–45*, edited by G. Wagner, Munich, 1972, p. 110, for 11 July 1940.

48. Halder, *Kriegstagebuch*, pp. 20f., for 13 July 1940; Klee, *Unternehmen*, p. 190.

49. *Weizsäcker-Papiere*, p. 213, for 10 July 1940.

50. See G. Schreiber, 'Zur Kontinuität des Groß- und Weltmachstrebens der deutschen Marineführung', in *Militärgeschichtliche Mitteilungen*, 26 (1979), pp. 101–71, here pp. 127, 142–7.
51. Bibliographical reference in Hildebrand, *Das Dritte Reich*, pp. 170–2.
52. Hillgruber, *Deutschlands Rolle*, pp. 108f.
53. Quoted from *Adolf Hitler. Monologe*, p. 55; also ibid., pp. 62f., 91, 110, 289.
54. Ibid., p. 389.
55. A. Hillgruber, 'England in Hitlers außenpolitischer Konzeption', in *HZ*, 218 (1974), pp. 65–84, here p. 78.
56. Hillgruber, *Hitlers Strategie*, pp. 214f.
57. See Allard, *Stalin*, pp. 228–31; Hillgruber, 'Der Faktor Amerika', pp. 510–13.
58. Halder, *Kriegstagebuch*, for 22 July 1940.
59. Ibid., pp. 33f.; on the conference see Hillgruber, *Hitlers Strategie*, pp. 217f.; on the under-estimation of the Soviet Union, see also *Weizsäcker-Papiere*, p. 219, for 22 July 1940: 'An attack by Russia on us is not to be feared. It is not strong enough in military terms nor as a regime'.
60. See W. Carr, *Hitler. A Study in Personality and Politics*, London, 1978, pp. 92f., which argues against Hitler's ideological fixation on the East.
61. Published in M. Salewski, *Die deutsche Seekriegsleitung 1935–1945*, Vol. 3 *Denkschriften und Lagebetrachtungen 1938–1944*, Frankfurt-am-Main, 1973, p. 137–44.
62. Critique of sources in Weinberg, 'Der deutsche Entschluß', p. 311.
63. In 1946 Jodl described the developments leading up to the Eastern campaign, as he remembered them, in very abbreviated and inaccurate form; see P.E. Schramm, *Hitler als militärischer Führer*, 2nd rev. ed., Frankfurt-am-Main, 1965, pp. 145–55.
64. Quoted from J. Toland, *Adolf Hitler*, Bergisch Gladbach, 1977, p. 797, information given by Warlimont to Toland; cf. Hillgruber, *Hitlers Strategie*, p. 219.
65. Quoted from W. Warlimont, *Im Hauptquartier der deutschen Wehrmacht 1939–1945. Grundlagen, Formen, Gestalten*, Frankfurt-am-Main/Bonn, 1964, p. 127; of direct relevance is *Kriegstagebuch des Oberkommandos der Wehrmacht* (Wehrmachtführungsstab) vol. 1: *1 August 1940–31 December 1941*, edited by H.-A. Jacobsen, Frankfurt-am-Main, 1965, pp. 3f., for 2 August 1940; ibid., p. 18, for 9 August 1940; cf. Hillgruber, *Hitlers Strategie*, pp. 222f.
66. See also S. Westphal, *Der deutsche Generalstab*, Mainz, 1978, p. 60.
67. See Halder, *Kriegstagebuch*, for 6, 7, 9, 12, 20, 23, 28 August, 1, 5, 6, 14, 16, 23 September, 1, 2, 8, 9, 11, 12, 16, 22, 28, 29, 31 October, 4, 7, 8, 11, 12, 13, 18, 19, 25, 29 November, 2, 3, 5 December 1940; cf. for the 'camouflage' (deception of the Soviet Union), *Weizsäcker-Papiere*, p. 219, for 27 September 1940: '. . . as I have been saying for some time, to simulate to the Russians the necessary autumn fog. It's still a long time to the spring'.
68. Raeder had left the discussion before the mention of the intended

attack on the Soviet Union. See M. Salewski, *Die deutsche Seekriegsleitung 1935–1945*, vol. 1, *1935–1941*, Frankfurt-am-Main, 1970, pp. 275f.

69. Quoted from Halder, *Kriegstagebuch*, pp. 46–50; cf. also *Kriegstagebuch des OKW*, pp. 3-5; Hillgruber, *Hitlers Strategie*, pp. 221-6.

70. See W. Schumann, G. Hass et al., *Deutschland im Zweiten Weltkrieg*, vol. 1, *Vorbereitung, Entfesselung und Verlauf des Krieges bis zum 22. Juni 1941*, Cologne, 1974, pp. 367f.; Hillgruber, 'Endlösung', pp. 99f.

71. E. Nolte, *Der Faschismus in seiner Epoche, Die Action Française. Der italienische Faschismus. Der Nationalsozialismus*, Munich/Zurich, 1979, p. 436.

72. Hillgruber, *Deutschlands Rolle*, p. 103.

73. See H. Diwald, *Geschichte der Deutschen*, Frankfurt-am-Main/Berlin/Vienna, 1978, pp. 152f.; P.W. Fabry, *Der Hitler–Stalin-Pakt 1939–1941. Ein Beitrag zur Methode sowjetischer Außenpolitik*, Darmstadt, 1962, pp. 249–68.

74. Hillgruber, *Hitlers Strategie*, pp. 223–42, 352–77.

75. Against, A. Görner, *Hitlers preußisches Engagement. Von der Feldherrnhalle bis Stalingrad. Zur Genealogie des Zweiten Weltkrieges*, Bellnhausen, 1966, p. 86; see also ibid., pp. 91–6.

76. Particularly typical of the exculpation of the National Socialist leadership, D.L. Hoggan, *Der unnötige Krieg 1939–1945: 'Germany must perish'*, Tübingen, 1974, pp. 437f.

77. According to Stegemann, *Die Errichtung* (note 43). In a very different vein, Hillgruber, *Hitlers Strategie*, p. 231, who says only that Hitler had 'no influence' on the preliminary work.

78. *Heeresadjutant bei Hitler 1938–43. Aufzeichnungen des Majors Engel*, edited by H.v. Kotze, Stuttgart, 1974, pp. 86f.; see also idem, p. 91, for 15 January 1940.

79. *Lagevorträge*, p. 137; ibid., p. 150, for 4 November 1940; ibid., p. 154, for 14 November 1940.

80. *Kriegstagebuch des OKW*, p. 18, for 9 August 1940; ibid., p. 176, for 14 November 1940.

81. Halder, *Kriegstagebuch*, pp. 165f.

82. Ibid., p. 49; cf. Hillgruber, 'Der Faktor Amerika', p. 512; for decision-making in the summer and autumn of 1940, see also R. Cecil, *Hitlers Griff nach Rußland*, Graz/Vienna/Cologne, 1977, pp. 69–86.

83. See *Staatsmänner und Diplomaten bei Hitler. Vertrauliche Aufzeichnungen über Unterredungen mit Vertretern des Auslandes 1939–1941*, edited by A. Hillgruber, Frankfurt-am-Main, 1967, pp. 134–8.

84. *Staatsmänner*, pp. 144–50, here p. 149.

85. Exhaustively covered in Böhme, *Waffenstillstand*, pp. 289–360; cf. R.T. Thomas, *Britain and Vichy. The Dilemma of Anglo-French Relations 1940–1942*, London, 1979, pp. 42–8.

86. *Staatsmänner*, pp. 150–62.

87. See Burdick, *Germany*, pp. 24–8; Halder, *Kriegstagebuch*, pp. 45f., for 30 July 1940.

88. *Deutschland im Zweiten Weltkrieg*, p. 368.

89. *Kriegstagebuch des OKW*, p. 11, for 7 August 1940.

90. Ibid., pp. 17f., for 9 August 1940; ibid., p. 20, for 10 August 1940.

91. Ibid., p. 31, for 14 August 1940; *Dokumente*, pp. 353f.
92. Halder, *Kriegstagebuch*, pp. 32, 45–8.
93. *Lagevorträge*, p. 146.
94. See also Warlimont, *Hauptquartier*, p. 127.
95. *Kriegstagebuch des OKW*, p. 18, for 9 August 1940; ibid., p. 32, for 14 August 1940; on Franco's attitude and Spain's demands for materials, see Detwiler, *Hitler*, pp. 32–6.
96. *Kriegstagebuch des OKW*, pp. 40f., for 20 August 1940; ibid., p. 48, for 24 August 1940.
97. Ibid., p. 41, for 21 August 1940; Halder, *Kriegstagebuch*, p. 75.
98. Halder, *Kriegstagebuch*, p. 72, for 21 August 1940.
99. *Kriegstagebuch des OKW*, p. 54, for 29 August 1940.
100. Ibid., p. 54, for 30 August 1940.
101. Bundesarchiv-Militärarchiv Freiburg i.Br. (BA–MA) RM7/15 *Kriegstagebuch* (KTB) 1. *Seekriegsleitung* (1.Skl.) T.A., pp. 328f., for 28 August 1940.
102. For a full account, see J.R.M. Butler, *Grand Strategy*, vol. 2, September 1939–June 1941, London, 1957, pp. 243–6.
103. BA-MA RM 7/16, KTB 1. Skl., T.A., p. 25, for 3 September 1940.
104. *Lagevorträge*, pp. 134–41; cf. Ansel, *Middle Sea*, p. 21.
105. *Kriegstagebuch des OKW*, pp. 63f, for 5 September 1940; ibid., p. 69, for 7 September 1940.
106. BA-MA RM 6/73 Oberkommando der Kriegsmarine. Ob. d. M. Persönlich. Großadmiral Raeder. 1.8.40–31.1.41, pp. 58–67, 70–82, 121–52: 'Betrachtungen zur Frage der Besetzung der atlantischen Inseln durch deutsche Wehrmachtsteile', 31 October 1940; directly on this subject, *Kriegstagebuch des OKW*, p. 90, for 25 September; ibid., p. 95 , for 28 September; p. 102, for 1 October; p. 124, for 23 October; p. 132, for 28 October; pp. 135f., for 29 October 1940.
107. BA-MA CASE GE 536 PG 32624 a, 'Die Bemühungen der Seekriegsleitung um ein deutsch-französisches Zusammengehen gegen England und um die Behauptung des französischen Kolonialreiches in Afrika', vol. 1, pp. 8f.
108. See on Operation Menace, Butler, *Grand Strategy*, pp. 313–19.
109. See G. Geschke, *Die deutsche Frankreichpolitik 1940 von Compiègne bis Montoire. Das Problem einer deutsch-französischen Annäherung nach dem Frankreichfeldzug*, Berlin/Frankfurt-am-Main, 1960, pp. 72–7.
110. BA-MA CASE GE 536, p. 9.
111. On the change in attitude, see *Kriegstagebuch des OKW*, pp. 50f., for 29 August; ibid., p. 51, for 30 August; p. 57, for 2 September; p. 61, for 4 September; p. 88, for 24 September 1940.
112. See E. Jäckel, *Frankreich in Hitlers Europa. Die deutsche Frankreichpolitik im Zweiten Weltkrieg*, Stuttgart, 1966, pp. 101f.
113. BA-MA CASE GE 536, pp. 16f.
114. BA-MA RM 7/16 KTB 1.Skl. T.A., p. 347, 25 September 1940.
115. See also *Kriegstagebuch des OKW*, pp. 88f., for 25 September; ibid., p. 93, for 26 September 1940; BA-MA CASE GE 536, p. 20.
116. *Lagevorträge*, pp. 143–6.
117. Hillgruber, *Hitlers Strategie*, pp. 200f.

118. See especially, W. Michalka, *Ribbentrop und die deutsche Weltpolitik 1933–1940. Außenpolitische Konzeptionen und Entscheidungsprozesse im Dritten Reich*, Munich, 1980, pp. 247–59.
119. See Hillgruber, *Hitlers Strategie*, p. 190.
120. Ibid., pp. 238–42; Michalka, *Ribbentrop*, pp. 295f.
121. See T. Sommer, *Deutschland und Japan zwischen den Mächten 1935–1940. Vom Antikominternpakt zum Dreimächtepakt. Eine Studie zur Vorgeschichte des Zweiten Weltkrieges*, Tübingen, 1962, pp. 426–49.
122. BA-MA MBox 1691 PG 33967 g Kriegswissenschaftliche Abteilung der Kriegsmarine (7 pp.).
123. *Staatsmänner*, pp. 229–47.
124. Those present were Bodenschatz, Brauchitsch, Halder, Jeschonnek, Jodl, Keitel, Milch, Puttkammer, Raeder and Schmidt; cf. E. Milch, 'Merkbuch' (photocopy in the MGFA), entry for 14 September 1940, 15.00 hours.
125. Halder, *Kriegstagebuch*, p. 98, for 14 September 1940.
126. Milch, 14 September 1940.
127. Halder, *Kriegstagebuch*, p. 98, for 14 September 1940.
128. Ibid., p. 136, for 15 October 1940.
129. See also *Adolf Hitler, Monologe*, p. 60 passim.
130. *Weizsäcker-Papiere*, p. 222, for 26 October 1940.
131. *Staatsmänner*, pp. 257–65; Geschke, *Frankreichpolitik*, pp. 86–9.
132. *Staatsmänner*, pp. 266–71; Detwiler, *Hitler*, pp. 56–62.
133. *Staatsmänner*, pp. 272–80; Jäckel, *Frankreich*, pp. 118–23.
134. See Hillgruber, *Hitlers Strategie*, pp. 285f.
135. *Weizsäcker-Papiere*, p. 221, for 25 October 1940.
136. *Staatsmänner*, pp. 280–94.
137. See K. Hildebrand, *Deutsche Außenpolitik 1933–1945. Kalkül oder Dogma?*, 4th (ext.) ed., Stuttgart/Berlin/Cologne/Mainz, 1980, pp. 104f.; idem, *Das Dritte Reich*, pp. 64f.
138. See Halder, *Kriegstagebuch*, pp. 155f., for 31 October 1940; *Kriegstagebuch des OKW*, pp. 142–7, for 1 November 1940.
139. For the discussion of 4 November 1940, see Halder, *Kriegstagebuch*, pp. 163–6; re the Anatolia Plan, ibid., pp. 152f., for 27/28 October, and p. 161, for 2 November 1940; for 4 November 1940, see further, *Kriegstagebuch des OKW*, pp. 148–52; *Lagevorträge*, pp. 148–51; Ansel, *Middle Sea*, pp. 50–4; Burdick, *Germany*, pp. 74f.; Hillgruber, *Hitlers Strategie*, pp. 323ff., 335f., 352–5.
140. *Weisungen*, pp. 77–82; cf. Hillgruber, *Hitlers Strategie*, pp. 325f.; N. Rich, *Hitler's War Aims. Ideology, the Nazi State and the Course of Expansion*, London, 1973, pp. 171f.
141. *Staatsmänner*, pp. 304–20.
142. Quoted from *Weisungen*, pp. 77–82.
143. See Gruchmann, 'Chancen', p. 466.
144. *Heeresadjutant*, p. 91, for 15 November 1940.
145. *Weizsäcker-Papiere*, p. 223, for 13 November; p. 224, for 15 November; pp. 224f., for 16 November 1940.
146. Ibid., p. 226.

147. BA-MA RM 7/18 KTB 1.Skl. T.A., pp. 102–6, for 8 November 1940.
148. Lagevorträge, pp. 151–65; *Kriegstagebuch des OKW*, pp. 174f., for 14 and 15 November 1940.
149. See Salewski, *Seekriegsleitung*, vol. 1, pp. 283f., note 53.
150. *Kriegstagebuch des OKW*, p. 177, for 15 November 1940, notes: 'The Führer sees the value of the Azores in two directions, wants to have them for intervention by America and in peace. Bombers with 6000 km range'. Thies, *Architekt*, pp. 142f., also pp. 136–47 for the long-range bomber project Me 261/264 in toto.
151. See also *Kriegstagebuch des OKW*, p. 184, for 20 November; ibid., p. 186, for 25 November and p. 193, for 30 November 1940.
152. *Weizsäcker-Papiere*, p. 228, for 8 December 1940.
153. Ibid., p. 229, for 8 December 1940.
154. See Hillgruber, *Hitlers Strategie*, pp. 326f.
155. *Staatsmänner*, pp. 320–30; *Akten zur deutschen auswärtigen Politik 1918–1945* (ADAP), Series D: 1937–1945, vol. II, 2, *Die Kriegsjahre (13 November 1940–31 January 1941)*, Bonn, 1964; see especially pp. 519–23, Doc. 357; Detwiler, *Hitler*, pp. 73–9.
156. *Kriegstagebuch des OKW*, p. 181, for 19 November 1940.
157. *Weisungen*, here no. 20, pp. 94f., for 13 December 1940.
158. See Halder, *Kriegstagebuch*, pp. 202f., for 2 December and p. 205, for 3 December 1940.
159. *Kriegstagebuch des OKW*, pp. 205f., for 5 December 1940.
160. Ibid., p. 196, for 1 to 4 December 1940; Halder, *Kriegstagebuch*, pp. 205, 207, for 3 December 1940.
161. *Kriegstagebuch des OKW*, p. 197, for 4 December; ibid., p. 206, for 5 December; p. 211, for 6 December; p. 219, for 8 December 1940; Halder, *Kriegstagebuch*, p. 209, for 5 December 1940; cf. A. Brissaud, *Canaris 1877–1945*, Darmstadt, 1977, pp. 363f.; H. Höhne, *Canaris, Patriot im Zwielicht*, Munich, 1976, pp. 419f.
162. *Weisungen*, pp. 86–90; Dankelmann, *Franco*, pp. 152–5.
163. Halder, *Kriegstagebuch*, pp. 211–14; *Kriegstagebuch des OKW*, pp. 203–9.
164. Directly on this subject, the information in Burdick, *Germany*, p. 98, note 5, according to which Hitler seems not to have been anything like as confident as he gave the impression of being on 5 December 1940.
165. Halder, *Kriegstagebuch*, p. 212.
166. Ibid., p. 214.
167. *Kriegstagebuch des OKW*, pp. 204f.
168. Ibid., pp. 196, 200, for 4 December 1940.
169. Ibid., p. 222; cf. Höhne, *Canaris*, pp. 420f.
170. See Dankelmann, *Franco, p. 155*.
171. *Weisungen*, here no. 19a, pp. 90f., for 11 December 1940.
172. Ibid., pp. 91f., for 10 December 1940.
173. See BA-MA CASE GE 439 PG 32485-32487 1. Skl. Folder VII, 1-3, 'Attila', pp. 12-21. Here, 1.Skl. Iop 2603/40 Geheime Kommandosache, Chefsache, Berlin, 16 December 1940 (response of the Skl. to Directive No. 19, re Attila).

174. BA-MA RM 7/19 KTB. 1.Skl. T.A., pp. 154f.
175. Ibid., pp. 234–40, quote on p. 235.
176. *Lagevorträge*, pp. 171–6.
177. *Kriegstagebuch des OKW*, p. 241, for 20 December 1940; ADAP, pp. 764f., for doc. 541, 10 December 1940.
178. *Lagevorträge*, p. 174.
179. *Kriegstagebuch des OKW*, pp. 243f., for 18 December 1940.
180. Ibid., pp. 245f., for 4 January 1941.
181. Ibid., p. 242, for 21 December 1940; ibid., p. 247, for 6 January, p. 250, for 7 January 1941.
182. Ibid.
183. Ibid., pp. 251f., for 8 January 1941.
184. Ibid., p. 253, for 9 January 1941.
185. Ibid., p. 270, for 20 January 1941; cf. *Staatsmänner*, pp. 435–52.
186. *Kriegstagebuch des OKW*, p. 326, for 15 February 1941.
187. Ibid., p. 254f., for 9 January 1941.
188. *Weizsäcker-Papiere*, p. 237, for 16 February 1941.
189. *Kriegstagebuch des OKW*, p. 257, for 9 January 1941.
190. Idem, p. 258, for 9 January 1941.
191. *Weisungen*, pp. 107f.
192. Schreiber, *Revisionismus*, pp. 168f.

BERNHARD R. KROENER

Squaring the Circle. Blitzkrieg Strategy and Manpower Shortage, 1939–1942

The course of the Second World War between September 1939 and the winter of 1941/2 is generally referred to as the phase of the Blitzkrieg.* However, this term has come to be used so indiscriminately that a clear definition no longer seems possible. Military historians agree only that every attacker must try to conclude the operations he begins as quickly as possible, as the Silesian wars of Frederick II clearly demonstrate.[1]

In its modern meaning, however, Blitzkrieg strategy is more than the operational-tactical principle of seeking a rapid decision. It means rather the optimal combination of military leadership principles with related economic and social factors necessary to achieve the overall strategic goal within a precalculated time period. Previously scholars have largely overlooked the fact that the element of a predetermined time period in German strategy underwent a decisive qualitative change during the first half of the Second World War. Whereas the German forces did not operate under such a time limit during the campaigns in Poland and France, it played an extremely important role in the planning and conduct of the war in the east. As the Scandanavian, Balkan and African campaigns made only limited

---

*This article is based on a more detailed analysis of the regimentation of labour and military personnel in Germany between 1939 and 1942. Details are to be found in vol. V of *Das Deutsche Reich und der Zweite Weltkrieg*, which is also the reason that extensive references have been omitted here.

Transl. from the German by Dean S. McMurry.

demands on German resources, they do not have to be considered here.

The practical realisation of the ideal, theoretical Blitzkrieg strategy was extremely vulnerable to the disruptive potential of individual factors, which often made considerable modifications necessary. Alan Milward has referred to the importance of these retarding elements in the inner structure of the Third Reich in German economic strategy during the first half of the war. In his opinion the National Socialist leaders developed an overall plan to mobilise the economic and military strength of the nation only to the extent considered necessary to defeat a supposedly inferior enemy.[2] On the other hand, Timothy Mason, who has subjected Milward's interpretation to a thorough critical analysis, believes that the German Blitzkrieg phase between 1939 and 1942 was determined by internal necessities of the National Socialist system, chance developments in foreign affairs and Hitler's *va banque* mentality. The initial military successes gave this mixture of largely independent factors an appearance of planning it did not really possess.[3]

While Milward maintains that the Blitzkrieg plan was followed, though not without difficulties, until the end of 1941, Mason is of the opinion that even the start of the war as well as the first spectacular successes were not the result of an overall plan but were rather necessitated by the economic and political dilemma in which the regime found itself and which made the use of the Blitzkrieg plan impossible. These two interpretations, which represent the extreme positions in this question, agree in two basic assumptions. Both claim there *was* a Blitzkrieg plan, to be used against a supposedly inferior enemy, and that economic and social factors played a greater role in it than immediate military considerations. This raises the very important question of the ability of the German population to bear the strains of war. It is therefore all the more astonishing that no comprehensive studies of the allocation of personnel between the armed forces and the economy during the war are available. While a number of such works have been published which deal with other states involved in the war,[4] only parts of the area under German control have been examined.[5] This situation can be explained in part by the fact that the historical sources seem at first glance to be scattered and only incompletely preserved.[6] There is, moreover, the problem that the allocation of personnel resources in a war involves all areas of life in a society, thus seeming to be many-sided, complicated and defiant of any attempt at a systematic survey. In addition, statistical material essential for a comprehensive account is incomplete and often incompatible because of different classification criteria. This makes any quantitative approach very difficult; nevertheless, an analysis of the use of available personnel resources in the German armed forces and economy can, by taking into consideration economic and social factors, be especially helpful in answering the question of whether or to what extent they interfered with or even prevented the realisation of a Blitzkrieg plan.

We should first note that the leaders of the Third Reich never had a clearly defined, generally accepted Blitzkrieg plan. Strongly in-fluenced by their very different individual experiences in the First World War, they developed, in the years before 1939, different ideas as to how Germany should conduct and win a future war.

As they considered it self-evident that any war based on the principle of attack should be won in the shortest possible time, German military leaders favoured an approach that would permit the peacetime creation of all preconditions to achieve victory through a brief, intense and total mobilisation of all resources. Through a 'rearmament in depth' and extensive organisational preparations, they hoped to avoid the problems of an inadequate personnel mobilisation, as had developed in 1914, and production breakdowns caused by bottlenecks in the final stages of manufac-turing, as had occurred at the start of the great battles over *matériel* in the First World War. The German lead in armaments had to be maintained for long enough after the start of a war to permit of a military decision before the superior production capacity of the enemy began to affect the situation on the battlefield.[7]

The political leaders of the National Socialist regime agreed with the military goal of a limited war, but their own interpretation of the First World War caused them to take another route to achieve this aim. Hitler and his regional party leaders in the administrative districts (*Gaue*) rejected the idea of even a brief total mobilisation because they believed the ability of the population to endure the hardships of war was very limited. Instead, they favoured a mobil-isation of part of all available resources, precisely calculated on the basis of the assumed strength of each enemy. This plan was actually a result of their almost traumatic experiences during the 'hunger winter' of 1917 and the revolution of late 1918. For this reason they wanted to avoid as far as possible any worsening of the living conditions of the population, especially in the industrial centres. Their plan required a 'broad rearmament', a very modern peacetime army which would be able to defeat an inferior enemy without a large-scale mobilisation of reserves. The success of limited military operations in the years between 1936 and 1939 seemed to confirm this theory.

For different reasons, industry and labour supported this view. The economic leaders feared the loss of their market shares in the consumer sector in the event of even a brief conversion to war production, as consumer goods and armaments factories were already working at full capacity.[8] For their part, many workers were convinced that under conditions of total war they would lose most of the few social concessions they had obtained since 1933. Moreover, most Germans who had experienced the First World War were strongly averse to any new military conflict.[9]

The political and military leaders of the Third Reich were thus agreed only in their conviction that a war would have to be waged against a weaker enemy and concluded as quickly as possible. As to how this aim should be realised, the two groups developed different answers based on different interests. As a result of the influence of National Socialist ideology, which assumed that the ability of an administrative organisation to function was best guaranteed by a Darwinistic struggle of various interest groups, there were no binding guidelines for conducting a 'short war'.

On the contrary, within the leadership élite there were at least two competing Blitzkrieg models in September 1939. The development of labour deployment policies in the first half of the war clearly shows whether and to what extent one of these two models was put into practice. The uninterrupted struggle for power between the Party and the armed forces, the leading exponents of the two conflicting plans for an optimal management of the war economy, was not decided until early summer of 1942 and resulted in particularly bitter disputes in this area.[10] Whereas the question of personnel replacements was of vital importance to the armed forces, the Party was, for the same reason, extremely sensitive to any change in the mood of the working population. Like a system of communicating tubes, labour allocation and military replacement policy were dependent on each other. Changes in either of these areas immediately affected the course of military operations. Even before the outbreak of the war the conviction that the German soldier felt himself to be racially superior caused Hitler to overlook obvious shortcomings in German units compared with the Polish enemy, as he later overlooked similar problems in planning the attack on the Soviet Union. On 14 August 1939 this attitude also caused him to give a rough estimate of the time required for the Poland campaign. However, this estimate cannot be regarded as a Blitzkrieg plan.[11]

In the following pages we shall attempt to outline the important phases of labour deployment and military personnel policy. It will become clear that, during the first half of the war, at least in these areas, Germany had neither a general Blitzkrieg plan nor the necessary administrative apparatus to carry one out.

Since the reintroduction of conscription, the leaders of the armed forces had demanded a comprehensive plan for the allocation of human resources in the event of war. Rising employment reduced the number of unemployed who could simply be conscripted or called to active duty, whereas, simultaneously, potential reserves were expanded. In August 1939 there were 34,000 unemployed males and about 2.66 million trained reservists and former soldiers.[12] Mobilisation would automatically mean that 2.5 million people would be taken away from their jobs. To avoid a repetition of the production stoppages in vital industries that had occurred in 1914, deferment measures had to be prepared early. In the armaments factories under the direct control of the armed forces the necessary preparations had been made, but in other sectors of the German economy not even the necessary index files had been prepared.[13] As the index files of the labour ministry included only persons who were not self-employed, those who were — primarily farmers, craftsmen and tradesmen and professional people — were not counted.[14] Files for the entire country which, in Göring's pithy phrase, would permit a mobilisation of every German 'national comrade' between the ages of fourteen and sixty, had not even progressed beyond the planning stage in 1939.[15] Altogether only about 58 per cent of the German working population was registered.[16] A Blitzkrieg plan such as the National Socialist regime had in mind, with a carefully calculated use of available forces, would have required particularly comprehensive advance personnel planning. Even this small detail shows the lack of any practical preparations for the realisation of the politically motivated Blitzkrieg plan. At the beginning of the war the situation was hardly more favourable for the total mobilisation demanded by the military. The armed forces had no clear guidelines for the processing of deferment applications. Until the autumn of 1940 they had to feel their way with a growing number of individual case decisions.[17]

The 'divided mobilisation', often considered part of the Blitzkrieg apparatus, was intended to maintain the government's complete political freedom of action until immediately before the outbreak of hostilities. This plan had proved to be of only limited effectiveness against Austria in 1938; in 1939 it revealed considerable shortcomings. The premature call-up of reservists for unlimited training in early summer and the mobilisation of the armed forces nine days before the corresponding measures for the economy were put into effect resulted in the call-up of many armaments factory employees in reserved occupations. In some cases considerable delays were involved before they were able to return to their civilian jobs.[18] This was a repetition of the events of August 1914, although the accompanying disruptions were not so serious. However, whereas the imperial German army had disposed of more than forty trained reservist classes, the German armed forces in 1939 had only four. These were the groups born during the First World War, when birth-rates had been unusually low. In some groups the number of able-bodied men was less than 50 per cent of the earlier classes from 1900–13.[19]

The still young German armaments industry, above all the aircraft industry, had recruited and trained skilled workers primarily from the age groups born during the First World War.[20] This, however, reduced the already small number of reservists from the youngest age group who were in reserved occupations.[21] The majority of those in the older and numerically greater age groups were, on the other hand, untrained and provided a considerable reservoir of labourers and recruits during the first years of the war. Because of their age and their lack of military training, they were not fit for immediate military service.

While this problem was a result of political developments and the demographic structure of the German population and had to be accepted, the German Labour Front (DAF), in co-operation with the regional party organisations and with the toleration of the national party headquarters, attempted to prevent any extensive reorganisation of the German economy to meet the requirements of the war. In order to avoid discontent among the population, the authorities generally refrained from any central direction of labour deployment, such as compulsory transfer of labourers to areas where they were needed, the elimination or restriction of the free movement of labour, the combing-out operations of the Reich Labour Ministry or the factory closing measures of the economics ministry.[22] By spreading armaments orders among as many suppliers as possible, the government and party leaders sought to avoid disrupting the economic structure of the country. Within a few months after the outbreak of the war, most small and medium-sized German firms had received at least one war-essential order, which permitted them to maintain their labour force more or less intact. The decision to avoid concentrating orders in relatively few firms meant that more skilled workers had to be exempted from military service than might otherwise have been necessary, but no firm was fully occupied with war-essential orders. Thus the production of consumer goods could continue, with few disruptions, by using available raw materials and semi-finished products.[23]

For ideological reasons the National Socialist regime resisted imposing compulsory work service for women, which was demanded by the armed forces; thus, the intention of the military leaders to make up for the loss of male labourers in this way, as had been done in the First World War, could not be realised. Even worse, the extremely high family support payments enabled many female industrial workers to stop working and get married at the beginning of the war.[24]

Although the German leaders had continued to hope until the declarations of war by the British and French governments that the conflict with Poland could be ended quickly, as a 'limited operation', they began at that time to prepare for a longer war. General Thomas, head of the war economy directorate (*Wehrwirtschaftsstab*, later *Wehrwirtschafts- und Rüstungsamt* (WiRüAmt)) in the armed forces high command (OKW) and an expert on armaments production in Germany, had warned earlier against designing a war plan exclusively for a short war.[25] By the end of October 1939 the head of the OKW had come to the conclusion that Germany should expect a long war,[26] while Field Marshal Göring was also of the opinion that no one could know how long the war would last.[27]

In October 1939 Hitler found himself in a dilemma which he had foreseen weeks before the outbreak of the war. In his opinion, there were many reasons why Germany had to strive for a short war, for example: the attitude of the neutral countries was uncertain — if the war lasted very long they could align themselves with the enemy, just as they had done in the First World War; the inner unity of the German people did not seem able to bear the strain of a long war;

unlike Poland's armed forces, the military strength of the Western powers, especially Britain, could not be estimated accurately, while an immediate threat to the German armaments industry in the Ruhr in the form of Allied air attacks certainly seemed possible.

In the first weeks after the end of the Polish campaign this uncertainty produced a strangely ambivalent estimate of the situation which alternated between the hope for a short conflict and the fear of a longer one.[28] Evidently influenced by Hitler's views and under the presumption of a stable situation in the west, this assessment began to change in November 1939, a change that can be clearly seen in the development of Keitel's views. In December he revised his estimation of the situation and pointed out that Hitler had realised that Germany could not sustain a long war and so intended to deliver the decisive blow before Christmas. 'We have to stake everything on one card', the dictator is supposed to have said.[29]

This important change of views between the end of September and the beginning of November 1939 was not limited to the political leaders; it was also noticeable in the general population. Incidents of refusal to work, which some historians claim had been widespread among German workers since the spring of 1939, actually showed considerable fluctuations. After the mobilisation they declined for a short time, increasing after the conclusion of the campaign in Poland and as a reaction to the 'phoney war' in the west.[30] This indicates that the population at first readily accepted the hardships of the war economy as an 'emergency situation', especially as the widespread anti-Polish attitudes and the declaration of war by the Western powers provided additional motivation to increase productivity. But when the conclusion of the campaign in Poland did not bring those conditions of peace which had always been reestablished after military action in previous years, and when at the same time an immediate threat did not become apparent on the Western Front, the industrial working class in particular began to fear that the regime wanted to use the situation to nullify the social progress they had made. It seems that it was not the attack on Poland, but rather the uncertain situation of the following months which caused unrest. Mason's thesis that German workers reacted to the outbreak of the war by working less hard thus requires correction.[31]

Several months later there were also differences in the assessment of the situation before the attack on France. After the experiences of 1914–18, General Thomas feared that the start of operations in the west would lead to battles of *matériel*.[32] The fear of suddenly facing great losses unprepared caused the military leaders to draft more and more recruits for five new waves of infantry divisions.[33] As the material losses of the Polish campaign and the gaps in supplies of ammunition could not at first be overcome for even the divisions of the first four waves, the situation of the new divisions and the replacement army was deplorable.[34] Nevertheless, until immediately before the attack in the west, more and more men in the 'white' age groups (born between 1900 and 1914) were trained. After eight weeks of training many of them had to be discharged and returned to civilian life, as the armed forces were unable to provide them with food and quarters.[35] Obviously the military leaders were still attempting to prepare for a total war.

Unlike the situation at the start of the Polish campaign, during which the military leaders, with one exception, agreed on their estimation of their own and their opponent's strength, there was no unanimity at the start of operations in the west. In contrast to the military technocrats (such as General Thomas), the aversion of the strategists to an attack on France decreased in direct proportion to the chances of success of the 'Sichelschnittplan'. This latent dissension among the various military leaders disappeared only shortly before the start of the war against the Soviet Union. Whereas the strategists considered the new operational plan the key to success, the technocrats in the army ordnance directorate, the organisation departments of the various branches of the armed forces and the general army directorate remained sceptical. As long as they defended their plan for a full mobilisation of all resources in constant disputes with the party, the personnel and material needs of the troops were generally met. Only after the technocrats became infected with the strategists' delusion that anything was possible, did a shift in the relationship between means and aims take place, with catastrophic consequences.

In September 1939, while the military leaders were attempting to mass sufficient forces for the attack on France that Hitler had ordered to be carried out as soon as possible, the military technocrats exhausted all possibilities in trying to avoid the execution of his order that 1.2 million soldiers who had served in the First World War be discharged.[36] The lack of trained reserves, which had become evident since the start of the war, was forcing the military planners to call up many men born between 1894 and 1899. Considerable powers of imagination are required to describe an army as a Blitzkrieg army if one-quarter of its soldiers are over forty years old and half of them have only a few weeks of training! The problems posed by a considerable disproportion of older soldiers as a result of an over-hasty rearmament was especially obvious in the age structure of the medium-rank officers. They constituted the mass of company and battalion commanders at the start of the war and had been for the most part junior officers in the First World War. In 1939 some of them were fifty-two years old. These officers were generally too old for the direct participation in actual fighting that their rank implied. A Blitzkrieg operation required energetic, younger company and battalion commanders.[37]

Although most of the former Front soldiers of the First World War were indispensable in rear areas and as non-commissioned officers, only a few of them were essential skilled workers in the armaments industry. Their discharge was therefore due exclusively to the desire of the regime to improve morale on the home front. The military technocrats, in co-operation with the commanders at the Front, used administrative manipulation to keep most of these soldiers until May 1940. This example shows the competing forces behind the two Blitzkrieg plans.

Not only was the equipment of the German armed forces generally unsatisfactory in the autumn of 1939, but also the organisation of the war economy was experiencing a crisis. After the war economy directorate in the OKW failed in its attempt to take control over war-essential and other vital industries away from the plenipotentiary for the economy (GBW), the chances of establishing an 'economic general staff' dominated by the military declined. This idea was itself a result of the experiences of the First World War.[38] Nevertheless, at the end of 1939 General Thomas made a new attempt to achieve a central direction of the war economy. As the position of the head of the OKW was considered too weak, Thomas regarded Göring, the head of the four-year plan, as a good man to advance the interests of the war economy organisations. It was hoped that, if he could be elevated to the position of armaments minister and the war economy directorate placed under his control, his influence on Hitler would help to neutralise the competing efforts of the party, the procurement offices of the service branches and the egoism of the leaders of the economy. This plan failed because of the distrust of the dictator, whom the increasing power of his henchman made uneasy, especially as it seemed out of all proportion to Göring's actual performance.[39]

When the munitions crisis threatened to become disastrous

shortly before the campaign against France, evidently even Hitler realised that the organisational anarchy of the different administrative centres entrusted with the management of the war economy offered no solution, although it had been deliberately promoted until then. A many-sided bureaucracy with numerous overlapping areas of responsibility was completely inadequate for the requirements of a functioning Blitzkrieg organisation. The appointment of Fritz Todt was not a step towards the necessary centralisation, but his closeness to Hitler did at least guarantee that the labour shortage in the supplier firms of the munitions factories would be quickly eliminated.[40] Barely a month after he assumed office, he achieved his first success in the 'Standstill Agreement for Special Tasks of the Defence of the Reich'.[41] This directive marked the end of the previous practice of individual exemptions from military service and the resulting innumerable individual instructions and exceptions. As long as the losses of the armed forces remained small, the exemption of entire work-forces in important armaments factories was possible in order to maintain continuous production over a long period of time.

After the rapid collapse of France, which surprised the German leaders as well as neutral observers, and the resulting victory, the chief of the army general staff, Halder, observed in a conference in Versailles that other nations were asking how the German victory had been achieved. The conduct of a war, he explained, was always a system of improvisations.[42] The organisation of the German war effort and war economy planning at the time could not be described more accurately.

The victory in the West marked an important psychological turning-point in the attitude of the German leaders as well as the German population towards the war. During the first ten months of the war, the leaders had generally based their planning on an accurate analysis of their personnel resources. This was the reason for the reluctance of the military technocrats to begin the attack on France early. Influenced by their experiences in the First World War, they regarded the French with considerable respect. With the passage of time after the previous campaign and the improved training and equipment of the German units, they became cautiously optimistic. The relief after the victory and the satisfaction of having eradicated the disgrace of 1918 soon led, however, to a new hubris and loss of all sense of proportion. After the lightning victory in the west, the idea of a Blitzkrieg seemed more realistic.

For this reason some scholars consider the redirection of the armaments programme against Britain, which went into effect with Hitler's order of 13 July 1940, as proof of a functioning Blitzkrieg organisation.[43]

If one considers only the central level of the decision-making process, this redirection may seem to have been a quick change in plans, but on the lower levels it generally did not proceed beyond the early stages. For example, the reduction in the size of the army demanded by Hitler changed imperceptibly into a qualitative improvement of the personnel situation. Some of the soldiers who had served in the First World War were discharged at this time. According to Hitler's instructions, they should have been sent home months before. The officer and non-commissioned officer cadres of inadequately equipped divisions were retained.[44] The army general staff prepared for a long war against an enemy in the east, whereas the political leaders placed emphasis on strengthening the navy and the air force in the war with Britain. As the army reduced its real strength only slightly, the strength of the navy and air force, which were especially important for Operation Sea Lion, rose only slightly (62,000/30,000).[45] In the armaments industry, orders for a conversion of capacity were not being issued. In this way considerable time was lost before the necessary manpower was transferred.[46] To judge the functioning of a Blitzkrieg economy by the chronology of central 'Führer' orders, as Milward attempts to do, is to overlook an important retarding factor. The administrative organisations, which he considers guarantors of a smoothly functioning Blitzkrieg economy, were partially responsible for the slowing of war production because of their bureaucratic rivalries. As a co-ordination of different programmes could be established only through the authority of a direct order from Hitler, the armaments industry usually had only a very short time for conversion, particularly as the political goals soon changed again. Only fourteen days after the order of 13 July 1940 had been issued, the chief of the OKW informed General Thomas of Hitler's intention to attack the Soviet Union.[47] As early as the beginning of August, Thomas stopped most of the conversion measures, which had just been started. This development can be clearly seen in the changes in the distribution of labourers within the main armaments programmes of the individual branches of the armed forces. On 1 August 1940 the emphasis in weapons production was still clearly on areas important to the army, whereas only small increases were made in those important or limited to the navy and air force. A comparison with production figures in March 1940 shows that no drastic changes had been made in the meantime. Production of signal and general equipment stagnated, but there were no signs of a change. Only munitions production declined significantly between March and August 1940. The situation remained unchanged until about the end of October. In this period production for the navy even declined noticeably, whereas that for the army and air force showed increases, that for the air force being greater than that of the army; this was due primarily to an increase in the flak programme. This was primarily of defensive benefit but had no immediate effect on the air war against Britain.[48] When, on 28 September 1940, Hitler demanded a change in armaments production to a main emphasis on equipment for the army, the industry had to increase its output but there was no need to redirect its capacity.

During the months after the conclusion of the campaign in France a change also took place in the attitude of the population towards the regime and the war. While the reports of the security service (SD) and the armament inspectorates repeatedly mentioned incidents of refusal to work and covert strike actions before May 1940, a clear feeling of satisfaction was now noticeable in broad sectors of the population. As had already become clear during the campaign in Poland, it seems that the population did not disapprove of the political aims of the regime in themselves but feared that attempts to achieve them might fail.[49] Even the Comintern admitted in the summer of 1940 that its agitation was meeting with less and less response among German industrial workers.[50] Thus the broad support of the population for the aims of the regime and the previous successes may actually have influenced Hitler to plan and attempt to conduct his war in the east as a Blitzkrieg. His decision was made easier by the military technocrats, who had abandoned their earlier caution and, after the overwhelming victory in the west, were now convinced that no power in Europe could stop Germany.[51] The German military leaders were aware of the personnel problems and shortages but believed that, because of German superiority to the Soviet Union, whose national character, political system, military strength and economy were considered completely inferior, these factors would present no significant difficulties.[52] Although development of Germany's human and material resources could not be measurably improved, the psychological situation and the political and ideological agreement within the leading élites and large segments of the population seemed more favourable than six months earlier.

By the summer of 1941 the area of labour deployment evinced several signs of a practical change to a Blitzkrieg plan with a precisely calculated use of resources. The expansion of the armed forces resulted in a further depletion of the available reserves in the 'white' age groups, especially as the liberal exemption policy was continued. At first there was no systematic recruiting of foreign workers, and the counter-intelligence services' fear of possible sabotage or subversion prevented a large-scale use of prisoners of war in the armaments industry. Ideological objections excluded an increased use of women and so a short-term plan was developed to overcome the shortage of skilled workers, primarily in the metal industry, by the extensive seconding of fully-trained troops to work in the armaments factories.[53] To enable soldiers to produce their own weapons seemed to make it possible to square the circle in the demographic situation in which Germany found herself. But this project, attractive at first glance, could succeed only if the planned military campaign did not result in high personnel and material losses. Such losses would have a double effect, as not only soldiers but also skilled workers in armaments production would have to be replaced. This risk could be accepted only by someone who believed absolutely in the success of his strategic planning. The attempt to realise this project in the winter of 1940/1 proved once again that the centrifugal forces in the bureaucracy of the National Socialist state made the carrying out of a Blitzkrieg plan impossible. The field army, which was supposed to provide the necessary workers, was scheduled to be expanded by 46 per cent. The mechanised divisions, which required the greatest number of soldiers from the metal industry, were to be almost doubled. Since the start of rearmament, Germany had used the principle of organic cell division in expanding its armed forces. This method involved the formation of new units with the help of trained or even experienced divisions. The manpower gaps of the new and the battle-tested divisions were filled by replacements trained in short courses. All units thus had a certain number of experienced officers, NCOs and older enlisted men. The disadvantage was that the internal cohesion of the divisions was lost for a time and could be restored only by extensive training. In the late summer of 1940 the political and economic leaders and influential military technocrats were of the opinion that a large number of soldiers could be discharged without danger. But this time the army units themselves opposed a further disruption of their training plans.[54] Their main objection was to the leave policy under which, as early as October 1940, 300,000 men were to be placed at the disposal of the armaments industry. Opponents of such policies again resorted to the administrative delaying tactics they had used successfully since the start of the war. They were able to prevent the departure of seconded soldiers until the middle of January and to hold the number to only a few more than 100,000, as opposed to the 300,000 originally planned.[55]

However, by that time the economic assumptions had undergone a basic change. On the basis of experience gained in the French campaign and the maxims of the Blitzkrieg plan with limited forces, the war economy directorate in the OKW reported at the end of November 1940 that a twelve months' supply of ammunition would be available at the planned start of the campaign against the Soviet Union; on the other hand, equipment for the eastern army was sufficient for only three months.[56] In spite of these time limits, the German planners thought that supplies for the armed forces were adequate. On 20 December 1940, only two days after signing the operational directive for Barbarossa, Hitler decided that, when the Blitzkrieg plan goals were achieved, the corresponding production capacity was to be converted to the manufacture of weapons for the air force and navy for the continuation of the war against Britain.[57]

Hitler's decision marked the first introduction of a typical factor of the Blitzkrieg plan in German calculations, the limited time period. While the armaments industry had produced exclusively for current operations before and during the French campaign, before the start of the war in the east basic decisions were made about the conversion of production for the continuation of the struggle with Britain.

The extent to which the planning in December 1940 began to have concrete effects even before the start of Operation Barbarossa can be seen in the further application of the policy of seconding members of the armed forces to work in the armaments industry. Instead of immediately being returned to the army for further training after their secondment, many of these soldiers were retained in the industry in the spring of 1941 to work in the navy and air force production programmes.[58] This contributed to the further rise in the number of persons in reserved occupations. At the start of operations in the east, there were more than 5 million people in this classification.[59] As a result of the Blitzkrieg plan with limited operational resources, the German field army, which had disposed of considerable operational reserves during the campaign in France, had to start the war in the east in the summer of 1941, almost without reserve formations, even though it had been enlarged in the meantime.[60]

With regard to the timescale envisaged, Operation Barbarossa clearly differed from the planning for the campaign in France. Before the start of operations in the west, the general army directorate had decreed a stop on exemptions for persons already serving in the field army, in order to preclude the removal of soldiers during the campaign. This was also done before the start of the campaign in the Soviet Union, but this time with the significant difference that the stop was limited to three months and was scheduled to be rescinded in September 1941.[61]

A few days before the attack in the east, Göring obtained a new order from Hitler that required a large-scale conversion of production capacity designated for the army to the needs of the air force.[62] This order, comparable in its content to that of 13 July 1940, was issued not after the conclusion of the Russian campaign but before it even started. After energetic protests by the navy, which felt threatened, Hitler issued another order on 14 July 1941 which reflected his elation at the apparently approaching victory over the Soviet Union and required an increase not only in armaments for the air force and the navy but also in production of the equipment for the army formations which were to advance on to the Middle East after the conclusion of Barbarossa.[63]

The inflexibility of the Third Reich bureaucracy and its inability to react to a changing military situation, as well as the rigidity of the German political leaders in their refusal to abandon the Blitzkrieg plan, can be seen in the fact that, in spite of constantly increasing losses in the east in the summer of 1941, the number of exemptions continued to rise and reached the very high figure of almost 5.6 million, in September 1941. By the end of 1941 it had levelled off and began to decline at the start of 1942. In the late summer of 1941 the leaders of the German war economy believed, as did the political and military leaders, in the possibility of making up for material losses and achieving the necessary new equipping of the armed forces by granting leave on an even larger scale than had previously been done. The Blitzkrieg plan began to perpetuate itself. At the beginning of December 1941 the Soviet counter-offensive finally revealed the bankruptcy of this strategy. It became clear that not only the material requirements had been underestimated from the very beginning, but also the necessary specialists for new production were no longer available. Reductions in the number of exemptions and the use of Soviet prisoners of war and foreign workers to cover personnel losses were the inevitable result. At the same time, the plundering of occupied areas had to be increased considerably. The economic bureaucracy also adjusted very slowly to the new situation this time. The 'Special Company Protection Agreement', whose liberal guidelines had left too many non-essential workers who were fit for military service at home, remained in effect until 31 March 1942.[64] The armed forces leaders and, primarily, the military technocrats paid for their generally uncritical support of Hitler's ideologically-influenced Blitzkrieg plan with an almost total loss of authority in 1942. With the establishment of Speer's ministry a concentration of all economic power was begun in order to prepare for the now inevitable 'total war'. Meanwhile, in November 1941 after the slowing down of the German advance in the east, Hitler had dissociated himself from the use of the term 'Blitzkrieg': 'I have never used the word "Blitzkrieg" because it is a very stupid word'.[65]

If one wishes to classify the major German campaigns of the first half of the war, they can be divided into three groups. Firstly, the attacks on Poland, Scandinavia and France were largely determined by the military demand for an optimal armaments production to achieve the required operational goals. Not the least important reason for their success was the fact that the military technocrats in some cases deliberately disregarded the domestic interests of the political leaders, who themselves had no exact idea of how long a given campaign would last. Secondly, there were the Balkan and African campaigns, which were limited operations and need not concern us here. Therefore the third campaign, the war in the east, remains a planned and, at first, successful Blitzkrieg. The spectacular and unexpectedly rapid victory over France created a specific psychological climate which was conducive to the development of the Blitzkrieg concept. This climate was the result of an overestimation of the political and military leadership of the Reich, whereas the population and the army, remembering the war of 1914 to 1918, over-estimated the military importance of the French defeat. An additional factor was the under-estimation of the Soviet Union as an inferior enemy, which was based more on irrational subjective prejudices than on factual knowledge. The precisely calculated time plan together with the limited mobilisation of resources based on supposedly exact estimations of the strength of the enemy produced a classic example of an attempt to apply Blitzkrieg theory to an actual war. When this attempt failed, the subordination of basic principles of military leadership to ideological premises was the inevitable result.

The highest-ranking German officers paid for their hubris of June 1940 and their support of the regime's Blitzkrieg plan by being forced to follow the path they had chosen to the bitter end without being able to exert a lasting influence on the course of events.

Notes

1. O. Hintze, *Die Hohenzollern und ihr Werk*, Berlin, 1915, p. 326.
2. A. S. Milward, 'Der Einfluss ökonomischer und nichtökonomischer Faktoren auf die Strategie des Blitzkrieges', in *Wirtschaft und Rüstung am Vorabend des Zweiten Weltkrieges*, edited by F. Forstmeier and H. Volkmann, Düsseldorf, 1975, pp. 189–201.
3. T. W. Mason, 'Innere Krise und Angriffskrieg 1938/1939', ibid., pp. 158–88.
4. H.M.D. Parker, *Manpower. A Study of War-time Policy and Administration*, London, 1957; B. Fairchild and J. Grossman, *The Army and Industrial Manpower*, Washington, 1959.
5. See, for instance, E. L. Homze, *Foreign Labor in Nazi Germany*, Princeton, 1967; U. von Gerstorff; *Frauen im Kriegsdienst 1914–1945*, Stuttgart, 1969; D. Winkler, *Frauenarbeit im 'Dritten Reich'*, Hamburg, 1977; D. Petzina, 'Soziale Lage der deutschen Arbeiter und Probleme des Arbeitseinsatzes während des Zweiten Weltkrieges', in W. Dlugoborski, *Zweiter Weltkrieg und Sozialer Wandel*, Göttingen, 1981, pp. 65–86; H. E. Kannapin, *Wirtschaft unter Zwang. Anmerkungen und Analysen zur rechtlichen und politischen Verantwortung der deutschen Wirtschaft unter der Herrschaft des Nationalsozialismus im Zweiten Weltkrieg, besonders im Hinblick auf den Einsatz und die Behandlung von ausländischen Arbeitskräften und Konzentrationslagerhäftlingen in deutschen Industrie- und Rüstungsbetrieben*, Cologne, 1966; L.J. Rupp, *Mobilizing Women for War. German and American Propaganda 1937–1945*, Princeton, 1981; D. Eichholtz, 'Zur Lage der deutschen Werktätigen im ersten Kriegsjahr 1939/40', in *Jahrbuch für Wirtschaftsgeschichte*, 1967, Part I, pp. 147–71; J. Kuczynski, *Die Geschichte der Lage der Arbeiter unter dem Kapitalismus. Studien zur Geschichte des staatsmonopolistischen Kapitalismus in Deutschland 1918–1945*, Berlin, 1963; D. G. Morgan,

Weiblicher Arbeitsdienst in Deutschland, Darmstadt, 1978.

6. The files held by the Bundesarchiv/Koblenz relating to compulsory labour contain much less than the holdings of the Bundesarchiv/Militärarchiv in Freiburg with its OKW Wehrwirtschaftsstab/ Wehrwirtschafts-und Rüstungsamt materials which we have barely begun to evaluate.

7. G. Thomas, *Geschichte der deutschen Wehr- und Rüstungswirtschaft (1918–1943/5)*, edited by W. Birkenfeld, Boppard, 1966. Thomas's views are also reflected in lecture notes by the head of the Lehrstab in the Wehrwirtschaftsstab, Lt. Col. Nagel, who articulated them in many variations before leading representatives of the Nazi Party, of industry and of the Wehrmacht. See the collection of speeches covering the years 1938–1939, in BA-MA, Wi/IF 5. 154.

8. File note of a meeting with General Thomas on 13 November 1939 at which representatives of the GBW, Reichsarbeitsministerium, Reichswirtschaftsministerium, Vierjahresplan and of the Wehrwirtschafts-und Rüstungsamt were also present. KTB, WiRü Amt/Rü Abt. Anlagen Bd. 1, Nr. 20, BA-MA, RW 19/261.

9. Speech by State Secretary Syrup (RAM) to the heads of the Beschaffungsämter der Wehrmachtteile, 22 November 1939. KTB, WiRü Amt/Rü Abt. Anlagen vol. 1, no. 20, BA-MA, RN 19/261.

10. Thomas, *Geschichte*, pp. 201–02.

11. Speech before the Oberbefehlshabern der Wehrmachtteile on 14 August 1939, in Max Domarus, *Hitler Reden und Proklamationen*, 2 vols., Würzburg, 1962, 1963, II, p. 1229; see also Hitler's Denkschrift of 9 October 1939, BA-MA, RW 4/v. 35.

12. OKH/Heereswaffenamt, Denkschrift über die personelle Leistungsfähigkeit Deutschlands im Mob-Fall of 18 March 1939, WaA, Nr. 170/39 gk Wa Stab Ia, BA-MA, Wi/IF 5. 844.

13. Contribution by Gruppe RüIV of WStb at the meeting of Wehrwirtschaft Inspectors on 12/13 October 1939, BA-MA, RW 19/305.

14. Speech by State Secretary Syrup before members of the Reichskriegsministerium in 1938 concerning the administration of labour, BA-MA, Wi/IF 5. 1232.

15. Generalfeldmarschall Göring before members of the Reichsverteidigungsrat on 18 November 1938 (stenographic excerpts) in: WWi Az. 11 k 20 WWi 10 g.k., 25 November 1938, BA-MA, Wi/ IF 5. 3452.

16. Minutes of the first meeting of the Reichsverteidigungsrat on 18 November 1938, S. 9, BA-MA Wi/ IF 5. 560, Vol. 1.

17. Heeresdruckvorschrift No. D 3/14 of 11 November 1940, 'Bestimmungen für Unabkömmlichstellung bei besonderem Einsatz'; Wehrwirtschaftsinspekteur VI (Münster) Az. 1 k 35/ Z Abt. Gr. Ib Br. Nr. 15758/39 geh., 14 November 1939, BA-MA, Wi/ IF 5. 375.

18. Der Generalbevollmächtigte für die Wirtschaft, 1/4013/39g, Rs., 2 August 1939, BA-MA, Wi/ IF 5. 672.

19. *Statistisches Jahrbuch für das Deutsche Reich*, 58, *1939/40*, Berlin, 1940; B. Mueller Hillebrand, *Das Heer 1933–1945*, vol. I, Darmstadt, 1954, p. 141; Der Reichsminister der Luftfahrt und Oberbefehlshaber der Luftwaffe – Chef der Luftwehr 12 d – 1074/41 g. Kdos (L Wehr 2

IVA), 14 October 1941; Ersatzlage der Luftwaffe im Rahmen der Wehrmacht, Stand 4 August 1941, MGFA, Microfilm 106 (Rhoden Collection).

20. FM-Verfahren für Facharbeiter der Reserve I und II, OKW/AHA/ Ag/E (Vb) Nr. 2880.39 g., 26 October 1939, BA-MA, Wi/ IF 5. 2621.

21. Memorandum by OKW/WiRüAmt/Oberst Jansen: "Der Arbeitseinsatz im Kriege produced by Rechtsanwalt Schulz, June 1940, BA-MA, Wi/IF 5. 1113, p. 11.

22. See note 8; OKW/WiRü Amt Stab Nr. 79/40 g.k.Ib 5 Az. 66 k 15, Kriegswirtschaftlicher Lagebericht Nr. 4 (December 1939), BA-MA RW 19/97.

23. OKW/WiRü Amt/Rü Abt., entry in War Diary on 3. 10. 1939, BA-MA, RW 19/253.

24. File note on negotiations between OKW/WiRüAmt and Reichsarbeitsministerium on 22 February 1940, KTB OKW/WiRüAmt/Rü Abt. Bd. 2, BA-MA RW 19/254.

25. Remarks by General Thomas before the Wehrwirtschaftsinspekteuren on 28 March 1939, OKW Az 34 x W Stb/W Rü (Ia¹) Nr. 1821/39p, 31 March 1939, BA-MA, Wi/IF 5. 384 Teil 2.

26. OKW/WiRü Amt Stab Ib 5, Interne Monatsberichte zur deutschen Rüstungwirtschaft, September 1939, BA-MA, RW 19/206.

27. Excerpts from a speech by Göring before Wehrersatzinspekteuren on 24 October 1939, circulated in Der Oberbefehlshaber des Heeres, Az. 1 k 35 AHA/Ag/E (Vb), Nr. 3412/39 geh. vom 6. November 1939, BA-MA, Wi/ IF 5. 2890.

28. Denkschrift of 9 October 1939, RW 4/v. 35, p. 14.

29. Discussion between Keitel and Thomas on 4 December 1939, KTB/ OKW/WiRü Amt/Stab, 4 December 1939, BA-MA, RW 19/164.

30. From among a wealth of material a few examples: File note of discussion of the heads of the air force departments in the Wehrwirtschafts inspections at the B.f.L. on 29. September 1939, here the statement by General Mooyer. WRü IVb, 2 October 1939, BA-MA, RW 19/312; Hauptmann Bodensiek, OKW/W Allg. (Ic), Report on morale in the Ruhr Area (Duisburg, Oberhausen, Mülheim, Essen), 11 September 1939, BA-MA, Wi/ I 316; Wehrkreiskommando VI Abt. Ic Nr. 25/39geh. Kdos., 30 August 1939, BA-MA, Wi/ I 316.

31. See also Mason, *Innere Krise*, pp. 186f.

32. Minutes of General Thomas' meeting with representatives of the Reichsbahn on 8 November 1939, KTB OKW/WiRü Amt/Stab, Anlagen Bd. 2, BA-MA, RW 19/172.

33. G. Tessin, *Verbände und Truppen der deutschen Wehrmacht und Waffen-SS*, vol. 1, *Die Waffengattungen-Gesamtübersicht*, Osnabrück, 1977, pp. 46–50.

34. OKH/GenStdH/Ausb. Abt. Nr. 30/39g, 28 August 1939, BA-MA, RH 54/99, Ausbildung im Ersatzheer.

35. Der Chef des Wehrwirtschafts- und Rüstungsamtes (IIa), Nr. 3925/ 39geh 13 November 1939, BA-MA, Wi/IF 5.384 Teil 2.

36. OKH/AHA/Ag/E (Va), Nr. 2900/39 geh. 19 September 1939, BA-MA, RH 19 III/95.

37. Heerespersonalamt (1. Staffel) Nr. 549/42 g.Kdos. of 6 July 1942. Summary of the composition and sociology of the officer corps and the consequences to be drawn from this in OKH/GenStdH Zentralabteilung, Die personelle Entwicklung des Generalstabes des Heeres während des Krieges 1939–19[42], vol. 3, Anlagen (June 1941–July 1942), here Anlage 3, BA-MA, RH 2/v. 155.

38. File note on discussion between General Thomas and Generalmajor von Hanneken (RWM) et al. on 18 November 1939, W Stb. Adj., 18 November 1939, KTB OKW/WiRüAmt/Stab, Anlagen, vol. 2, BA-MA, RW 19/172.

39. KTB OKW/WiRüAmt/Stab, entry for 21 November 1939, BA-MA, RW 19/163.

40. KTB OKW/WiRüAmt/Stab, entry for 1 April 1940, BA-MA, RW 19/164.

41. OKW/WiRüAmt/Stab Ib 5, Interne Monatsberichte zur deutschen Rüstungswirtschaft, April 1940, BA-MA, RW 19/205; 'Stillhalteabkommen für besondere Vorhaben im Interesse der Reichsverteidigung' first circulated in Fernschreiben OKW/AHA/Ag/E (Vb) Nr. 554/40 geh. 19 April 1940, KTB OKW/WiRüAmt/Rü Abt. Anlagen Bd. 3, Nr. 50, BA-MA, RW 19/263.

42. Speech by Chef des Generalstabes des Heeres before the generals at Versailles on 28 June 1940, HGr. C Ia Nr. 1119/40 gk, 29 June 1940 (summary in note-form), BA-MA, RH 19 III/141.

43. A. S. Milward, Die deutsche Kriegswirtschaft 1939–1945, Stuttgart, 1966, p. 39.

44. GenStdH/Org. Abt. (1.St.) (I), Nr. 2899/40 geh. to Chef HRüst und B.d.E./AHA, Betr. Demobilmachung des Heeres, 1 July 1940, BA-MA, RH 2/v. 1112.

45. Notes by OKW/WiRüAmt/ Gruppenleiter Rü IV, Major Dr Krull, for his speech at a meeting on 12 August 1940, BA-MA, RW 19/307.

46. Meeting at Rüstungsinspektion III (Berlin) on 31 July 1940, KTB OKW/WiRü Amt/Rü Abt. vol. 4, p. 188, BA-MA, RW 19/256.

47. Keitel to Thomas, 29 July 1940, quoted in Colonel Dr Hedler, 'Die Umsteuerung der Wirtschaft', December 1940, p. 44, OKW/ WiRüAmt, BA-MA Wi/IF 5. 2276.

48. Milward, Kriegswirtschaft, p. 39; and note 43.

49. Report by Rüstungsinspektion IX, 13 July 1940, BA-MA, Wi/IF 5. 2699; Meldungen aus dem Reich, no. 116, 19 August 1940; no. 104 11 July 1940, BA-MA Wi/IF 5. 2748.

50. H. Focke and U. Reimer, Alltag der Entrechteten. Wie die Nazis mit ihren Gegnern umgingen, Reinbek 1980, pp. 24–25.

51. OKH/Org. Abt. (I), Nr. 507/41 g. Kdos. Chef-Sache, 7 April 1941, attached to OKH/Op. Abt. Nr. 675/41 g. Kdos. Chef-Sache, BA-MA, RH 2/v. 427.

52. J. Förster, in Das Deutsche Reich und der Zweite Weltkrieg, edited by Militärgeschichtliches Forschungsamt, vol. 4, Der Angriff auf die Sowjetunion, Stuttgart, 1983, pp. 188ff., 440ff.

53. Reichsminister Dr Ing. Fritz Todt, G I Nr. 3986/40Dem., to Generalfeldmarschall Keitel, 27 September 1940, BA-MA, Wi/IF 5. 120 Teil 1.

54. OKH (Chef HRüst u. BdE) AHA/Ag/H/ Id Rü, 27 November 1940, circulated in Div. 157 (Wehrkreis VII) Tgb. Nr. 2499/40geh. of 2 December 1940, BA-MA, RH 54/118.

55. Zentralstatistik OKW (3) geh., 1 July 1941, Die Entwicklung des Einsatzes von Wehrmachtangehörigen in der Kriegswirtschaft. BA-MA, RW 19/330.

56. Response to Wi und Rü Amt file note of 30 November 1940 betr. Überprüfung der Rüstungsprogramme. OKW/WFSt. 3 December 1940, in *Kriegstagebuch des Oberkommandos der Wehrmacht (Wehrmachtführungsstab)* edited by Percy Ernst Schramm, Vol. I, Frankfurt 1965, p. 981.

57. Discussion between Halder and Fromm on 23 December 1940 in F. Halder, *Kriegstagebuch Tägliche Aufzeichnungen des Chefs des Generalstabes des Heeres 1939–19*, 3 vols., Stuttgart, 1962–1964, II, pp. 240–1.

58. KTB/OKW/WiRü Amt/Stab, entry for 12 March 1941, BA-MA, RW 19/164.

59. OKW Az. 1 i 15 (305) Wi Rü Amt/Rü IV f/(Rü Z St) Nr. 1524/42 g. II Ang., 31 March 1942, Ergebnisse der volkswirtschaftlichen Kräftebilanz, Stand 31 May 1941, BA-MA, Wi/IF 5. 1123.

60. *Das Deutsche Reich und der Zweite Weltkrieg*, edited by Militärgeschichtliches Forschungsamt, vol. 4, Stuttgart, 1983, Beiheft, Anlage 2.

61. Der Chef des Oberkommandos der Wehrmacht 12 i k 10 WFSt/Abt. L (II Org) Nr. 1261/41 geh. of 12. Mai 1941, Massnahmen zur Deckung des Ersatzbedarfs für die Wehrmacht, BA-MA, Wi/IF 5. 2254.

62. Der Führer und Oberste Befehlshaber der Wehrmacht, 20 June 1941, BA-MA, Wi/ IF 5. 120, part 2.

63. Der Führer und Oberste Befehlshaber der Wehrmacht WFSt/Abt L (II Org) Nr. 441219/41g. Kdos. Chefs. 14 July 1941, BA-MA, Wi/IF 5. 321; also printed in Thomas, *Geschichte*, pp. 452–5.

64. KTB OKW/WiRü Amt/Stab, entry for 12 December 1941, Report by Gruppenleiter Rü IV Major Dr Krull to General Thomas, BA-MA, RW 19/166.

65. Hitler on 6 November 1941 in the *Löwenbräukeller* in Munich, in M. Domarus, II, p. 1776.

JÜRGEN FÖRSTER

New Wine in Old Skins? The Wehrmacht and the War of 'Weltanschauungen', 1941

Hitler launched his war against the Soviet Union on 22 June 1941. The Führer was well aware that this new war would entail the mass slaughter of Jews and Communists; moreover, he was not the only German who knew it. Operation Barbarossa cannot be compared to the earlier campaigns. In spite of the efforts of National Socialist propaganda to view it as a necessary defensive action against an imminent Soviet attack and to praise it as 'Europe's crusade against Bolshevism', Barbarossa was a carefully planned war of extermination.[1] This totally different character of the German–Soviet war resulted from Hitler's determination to realise his idea of Lebensraum, in which German expansion to the east, the extermination of Bolshevism and the annihilation of Jewry were all inextricably intertwined.[2] Hitler's 'Weltanschauung' encompassed race, autarky, living space and world politics. His goals were to be achieved through war, wherein Germany would face the grand alternative: victory or total destruction.

Hitler's concept of Lebensraum must be understood as forming the basis for all his political decisions during the years 1933–45, despite tactical improvisations. The importance of his Weltanschauung is clearly demonstrated in a seldom-cited speech to army field commanders on 10 February 1939. With this address, Hitler intended not only to make propaganda for his risky expansionist policy against Czechoslovakia, but also to disclose to his military commanders the National Socialist world view in more detail than he deemed politic to reveal to the general public.[3] A general, Hitler pointed out, must know each category of his leader's policy in order to understand the Führer's further manoeuvres. One could, after all, answer 'very rigorously and courageously' only for something which one comprehended. Hitler then began to explain why the existing German living space was insufficient for his people: there was not enough land to produce the necessary food stuffs, nor to provide the economy with necessary raw materials; he could conceive of no other possibility than to adjust the living space to the anticipated growth of population; he was determined to solve this problem; this thought would govern his entire life; now that the recognition of the importance of race was forcing mankind into conflict, the next war would be 'purely a war of Weltanschauungen, that is, totally a people's war, a racial war". Hitler also demanded that his generals acknowledge him as supreme ideological leader. As officers, they owed allegiance to him as supreme commander of the Wehrmacht, now they were to pledge themselves to him unconditionally as their ideological 'Führer'. Even if the remainder of the German people should desert him in his fight for this ideology, the German soldier and the entire officer corps, man for man, should stand beside him, shoulder to shoulder. The reaction of the audience was partly enthusiastic and partly very sceptical.[4]

Hitler's clear-cut demand that the entire officer corps form his 'guard to the bitter end' to aid him in achieving specific ideological objectives is extremely significant for an understanding of the relationship between himself and the Wehrmacht. Hitler only repeated what the commander-in-chief of the army, Colonel-General von Brauchitsch, had demanded on 18 December 1938 in his directive on education:

> The officer corps must not allow itself to be surpassed by anyone in the purity and genuineness of its National Socialist Weltanschauung. It is the standard-bearer, remaining unshakeable if everything else should fail. It stands to reason that in every situation the officer acts according to the ideas of the Third Reich, even if such ideas have not been laid down in legal terms, decrees or official orders. He must also be the leader of his subordinates politically. That does not mean that he should talk with them much about politics, but that he must be master of the great fundamental ideas of National Socialism, otherwise he will not be able to answer questions put to him and not to explain and discuss in line of these ideas questions of the day properly.[5]

Brauchitsch's and Hitler's demands are significant too when viewed against the background of the latter's address to the generals on 30 March 1941 and his 'prophecy' to the Reichstag on 30 January 1939: 'If the Jews of international finance, inside and outside Europe, should once more succeed in plunging the people of the Continent into another World War, the consequence will be not the Bolshevisation of the world and thus the victory of Jewry, but the annihilation of the Jewish race in Europe.'[6] The minutes of the Reichstag note 'long and vigorous applause' at this point. It was in this light that Hitler viewed the British and French declaration of war on Germany on 3 September 1939. Consequently he declared before his military leaders on 23 November 1939 that 'a racial war has broken out and this war shall determine who shall govern Europe, and with it, the world'.[7]

German expansion to the east had long been justified not only in economic, political and geographic terms, but also in the social Darwinistic sense of the right of the stronger in the struggle for survival. Lately it had also been justified as a defence against the radical enemy images conjured up by the words 'Bolshevism' and 'Jewry'. 'Domestic and foreign Bolshevism' and the influence of Jewry were both seen by the conservative military leaders not only as a threat to the German national state, but also as a necessary component in their assessment of the Red Army in 1940/1.[8]

The relevant remarks of General von Fritsch and Rear-Admiral Fricke are well known. Almost unknown, however, are the reflections of a major in the general staff who later joined the military opposition to Hitler and was executed in 1944. Three weeks after the beginning of Barbarossa Major Bernardis declared:

> Now the conflict with Great Britain which is being fought for political, ideological and economic reasons (democracy, Jewry and capitalism) must take a back seat. Germany is fighting the Soviet Union for her very existence and influence. I believe that these considerations were already taken into account by the Führer before the outbreak of the war and that the war in the west had to be waged in order to secure the German rear. The Führer would certainly have accepted a compromise with England. He believed that he had to fight a war against Russia in order once and for all to free the German people from this menace.[9]

Bernardis explicitly blamed the Jews as the enemies of Germany in her struggle for a New Order in Europe, for the purpose of securing her living space and her vital needs. This officer had a full understanding of Hitler's programme. There was, in fact, a short time after the fall of France during which Hitler was convinced that London 'would cave in' and be ready for a 'division of the world'.[10] Not until Britain had made it clear that she would not submit to Hitler did he give verbal orders to prepare planning to tackle the Soviet problem. In 1940/1 the strategic necessity of safeguarding the German sphere of influence *vis-à-vis* the Anglo-Saxon naval powers and of eliminating the latent threat by the Soviet Union were combined with the realisation of the objectives of his Weltanschauung.

From the end of February 1941 onwards, when military preparations for Operation Barbarossa were already far advanced, Hitler articulated — first within a small circle of his advisers and then before a wider military public — his decision to conduct the approaching campaign as a war of extermination. On 3 March 1941 Hitler rejected the OKW's (armed forces high command) 'Guidelines for Special Fields to Directive No. 21 (Case Barbarossa)' that had provided for military administration in the territory to be occupied. The campaign, as Hitler pointed out, was to be more than a battle between two armies, it would also lead to a struggle between two ideologies. The Soviet Union must be demolished, and the 'Jewish–Bolshevik intelligentsia' that had oppressed the people must be 'liquidated'.[11] General Jodl gave instructions to his staff as to how the guidelines were to be altered. Military administration was to be restricted to the area of operation, that is the combat zone and the rear areas of the armies and the army groups. 'The necessity for immediate liquidation of all Bolshevik bosses and commissars' would entail the use of the SS in the area of operation in addition to the army's secret field police. Courts martial should be excluded from this sphere. Two days later the new draft passed on to the OKH (army high command) for comment. The army command accepted the order that Himmler be entrusted with 'special tasks' in the area of operation, even though they had known since Poland what this signified. Thus the OKW's 'Guidelines for Special Fields' could be issued on 13 March and also conveyed special orders governing the conduct of soldiers and the functions of courts martial.

Can one argue that the Wehrmacht senior officers and their legal advisers were, as in 1939, happy to be permitted to concentrate on military matters and not to be held answerable for the National

Socialist programme of extermination? Did they turn a blind eye to such policies, as the draft agreement between the army and the SS of 26 March 1941 may suggest? Or did they accept the Bolshevik–Jewish identification as an unquestioned dogma of Nazi ideology? It is significant that, on 27 March, Field Marshal von Brauchitsch, commander-in-chief of the army, instructed his commanders-in-chief to regard the German–Soviet war as a struggle between two different races, requiring their troops to act with all necessary harshness.[12] Even more striking is the fact that, shortly after the Belgrade putsch and Hitler's relevant speech of 30 March, not only was the draft agreement between the army and the SS validated for the operations in the Balkans, but Jews and Communists were also explicitly included among those of Germany's enemies who were to be handled by the SS.[13]

Hitler was determined to convert the Wehrmacht into an instrument of extermination alongside the SS. Thus he wanted to erase the boundary between military and political-ideological warfare in the east. He made his intention known in a long address to the commanders-in-chief and their chiefs of staff in the Reich Chancellery on 30 March. Halder noted down in his diary:

> Clash between two Weltanschauungen .... Bolshevism equals antisocial crime .... We must get away from the standpoint of soldierly comradeship. The communist is no comrade, either before or after. It is a war of extermination .... We do not wage war in order to preserve the enemy .... Extermination of the Bolshevik commissars and communist intelligentsia .... The battle must be conducted against the poison of decay. This is not a question of courts martial. The leaders must know what is involved. They must take the lead in this struggle! The troops must defend themselves with the methods with which they are attacked. Commissars and secret service personnel are criminals and must be treated as such. The troops need not get out of their leader's control. The leader must give his orders in accordance with the feelings of the troops. The leaders must make sacrifices and overcome their scruples.[14]

Many a general must have remembered Hitler's demand of 10 February 1939 to be acknowledged as their supreme ideological leader.

Although it was Hitler who wanted to transform Barbarossa into a war of extermination against Bolshevism and Jewry, it was the

Wehrmacht senior officers and their legal advisers who cast his ideological intentions into legally valid form: 'Decree concerning the Exercise of Military Jurisdiction and Procedure in the Barbarossa area and Special Measures of the Troops in Russia' of 13 May 1941; 'Guidelines for the Treatment of Political Commissars' of 6 June 1941. Those directives which gave the war in the east its special character emerged out of a routine bureaucratic process within the relevant departments of the Wehrmacht. In the centre of the army's preparations for the struggle against the 'deadly enemy of National Socialist Germany' stood Halder, not Brauchitsch or his oftenmentioned 'general officer on special duties attached to commander-in-chief', General Eugen Müller. After October 1940 Müller was subject to directives 'regarding the military jurisdiction within the army and against the population of occupied territories'. Regardless of Müller's title those directives came from *Halder* and not Brauchitsch.[15]

The army's draft for a decree concerning the restriction of military jurisdiction and the treatment of political commissars of 6 May 1941 was not simply a minimal compliance with Hitler's intentions. Since Halder was willing to let the troops participate in the intended ideological war, the OKH not only drafted its own instructions to the troops to shoot suspected guerrillas 'while fighting or escaping', but also took the initiative against the 'bearers of the Jewish–Bolshevik world view' in the Red Army and provided for the execution of the commissars. The army leadership saw an inherent connection between the two drafted measures which it justified with the need for ensuring absolute security for the German soldier and with post-1918 German history.

While the bureaucratic process within the top commands continued, some officers took Hitler's suggestion of 30 March seriously and defined their own standpoint towards the antagonistic ideology. For example, in an address to his divisional commanders on 25 April 1941 the commander of the Eighteenth Army likewise stressed the point that the Soviet political commissars and secret service personnel were criminals. They should be court-martialled and sentenced. General von Küchler considered those measures an appropriate means of driving a wedge between the political leadership and the assumed decent Soviet soldier. By this he hoped for a speedier and less costly advance.[16] Another general who justified the coming war on the same grounds as Hitler and included a relevant paragraph in a deployment directive was General Hoepner, commander of Panzer Group 4 until his recall in the winter crisis of 1941/2. He was later an active member of the military resistance. On 2 May 1941 Hoepner declared that

> . . . the war against Russia is an important chapter in the struggle for existence of the German nation. It is the old battle of the Germanic against the Slavic peoples, of the defence of European culture against Moscovite–Asiatic inundation, and the repulse of Jewish Bolshevism. The objective of this battle must be the destruction of present-day Russia and it must therefore be conducted with unprecedented severity. Every military action must be guided in planning and execution by an iron resolution to exterminate the enemy remorselessly and totally. In particular, no adherents of the contemporary Russian Bolshevik system are to be spared.[17]

In the formulation of the final decrees of 13 May and 6 June 1941 the OKW followed this path and accepted concepts offered in the drafts of the OKH. Since officers, judge-advocates and other officials of the supreme command recognised that they had twisted the law of war into a function of political expediency they acknowledged the necessity of cloaking these measures as 'preventive reprisals'. Brauchitsch made amendments to both the OKW's decree for the exercise of military jurisdiction and to the guidelines for the treatment of the political commissars before he passed them on to the army. On the one hand, he shifted the burden for segregating and executing the commissars 'inconspicuously' on to the shoulders of the officers. On the other hand, he stressed the duty of all superiors to prevent arbitrary excesses by *individual* soldiers against civilians. 'Timely action by every officer must help to maintain discipline, the basis of our successes.'[18]

Concern for the discipline of the troops was obviously more important than scruples about illegal shooting of captive commissars or of civilians who were merely suspect. The whole concept of *ius in bello* was viewed as an irksome obstacle to warfare[19]. This becomes evident from the personal instructions given to intelligence officers and judge-advocates of army level by General Müller and his legal adviser, Dr Lattmann. On 10 June 1941 Müller stated that in the war against the Soviet Union 'feelings of justice must in certain circumstances give way to military necessity'. As long as the military jurisdiction would be suspended, it would be necessary that the troops help themselves against guerrillas, 'that is reversion to the old customs of war. . . . One of the adversaries must remain dead on the field. Adherents of a hostile attitude must not be preserved, but liquidated'. Any civilian impeding or inciting others to impede the Wehrmacht was to be considered a guerrilla and executed by the troops. Müller stressed, however, that there should be no acts of revenge or wholesale slaughter. Everything must be done for the security of the troops and the speedy pacification of the country. All actions against 'enemy civilians' after battle should only be taken upon direct orders from an officer.[20]

Returning from the instructions on those two decrees, the judge-advocate of the Eleventh Army summed up on 18 June:

> Each soldier must know that he has to defend himself against all attacks in battle; that in cases of doubt he can either liberate or shoot arrested persons. Each officer must know that he can shoot or liberate arrested persons, but that political commissars must be segregrated and liquidated. Each battalion commander must know that he can order collective punishments.[21]

In fact, this particular paragraph of the decree on military jurisdiction stemmed from one of Halder's suggestions. Thus the burning of villages and mass executions were to become common features of the anti-guerrilla operations carried out by the armed forces. Although there seem to have been very many law-abiding German officers in the war against the Soviet Union one cannot agree with Geoffrey Best, who asserts 'that in no army was the law of war more a matter of concern than in the German one'.[22] Henning von Tresckow's judgement of 10 May 1941, 'if international law has to be broken, the Russians shall do it, not we', simply ceased to be shared by many of his fellow officers.[23]

The decree on military jurisdiction and the guidelines on political commissars cannot be viewed simply as examples 'of systematic projection of National Socialist legal theory on to an ideological foe'.[24] Experiences with Russian forces in East Prussia in the First World War also played a significant role. These rigorous measures were not forgotten and had already been defined, in the 1925 official history, as the transfer of Asiatic customs to civilised German soil.[25] Another factor which dictated the treatment of Soviet political commissars was the fear that such hardliners would organise resistance behind German lines or, if taken prisoner of war, would continue disseminating propaganda in the Reich. The commander-in-chief of the army later ordered officers to scrutinise prisoner of war camps continuously.

Why did the military leaders and their legal advisers issue orders that twisted the rules of war to suit Hitler's concept of a war of extermination against the Soviet Union? An all-absolving principle of obedience or lack of civil courage offers an inadequate explanation for this attitude. The same applies to contemporary and *ex post facto* characterisations of the generals as 'military technicians' (H. v. Moltke), 'hopeless sergeants' (U. v. Hassel) or 'corps of postmen' (R. Kempner). They were not mere victims of their own military tradition. The relationship between the Wehrmacht and Hitler with regard to the Soviet Union was determined in large measure by a consensus on both ideological matters and Germany's role in Europe and in world politics. Was it not General von Küchler, commander of the Eighteenth Army, who had instructed his divisional commanders on the aims in the coming war: 'to bring about a pacification of Europe for a long time in which the German people would rule over a space that would secure adequacy of food supplies for them and the other European nations . . . Germany and Russia are, ideologically and racially, separated by a deep gorge.' Küchler considered the Soviet Union as an Asiatic state. 'If Germany wants to feel safe for generations from the threatening danger in the east, it will not be enough to push Russia back, not even for hundreds of kilometres, but to aim at the destruction of European Russia, the disintegration of the state.'[26]

The contribution of generals to the Wehrmacht's integration into the National Socialist concept of an ideological war described above challenges the myth that the German soldier's behaviour in the east was no more than a response to circumstance. At the Sixth Annual Conference of the Western Association for German Studies at El Paso, Texas, in October 1982 Dennis Showalter called attention to the point that 'a neglected but important continuity in German history from 1871 to 1945 is a significant gap between rhetoric and behavior. Accepting this can be difficult for German intellectuals, who are quicker than their American counterparts to assume a direct correlation of ideas and actions'.[27] We shall have occasion to look at this closely.

On the eve of the attack, the German soldiers were informed about Hitler's order of the day and about the 'Guidelines for the Conduct of the Troops' of 19 May 1941. These instructions declared Bolshevism to be the deadly enemy of the National Socialist

German nation. 'It is against this destructive ideology and its adherents that Germany is waging war. This battle demands ruthless and rigorous measures against Bolshevik inciters, guerrillas, saboteurs, *Jews* and the complete elimination of all active and passive resistance.'[28] Stalin countered the German notion of an ideological and ruthless fight with his own concept of a merciless people's war against 'German Fascism', a war which would decide the future of Socialism. This people's war was to be led by the Communist Party. Stalin's appeal for a partisan war behind the Front was viewed immediately by Hitler as an excuse to mask the true purpose of his extermination programme as a military necessity.[29] Stalin's radio speech of 3 July 1941 was made public to the German troops by leaflets printed in German[30] and encouraged them in their 'special measures' already under way. Moreover, the excesses of the Soviet state police's special forces against captive German soldiers and Soviet political prisoners seemed to demonstrate to the German soldier that the Red Army in fact employed 'Asiatic-barbarian' methods, as had been assumed before the outbreak of the war.[31]

On 9 July 1941 Field Marshal von Brauchitsch rejected the Sixth Army's request for reprisals against Soviet prisoners of war for the shooting and mutilating of German captives, 'because even the execution of large numbers of them would have — in contrast to the Western allies — no effect on the Russians', it would lead only to more 'violent anger' on both sides.[32] Yet only a few days later, the commander-in-chief ruled differently. Brauchitsch had learned of detailed Soviet directives which instructed political functionaries to form partisan units, and he believed that the German troops had not dealt energetically enough with partisan activities. These grounds were reason enough for him to supplement the earlier directives of May and June 1941 with a special order for the 'treatment of enemy civilians and of Russian prisoners of war' in the army group rear areas.[33] Within this order Brauchitsch mixed military and ideological, punitive and preventive measures. He accused those whose devotion to the Jewish–Bolshevik system had led to the renewal of fighting in already pacified areas. 'The essential rapid pacification of the country can be achieved only if every threat on the part of the hostile civilian population is dealt with ruthlessly. All pity and softness are weakness and constitute a danger.' The leading principle in all actions should be the 'absolute security of the German soldier'. Brauchitsch expressly stated that the preventive taking of hostages as a guarantee against future violation was not necessary. Instead he justified reprisals and collective punishments. The shooting of civilians and the destruction of villages was to be the normal reaction against any unidentified instance of sabotage. That reprisal executions exceeded the set frame becomes evident from an order of Army Group 'centre' of 7 August 1941. The understandable irritation of the troops after attacks by guerrillas must not lead to retaliation against localities 'just because they are in the vicinity' of the place of action.[34] Significantly the Second Army pointed out that the troops would give up overreaching collective punishments, if they were given a guarantee that the 'experienced specialists', that is SS–*Sonderkommando* 7b, would carry out energetic measures against the 'dangerous elements' in their rear.[35]

Brauchitsch's order of 25 July 1941 has to be seen in connection with an earlier directive of the army high command.[36] This had consciously aimed at the avoidance of measures which would drive the population back into the hands of the Bolsheviks. It was admitted frankly that the reason behind the still small number of sabotage incidents in the western parts of the Soviet Union was to be found in a 'bargain' struck between the interests of the Wehrmacht and the peaceful population. Let the latter only be still, work and obey orders, and the suffering would be minimised by combatting resistance activities with reprisal executions chiefly of Communists, Russians and Jews. In the Ukraine or in the Baltic states the military appropriated minorities for its own use, thus trying to separate 'the remainder of the population the more decisively from connexion with hostilities, in order (in effect) to ensure its taking no part in them'.[37]

In consequence of the two orders, the commander of the Seventeenth Army, General Karl-Heinrich von Stülpnagel, explained:

> Collective punishments must not be made indiscriminately. If the Ukrainian inhabitants of a locality cannot be convicted of the initial act of violence, the village mayors will be requested to name Jewish and communist inhabitants in the first instance . . . In particular, the Jewish Komsomol members are to be considered the main exponents of any sabotage movement and of the forming of youth bands.[38]

So it was not only Hitler or the SS who construed a connection between 'Jewish Bolshevism' and the 'partisan' movement; military commanders also saw in the Jews special adherents of the hostile system of government, and they acted accordingly. This happened in the Soviet Union and in Serbia.[39] As long as the anti-Jewish measures in both occupied countries were 'perceived and construed as military measures against Germany's enemies, it did not require nazified zealots (though surely such were not lacking), merely conscientious and politically obtuse professional soldiers to carry them out'.[40] Thus after a mopping-up operation near Mirgorod in the rear area of army group 'south', the 62nd Infantry Division shot the 'entire Jewish population (168 souls) for associating with partisans', in addition to executing forty-five partisans.[41] In Šabac (Serbia) 'central-European Jewish refugees, mostly Austrians, were shot by troops predominately of Austrian origin in retaliation for casualties inflicted by Serbian partisans on the German Army!'[42] Such anti-Jewish measures by the Wehrmacht sever the German occupation policies in the Soviet Union and Serbia from that in France. In the West it was not obvious to the military that the Jews would assuredly be among Germany's enemies. Thus the directives for the military administration of France stated that 'special measures' against civilians could not be justified solely by the fact that they happened to be Jews.[43]

The intermingling of political-ideological warfare with military action in the east, which Hitler had striven for and Halder had consciously accepted, becomes especially self-evident from the well-known orders of the commanders of the Sixth and Eleventh Armies, Field Marshals von Reichenau and von Manstein, of 6 October[44] and 20 November 1941.[45] Reichenau's order concerning the 'Conduct of the Troops in the Eastern Territories', which was termed 'excellent' by Hitler and immediately taken over by other commanders, was later distributed by the army high command to all armies and army groups, with the request to issue similar directives. Manstein acted upon this suggestion of 28 October 1941. Less well-known is the similar order of the commander of the Seventeenth Army, General Hoth, of 17 November 1941.[46] He thought that the eastern campaign ought to be concluded differently from the war against France. In the east, two irreconcilable world views were in combat: 'German feelings of honour and race, and a centuries-old German soldierly tradition against Asiatic thought and its primitive instincts stirred up by a few, mostly Jewish, intellectuals.' By this order, Hoth not only wanted to guarantee a unified view of the duties of the German soldier in the Soviet

Union, but also strove to render Hitler's unequivocal maxims in terms which were to become the only guidelines for the Wehrmacht. Hoth had been present at Hitler's address in the Reich Chancellery on 30 March 1941. He took the lead in this struggle against the antagonistic Weltanschauung, as Hitler had then demanded. Inspired by a sense of Germany's mission, Hoth defined the essence of the war:

> More strongly than ever we carry within us the belief of a changing age in which, because of their superiority of race and deeds, the German people are meant to lead Europe. We see clearly our mission to save European culture from Asiatic barbarism. We know now that we have to fight against a fierce and stubborn enemy. This fight can be ended only by the destruction of one or the other of us. There is no room for compromise.

Similar to the orders of Reichenau and Manstein, Hoth's directive called for the complete extermination of the Soviet war machine, as well as the annihilation of the Jewish–Bolshevik system, and instructed his soldiers to show understanding for the 'necessity of the harsh punishment of Jewry'. This could only be understood by the troops as justification of the mass executions carried out by the *Einsatzgruppe C*. Yet stronger than Reichenau and Manstein, Hoth turned his soldiers' eyes to German history, to the alleged guilt of the Jews for the domestic conditions after the First World War: 'The annihilation of those same Jews who support Bolshevism and its organisation for murder, the partisans, is a measure of self-preservation.'

There were, of course, other voices. General von Mackensen, commander of the III (motorised) Army Corps, issued a different communication from Reichenau, Manstein and Hoth. Although he demanded the 'ruthless combatting and annihilation of hostile elements', Mackensen also warned the troops not to consider every one as their enemy just because he would look like a Bolshevik — in rags, unhygienic, unkempt.[47] The decision would rest with the officers, who should be careful of denunciation. But this was only one paragraph among ten; the other nine were guided by the traditional understanding of the treatment of the population of an occupied country. The fact that their initially friendly attitude towards the Wehrmacht had nearly come to an end was explained by the unjust or psychologically wrong conduct of the German troops in the rear areas, as well as to the unavoidable consequences of warfare. The troops should not transfer their hate of Bolshevism on to the Soviet people. They were not an 'object of exploitation', but a 'necessary part of the European economy'. The German soldier should treat civilians and prisoners of war in the same manner in which he wished to be treated in hard times. The important question here is how representative this order may be when compared to those of Reichenau, Manstein, Hoth and others. That question can be answered by quantification.

The reports of the 707th Infantry Division, responsible to the *Wehrmachtbefehlshaber Ostland*, represent another example of self- corroboration and self-fulfilling prophecy in the extermination of 'Jewish Bolshevism':

It was noticed with the Jews that they tend to leave their homes in the flat country, probably for the south, whereby they seek to escape the operations introduced against them. Since, then and now, they *make common cause with the communists and parti- sans, the complete extermination of this alien element is being carried out* (monthly report of 1 October to 1 November 1941).

The measures introduced against the Jews, *as bearers of the Bolshevik idea and as leaders of the partisan movement*, have shown tangible results . . . . During this month the raiding- parties repeatedly noted and *confirmed the association of the Jews with the partisan movement* (monthly report of 1 November to 30 November 1941.

In the situation report of mid-February 1942 the division went further and declared that, without a single exception, Jews and partisans were identical.[48] These reports, of course, contained the measures carried out by the SS and Ordnungspolizei (Orpo) in White Ruthenia, for example in Sluzk. The connection construed between the mass murder of Jews and the reprisal policy must on no account induce us to justify the extermination of the Jews in the occupied territories. A distinction should be made between the Soviet Union and Serbia. While in the latter, 'the mass murder of male Jews was accomplished primarily by the German Wehrmacht, though it certainly received willing help from the Ordnungs- and Sicherheitspolizei of the SS'[49], in the former it was the other way round. Babi Yar, the name of a gorge near Kiev, has become the symbol not only of the crimes of the *Einsatzgruppen* in the Soviet

Union, but also of the support they received from the Wehrmacht.[50]

It is not sufficient to explain the arbitrary reprisal policy of the Wehrmacht in the Soviet Union by the motto of 'absolute security for the German soldier' against partisan attacks or acts of violence by an incited population. Nor can it be explained by the fact that German military doctrine since 1871 had advocated policies of indiscriminate retaliation and of preventive repression as the best means of checking partisan activity.[51] The considerable discrepancy that exists between the number of partisans killed and German casualties, on the one hand, and the minor difference between the number of those arrested and later executed, on the other, in the reports of German combat or security divisions, both serve to underline the ideological background of the Wehrmacht reprisal policy. The armed forces did not confine themselves to 'normal' warfare. In their effort to eliminate 'all active and passive resistance' they deliberately struck, along with the SS, a fatal blow at the phantom of Jewish Bolshevism.[52] Total exoneration of the army is no more of an aid towards the understanding of this chapter in German history than is total condemnation. There were, of course, commanders who tried to draw a distinct line between military actions and police measures, who issued orders to prevent individual soldiers from taking part in the executions of Jews by the SS. But it was a futile fight against the ordered 'constant close co-operation' with the *Einsatzgruppen*, against the deliberate mix-ups of military actions with political warfare ordered by the Wehrmacht leadership and enforced by many a commander. The mere suspicion of actual or potential anti-German activities led to the shooting of civilians and Soviet soldiers who, cut off from the main body of their army, had not reported to German authorities by set date. Jews and Communists were in fact and a priori classified as suspected partisans and shot. The legal basis for thus suspending the rules of war was the decree on military jurisdiction and 'special measures' of the troops of 13 May 1941 and its successive communications. This disproportionately savage reprisal policy of the Wehrmacht in the Soviet Union is most strikingly demonstrated by one report of the 707th Infantry Division, already mentioned above. In its area in White Russia 10,431 out of a total of 10,940, 'captives' were shot in one month, while in combat with partisans the division suffered only seven casualties, two dead and five wounded![53] Among those 'captives' were former Soviet soldiers, escaped prisoners of war and civilians arrested by mopping-up operations. This practice closely approached Hitler's formula of 16 July 1941 for the pacification of the Eastern Territories: to shoot every one 'who merely looks suspicious'.[54]

It has been suggested that the 'mere Gook' mentality is hardly a German monopoly, and that Japan and the United States applied their own versions of it during the Pacific war. In this respect one needs only to remember General Sherman's views in 1863 about restraining his subordinates in a war which, as he understood it, was fought between peoples and not just between armies:

> The government of the United States has in north Alabama any and all rights which they choose to enforce in war, to take their lives, their houses, their lands, their everything, because they cannot deny that war exists there, and war is simply power unrestrained by constitution or compact. If they want eternal warfare, well and good.[55]

Dennis Showalter rightly pointed out that we need patterns and dimensions of comparison in order to evaluate the armies' conduct *vis-à-vis* the occupied civil populations during the Second World War. Who is going to write a comparative history of international occupation policies that could serve as a starting-point for a typology? Yet it must be the task of a German historian to breach the walls of self-deception which we Germans are still constructing, by confronting us with the unconstrained or distorted past. German contemporary history has far too long been preoccupied with the 'German Catastrophe' (F. Meinecke) and has thus overlooked the 'Jewish' and 'Soviet' catastrophes.[56] If we establish the fact that the essential relationship between Wehrmacht and National Socialism in regard to the Soviet Union was an ideological rather than an instrumental one, then we shall understand the totally different character of the German–Soviet war as compared to that waged against France. Military action for the sake of conquest and police measures to safeguard the acquired Lebensraum were different aspects of one single war of extermination, in which the Wehrmacht also played a significant role.[57] But this is only one side of the coin. The other is the Soviet reaction to the German invasion. The orders to execute and mutilate German captives, to shoot the so-called political prisoners and the deliberate people's war behind the German lines seemed to justify the intended German measures and led to a radicalisation of warfare between the two antagonistic Weltanschauungen. 'No longer on the eastern front existed that sense of a residual community of interests between states which the old law of war presupposed.'[58]

Notes

1. See *Das Deutsche Reich und der Zweite Weltkrieg*, vol. 4, *Der Angriff auf die Sowjetunion*, Stuttgart, 1983, pp. 3–25.
2. K. D. Erdmann, *Die Zeit der Weltkriege*, Stuttgart, 1976, p. 327. Cf. E. Jäckel, *Hitlers Weltanschauung: Entwurf einer Herrschaft*, Stuttgart, 1981.
3. *Bundesarchiv* Koblenz, NS 11/28, Bl 86. J. Thies first drew attention to this speech, though in a different context: *Architekt der Weltherrschaft. Die 'Endziele' Hitlers*, Düsseldorf, 1976, p. 112.
4. *Heeresadjutant bei Hitler 1938–1943. Aufzeichnungen des Majors Engel*, ed. H. v. Kotze, Stuttgart, 1974, p. 45.
5. M. Messerschmidt and U. v. Gersdorff (eds.), *Offiziere im Bild von Dokumenten aus drei Jahrhunderten*, Stuttgart, 1964, p. 276. This directive was once more distributed to the troops after the fall of France.
6. M. Domarus, *Hitler: Reden und Proklamationen 1932–1945*, vol. 2, Wiesbaden, 1973, p. 1,058.
7. H. Grosscurth, *Tagebücher eines Abwehroffiziers 1938–1940*, ed. H. Krausnick and H. C. Deutsch, Stuttgart, 1970, p. 414.
8. See *Der Angriff auf die Sowjetunion*, pp. 23–4, 201.
9. *Bundesarchiv-Militärarchiv* Freiburg (hereafter cited as BA-MA), LI. Armeekorps, 15290/23, notes of a speech of 11 July 1941.
10. See *Der Angriff auf die Sowjetunion*, pp. 3–4.
11. For the following see now ibid, pp. 414–47. Cf. N. Rich, *Hitler's War Aims: The Establishment of the New Order*, vol. 1, London, 1973, pp. 212–20 and R. Cecil, *Hitler's Decision to Invade Russia 1941*, London, 1975, pp. 156–66.
12. BA-MA, 18. Armee, 19601/2, note of the Ia.
13. BA-MA, RH 31-I/v. 23, OKH/GenStdH/GenQu/Abt. Kriegsverwaltung, Nr. II/0308/41 geh. of 2 April 1941. It is signed for Brauchitsch by the chief of the general staff, General Halder, who since 1938 had been the former's 'permanent deputy in ministerial functions'.
14. Generaloberst Halder, *Kriegstagebuch*, ed. H. A. Jacobsen, vol. 2, Stuttgart, 1963, pp. 336–7.
15. BA-MA, RH 19 III/146, ObdH/GenStdH/GZ (I^2) 1.St.Nr. 2182/40 geh. of 29 September 1940, annex 1. Cf. *Der Angriff auf die Sowjetunion*, pp. 255, 428–9.

16. BA-MA, 18. Armee, 19601/2, Küchler's notes.
17. BA-MA, LVI. Armeekorps. 17956/a, Kdr. PzGrp 4, Ia Nr. 20/41 g.Kdos. of 2 May 1941, annex 2.
18. See *Der Angriff auf die Sowjetunion*, pp. 432–3, 438.
19. To the complex of *ius in bello*, see G. Best, *Humanity in Warfare: The Modern History of the International Law of Armed Conflicts*, London, 1980.
20. *Der Angriff auf die Sowjetunion*, pp. 433–4.
21. BA-MA, 11. Armee, RH 20-11/11, notes of the judge.
22. G. Best, 'World War Two and the laws of war', *Review of International Studies*, 7(1981), p. 73.
23. *Heeresadjutant bei Hitler*, p. 103.
24. M. Messerschmidt, *Die Wehrmacht im NS-Staat: Zeit der Indoktrination*, Hamburg, 1969, p. 409.
25. *Der Angriff auf die Sowjetunion*, pp. 431–2.
26. BA-MA, 18. Armee, 19601/2, Küchler's notes of 25 April 1941. Cf. General Hoth's order of 17 November 1941 (see n. 46).
27. Commentary to papers of M. Messerschmidt and J. Förster.
28. BA-MA, RH 31-I/v. 40. Italics mine.
29. International Military Tribunal, Trial of the Major War Criminals, Nuremberg 1947, vol. 38, p. 88 (hereafter cited IMT).
30. BA-MA, RH 24-3/134.
31. See *Der Angriff auf die Sowjetunion*, pp. 437, 781–5, 1035–6.
32. BA-MA, RH 20-2/1090.
33. BA-MA, RH 22/271, order of 25 July 1941. Müller had signed it by order of Brauchitsch.
34. BA-MA, RH 20-2/1091.
35. Ibid., communication of 11 August 1941.
36. BA-MA, RH 27-7/156, order of 12 July 1941.
37. Best, *Humanity in Warfare*, p. 180.
38. BA-MA, Alliierte Prozesse 9, NOKW-1693, order of 30 July 1941.
39. See H. Krausnick and H. H. Wilhelm, *Die Truppe des Weltanschauungskrieges: Die Einsatzgruppen der Sicherheitspolizei und des SD 1938–1942*, Stuttgart, 1981.
40. C. Browning, 'Wehrmacht Reprisal Policy and the Mass Murder of Jews in Serbia', *Militärgeschichtliche Mitteilungen (MGM)*, 1/83, p. 38. Cf. *Der Angriff auf die Sowjetunion*, pp. 1,037–49.
41. BA-MA, RH 22/3, entry of 3 November 1941. Cf. J. Förster, 'The Wehrmacht and the War of Extermination against the Soviet Union', *Yad Vashem* XIV (1981), pp. 29–30.
42. Browning, 'Wehrmacht Reprisal Policy', p. 39.
43. BA-MA, RH 24-3/218, military administration, no. 6.
44. IMT, vol. 35, pp. 84–6.
45. IMT, vol. 34, pp. 129–32.
46. BA-MA, 17. Armee, 14499/15.
47. BA-MA, RH 24-3/136, communication of 24 November 1941.
48. BA-MA, RH 26-707/v. 1.
49. Browning, 'Wehrmacht Reprisal Policy', p. 42.
50. See *Der Angriff auf die Sowjetunion*, pp. 1,044–9.

51. See Best, *Humanity in Warfare*, and M. Howard, *The Franco-Prussian War: The German Invasion of France, 1870–1871*, London, 3rd ed., 1962, pp. 249–56, 379–81.

52. See M. Cooper, *The Phantom War: The German Struggle against Soviet Partisans 1941–1944*, London, 1979, p. 56.

53. BA-MA, RH 26-707/v. 1. Monthly report of October–November 1941. See also T. P. Mulligan, 'Reckoning the cost of people's war. The German experience in the central USSR', *Russian History*, 9 (1982), pp. 30–3.

54. IMT, vol. 38, p. 88.

55. W. F. Fleming, *Civil War and Reconstruction in Alabama*, New York, 1905, p. 76. I should like to thank Prof. W. Murray, Ohio State University, for this information.

56. Cf. K. Kwiet, 'Zur historiographischen Behandlung der Judenverfolgung im Dritten Reich', *MGM* 1/1980, pp. 149–53.

57. Cf. O. Bartov, 'The barbarisation of warfare. German officers and soldiers in combat on the Eastern Front, 1941–1945', Ph. D. Thesis, St Antony's College, Oxford, 1983.

58. Best, 'World War Two', p. 77.

MANFRED MESSERSCHMIDT

German Military Law in the Second World War

Those who remember the impact of National Socialist propaganda concerning the 'New Germany', the new people, their common spirit and the certainty of Germany's final victory might think that far fewer disciplinary and criminal difficulties would have occurred in the German forces than in those of the other powers engaged in the Second World War. The common spirit of the German people, the so-called 'Volksgemeinschaft', was regarded even by conservative officers as a guarantee of voluntary discipline.

Military leaders, lawyers and above all Hitler himself had argued that in a future war there must be no repetition of the events of 1918. They firmly believed in the famous 'stab in the back' story which was developed at the end of the First World War by the military (above all by former leading figures such as Ludendorff, right-wing party members, antisemites and the Nazis) to explain Germany's defeat in psychological and political terms that did not damage the reputation of the Wilhelmine system, especially its military arm. In their view, Germany did not lose the First World War on the battlefield, or even on the economic front but rather, simply, because Socialists, Democrats and Jews had so managed to undermine discipline and morale at home as to influence the army in the field.

If there was criticism of military institutions, it was directed primarily against the government for not allowing these institutions to function in the way they wished. This was deemed particularly true in the case of the military courts.[1] During the First World War only 150 German soldiers were sentenced to death by military courts, and of this number only 48 were actually executed. In contrast the British and French military courts appeared to hand down sterner sentences: British courts martial dispensed 3,080 death sentences, of which 346 were carried out, and the French about 2,000 death sentences which resulted in approximately 700 being executed.[2] During the interwar years, therefore, German military law of the First World War came to be looked upon by many as a feeble and weak instrument of warfare. It was a common belief of soldiers, former military lawyers and National Socialists that this must be changed in the framework of a new army. Hitler himself hinted at the connection between Germany's breakdown in 1918 and the failure of the military legal system. This system, he argued, had lost the war by not applying its military laws effectively and by virtually eliminating capital punishment.[3]

When military courts were re-established in the armed forces in 1933, the adaption of the civilian legal code to the principles of National Socialist ideology was already in full progress. The new body of military lawyers and judges participated fully in these legal reforms, and their impact should not be underestimated in the decisions of military courts during the Second World War. However, before analysing the process of adapting the military laws to the political aims of the Nazi state it is useful to look at the results. Second World War statistics reveal what actually happened behind the propaganda image of Volksgemeinschaft. In them can be seen the real nature of the political system and its technique of mastering problems, in a manner which is unimaginable in liberal and democratic societies.

When compared with those of the First World War, Second World War statistics indicate a total change in German law theory and practice. While the British army in the Second World War carried out forty death sentences (thirty-six for murder, three for mutiny and one for treason)[4] and the French army just over a hundred,[5] Wehrmacht statistics reveal 9,732 executions up till the end of 1944.[6] Even this figure, for several reasons, cannot be regarded as final for the period mentioned. As there were more German soldiers serving in fighting units than was the case with Britain and France, a higher German figure should be expected. Nevertheless, this fact cannot explain the 'explosion of death sentences' which resulted in a grand total of between 13,000 and 15,000 executions — or even more — by the end of the war. Furthermore, there was a rather small discrepancy between the number of death sentences and the number of executions. In mid-June 1944 the statistics reveal that 85 per cent of death sentences were carried out, although this percentage is probably too high.

Death sentences were handed down mainly for desertion and for the offence of *Wehrkraftzersetzung*, which can be translated loosely as 'attempting to subvert the will of the people to fight'. In August 1938, when the outbreak of war seemed imminent, a new anti-sedition law was introduced. Jointly conceived by lawyers and the armed forces high command (OKW), the *Kriegssonderstrafrechts-verordnung* (KSSVO) called for capital punishment for anybody who tried publicly to induce soldiers to refuse to carry out their duties as well as for individuals who attempted to paralyse the resolution of the German people to continue the war effort until victory was achieved.[7] By this means Hitler and the military believed that at least one lesson had been learnt from the First World War. Of the 1,640 death sentences handed down between 1 January 1940 and 31 March 1942, 1,299 were for desertion, 216 for *Zersetzung der Wehrkraft* and 57 for violations of the so-called 'law against enemies of the people' (*Verordnung gegen Volksschädlinge*),[8] which was issued on 5 September 1939.[9] These statistics reveal that nearly 80 per cent of all death sentences were inflicted for offences that can be regarded as political ones. Desertion, for instance, was seen as an offence against the Führer and the Volksgemeinschaft. Some military courts and judges saw a connection between desertion and *Wehrkraftzersetzung*. In their view, deserters belonged to what they called 'people's or army's enemies' (*Volks- oder Wehrmachtschädlinge*).[10] Such judges did not belong, as has been argued, exclusively to the group of younger lawyers who had entered the army only after the outbreak of war. On the contrary, they were to be found in the peacetime military legal personnel as well.[11] Heinrich Dietz can be taken as a good example of this latter type.

Dietz, who had been a member of the Prusian Army's legal service since 1901, was one of the leading advocates for the re-introduction of the military law during the interwar years. From 1933 he was the editor of *Zeitschrift für Wehrrecht*, the journal for military lawyers, and subsequently was a high-ranking official in the war ministry. In an article on the legal code written shortly after 1933 Dietz pleaded for the union of military and National Socialist principles, motivation and character,[12] calling for a new and greatly strengthened system of military law, since what the state was lacking was an effective, abbreviated procedure which permitted capital punishment. Doubtful thinking, hesitation, a lack of belief in the state and the actions of its leadership (as had occurred during the First World War) must be rooted out through military law in order to prevent any weakness at home affecting the fighting forces. Briefly, action must be taken to forestall another 'stab in the back'. Dietz wanted a model for the unity of state, people and armed forces to be established in which military law would be used as a powerful mental weapon to stabilise the will to fight of both the people and the army so as to allow them to overcome any wartime setback.

German military law followed this line despite the efforts of individual judges and commanders to limit the influence of ideological thinking. There are examples of courageous attempts to leave matters within the framework of 'normal arguments', which were looked upon during those years as being 'non-conformist'. There was also a zone of 'grey normality' facing this kind of non-conformity. Thus, on the whole, the statistics mentioned above can be explained only by processes of thinking and acting which made perversion of justice a 'normal' phenomenon inasmuch it fitted into the supposed requirements of Volksgemeinschaft in wartime.

German military legal procedure did not provide for any such institutions as courts of appeal. The decision whether to confirm or annul a sentence lay with the army commanders, the supreme commanders of the army, navy and air force or Hitler himself as supreme commander of the Wehrmacht (since 1941 also army supreme commander). This characteristic arrangement, inherited from the old army, gave the decision as to (literally) life or death to a group of military commanders, the 'Masters of the Court' (*Gerichtsherren*). In theory, they could annul a sentence and order new trials until they obtained the sentence which they thought was correct. In order to make decisions on sentences of over one year's imprisonment, they were required to ask for expert advice which was normally delivered by senior judges;[13] they were not bound to follow this advice. However, judges were still free from any direction from military commanders during the course of trials. Generally military commanders followed the summations of their senior judges, whose influence must be considered as far-reaching. Indeed, it was often the judges themselves who initiated new trials in order to impose harsher punishments. These senior military judges were very well aware of the kind of ideological mission the political system intended them to fulfil. As with attitudes in the navy, there is in their thinking a fear of failure which stemmed from the criticism of the courts-martial during and after the First World War. Many of them became guardians of a merciless jurisdiction. It was, after all, easy to implement such a policy in an advisory capacity; the responsibility for carrying it out was left to the courts and the *Gerichtsherren*.

In analysing the position of the military judges in the armed forces it must be remembered that, notwithstanding their freedom of action during the periods of trial and deliberation, they did not live in a vacuum; their independence was only relative. They were surrounded by decrees, edicts and official interpretations of the law as well as being subject to the outspoken will of Hitler. Beyond this there was also the vital need to speed up procedures (another lesson from the First World War). Combined with these factors was another sinister development, initiated before the war by the legal profession itself but greatly intensified during the course of the war. This was the creation of an autonomous, self-fabricated structure of legal interpretations which acknowledged National Socialist ideology and demanded even 'better' laws. These elements came together in the fundamental judgments of the *Reichkriegsgericht* and in the conclusions of numerous contemporary books and articles written by professors of law, judges and lawyers both inside and outside the armed forces. The establishment of this network helps to explain the new developments in German military law during the Second World War.

To enlarge a little on this point; it must be remembered that, from the nineteenth century until the end of the First World War, the German Army, in common with the armies of most of the Western powers, saw as the main concern of military law the protection and preservation of military discipline. Soldiers were punished for violations of their *military* duties. After 1933 German lawyers began to argue that this was not sufficient and sought another interpretation of the notion of both civil and military guilt. To them, at that time, it seemed clear that a soldier's guilt could not consist simply in having violated a specific rule or order, but should also be seen in terms of the damage his crime had done to the people, that is, to the Volksgemeinschaft. Thus the law and its meaning had to be brought into line with 'the new ethos of our people'.[14] Nothing seemed more important than to do away with liberal legal interpretation with its concept of individual ethics and personal guilt. As early as 1937 Erich Schwinge, a prominent authority on military law, noted that the Wehrmacht's new task as a pillar of the new state had changed the concept of undutiful behaviour. Another well-known military lawyer argued that the military judge's objective was to apply, by using a 'purification procedure', the principles of the National Socialist community against the accused.[15]

These endeavours must be seen in the context of the general ideas on law and justice that were developed in the Führer state. Well-known authorities on subjects such as constitutional, international and criminal law played a leading role here, together with younger academics. If it is possible to single out an individual, that must be Carl Schmitt, who influenced many others by his writings on 'konkrete Ordnung', as which, of course, the National Socialist system was seen.[16] Another very productive academic, Ernst Rudolf Huber, perverted the notion of law by saying that it was the unfolding of 'völkisch' life according to the Führer's plan and decision.[17] For National Socialists and their lackeys in the different branches of the judiciary, the ministry of justice, the universities and the armed forces there was no doubt that criminal law and procedure would and must become special tools in the hands of the state and its organisations. So military justice became a strong link between the National Socialist system and its armed forces, working for the sake of German Volksgemeinschaft.

Owing to the loss of legal and other archives, it is not possible to give an overall picture of the workings of the military legal system during the Second World War. However, the central archives in Kornelimünster near Aix-la-Chapelle hold far more than 100,000 case files and some are also to be found in Vienna. It is also likely that other records exist in East Germany and elsewhere behind the Iron Curtain. Taken together the documents still existing represent only a small portion of the original number.

As early as 23 September 1938 Hitler had ordered the keeping of criminal statistics as they might be of use when mobilisation occurred; furthermore he wished to obtain a clear picture of how military law was being administered. Hitler was interested primarily in political cases, that is those concerning desertion, *Wehrkraftzersetzung* and charges against officers. In December 1939 Brauchitsch, the commander-in-chief of the army, ordered reports be made on cases which would indicate the morale of the army (particularly those involving desertion, threats against superiors, attacks on superiors and mutiny).[18] From the beginning of 1940 the legal department of the Wehrmacht published quarterly statistics.[19]

From these reports it is possible to plot general trends as well as to gather many interesting details. However, in noting the rising numbers of trials, it must be remembered that until the end of 1942 the total numbers of soldiers, of courts and of judges was also rising. It should also be borne in mind that the conditions of warfare in the Soviet Union induced many soldiers to try to find ways of escaping from the hardships and dangers of the Eastern Front. From December 1939 statistics reveal a steady and continuous increase of trials:[20]

December 1939	12,853
December 1940	21,421
December 1941	22,022
December 1942	26,475
December 1943	36,675
December 1944	44,955

From these figures one must apparently come to the conclusion that the total of all trials must have been far greater than the detailed statistical report of the Wehrmacht mentions (628,032 until June 1944).[21] As the number of cases increased so did the number of courts and judges. In December 1939 the Wehrmacht instituted 290 courts with 463 judges. By December 1943 this had been increased to 687 courts with 1,139 judges, although after 1944 the rate of addition of new courts began to slow down.

The majority of trials dealt with ordinary contraventions usual in wartime: absence without leave, theft and fraud. According to the obviously not comprehensive criminal statistics of the Wehrmacht, by mid-1944 there had been approximately 107,000 completed cases of each of these offences. Below them came disobedience and contraventions against guard duties with 49,000 and 46,000 cases respectively. Next came drunkenness, with 19,000 cases. This was followed by charges of incautious handling of arms and ammunition, sacking and wilful spoiling which each accounted for some 13,000 to 15,000 cases. At the same level (13,000 to 15,000 cases) ranged desertion and *Wehrkraftzersetzung*. The nine offences mentioned above represented the main bulk (61 per cent) of all trials, whereas typical wartime offences such as mutiny (442), attacks against superiors (2,493), cowardice (3,533) and abuse of military position (2,074) combined made up only 1.37 per cent.[22] Most of these offences were punished with imprisonment. This is clearly shown by the statistics (up to mid-1944):

Capital punishment	11,664
Penal servitude	23,164
Imprisonment for more than one year	84,346
Six months to one year	84,393
Less than six months	232,259

Despite the high number of capital punishments, these figures alone cannot explain the ideological stance of military courts during the Second World War. To go further, one has to examine the arguments used by judges, *Gerichtsherren* and legal advisers in their sentences and statements. Of special interest are those cases in which death sentences were handed down. Cases involving desertion and *Wehrkraftzersetzung* will always remain, of course, the main charges from which historians and lawyers will try to establish what went so wrong with the German military legal system during the Second World War. One should also not forget to ask why some soldiers were condemned to death for theft and other minor offences, while others were only imprisoned for similar charges.

During the Second World War German military courts were composed of one professional judge (a lawyer who, at the least, had the legal qualifications to become a judge) and two soldiers whose rank depended upon the rank of the accused. As discussed above, these courts were not expected to uphold an abstract idea of justice but had the concrete aims of serving the advantage of the people and military discipline. This was also the case in the navy: thus Vice-Admiral Warzecha, chief of the *Allgemeines Marineamt*, a branch of the navy supreme command, saw their function. Even the highest-ranking lawyer in the Wehrmacht, Rudolph Lehmann, argued that it was not the mandate of these military courts to find truth as such — which did not exist — but rather to guarantee the existence of the community that had given power to the court.[23] The law, according to Lehmann, was simply 'the most distinguished form of the Führer's orders' and nothing more. In February 1942 Vice-Admiral Warzecha explained to a meeting of naval judges that German 'legislation', because it permitted practically unrestricted capital punishment as well as the establishment of 'special camps' for convicts, had now effectively provided for those cases in which imprisonment alone would be considered an ineffectual sentence.[24] Three years earlier, in December 1939, Hitler had stated that ruthlessness against subversive elements was in political terms the greatest clemency.[25]

How did the courts work? The full story will never now be known. However, it is possible to illustrate what German soldiers were likely to experience when summoned before a court martial by investigating some cases in detail.

Firstly, let us consider *Wehrkraftzersetzung* (subversion of the will to fight); this type of offence revealed the rather special National Socialist ideas of the law. In the early stage of the war, the *Reichskriegsgericht* set out to formulate a binding interpretation: *Zersetzung der Wehrkraft* was described as troubling or damaging the firm resolution of the people to continue fighting until the final victory.[26] A case was judged from the point of view of a people engaged in a war for their very existence. The special circumstances of the war made it necessary for the courts to disregard mitigating factors. There was no leeway for pleas of partial responsibility. To take an example: in 1943 an army private in a hospital at Amiens had said in the presence of some *Waffen-SS* soldiers that National Socialism would be forced 'to go' as had already been the case with Fascism. The private was accused of *Wehrkraftzersetzung*. General von Boineburg, then commander of Greater Paris, reported to General von Stülpnagel, the territorial commander in France, that just before making his remarks the private had received news that his wife had been killed in an air raid and his house destroyed. Boineburg argued that therefore his offence should be considered as a 'less serious' case. It was hoped that the military prosecutor would ask for two years' imprisonment. However, in February 1944 the prosecutor (a lawyer, as was normal) demanded the death sentence and the court followed him. The private's remarks were regarded as being malicious and hostile to the state. As the soldier happened to have had some dealings on the black market, he was described as being an 'inferior human being'. In the eyes of the court the death sentence was seen as the fit punishment. General von Stülpnagel overruled the sentence. The records do not indicate what happened after that.

Secondly, desertion: in a decree of 14 April 1940 Hitler ordered strict guidelines to be followed in dealing with deserters. These guidelines laid down that capital punishment was to be considered normal for desertion. In April 1943 Dönitz, commander-in-chief of the navy surpassed even Hitler by telling the courts that he would never lend his voice to acts of mercy.[27] This was the framework in which military courts were expected to work. In April 1941 a

21-year-old sailor was condemned to life imprisonment for desertion and threatening a superior. The summation of a high-ranking navy lawyer concluded that capital punishment was necessary. The accused was described as a 'noxious person' (*Schädling*). For disciplinary reasons the death sentence was called for.[28] Admiral Warzecha accepted this argument and added a warning against 'inferior elements'. Raeder, then commander-in-chief, annulled the previous prison sentence. A new court was formed which condemned the sailor to death.

Finally, theft: there was a tendency in German law to interpret the theft of soldiers' parcels as a serious offence. Some judges even saw a connection between such offences and serious dangers to the German Volksgemeinschaft. Hitler in one of his headquarters table talks put it this way: what would a wife sending parcels to her husband say in the case of their theft? Kill the thieves; that is the sane feeling of the people (*gesundes Volksempfinden*).[29] One of the high command decrees stated 'that it was possible in serious cases' to use 4 *Volksschädlingsverordnung* and 5a *KSSVO*, that is laws which would enable courts to pass death sentences on so·called 'army post weasels'.[30] In October 1942 a court martial of the 291st Infantry Division used these laws against a private. The soldier was found guilty of stealing twenty-six parcels, seven letters, some soap, chocolate, a scarf and a lighter. He had been his unit's post-carrier. The sentence is unknown, but the legal summation has been preserved. In this the senior legal adviser of the army commander stated that the death sentence was justified and that the slight mental debility of the accused made no difference. It was no loss to expel this 'inferior' from the community of the people (Volksgemeinchaft). The legal adviser therefore proposed execution and on 18 October the commander of the Eighteenth Army agreed with him.[31]

Examples like those given above reveal that German military law had its share in the National Socialist system. To say that many members of the legal personnel of the forces did not belong to the Nazi Party does not explain what really happened in the Second World War. Of course there are many examples of 'normal' behaviour and even of courageous conduct. In general, nevertheless, it is correct to emphasise that German military law acted in conformity with the principles of National Socialist Volksgemeinschaft, which in itself was not invented by the Nazis. The idea of a German nation, united in will and belief, following a strong government, doing away with parliament, political parties, trade unions and so on, was older than National Socialism. This political aim joined together conservative nationalists among whom were many lawyers and Nazis. It therefore made no real difference for soldiers, after committing offences which were categorised as 'political', whether the judge was a conservative nationalist or a card-carrying member of the Nazi Party. For there to be any chance of a fair trial, the prosecutor, court and *Gerichtsherr* must agree and come to a common conclusion. Very often this was not the case. Too many of them belonged to the 'conformist school', like the senior judge who told the judges of his circuit (*Kassel*) to hand down death sentences so that he could write a report in which he was able to stress that capital punishment as practised in the army was a 'rite of purification', done with great responsibility and with the aim of cleansing the armed forces of 'inferior and decomposing elements'.[32]

To take a similar example; as late as January 1945 von Friedeburg, the commanding admiral of submarines, went against the general practice by ordering that soldiers being sentenced to death must not have a last wish to die without eye bandages fulfilled because they had offended the people, community and military duties.[33] These examples illustrate that it was not mere theory when Hitler and many lawyers declared that 'guilt' must be defined from the standpoint of the needs of the people. In November 1944 this idea was illustrated by the chief of the personnel branch and National Socialist education in the Luftwaffe who noted that it had long been self-evident that anybody who doubted Hitler's ability or criticised his decisions was infamous and therefore deserved death.[34]

It was in this atmosphere that German military law operated. Whether the people responsible for the maintenance of the military legal system were Nazis or not, it is plain that its philosophy was underpinned by its compliance with Nazi war aims and ideology. Death sentences rained down faster and faster every year.

	Army	*Navy*	*Air Force*	*Total*
1939–40	485	8	26	519
1940–1	392	15	40	447
1941–2	1,394	144	135	1,673
1942–3	2,282	218	274	2,769
1943–4	3,224	400	494	4,118[35]

The exact figures for 1944–5 are unknown, but one must expect them to be several thousands, bringing the total up to more than

13,000. To these one should add those soldiers who received sentences of imprisonment and were then sent to *Frontbewährung*, that is, to special units which were used in dangerous areas and were treated most severely. The losses of these *Strafbataillone* were extremely high. The intention was that those soldiers who survived would go to prison after Germany's final victory. There is no detailed study of all these cases. But one is surely entitled to say that in this manner the number of victims of the special ideological function of German military jurisdiction was enlarged enormously.

Notes

1. See for instance E. Ludendorff, *Kriegführung und Politik*, Berlin, 1922, p. 149; v. Wrisberg, *Heer und Heimat 1914–1919*, Leipzig, 1921, p. 194.
2. *Statistics of the military effort of the British Empire during the Great War 1914–1918*, London, 1922, p. 648; G. Pedroncini, *Les Mutineries de 1917*, Paris, 1967; A. Juin, *Trois Siècles d'Obéissance Militaire*, Paris, 1964.
3. Speech of 13 July 1934, cf. M. Domarus, *Hitler: Reden 1932–1945*, Munich, 1965, p. 421; *Mein Kampf*, commemorative ed., 1939, p. 518.
4. Figures given to author by Judge Advocate General, JAG/733, 12 June 1980.
5. Magistrat Général F. Le Gallais, letter dated 11 June 1980.
6. O. Hennicke, 'Auszüge aus der Wehrmachtkriminalstatistik', in *Zeitschrift für Militärgeschichte* 1966, p. 444.
7. *Kriegssonderstrafrechtsverordnung*, d. 17 August 1938, *Reichsgesetzblatt* (RGBl) 1939 I 1455.
8. *Kriegskriminalstatistik für die Wehrmacht, OKW, Sonderheft Zusammenfassung der kriminalstatistischen Ergebnisse des ersten Kriegsjahres*, Berlin, 1941, and *Quartalsberichte* from 1 January 1940 to 31 March 1942, see BA-MA, RW6/v. 129, and Hennicke, *Auszüge*.
9. RGBl I 1679.
10. Examples in BA-MA / ZNS, OKM, Documents concerning *Feldkriegsgerichte*, April–November 1941, fol. 232ff.
11. See O. P. Schweling, *Die deutsche Militärjustiz in der Zeit des Nationalsozialismus*, Marburg, 1977 — a book filled with apologies.
12. H. Dietz, *Das Strafrecht der Wehrmacht im neuen Reich. Zur Neuordnung der Militärgerichtsbarkeit*, in *Deutsches Recht (DR), Zeitschrift des Bundes Nationalsozialistischer Deutscher Juristen*, 1933, pp. 163–72.

13. 83 *Kriegsstrafverfahrensordnung* (*KStVO*), 17 August 1938, RGBl I 1457 — a law which introduced considerable changes in the military criminal procedure.
14. E. Schwinge, *Zum Schuldbegriff des Militärstrafrechts*, in *Zeitschrift für Wehrrecht* (*ZWR*) 1937/8, pp. 443–8. Schwinge followed Carl Schmitt's idea of 'konkrete Ordnung'.
15. W. Hülle, *Die Stellung des Militärrichters und seine Aufgaben im künftigen Verfahrensrecht*, in *ZWR* 1937/8, vol. 2, pp. 97–111.
16. C. Schmitt, *Uber die drei Arten des rechtswissenschaftlichen Denkens*, Hamburg, 1934.
17. E. R. Huber, *Der Führer als Gesetzgeber*, in DR 1939, pp. 275–8.
18. *Verfügung OKH*, Ch H Rüst v. BdE 7 December 1939, BA-MA RH 14/30.
19. Cf. n. 8.
20. Hennicke, *Auszüge*, p. 443.
21. Ibid.
22. These figures can be assumed from the statistics.
23. R. Lehmann, *Die Aufgaben des Rechtswahrers der Wehrmacht*, in DR 1939, pp. 1265–9.
24. BA-ZNS *Vorschriften* o.Nr.
25. OKW — 14n 16WR (2), 21 December 1939, BA-MA RH 14/28 v. 96, 62.
26. Special issue of *Rechtsgrundsätze des Reichskriegsgerichts* on 5 KSSVO.
27. See R. Absolon, *Das Wehrmachtstrafrecht im 2. Weltkrieg*, Kornelimünster, 1958, pp. 77ff.; M. Messerschmidt, *Die Wehrmacht im NS-Staat*, Hamburg, 1969, pp. 367f.
28. BA-ZNS-6G2, *OKM, Akten betr. Bestätigung von Urteilen der Feldkriegsgerichte*, April–November 1941, pp. 232ff.
29. A. Hitler, *Monologe im Führerhauptquartier 1941–1944*, W. Jochmann (ed.), Hamburg, 1980, p. 350.
30. *Mob-Sammelerlaß*, no. 10.
31. BA-ZNS, *Sammelakte BAL 1942, Gericht der 18. Armee*, Archiv Nr. 43.
32. Order dated 28 September 1943, BA-ZNS, 'Sammlung Todesurteile in der Wehrmacht'.
33. Order from 4 January 1945, BA-MA K1/139, sheet 64.
34. See Absolon, *Wehrmachtstrafrecht*, pp. 90–3.
35. Hennicke, *Auszüge*, p. 444. For the period October–December 1944 Hennicke mentions an additional number of 206 executions, which brings the total up to 9,732.

WILHELM DEIST, MANFRED MESSERSCHMIDT, HANS-ERICH VOLKMANN, WOLFRAM WETTE

Causes and Preconditions of German Aggression

The historical controversy on the causes of the Second World War has never produced such diverse points of view as has research into the causes of the wars of 1864–6, 1870 and 1914–18.[*] Even the provocative theses of a few revisionist historians, which have led to a re-examination of prevailing opinions, have not been able to shake the generally accepted conclusion that it was German policy in the years before 1939 that was the basic cause of the Second World War. Moreover, broadly based research in the field of German history of the last 150 years has shown that the founding of the German Empire and the attempt to maintain and enlarge it, as well as the renewed efforts to achieve a Great Power, even world power, position after the catastrophe of the First World War, involved a policy of expansion and preparation for war which fundamentally changed Europe and its political weight in the world. Wars marked the beginning and the end of the seventy-five-year history of the united German state.

[*]This essay is taken from the series *Das Deutsche Reich und der Zweite Weltkrieg* (Stuttgart, 1979 et seq.). It was published as the conclusion of the first volume (*Ursachen und Voraussetzungen der deutschen Kriegspolitik*, pp. 703–16), which has four authors. Another early version was published under the title 'Der Weg in den Krieg' in *Aus Politik und Zeitgeschichte. Beilage zur Wochenzeitung Das Parlament* (34–5/79), 25 August 1979, pp. 3–15. In accordance with the original character of the conclusion, no footnotes have been added.

Transl. from the German by Dean S. McMurry.

This perspective is an important result of the continuing discussion as to the decisive structural elements of that state. These political and economic elements developed primarily as a result of specific conditions in the years after 1871, of the accelerating industrialisation and of combinations of both factors. The question of the continuing importance of these elements has been dealt with in numerous historical studies of Imperial Germany. The preliminary conclusion of most of these studies is that in the dominant military, political and social groups a continuity of foreign and domestic policy aims and supporting ideologies can be seen and that this exerted a powerful influence long after 1918.

To understand the history of the years before the Second World War it is necessary to place these insights in a clear historical framework. The detachment thus achieved permits a more differentiated judgement of the developments, trends and events of the 1930s which must be considered integral parts of the relatively short history of the united German state. It enables one to see both the continuity and discontinuity of this historical development in which stability and also the change of the structural elements mentioned above are reflected.

The effects of the German military defeat of 1918, the Revolution of that year and the Treaty of Versailles must be considered starting-points for an analysis of the causes of those German policies which led to war in September 1939. The decline of earlier political and military power structures, the assumption of power by Social Democrats — former 'Reich enemies' — the limiting of the German armed forces to a professional army of 100,000 men and a navy whose only mission seemed to be coastal defence clearly shook traditional German values and ideas of order. Economic and social areas seemed at first less affected, although even during the war large segments of the middle class had experienced economic difficulties which threatened their livelihoods and were aggravated considerably by the inflation of 1923. Quite apart from the question of whether these changes in political and social conditions were actually 'revolutionary', they were felt to be so by those members of the bourgeoisie who shaped public opinion and especially by the educated middle class.

The demand for a revision of the Treaty of Versailles played a fundamental role in further developments and in the justification of National Socialist policies after 1933. The issue was raised by all political groups and supported by the mass of the population under the influence of the harsh conditions of the treaty. As a slogan for political programmes, 'revision' only had a socially unifying effect in the beginning. Very soon it came to be associated with the most varied foreign and domestic policy aims, a shining symbol and catchword for political propaganda. In nationalistic circles the demand for revision acquired a distinctly domestic political emphasis. Many nationalistic Germans simply refused to accept the fact that Germany had been defeated by its enemies in the war and spoke of 'revolutionary wire-pullers' who had 'stabbed' the undefeated German army 'in the back' and caused the military and political 'collapse'. The condemnation of the 'Versailles *Diktat*' thus came to be allied with traditional German anti-parliamentarianism and anti-republicanism.

All revisionists were primarily interested in such foreign policy goals as eliminating reparations, re-establishing German military sovereignty and regaining territory lost at Versailles. Here too the number and scope of demands differed from party to party. The important differences were usually to be found in the long-range political goals and the methods with which they were supposed to be realised. In these goals it became clear that, in spite of the completely changed conditions, the thinking and actions of many parties in the Weimar Republic, even the Social Democrats, were still determined by various continental Great Power plans which had been propagated and tried out with varying degrees of success before 1918. Moreover, compared to the situation at the beginning of the century, the long-range prospects for a German Great Power role had improved considerably. The fundamental ideological conflict between Britain and the Soviet Union appeared so deep as to be unbridgeable, the United States had dissociated itself from Versailles, the states of east-central Europe were interested in better economic and political relations with Germany and, finally, the Anglo–French relationship had lost much of the closeness of the war years, especially after the French occupation of the Ruhr in 1923.

In the German press and the thinking of almost all politically prominent persons of the Republic, these developments were less important than the mistaken belief that Germany had almost no freedom to manoeuvre in foreign policy. Even after the Treaty of Rapallo with the Soviet Union (1922) and Germany's admission to the League of Nations (1926) this assessment of the political situation hardly changed. Stresemann's promising attempts to exploit economic factors and the advantages of the League's collective security system to create a new basis for a German Great Power policy were dismissed by the right-wing parties and similar groups as merely a 'policy of fulfilling the conditions of Versailles'. Liberals and Social Democrats as well as several moderate conservatives, who pursued with different aims a policy of understanding and compromise within the international system represented by the League, ultimately failed because they were unable to maintain majority support for this policy. The continued vehement rejection of Versailles and the League (the latter was seen as an 'organisation of the victors'), the struggle for equality for Germany in armaments questions and demands for a reduction of reparations strengthened those political groups favouring traditional power politics.

While the German Revolution of 1918–19 and the Treaty of Versailles may be taken as possible starting-points for a discussion of the causal context in which German policy after 1933 must be analysed, the Depression after 1929, with its political, economic, social and psychological consequences, must be regarded as the decisive development which contributed to the concentration and strengthening of those forces which determined German foreign policy until 1939. The clearly strengthening tendencies towards a breaking away from the multilateral system of the League were themselves a consequence of changes in the German domestic situation brought about by the economic crisis. These tendencies were accompanied by changes in the military policies of the Reichswehr.

The earlier attempts by General Hans von Seeckt, chief of the army high command (OKH), to break out of the Versailles system with the help of the Soviet Union and create a basis for German Great Power policy had not, in spite of Rapallo, produced the desired results. In the years after Seeckt's dismissal in 1926 the Reichswehr took the real political and military situation more into account in its plans and actions. The Reichswehr leaders attempted to draw the proper conclusions from the experiences of the First World War by pursuing systematic armaments planning, but actual rearmament programmes were very limited. The government's approval of the first armaments programme in 1928 was due to the efforts of the Reichswehr minister, Groener, to make the Reichswehr part of Stresemann's general revisionist policy, whose goals Groener even wanted to adopt as a framework for operational planning. This relatively consistent policy was gradually abandoned as the foundation of Reichswehr planning after the autumn of 1931. By January 1933 the general political crisis had led to the balance of power in the Reichswehr ministry shifting in favour of those who believed that the only way to achieve ambitious military aims and provide a solid base for Germany's claims to be a Great Power, was to abandon the system of collective security. Groener himself did not basically reject such aims, representing as they did a continuation of Seeckt's foreign policy, which in turn was based on the Prusso-German military traditions rendered obsolete by the First World War. In this context it is possible to claim that Groener's programme was defeated by reactionary forces.

At the same time the political influence of the Reichswehr increased noticeably. In the autumn and winter of 1923 the attempts of the Reichswehr leaders under Seeckt to use the state of emergency to regain the traditional supremacy of the armed forces within the general power structure, and which had been lost at the end of the war, had failed. After an interval during the relatively stable years of the republic, this development culminated in the appointment of General Schleicher as Reichswehr minister and then chancellor. Schleicher's appointment represented an attempt to achieve the goal of supremacy of the military with a broad organisational base; favoured by the decline of parliamentary government caused by the economic crisis, this had greater chances of success. Under Schleicher, who enjoyed the confidence of President von Hindenburg, Germany moved towards becoming a military state. After the break of 1918–19 this traditional factor in German political development seemed to be regaining its former influence.

The crisis of the parliamentary system found its expression in presidential governments. The system collapsed under the political, economic and, above all, the social problems resulting from the economic crisis. These problems were accompanied by a wave of nationalistic and anti-democratic ideas which generally favoured the Nazi Party (NSDAP). A decisive role in the propagation of these ideas was played by the so-called National Opposition. This included the NSDAP; the *Stahlhelm*, a league of former Front soldiers; the German National People's Party (DNVP); the influential literary group Soldierly Nationalism around Ernst Jünger; the largest German student organisation and a number of paramilitary organisations and groups. In domestic policy, the National Opposition sought to introduce a 'Front-soldier state' organised along military lines, an authoritarian state based on military power. The foreign policy of the National Opposition was based on a less clearly formulated but nevertheless loudly proclaimed military imperialism supported by rather vague arguments which stressed national defence and military readiness above all else. The two main churches, the Protestant more than the Catholic, also tended to support the nationalistic groups and not the democratic-republican organisations. The churches' traditional teaching of the 'just' war prevented the Christian principle of non-violence from influencing political developments. In spite of the horrors of the First World War, the German churches tended to accept war uncritically, as a result of a natural or divine law. The Catholic Centre Party, the right-liberal German People's Party (DVP), the left-liberal German Democratic Party (DDP) and organisations close to them became increasingly nationalistic during the crisis years of the Weimar Republic and dissociated themselves from a foreign policy of peaceful compromise. Only the Social Democrats, who were kept out of power, the Reichsbanner Black-Red-Gold, and the labour unions continued to support that policy. Pacifist organisations, especially those which were clearly anti-military, were completely isolated. The German Communists warned constantly of the dangers of an 'imperialist' war, but since their argument was that new wars were inevitable, this only contributed to the development of a certain fatalism.

The flood of nationalistic books and war films which began in 1929 and increased steadily until the end of 1933 also changed the political climate; the decline in the number of artistic and literary works with pacifist themes at this time reflected a general trend. In spite of the Kellogg–Briand Pact of 1928 outlawing war, the view that military force was a legitimate means of policy was accepted as self-evident. The German press as a whole tended to support the strong trend towards a militarisation of society which was in accord with and promoted the intentions of the Reichswehr under Schleicher. In this respect the developments of 1933 did not represent a break; rather the National Socialist regime was able to exploit this favourable climate of opinion in its practical policies.

This survey of the German political situation at the end of 1932 supports the view that, in almost all areas of domestic and foreign policy, groups and individuals who followed traditional lines, as they had developed since 1867–71, had gained influence and increasingly determined developments, even though conditions at home and abroad had changed completely since 1918. This trend could be observed also in the ideologies of most of these groups and individuals, as well as in certain economic developments. The Depression represented a crisis of the liberal world trade system. It resulted in a revival of ideas and plans for more or less closed economic areas. In Germany such ideas were a continuation of similar plans of the Wilhelmine era. The idea of a large, autarkic European economic area as an alternative to the disintegrating world trade system gained new significance when the NSDAP adopted it as the foundation of a new German economic programme, and was thus able to obtain the support of important economic circles even before Hitler's appointment as chancellor.

It may seem logical to conclude that after January 1933 the policies of the National Socialist regime were essentially a continuation of traditional tendencies and lines of development and were new only in their extreme radicalism, but such an interpretation would be superficial and would carry the continuity thesis too far. It would disregard the 'programme' and political acts of the man who within a few years led the NSDAP to victory over powerful rivals and who was the dominant figure in German policy until 1945: Adolf Hitler. Although individual elements of his world view may seem heterogeneous and even contradictory, both his social Darwinist conviction that 'struggle in all its forms' determined the life of the individual as well as national development and his race ideology must be considered the unchanging foundations of his political decisions. Hitler's foreign policy aims, of which the most important was the conquest of 'Lebensraum' in the east, were also determined by this ideological perspective. Peace was desirable only as an opportunity to prepare for war; alliances were valued only in so far as they might be useful in future wars. The ideological determinant in Hitler's political views and decisions after 1933 constituted a break with previously accepted official aims and ideas of international order in German policy. In the years after 1933, however, Hitler was careful to conceal the real extent of this change. He was able to avoid conflicts by concentrating on broad areas of agreement with strong revisionist groups in short-term domestic, foreign policy, economic and military goals. In the years after 1933 no one talked more about peace than Hitler himself; his broad programmes to 'rebuild Germany's defence capability' made that necessary. Only in this way could he hope to achieve an agreement with Britain, an essential element of his programme since the 1920s and a precondition for German expansion in the east. But the rapid German rearmament made the attaining of this goal uncertain and thus endangered the political and strategic assumptions of Hitler's policy of aggression.

The essays in *Ursachen und Voraussetzungen der deutschen Kriegs-politik* show that the extent and dynamism of the rearmament programme shaped the development of German domestic and foreign policy in the years between 1933 and 1939 to a much greater extent than has previously been assumed. All important measures of the regime supported rearmament directly or indirectly; this was especially true of economic policy and to a lesser degree of foreign policy.

In a conference with the commanders of the Reichswehr on 3 February 1933 Hitler mentioned an additional precondition for successful rearmament: the 'rebuilding of Germany's defence capability', the strengthening by all means of the will of the population to defend the country. In Hitler's view this could be achieved only through a 'complete reversal' of domestic conditions, by a strict, authoritarian leadership. In this respect the interests of the party and the Reichswehr were identical. The domestic policies of the National Socialist regime clearly served the aim of reorganising German society for war. Political measures — the elimination of parliamentarianism and political parties, the forcing of all interest groups into line and the establishment of an authoritarian Führer state — were not ends in themselves but only means serving the preparations for war. One consequence of this policy was the corruption and finally the dissolution of the rule of law. Despite certain similarities with Imperial Germany, the National Socialist break with German national traditions is most clear here.

Even the social policies of the National Socialist regime did not remain unaffected by the general preparations for war. In this area the NSDAP was strongly influenced by the First World War, during which it had been especially the working class who had protested with increasing force against the continuation of the war and the economic sacrifices required and had ignited the revolution after the military defeat. Fear of revolution was the main motive of Hitler's policy of maintaining the production of consumer goods in spite of intensive rearmament. But the workers could not be kept in line by propaganda alone; economic concessions were required. When the social 'bribery strategy' did not work, obedience was enforced by brutal terror.

Hitler left the planning and concrete aims of rearmament largely to the military. The new Reichswehr minister, von Blomberg, who had determinedly opposed Groener's military policy since 1929, successfully advocated unilateral rearmament. He rejected multilateral or even bilateral armaments agreements which might lead to restrictions on German armaments plans. The senior officers of the German army and navy quickly took as their point of reference the level of armaments achieved before the First World War. In view of the existing levels of military forces in Europe, and the danger of political isolation, it was the first German steps towards this goal which were the most dangerous. Hitler himself pointed out the danger of a French preventive strike to the commanders of the Reichswehr at the beginning of February 1933. The military leaders, particularly Generals von Fritsch and Beck, were of the opinion that this danger, could be met only by accelerating the tempo of rearmament; Hitler's intentions thus agreed with those of the military leaders. The rejection of all international restrictions on German armaments, the resulting feeling of being in an endangered military position and the military conclusions drawn from this assessment of the situation gave the rearmament programme a dynamism of its own whose political and economic effects in the period 1933–9 can hardly be overestimated.

The form in which the rearmament of the Wehrmacht was carried out until 1939 was marked by a pronounced lack of co-ordination among the service branches, which reduced its effectiveness considerably. No attempt was made to co-ordinate the armaments programmes of the army, navy and air force through clear policy and strategic directives. The army armaments programmes of December 1933 and August 1936 were based on the assumption of a European war on several fronts. After the completion of its armaments programme, Germany would be able to fight such a war with 'some prospects of success'. The offensive aims of the armaments plan of 1936 were obvious. As early as the end of 1935 Beck had spoken of a 'strategic defence' to be carried out in a war in the form of attacks on several fronts. In August 1936 the chief of the army general office considered the armaments plan to be justifiable for military and economic reasons only if the armed forces would actually be used after its completion.

At that time the navy had not developed such a comprehensive programme, even taking into account the length of time necessary for the long-term planning for its main resources — ships. Since the pre-planning for the Anglo-German naval agreement of June 1935, as well as after its signing, the navy leaders had been involved in the difficult task of developing new strategic premises. As with the army, the navy planners considered France and Poland the probable enemies, until the conclusion of the German–Polish non-aggression pact. The strategic consequences of the German demands for armaments parity with France raised at the beginning of 1934 show that the navy already considered Britain as a possible long-term enemy. The 'Tirpitz fleet' ideology, to which the leading German naval officers felt bound by tradition, acquired a new relevance. But the change from an orientation towards Britain, which had not been previously questioned, to a policy directed against the superior sea power was a lengthy one. A taboo had to be broken. Only in the summer of 1937 did the naval leaders officially begin to concern themselves with the strategic consequences of a confrontation with Britain. The result of this lack of clarity regarding strategic requirements was a curiously vacillating armaments policy determined more by the impulses of the moment than by the navy's basic long-term aims.

There is no evidence of even a basic co-ordination of armaments efforts between the army and the navy. In contrast, there seemed to be at least the beginning of co-operation between the army and the air force. This was due primarily to the fact that almost all the senior air force officers had come from the army. The two services also shared common strategic ideas; both expected a war on several fronts in Europe, with France, Poland and/or Czechoslovakia as the most important states on the other side. The air force considered its main task to be the support of the ground forces and not the conducting of an independent air war. In spite of these common views there was no co-ordination, as the air force regarded its own armaments programme and related industrial activities as its exclusive domain. The large-scale, well-planned development of the aircraft industry made possible the creation, between 1933 and 1936, of an air force which completely fulfilled its function of deterring other states from taking preventive measures against German rearmament. However, this neither solved the military problems of the new service branch, nor helped to master the difficulties resulting from the necessary modernisation of aircraft and the systematic application of technical advances to industrial production. After a rapid initial increase, aircraft production stagnated in the years 1937 to 1938, a point at which the British Royal Air Force became the potential enemy. For this war, however, the German air force lacked the basic weapons, such as strategic bombers.

The rearmament of the German armed forces can be described as an almost uninterrupted build-up and expansion of the service branches which was unprecedented in its speed and dimensions. In

1936–7 economic difficulties necessitated bureaucratic management of the armaments programme in the form of allocations of raw materials. However, such difficulties led neither Hitler nor his military leaders to base their armaments aims on political goals and resulting strategic perspectives. The generally accepted principle was to produce as much as possible as rapidly as possible. Hitler attempted, with some success, to overcome the resulting crises in armaments production by ideological appeals to the armed forces, descriptions of future political perspectives and excessive production demands. Such efforts, however, also intensified interservice rivalries. Undoubtedly the armed forces had achieved a very high level of rearmament by the outbreak of the war, when Germany was the strongest military power on the Continent, with the most modern equipment. But the level of armaments did not meet completely the wishes of the military, it was, rather, the result of an unrestrained rearmament of individual service branches. Available resources were thus wasted, although they would certainly have been adequate for a thorough rearmament based on a realistic estimation of the country's economic potential. The causes and preconditions of German aggression can be explained to a considerable degree by this complex conclusion and its implications for German foreign, economic and social policy. In comparison, the ideological differences between the armed forces and the NSDAP, the authority conflicts within the armed forces themselves and the innumerable organisational problems were of only peripheral importance.

Rearmament was in keeping with Hitler's programmatic aims of struggle, war and Lebensraum. At the beginning of 1933, however, the reality in Germany was still marked by a depressed economy and several million unemployed, in spite of the nationalistic enthusiasm which constituted the ideological and propaganda basis for the fulfilment of the National Socialist programme. Solving this economic problem was a precondition for the consolidation of the regime's domestic power and for giving it the opportunity to realise its military and foreign policy aims. As Papen and Schleicher had done before him, Hitler adopted a policy of using government funds to stimulate the economy and create new jobs. Typically, however, he saw to it that the corresponding programmes served rearmament directly or indirectly. The close connection between economic recovery and rearmament meant that certain risks had to be taken. The president of the Reichsbank (the German central bank), Schacht, who became the central figure in the first phase of

National Socialist economic policy, sought to limit the risks from the very beginning. The funds obtained for rearmament by the well-known Mefo Bills were limited. Although financing for rearmament could be guaranteed in this way for a few years, serious difficulties were soon encountered in obtaining sufficient foreign exchange for imports of essential raw materials and even foodstuffs. Schacht attempted to solve this problem through a reorientation of German trade policy. Germany largely restricted its exports to countries that could pay for them with the desired raw materials and foodstuffs. The constantly shrinking foreign exchange reserves could thus be concentrated on rearmament needs. This new element in German economic policy complemented almost perfectly the efforts to achieve autarky, as economic relations with the less industrialised states of eastern and south-eastern Europe could now be used to make them more dependent on the German market.

The state regulation of foreign trade which accompanied the 'New Plan' of 1934 had some features of a planned economy, but Schacht and those members of the National Socialist regime concerned with economic questions continued to emphasise the basic responsibility of the employers. In accordance with their view of the economy as a 'defence economy' they did claim the right to intervene for the purpose of guiding the economic process; they wanted to establish centralised control of all economic organisations. The consideration with which the regime treated both companies and individual capitalists was in sharp contrast to the workers' complete loss of political and economic power. Only in the course of time did the German Labour Front, which had replaced the trade unions, develop social policy initiatives going beyond its original supervisory function.

The successes of Schacht's economic policy were overtaken by the speed and extent of rearmament as early as the second half of 1935. The National Socialist leaders, above all Hitler and Göring, reacted to the new raw materials crisis caused by the exhaustion of foreign exchange reserves by proclaiming an economic mobilisation, the Four-Year Plan, in September 1936. More than ever, economic policy was subordinated to preparations for war. The programme of exploiting all sources of raw materials within Germany without regard to the profit principle, the build-up and expansion of synthetic materials industries at almost any cost and, finally, the goals of achieving a high degree of self-sufficiency in those raw materials of especial importance for armaments and of preparing the whole economy for war within four years must be seen in connection with the army armaments programme of August 1936. As a whole this programme shows quite clearly the basic social Darwinist nature of Hitler's ideas and actions: his only solution for economic problems was the conquest of new Lebensraum.

Hitler's appeals and his new programme made little difference to the total economic situation. Certain improvements in some sectors of the economy could be expected from individual projects, but the short-term effects achieved by Hitler's dramatic announcement and Göring's energetic efforts soon came to nothing. The raw materials allocation measures introduced in 1937 completely failed to satisfy the armed forces; it became clear that Hitler himself would have to determine the distribution of available raw materials. Instead on 5 November 1937 he lectured the commanders of the armed forces on his political ideas for the future. His decisions regarding pressing economic and armaments questions were improvised and provisional. Until the outbreak of the war there was no comprehensive armaments programme for all the armed forces. Hitler had already indicated that he did not have much faith in systematic preparations for a total war, as advocated earlier by Ludendorff. As the experiences of the First World War had shown, such a programme made it necessary to prepare the entire economy for a 'long' war. Hitler considered it much more important always to have at his disposal well-equipped, formidable armed forces ready for war; maintaining supply depots and logistics capacity were in his eyes matters of only secondary importance.

In the winter of 1937/8 it became increasingly clear that available resources were not sufficient to maintain the volume and speed of rearmament and at the same time overcome the economic crisis, which was now aggravated by a labour shortage. Consequently German economic planners developed a growing interest in neighbouring states, especially Austria and Czechoslovakia. They saw the only possibility of maintaining the desired pace of rearmament and economic recovery in territorial expansion and a resulting enlargement of Germany's economic base. Undoubtedly these economic arguments influenced the motives and even the timing of Hitler's political decisions to annex Austria and 'smash' Czechoslovakia. The improvement of the general economic situation could not, however, conceal the fact that the crisis persisted and restricted Hitler's freedom of action in making further political decisions. The Führer, of course, considered the economy a mere instrument to be used in the support of his expansionist policies.

A policy directed towards war was also a means of avoiding those social consequences of the constant strain on the economy which Hitler feared. In 1938 and 1939 signs of social unrest among workers and of a general economic dissatisfaction among farmers increased. Refusals to work overtime, high rates of absenteeism due to illness, a decline in productivity and complaints about the catastrophic migration from rural areas to the cities and the disadvantages of price controls were all symptoms of a development which could endanger the domestic political stability of the regime. Although it is not accurate to speak of a dangerous worsening of these conditions in 1939, the possibility of domestic political motives in the policies which led to war cannot be completely excluded. The consequences cited above also show the basic reversal of the traditional values and aims of economic policy that took place under National Socialism.

Preparations for war were the common denominator of the basic decisions of the regime in the areas of domestic, military and economic policy. It was therefore logical that foreign policy should also be determined by this factor. In accordance with his ideological premises, Hitler never accepted an international order which had as its goal a permament peaceful coexistence of the various states. In the phase of 'rebuilding Germany's defence capability', foreign policy assumed the function of providing diplomatic cover for the programme of the new regime. Hitler and the foreign ministry, which was happy to accept this task under the banner of revisionism, were able to avoid international isolation through numerous bilateral initiatives and even to achieve significant successes, such as the conclusion of the Concordat and the Polish–German non-aggression pact.

This policy was accompanied by the extremely effective use of propaganda under the direction of Joseph Goebbels, whose task was to conceal the personnel and material rearmament measures both from other countries and the German population or, if that was not possible, to play them down as for self-defence. For this purpose Goebbels used catch-phrases that had been popular in all German right-wing groups since the 1920s — 'revision of Versailles', 'the struggle against Bolshevism', 'equal treatment' (for Germany) and 'rebuilding Germany's defence capability'. Hitler stressed his peaceful intentions at every opportunity, and his propaganda minister saw to it that he received vocal mass support. This deception proved effective at home and abroad.

Public opinion abroad generally believed that National Socialist foreign policy differed from that of the Weimar governments only in its greater determination to realise the same well-known demands. The united front of the Versailles victors had begun to crumble during the 1920s. Even at that time the reaction to German wishes for revision had been varied, even positive. In this situation and in view of the generally weakened condition of most countries as a result of the Depression, energetic, forceful joint action against German treaty violations was not to be expected. The other powers vacillated between attempts to isolate Germany completely, partial co-operation and efforts to preserve peace by drawing Germany into the international system in spite of her treaty violations.

Hitler and the foreign ministry recognised and thoroughly exploited the opportunities this international configuration offered them for an active foreign policy. The occupation of the demilitarised Rhineland in March 1936 was the high point and also the successful conclusion of the first phase of National Socialist foreign policy. Thereafter the shielding function of German foreign policy was largely replaced by attempts to create the diplomatic preconditions for the planned war for Lebensraum in the east. German trade policy towards south-eastern Europe was, in terms of its effects, as much a part of these attempts as the generally less successful courting of Italy and Japan.

The relationship with Britain was a decisive factor in Hitler's programme aims, as he was convinced of the unchanging hostility of France and considered her elimination or neutralisation before the start of his war of expansion in the east absolutely necessary. Hitler never really understood the place of Europe in British foreign policy. After 1933 he seems to have assumed that Britain would accept a German hegemony on the Continent if her overseas interests were not affected. The influence of earlier ideas about a possible arrangement of interests between the land and the sea power, about world-wide co-operation, is obvious. But the uncertainty remained. Hitler and the German naval commanders considered the Anglo-German naval agreement of 1935 as a relatively short-term, interim solution, and Britain kept her distance in the following years. This threatened to disrupt Hitler's timetable; an unencumbered rear in the west was the decisive prerequisite for the conquest of the European part of the Soviet Union, whose military strength he completely underestimated.

Hitler rejected all British offers to co-operate in a mutually satisfactory peaceful change of the status quo in eastern and south-eastern Europe. Such a policy would have enabled him to achieve the main revisionist goals in Poland, Czechoslovakia and Austria peacefully — a very generous concession of the appeasement policy. Hitler's refusal to accept such a solution showed his determination to achieve his larger goals by force. His talks with the British foreign minister, Lord Halifax, fourteen days after he had revealed his belligerent intentions to German military leaders in November 1937, show that even at that point he was not prepared to accept what he regarded as a temporary solution. Unusually by diplomatic standards, it was made quite clear in the conversation that Hitler was pursuing a policy of war which was completely incompatible with the peace plan proposed by Halifax.

Hitler was now carried along by the dynamism of the policy he had initiated. The course of events was accelerated not only by the reactions of Germany's threatened neighbours but also by a combination of psychological causes and a variety of factors in military policy and the armaments industry. The events of February and March 1938 and of May and September later that year quickly made the timetable of November 1937 obsolete. The British guarantee to Poland in March 1939 reduced Hitler's room for manoeuvre even more, as he refused to consider the alternative of a peaceful compromise.

To ask about a connecting link between Hitler's programme and the rapid rearmament programme is implicitly to seek a general plan and a timetable agreed upon by Hitler and the military leaders. Hitler was obviously incapable of proceeding in that manner. To do so he would have had to have the co-operation of the partners envisioned in his programme. Even Italy was not prepared to go as far as he wanted; Britain deliberately avoided a definite answer and made it clear in 1937 that she had no intention of agreeing to military solutions of continental problems. Whatever may be said against appeasement, the British refusal did force Hitler to improvise an alternative. In the autumn of 1938 and the spring of 1939 it included the attempt to come to an agreement with Poland. The idea of a political triangle consisting of Berlin, Rome and Tokyo, which remained an illusion, can also be explained only as a reaction to British policy, an attempt to exert pressure on Britain.

Britain's refusal to co-operate forced Hitler to conclude a pact with and made him dependent on Stalin, which was completely incompatible with his long-range aims. In the first Blitzkrieg (against

Poland) the deterrence component of the 'Blitzkrieg strategy' was a political failure: the Western powers declared war on Germany, making it impossible for Hitler to prepare his next move according to plan. He could only attempt to improve his military starting position for the realisation of his programme. But the qualitative and quantitative German superiority in armaments was sufficient for only the first stages. It permitted solutions on the Continent which only fed a short-lived optimism. Germany was unable to conduct a world war, which is what the conflict rapidly became.

In seeking the causes of the German policy of aggression in September 1939 we must note that, unlike August 1914, there was no significant enthusiasm for the war in the German population at that time. Contemporary reports indicate the exact opposite. As early as the Sudeten Crisis in the autumn of 1938 the National Socialist propagandists noted the widespread fear of war among the population. For this reason Hitler ordered in November 1938 that the 'pacifist record' be turned off and the nation prepared for military solutions. Consequently the propagandists tried an entirely different approach in 1939. As in 1914 the country was warned of an alleged encirclement by hostile powers; it was claimed that Germany was a nation without enough Lebensraum. To conceal the aggressive intentions of their own government, the German propagandists tried to place the blame for 'what is to come' on other countries. Whatever the reasons for the negative attitude of the German population, we can conclude that, in contrast to the situation in 1914, the belligerent policy of the regime did not enjoy widespread support.

This conclusion again raises the question of the real forces behind the German policy of aggression. In seeking an answer we cannot ignore the bourgeois-nationalist groups and their representatives in the foreign ministry, the armed forces, industry and the universities. In their thoughts and deeds the traditions of the German Empire lived on. They had experienced Germany's rise to world power status before 1914 and their attitudes had been shaped by it; they were familiar with all the variations of German Great Power foreign policy and its economic and military principles. They had welcomed and supported rearmament, the 'rebuilding of Germany's defence capability' and the concentration of the economy on preparing for war. Their aim was an expansion of Germany's position as a Great Power over and above a mere revision of the limitations imposed by the Treaty of Versailles. They hoped that Germany would be able to dominate eastern Europe and establish an imperium in the east and thus an autarkic defence economy. In these policy calculations, the use of military force was taken for granted. Differences that developed between Hitler and the German diplomatic, economic and military leaders after 1936–7 involved only the question of the speed at which one should attempt to achieve these goals. Hitler's Lebensraum programme, the axiomatic basis of his policy, as well as its social Darwinist and race-ideological justification, were simply beyond the framework of traditional German Great Power policy and were ignored, played down or simply not understood by the old leadership groups.

Thus Hitler's programme functioned as a point of orientation which could be approached in different ways determined by tactical considerations. The precondition for a policy of hegemony, the rebuilding of the nation's military capability, affected all areas of life and society and was carried out as a constantly accelerating process with the participation of a growing number of institutions and organisations. The forces unleashed by this process penetrated the traditional state bureaucracy, competed with and checked each other, but always regarded the 'Führer and Chancellor' as the real centre from which they derived their power. The essays in *Ursachen und Voraussetzungen der deutschen Kriegspolitik* leave no doubt that even Hitler's decisions were affected by the dynamism of the power structure which developed as a result of these authority conflicts.

The step-by-step realisation of Hitler's continental programme, in historical perspective a new attempt to establish Germany as a Great Power and a world power, entered a new phase with the German attack on Poland on 1 September 1939. The unfounded expectation that the subjugation of Poland would provoke only formal protests from the Western powers was shattered by their declarations of war on Germany on 3 September. Twenty-five years after the outbreak of the First World War the lights in Europe went out again. A military machine was set in motion whose destructive power exceeded anything previously known and affected almost every corner of the European continent. This catastrophe was the result of policies pursued by Germany since 1933, which were aimed at expansion and war. These policies not only were based on Hitler's Lebensraum ideology but also were an expression of the persistent self-aggrandisement of various German élites and their continuing demands for the acceptance of Germany as an international and even world power since the turn of the century.

Notes on the Contributors

Lothar Burchardt (b. 1939) studied at the Universities of Heidelberg and Tübingen and took his Ph.D. in 1966. He is currently Professor of History at the University of Konstanz. His publications include *Friedenswirtschaft und Kriegsvorsorge* (Boppard, 1968), *Wissenschaftspolitik im Wilhelminischen Deutschland* (Göttingen, 1975) and *Hitler und die historische Größe* (Konstanz, 1979).

Wilhelm Deist (b. 1931) completed his doctorate at the University of Freiburg in 1956 and is now a member of the Militärgeschichtliches Forschungsamt and co-editor of the *Militärgeschichtliche Mitteilungen* and of the *War and Society Newsletter*. His publications include *Militär und Innenpolitik im Weltkrieg 1914–1918* (Düsseldorf, 1970), *Flottenpolitik und Flottenpropaganda. Das Nachrichtenbureau des Reichmarineamts 1897–1914* (Stuttgart, 1976) and *The Wehrmacht and German Rearmament* (London, 1981). In 1978 he was Visiting Leverhulme Fellow at St Antony's College, Oxford.

Jost Dülffer (b. 1943) took his Ph.D. at the University of Freiburg in 1972 and is now Professor of History at the University of Cologne. His publications include *Weimar, Hitler und die Marine. Reichspolitik und Flottenbau 1920–1939* (Düsseldorf, 1973) and *Regeln gegen den Krieg? Die Haager Friedenskonferenzen von 1899 und 1907 in der internationalen Politik* (Frankfurt, 1981).

Jürgen Förster (b. 1940) was educated at the Universities of Nottingham and Cologne, where he took his Ph.D. in 1974. He has been a member of the Militärgeschichtliches Forschungsamt since 1970. He is the author of *Stalingrad. Risse im Bundnis 1942/43* (Stuttgart, 1975) and has co-authored *Der Angriff auf die Sowjetunion* (Stuttgart, 1983). In 1982 he was Visiting Professor of History at Arizona State University, Tempe, Arizona.

Michael Geyer (b. 1947) was educated at the University of Freiburg and is currently Associate Professor of History at the University of Michigan. He is the author of a variety of articles on German militarism and rearmament.

His study *Aufrüstung oder Sicherheit. Die Reichswehr in der Krise der Machtpolitik 1924–1936* was published in 1980. A further study, *Deutsche Rüstungspolitik 1860–1980*, appeared in 1984.

Bernhard R. Kroener (b. 1948) was educated at the Universities of Bonn and Paris. He took his Ph.D. in 1977 and has been a member of the Militärgeschichtliches Forschungsamt since 1978. His study *Les Routes et les Etapes. Die Versorgung der französischen Armeen in Nordostfrankreich (1635–1661)* was published in 1980. His main interests focus on the economic and social history of the seventeenth and eighteenth centuries.

Klaus A. Maier (b. 1940) completed his doctorate at the University of Tübingen in 1970 and has been a member of the Militärgeschichtliches Forschungsamt since 1972. He is co-editor of the *Militärgeschichtliche Mitteilungen*, and of *Militärgeschichte* (Stuttgart, 1982). His study *Guernica 26.4.1937* was published in 1975. He co-authored *Die Errichtung der Hegemonie auf dem europäischen Kontinent* (Stuttgart, 1979). His main interests focus on German air policy and air operations in the Second World War.

Manfred Messerschmidt (b. 1926) is Chief Historian at the Militärgeschichtliches Forschungsamt. His publications include *Die Wehrmacht im NS-Staat* (Hamburg, 1969), *Die Politische Geschichte der preußisch-deutschen Armee* (Munich, 1975) and *Militär und Politik in der Bismarckzeit und im wilhelminischen Deutschland* (Darmstadt, 1975). He co-authored *Offiziere im Bild von Dokumenten aus drei Jahrhunderten* (Stuttgart, 1964) and *Ursachen und Voraussetzungen der deutschen Kriegspolitik* (Stuttgart, 1979).

Rolf-Dieter Müller (b. 1948) was educated at the Universities of Braunschweig and Mainz, where he took his Ph.D. in 1981. He has been a member of the Militärgeschichtliches Forschungsamt since 1979. His study *Das Tor zur Weltmacht. Die Bedeutung der Sowjetunion für die deutsche Wirtschafts- und Rüstungspolitik in der Zwischenkriegszeit (1919–1939)* was published in 1984. He co-authored *Der Angriff auf die Sowjetunion* (Stuttgart, 1983) and *Chemische Kriegführung — chemische Abrüstung* (Berlin, 1984).

Wolfgang Petter (b. 1942) was educated at the Universities of Marburg and Freiburg, where he took his Ph.D. in 1975. He has been a member of the Militärgeschichtliches Forschungsamt since 1971. His publications include *Die überseeische Stützpunktpolitik der preußisch-deutschen Kriegsmarine 1859–1883* (Freiburg, 1975) and *Deutscher Bund und deutsche Mittelstaaten* (Munich, 1976).

Gerhard Schreiber (b. 1940) completed his doctorate at the University of Hamburg in 1976 and since then has been a member of the Militärgeschichtliches Forschungsamt. His publications include *Revisionismus und Weltmachtstreben. Marineführung und deutsch-italienische Beziehungen 1919 bis 1944* (Stuttgart, 1978), *Die Zerstörung Europas im Zweiten Weltkrieg* (Tübingen, 1983) and *Hitler – Interpretationen 1923–1983* (Darmstadt, 1984). He co-authored *Der Mittelmeerraum und Südosteuropa. Von der 'non belligeranza' Italiens bis zum Kriegseintritt der Vereinigten Staaten* (Stuttgart, 1984).

Hans-Erich Volkmann (b. 1938) has been a member of the Militärgeschichtliches Forschungsamt since 1971 and is currently Professor of History at the University of Freiburg. His publications include *Wirtschaft im Dritten Reich. Eine Bibliographie*, 2 vols. (Stuttgart, 1981, 1983). He is co-editor of *Wirtschaft und Rüstung am Vorabend des Zweiten Weltkrieges* (Düsseldorf, 1975) and *Kriegswirtschaft und Rüstung 1939–1945* (Düsseldorf, 1977). He co-authored *Ursachen und Voraussetzungen der deutschen Kriegspolitik* (Stuttgart, 1979).

Bernd Wegner (b. 1949) was educated at the Universities of Tübingen, Vienna and Hamburg, where he took his Ph.D. in 1980. He was a Research Fellow at St Antony's College, Oxford, in 1979/80 and since then has been a member of the Militärgeschichtliches Forschungsamt. His study *Hitlers Politische Soldaten: die Waffen-SS 1933–1945* was published in 1982.

Wolfram Wette (b. 1940) completed his doctorate at the University of Munich in 1971 and since then has been a member of the Militärgeschichtliches Forschungsamt. His study *Kriegstheorien deutscher Sozialisten* was published in 1971. He co-authored *Ursachen und Voraussetzungen der deutschen Kriegspolitik* (Stuttgart, 1979) and *Bomben und Legenden. Die schrittweise Aufklärung des Luftangriffs auf Freiburg am 10. Mai 1940* (Freiburg, 1981). He is co-editor of *Pazifismus in der Weimarer Republik* (Paderborn, 1981) and *Unternehmen Barbarossa* (Paderborn, 1984).

Index